How are

by Arthur T. Hadley

Prentice-Hall, Inc., Englewood Cliffs, N.J.

THE INVISIBLE PRIMARY
by Arthur T. Hadley

Printed in the United States of America

Prentice-Hall International, Inc., London
Prentice-Hall of Australia, Pty. Ltd., Sydney
Prentice-Hall of Canada, Ltd., Toronto
Prentice-Hall of India Private Ltd., New Delhi
Prentice-Hall of Japan, Inc., Tokyo

10 9 8 7 6 5 4 3 2 1

Library of Congress Cataloging in Publication Data

Hadley, Arthur Twining
  The invisible primary.

  Includes index.
  1. Presidents—United States—Election—1976.
I. Title.
E868.H32   329'.023'730925   76-828
ISBN 0-13-504654-8

For
Stewart J. O. Alsop *(1914–74)*,
in war, life,
and craft a gentle hero,
and for
Susan

by Arthur T. Hadley

CONTENTS

The sun goes round and the stars go round
the nature of eternity is circular
and man must spend his life to find
all our successes and failures are similar.

Keith Douglas
"Wadi Natrum," 1942

INTRODUCTION

This is a book about that period of political time between the election of one President and the start of the first state primary to determine the next presidential candidates. Specifically it deals with the people, winners and losers, and politics of presidential selection from 1973 through December 1975. I have called this period of time "the invisible primary." During it we select from all those in the nation eligible to be President the three or four people who will become candidates in both parties. And those who choose to run make the critical decisions in politics and their own lives that determine whether they will win or lose in the state primaries that follow. I am certain and will attempt to show, primarily in today's world but also historically, that the invisible primary is where the winning candidate is actually selected. The state primaries, caucuses, and party conventions have become largely media events with their outcomes predictable.

The first sparse notes and tentative interviews for this book were begun in November 1973. The work continued with ever growing intensity until the 15th of December 1975, except for two pages that closed December 28 to include the final Gallup Poll. As the candidates emerged I traveled with them, watched their staffs and supporters, covered their meetings, read what they had said in the past and what others had said about them, and interviewed their friends and many not so friendly. Rather than holding all the writing to the end, I wrote the chapters on the various candidates, losers and winners, and the principles they embodied, sequentially as these people entered or left the race. In this way the book itself becomes a test of the existence and meaning of the invisible primary and, I hope, retains the excitement of a race still fluid and undecided.

As pressure and time altered the original candidates and their positions I have recorded these changes in the later chapters and have explored the character and strategies of the new entries. In the first chapter I have taken a very brief look at the history of presidential candidate selection up to the 1950s. I have also outlined a method by which to judge the strengths of the various candidates. I did not begin this book with such matrices in mind. Rather it grew out of my need to have a framework in which to arrange the masses of data, feelings, and thoughts I was gathering about so many people, theories, and events.

In the last chapter, actually written in October before Chapters 8 and 9, I have dollied back to take a panoramic view of this irrational marathon we call presidential selection. That chapter also examines some of the magic nostrums being advanced by the self-serving to cure the ills from which our presidential politics suffer. In the penultimate chapters I try to give some indication of how this invisible primary has turned out and why, and also to explain certain signposts that will be uncovered in the period from February to April. These indicate how successfully the candidates have used their energies and skills.

A book such as this usually begins with a list of distinguished people alleged to have helped the author. The hope appears to be (I've used such lists myself) that the famous presences will lend cachet to whatever varied fare follows. Obviously, to do this book I have had to spend time with many, many people involved in politics at all levels, some famous, some not, including every one of the candidates. But a fair number of those who gave me the most help do not wish to be listed. So it seems fairest to mention no one. My gratitude to those who did help is immense. Quite literally I could not have done this book without you. Thank you.

However, outside of the ranks of politicians, their staffs and helpers, with whom this book largely deals, there are a few people who have aided me so much with ideas, information, and time that I would be remiss not to name them. Politics in America is covered by some very fine craftsmen, reporters whose work I read constantly and whose company I enjoy. Since I could not, obviously, be everywhere for this book, I have benefited from their work and their generous fill-ins. Thank you all, particularly David Broder, Robert Boyd, Dean Fischer, Martin Nolan, and Christopher Lydon in Washington; Jim Gritzner and James Flansburg in Iowa; Andrew Schneider in New Hampshire; and the team of James Barron and Marjorie Arons in Massachusetts.

Mark Siegel's unpublished Ph.D. thesis on delegate selection first caused me to wonder if the process that I later came to call the invisible primary did exist. Stewart Alsop, to whom this book is dedicated, by his enthusiasm encouraged me to risk the time and effort to find out. Sterling Lord, my good friend and agent, and my editor at Prentice-Hall had faith enough to provide generous support and advice. I do not know as much about statistical analysis as I wish I did, and Peter Hart of Hart Research, Charles W. Roll, Jr., of the Gallup organization, and Robert Teeter of Market Opinion Research helped me through the statistics in Chapter 6 about who we are as Americans and which of us vote and for what reasons. Many of these statistics were developed at a conference held in Cambridge, Massachusetts, on June 20–23, 1975, by the Institute of Politics in the John Fitzgerald Kennedy School of Government, Harvard University, attended by, among others, Walter De Vries, V. Lance Tarrence, Jr., and Patrick Caddell.

George Hirsch and Jon Larsen at *New Times* gave me the time off from what I should have been doing for them to travel, question, investigate, and write. Lindsay McKelvie did practically all the research and a liberal share of the reporting. Her work and patience grace most of this book.

A lovely and generous person, for reasons I am not fully able to understand, stepped out of a yellow Volkswagen convertible and into my life some time ago and this book is also dedicated to her.

Oh yes, there are usually some final smarmy words in an introduction about the excellence of the book being the work of others but the mistakes being all the author's. I don't know any author who believes that. Why should I say it? I know I have made mistakes. But you should have seen some of the garbage I was given. Let me say with Voltaire, *"J'ai fait de mon mieux,"* and let it go at that.

> Arthur T. Hadley
> Washington, D.C., February 1976

CHAPTER 1

The Invisible Primary

July 1974—two full years before Republicans and Democrats will meet in their conventions to nominate "the man who," the thirty-ninth President of the United States.

The brief attention span of the news focuses almost exclusively on Washington and impeachment. President Nixon, like a badly gored matador, has twice dragged the cape of foreign affairs in front of the angered press, hoping to draw the public gaze off Watergate with trips to Egypt and Russia. No eye wavers. Fifty Nixon supporters fast on the Capitol steps. Others, mostly older people and high-schoolers, march quietly before the White House in the unusually cool nights.

In the Ebenezer Baptist Church in Atlanta, Georgia, Marcus Wayne Chenault, an easygoing twenty-three-year-old from Ohio State who used to harass his neighbors with electrically amplified foul language, heeds the voice of his private god and shoots Mrs. Martin Luther King, Sr.

From the closed hearings of the House Judiciary Committee, whose members are still unrecognized and unknown, spurt small driblets of information about the presidential tapes. Before the Supreme Court, presidential counsel James St. Clair and special prosecutor Leon Jaworski argue whether the President must turn over to the grand jury an additional sixty-four tapes of White House conversations involving the Watergate cover-up. Predicting the Senate vote count for or against impeachment is the inside Washington game.

Yet, defying the Washington impeachment focus, a small group of politicians this July is jetting crisscross about the country. Senator Henry M. "Scoop" Jackson is in Omaha, Nebraska; Senator Lloyd Bentsen is in New York City; Senator Charles Percy is in the Bohemian Grove, California; citizen Elliot Richardson, no longer attorney general since his refusal to fire Jaworski's predecessor, Archibald Cox, speaks in Lansing, Michigan; Congressman Morris K. "Mo" Udall is in Marshall Field, Wisconsin; Senator Edward Kennedy has just returned from Moscow. What are these men doing? They are running for President. Two years before the convention? Yes.

The conventional wisdom holds that those in the presidential race make their first halting start sometime in the year before the election. Theodore H. White writes in *The Making of the President 1960:* "Thus in the spring, summer and fall of 1959 the rivulets of hope and ambition began to descend from their secret places, tributaries ambling, rushing and twisting toward the two great political streams, Republican and Democratic, that would make in their meeting *a year later,* the campaign of 1960."

David Broder, the Washington *Post*'s justly famed expert on politics, political parties, and politicians both illustrious and obscure, says: "Nothing that happens before the first Presidential primary has any relevance at all," though he goes on to add that the rules change from year to year.

Even presidential candidates themselves sometimes talk of "waiting to see what happens after the first few primaries," as if there were still a possibility of entering the race that late.

The burden of this book is that the critical battles for the presidency are fought long before the first state primaries. Far from being decisive politically, the primaries appear more as a ritual encounter, a symbolic show whose results reinforce a victory already decided. That is why candidates were on the road for 1976 as early as 1973. History proves them right. Modern political polling began in 1936. Since then the active candidate who ranked as most popular within his own party in the Gallup poll taken one month before the New Hampshire primary has won his party's nomination 85 percent of the time.

In other words, since 1936 in seventeen out of twenty presidential contests the race was over before we paid our money to watch, or reporters and TV crews pulled on their galoshes and headed for the New Hampshire snows. The three exceptions were Wendell Willkie over Thomas E. Dewey in 1940, Adlai Stevenson over Estes Kefauver in 1952, and George McGovern over Hubert Humphrey in 1972. None of these three upset victors went on to win the general election that followed. Since 1936 we have always elected as President one of the two active candidates ahead in the polls the month before the primaries began—not a good course for a dark horse.*

A metaphor often used to describe the state primaries is that "they are the stepping stones to the White House." Closely examined, this phrase contains an exact truth. The primaries are true stepping stones. A candidate must cross on them to get to the far bank, and he may stumble on one of the stones. Muskie fell in New Hampshire when he cried over the infamous "Canuck Letter"; Romney was thrown by his claim he was "brainwashed" in Vietnam. But unless a candidate trips, his arrival at the far bank to receive his ballot-studded crown will be determined by his unnoticed maneuvering to be first in line at the near bank, not by his widely reported leaps from primary to primary.

This book is about that unnoticed maneuvering, the invisible primary: what a candidate does before the state primaries to assure himself of victory;

---

*In 1952 and 1968 Presidents Truman and Johnson respectively led the Democratic poll. But neither man was an active campaigner. Similarly in 1964 Nixon was more popular with his party than either Senator Barry Goldwater or Governor Nelson Rockefeller. But he too declined to campaign.

in particular, what those people who ran successfully or unsuccessfully in 1973–76 were doing. It begins where most people have not looked and ends where the supposedly decisive race begins, at the New Hampshire primary. In reporting the present race and others in the more immediate past, I shall try to show some of the principles beneath the mumbo jumbo of our present presidential selection. I will also outline a method by which to test the worth and political power of those contesting for our vote. The belief that from a thousand rubber chicken dinners magically arises the man best qualified to lead us seems obviously contradicted by memories we all share. Something is wrong with the selection method. What is it? What can we do?

In exploring the invisible primary this book will cover many more losers than eventual winners. This is as it should be. Often the reasons why a man loses reveal more about the nature and rules of a race than an analysis of the victor's strategy. "No Cannae without a Varro." To comprehend the slaughter of the Roman troops below Lake Trasimene, one must understand the system that could elevate an incompetent like Varro to command, as well as the military genius of the Carthaginian, Hannibal. The precise individual ingredients of a victory often get submerged in the juggernaut of success. Besides, the losers are often at least as attractive and able as the winners. We all have been both.

When does a person start to run for President? Undoubtedly some start when they plan their careers in their twenties; or before. Legend tells us that Ambassador Joseph Kennedy, ambitious leader of his star-crossed house, had determined that one of his sons would be President before they were born. Surely other fathers and mothers—particularly mothers, for the majority of the 1973–75 candidates would cite their mothers as the dominant factor in their lives—must have dreamed the same dream.

Paratroop Captain Stuyvesant Wainwright II, himself later a congressman, found crouched in a D-Day foxhole the figure of a major he knew was meant to be back in England.

"Major, what are you doing here?" he asked.

"Captain, being in on this here D Day is goin' to be worth 250,000 votes back home," replied Major Strom Thurmond, now senator from South Carolina and third-party candidate for President in 1948. But to go that far back in a man's life is the subject of biography rather than presidential politics. As Horatio remarked when asked by Hamlet to trace the noble dust of Alexander, till he find it stopping a bung-hole: " 'Twere to consider too curiously, to consider so."

Logically the 1976 presidential campaign can be said to have started the day the votes were counted in 1972. This holds true even though some candidates may have looked on their '72, or even '68, efforts as mere openers for '76. "We never stopped running after '72," said Brian Corcoran, the unflappable former sportswriter who handles press and politics for candidate Scoop Jackson. John F. Kennedy sought the vice-presidency in 1956 not because he thought Stevenson had a chance against Eisenhower, but for the help the media exposure then would give his own campaign in 1960.

As soon as a person has spent or received over a thousand dollars to run for President, the law requires that he register with the General Accounting Office. Using this standard, the first off the mark for 1976 was George Wallace, governor of Alabama. He never closed out his registration for the 1972 campaign. Next to register, in September of '73, was Senator Charles Percy, the moderate Illinois Republican. Then in January of '74 came two Democrats, Walter F. Mondale of Minnesota and Lloyd M. Bentsen of Texas. Terry Sanford, the former governor of North Carolina who was chairing the commission to write a new charter for the Democratic party, filed in May '74. Senator Henry M. "Scoop" Jackson became the final official '74 candidate in July.

Since tradition then held it indecent to begin the race for President until just before New Hampshire, none of these men admitted what they were doing, even though they had created committees to do it. "Testing the presidential waters," "exploring the situation," "studying the feasibility of becoming a candidate," is the uninspired jargon of the hour. The first person actually to admit to the disease of candidacy was President Gerald Ford on November 15, 1974. Next came Representative Morris "Mo" Udall on November 23, followed by Governor Jimmy Carter of Georgia on December 12. Then Senators Jackson and Bentsen on February 6 and February 17, 1975. In the 1972 campaign George McGovern was the first to announce, on January 18, 1971, a year and ten months before the election—something that totally shattered precedent. His chief rival, Senator Edmund Muskie, didn't announce until the month before the New Hampshire primary.

In addition to those actually registered in the race, early 1974 saw the dust of other runners rising across the land. Elliot Richardson, Nixon's forceably retired attorney general, was on the road financing himself and a staff of two from lecture fees. Ex-Senator Gene McCarthy of the '68 antiwar campaign was running with the Committee for a Constitutional Presidency and $50,000, but hadn't registered because he believed the law unconstitutional. Gerald Ford, still just Vice-President, traveled about ringing the changes on never wishing to replace Nixon. Senator Edward Kennedy hadn't committed himself one way or the other and had everyone on edge. Congressman Morris Udall, Democrat of Arizona, campaigned but hadn't raised money. The most invisible candidate was ex-Oklahoma Senator Fred Harris, populist candidate of the innocent, representing the eternal Parsifal in each of us. He not only had not raised money but traveled in borrowed cars and slept in supporters' homes.

On any weekend in the summer of '74, two years before the first primary, some science-fiction satellite orbiting America with its detectors geared to politics would have observed a series of continually repeating vignettes.

Salt Lake City: Seven P.M., after two press conferences in Colorado, a speech on energy to the Edward Teller Center in Denver, and an airport press conference in Salt Lake City. Congressman Morris K. Udall is carrying his suitcase and clothes bag into the plush red lobby of the Hotel Utah. He has one aide with him. No press.

"Name, sir?" asks the room clerk.

"Udall."

The clerk turns away to the tall wheel of names. Spins it several times. Looks puzzled.

"How do you spell that?" he asks.

"How's that for national name recognition?" says Udall.

Waterloo, Iowa: Six P.M., the ballroom of the Ramada Inn. A high school choir, girls in white, boys in tux with wide lapels, is singing "Yankee Doodle Dandy." Senator Percy is sitting on the stage before some two hundred people, smiling. The two congressional candidates he is in Iowa to help have left the room to go somewhere else important. The fund-raising cocktail party, twenty-five dollars a head, attended by seventy-five people, was so undersubscribed that people were let in free; and the Black Hawk County Republican chairman complains the fund raiser will cost money. Suddenly a compressed air pipe in the back of the room lets go with a roar. The choir keeps belting out "Yankee Doodle" in the best show-biz tradition. Percy keeps smiling. Ten minutes later the pipe is turned off. The Republican chairman of Black Hawk County rises to introduce the state chairman, who gets the name of the high school choir wrong. In the back of the room three members of the National Rifle Association position themselves to blast Percy with questions on gun control.

Canton, Ohio: Ten fifteen P.M., the Akron-Canton Airport, a fat, hazy night, with the red half-moon looking hot and unwalked on. A United Air Lines jet is keeping one engine whining so a cleaning woman inside has light enough to sweep. Vice-President Ford is about to arrive in a two-engine Air Force Convair. State police, sheriff's deputies, airport police, and secret service guard the runway. The security is so Mickey Mouse tight that when Ford's chief advance man, Jim Gustafson, goes inside the terminal to the bathroom, a sheriff's deputy won't let him back onto the field. Ford's Convair taxies up, and an airport cop racing out to the plane gets so excited he runs over the foot of a sheriff's deputy. As Ford comes down the ramp, the specially rigged floodlights break down.

The next afternoon Ford stands in the blazing ninety-degree heat before the front entrance to the Football Hall of Fame, a building that, for those fortunate enough not to have seen it, resembles a cross between a chichi modern church and a small-town aquarium topped by a scoop of melting ice cream. Above its glass front doors is fixed a mural in which three footballers dressed in space suits kick each other in the crotch. The 350 people in the audience, mostly male and white, hold their programs over their heads to protect themselves from the sun. Ford says of the ballplayers: "They have achieved an excellence that deep down in my own heart I would rather have achieved than the office I now hold."

Washington, D.C.: Four thirty P.M., a vaulted stone corridor in the basement of the Old Senate Office Building; the sign on the office door reading, "Subcommittee on Refugees." Inside in the cramped space two of the three men working there answer the phone "Senator Kennedy's office," the third, "Subcommittee on Refugees." The phones ring continually with requests for speeches and appearances by the senator. That is not a figure of speech; as soon as a phone is returned to its cradle it rings again. Paul Kirk, who began working for Teddy in local Massachusetts campaigns, and who keeps the name and date file for the Kennedy organization, makes little notes in his black engagement book and tells each caller, "I'll get back to you." The senator is "keeping his options open," says Kirk.

Rochester, N.Y.: Seven A.M., the cramped counter of the Flagship Rochester Coffee Shop. Elliot Richardson, isolated and self-contained as always, his carefully folded handkerchief in the exact center of his left-hand suit pocket, is eating eggs and bacon.

"Do you know who that is?" One waitress behind the counter nudges another staring at Richardson. "That's our congressman." Standing behind Richardson waiting to take him to a 7:30 local TV show is Congressman Frank Horton of Rochester, one of the lesser known lights of the lower chamber. The night before Richardson has lectured six hundred Republicans at a sixty-dollar-a-plate fund raiser. On the TV show Richardson praises Horton and says of himself for the one-hundred-thousandth time, "I'm glad to be mentioned for President; but we will have to wait and see."

Las Vegas, Nevada: Two twenty P.M., a suite on the twenty-second floor of the Dunes Hotel, desert sunlight outside, filtered air and artificial grapes inside. Jerome Mack, banker and former part-owner of the Riviera Hotel, sits on the imitation Louis IV console TV swinging his legs. Senator Henry "Scoop" Jackson and his aide, Brian Corcoran, relax on a couch, their ties loose. Under discussion is a plan to raise $10 million in the period to be covered by this book—*before* the first state primary. They discuss the new laws that restrict individual gifts to $1,000 a candidate. Mack is to help organize two thousand Westerners to give $1,000 apiece. As always in politics the conversation comes back to people, who will go where to raise how much. Mack has a plan to charter a plane and lease it to the Jackson campaign.

Jackson shakes his head: "That would count as a gift, Jerry."

Mack looks surprised, shakes his head.

"Politics is getting complicated," says Brian.

All these men were deep in the invisible primary, hurtling round the country, appearing on television, energizing future supporters, taking names, neglecting their jobs and families, trying to raise money. What they and other candidates were forced to do and the length of time for which they were forced to do it reveals the present irrational state of American presidential selection.

Our Chief Executive has not always been chosen by such a punishing, lengthy, and convoluted system: this mix of state caucuses and state primaries that ends in a party convention. State presidential primaries did not even exist until the early 1900s. The first presidential candidate actually to enter a state and campaign was Theodore Roosevelt in 1912. After Roosevelt's defeat no candidate campaigned within a state for thirty-two years until Wendell Willkie did so in 1944. And Willkie entered only one state, Wisconsin.

The real creation of our present system of long, grueling primary campaigns in many states was in 1950 with the campaign of Senator Estes Kefauver. Then in 1974 came another mammoth change. Without fully realizing what we were doing we altered the structure of our political parties to vastly increase the number of state primaries: from sixteen in 1968 to thirty-four today.* At the same time, through the Federal Election Campaign Act of 1974, which took effect in 1975, we shifted and restricted the financing of a candidate's drive for the nomination. These two changes reinforce each other to make the 1976 presidential campaign profoundly different from those before. Both the innovations of Senator Kefauver in 1950 and the new laws and rules greatly increase the importance of the invisible primary.

How the invisible primary of 1973–75 works, who were the candidates and other principal players, what fates befell them and powers moved them, is the subject of this book. But before plunging into today, this chapter will take a brief look at the history of presidential candidate selection. It will also present a system by which to judge the strengths and weaknesses of the various candidates hacking their way through the political savannahs.

The ideal political location in which to place the power to choose the President perplexed the Founding Fathers. At the Constitutional Convention in 1787 it took over sixty ballots to decide the matter. The

*The number of primary states is sometimes given as low as twenty-eight, sometimes as high as thirty-five. The low figure results from defining primary states as those where delegates are elected at polling places supervised by the state, for example, New Hampshire and California. The high figure comes from defining primary states as those where delegates are elected at the polls whether supervised by the state or the political party. These latter party-supervised states are sometimes called "firehouse primaries," for example, Arizona and Connecticut. I include them since the "primary" method of selecting delegates is still at the polls. However, I do not include Wisconsin, whose Laocoon convolutions designed to protect the incumbent governor will probably be found illegal. Result: thirty-four.

members' diaries and private correspondence record their grave doubts about the final compromise. The method by which we choose our Presidents has been in flux ever since. It stabilizes for a period of time, then shatters under some new set of political pressures. And with each change the power to choose the candidates for President shifts to a new location in the political system.

The method of selecting Presidents chosen by the Constitutional Convention was the Electoral College, still nominally in effect today. But the only two Presidents chosen by this method were Washington and Jefferson. The political battles between Thomas Jefferson and his Vice-President, Aaron Burr, caused the functioning of the Electoral College to break down. Though the college remained as a symbolic presence, the actual power of choosing a President next moved to the Congress, specifically the Congressional Caucus. James Monroe, James Madison, John Quincy Adams, and Andrew Jackson were all selected by this method. No one with sense ever advocates a return to the past; and I don't. Still I find it hard to argue on the basis of product reliability that our present method of presidential selection is superior to the old.

The Congressional Caucus had begun to fail in 1824 when John Quincy Adams, Henry Clay, Andrew Jackson, and W. H. Crawford, the fading heir of the fading Virginia dynasty, were all battling for the presidency.* Eight years later it was dead: killed by Andrew Jackson's maneuvering to deny the presidency to the southern secessionists led by John C. Calhoun and by the regional pressures of a nation expanding westward. President Jackson engineered the first National Party Convention in 1832, because he could control such a convention, gain his own renomination, and choose his own man, Martin Van Buren, as Vice-President. The delegate representation at this first convention was based on the Electoral College and so overrepresented the small states. Traces of this discrimination still linger in today's conventions.

By 1840 and the election of William Henry Harrison the Party Convention had become firmly established as the method of candidate selection. This made candidate selection an important function of a national political party, along with patronage and ideas. The convention delegates were chosen by the state party leaders. Astute politicians soon realized that to control the party machinery and therefore the convention assured them the presidential candidate of their choice. In the immortal words of Boss Tweed of New York's Tammany Hall, "I don't care who does the electing, as long as I do the nominating."

By the late 1800s, the convention system was being attacked by reformers in both parties as being under boss control. The Cook County, Illinois,

---

*The account by the then boss of New York, Senator, later President, Martin Van Buren, of the wheeling and dealing in this caucus is one of the better treats in American history.

delegation of 1896 (believe it or not, before Mayor Richard Daley's time) was described by a contemporary as: "Among the 723 delegates, 17 had been tried for homicide, 46 had served terms in the penitentiary for homicide or other felonies, 84 were identified by detectives as having criminal records." To improve the conventions and therefore the quality of presidential candidates, reformers turned to the direct state primary. This method of choosing candidates by the vote of all party members rather than by party leaders began in local politics. By 1875 six states (California, Missouri, New York, Ohio, Pennsylvania, and Virginia) employed some form of direct primary in their local government.

In the early 1900s the next wave of reforming populism extended this method of choice to presidential primaries so that delegates to the party convention were elected by party members as they are in most states today. Liberals in both the Republican and Democratic parties joined to battle for more primaries. The "steal" of the nomination of 1912 from Theodore Roosevelt by the followers of William Howard Taft, who controlled the convention, though Roosevelt had won the primaries, fueled the reforming zeal. By 1916 twenty-six states, led by Florida and Oregon, had passed laws that gave them the present direct primary method of selecting national convention delegates.

After 1916 the high tide of reform that had brought direct primaries began to ebb. People questioned whether the direct primary did not intensify the evils of politics by adding a new layer of elections on which bosses and spoilsmen could operate. Primaries were seen as breaking down party responsibility and keeping good men out of politics by increasing the expense and difficulty of campaigns, precisely the same arguments leveled against them today. President Woodrow Wilson, who had lost in the primaries to Champ Clark, was against further expansion of the primary system.

In addition to being attacked on theoretical grounds, practical political experience had shown that winning primaries did not mean gaining the nomination. In fact it meant the opposite. Of the 388 delegates elected by primaries to the Republican Convention of 1912, Theodore Roosevelt won 221. Even the third GOP candidate, Senator Robert La Follette, won more states than William Howard Taft, who gained the nomination. At the same time Wilson was being defeated in the Democratic primaries by Clark.

As a result, within the next thirty years only one more state, Alabama, took up the direct primary, while eight states reverted to the caucus method of selecting convention delegates. Politics and theory combined to produce "back to normalcy." Both boss and reformers had found the direct state primary unreliable—that is, not always producing the candidate they preferred—just as today's Democratic party reformers in their drive for more primaries have found to their horror they have opened up their party not to some philosopher-king, but to George Wallace.

The belief that the direct primary favors the insurgent over the boss dies hard. The bright energetic reformer is certainly favored over the dumb, lethargic boss. But other variables being equal, political organization and a telegenic smile probably exercise more clout in a direct primary than in a state caucus, where a small group of activists can have an effect out of proportion to their numbers.

With the election of 1916 began the strange, for today, political habit of candidates entering their names in state primaries to prove their popularity, but not themselves campaigning in those states. Instead, un-American oddballs that they must have been, they stayed home and did their job, letting their supporters campaign for them.

President Calvin Coolidge, the organization's choice in 1920, secured his first nomination in his own right by entering seventeen state primaries against insurgents and winning fifteen, excluding one against Robert La Follette, the father of the direct primary. He never left the White House. Mr. Normalcy himself, Warren Harding, entered two state primaries, losing one and just squeaking by the other in his home state of Ohio. In 1928 Herbert Hoover entered eight primaries and Al Smith seven, both men winning the majority of those they entered. Again one stayed in Washington, the other in New York. Smith's win included West Virginia, a fact of significance in 1960, since Smith, like John Kennedy, was a Catholic and he defeated a Protestant, Senator James A. Reed of Missouri. As with Kennedy, Smith's victory demonstrated to the professionals that Smith actually had the Protestant support he claimed. In 1932 Governor Franklin D. Roosevelt, who remained in Albany, won eleven state primaries, including New Hampshire, already a key early state, which he carried against Smith. However, Roosevelt also went down to defeat in the key states of Massachusetts, Pennsylvania, and California. While state primary victories were important in this period, the real power remained with the party bosses in the state caucuses.

Yet the myth that the state primaries are all-important remains stronger than historical fact. "The winner of the critical primaries has invariably won the nomination. Taft and Eisenhower 1952, Kefauver and Stevenson 1956. . . ."* Not so. In 1952 Eisenhower actually finished behind Robert Taft in the primary battles, 4 to 5, or 406 delegates to 458. And while Adlai Stevenson finished ahead of Estes Kefauver in the 1956 primaries, in 1952, the first time he won the Democratic presidential nomination, Stevenson finished behind Kefauver 0 to 9—including a loss in his own state of Illinois. In 1968 many of the big state primaries—California, New York, Ohio—went uncontested because there were favorite sons in the race. These states were approached on a political basis rather than on personal popularity. In the face of this evidence it is difficult to maintain that the state primaries are "crucial."

This is not to minimize the risks involved in entering the primaries. A man

---

New York Times Magazine, March 23, 1975.

can still trip on those stepping stones—witness George Romney and his famous "I was brainwashed" gaffe. And the risk must usually be taken. Richard Nixon led both Nelson Rockefeller and Barry Goldwater in the Republican polls in 1964, but refusing to risk his popularity in any primaries, he was forced to bow out of the race. On the other hand, in 1968 Hubert Humphrey defeated the forces of Gene McCarthy without ever having entered a single primary.

The modern primary campaign as we know it was started by Wendell Willkie in 1944, making his comeback try. He became the first presidential candidate since Theodore Roosevelt to enter a state and actively seek votes. Traveling through Wisconsin, running hard and shaking hands fourteen hours a day, Willkie failed to pick up a single delegate and quit the race after that one primary. But even in defeat he had shown the possibility of a primary campaign. Once again the loser, not the victor, had pointed the way. In 1948 Harold Stassen campaigned in almost every state of the Union, winning three primaries before he was defeated decisively in the Oregon primary by the eventual winner, Thomas Dewey.

In the 1950s the liberal Republicans began to push for more state primaries, re-creating them in Montana and Indiana, as part of their drive to secure the nomination of General Dwight Eisenhower over Robert Taft. Ironically, at this time liberal Democrats were battling to keep states in the caucus system. In those years they had a candidate, Adlai Stevenson, who wasn't particularly adept at winning primaries. "What's best for the country" and "what's best for my candidate" have a tendency to jumble in a person's mind. In the 1950s the candidate both Democratic bosses and reformers feared was the coonskin-capped populist from Tennessee, Estes Kefauver, one of the most neglected political figures of recent times.

Senator Estes Kefauver was the first politician to realize that the open primaries, plus the new invention of television, had radically altered the presidential race. He discovered that a senator who, instead of legislating, got hold of an investigation that made good TV viewing could become a major public figure. And then he could take his name recognition and, through campaigning, turn that popularity into votes in the state primaries. To be blunt, Kefauver, a more or less average senator who drank, almost parlayed exposing a few crooks on TV into the presidential nomination of the Democratic party. He did this though he was hated by the Democratic bosses for exposing the ties of certain city machines to organized crime, despised for his uncouth populism by the intellectual reformers who preferred Stevenson, and denigrated by his peers in the Senate for neglecting the duties of legislation. I remember the mythic Texas Senator Tom Connally, who headed the Foreign Relations Committee, calling his committee to order during a debate on NATO and finding Senator Kefauver absent. "Kefauver . . . Kefauver," rumbled Connally, "where is that gonfalonier of gasconade; out chasing a crapshooter somewhere?"

Yet it took the combined strength of President Harry Truman, the city bosses, and the reformers to keep the nomination from Kefauver, who had swept the major state primaries. In accomplishing this, Kefauver brought a new dimension to the invisible primary by uncovering the importance of TV and destroying the myth that the Senate was a poor place from which to run for the presidency. Again a loser blazed the way. In 1960 John F. Kennedy was astute enough to read the blazes. To quote that justifiably famous pioneer of in-depth campaign reporting, Theodore H. White, again: "Between 1956 and 1960 no Democrat, not even Adlai Stevenson, spoke in more states, addressed more Jefferson-Jackson day dinners, participated in more local and mayoralty campaigns of deserving Democrats, than did John F. Kennedy." Kennedy had the perception to expand Kefauver's pioneer efforts while at the same time he remained popular with the professionals.

The examples of Kefauver and Kennedy have transformed the Senate, leaving a legacy that has come close to devastating that body. Few senators any longer concern themselves with passing legislation. Instead they chase frantically after the sexy investigation or simplistic program that will get them on the tube again and again and again. For much of the week the presidentially ambitious senators are not even in Washington but jetting around the country to meet the local leaders and other activists who will form their constituency at primary time. Since Kennedy and Kefauver, senators have been mesmerized by the ease with which they can use their office as a presidential launching platform. And the press has helped them by focusing on senators as candidates: Barry Goldwater, Eugene McCarthy, Robert Kennedy, Hubert Humphrey, Edmund Muskie, Fritz Mondale, George McGovern, Scoop Jackson, all senators. All men with little to do but spend time in the invisible primary.

Had there been the number of state primaries in 1952 that there are today (thirty-four), Estes Kefauver would most probably have become the Democratic presidential candidate. But there were only sixteen, of which Kefauver entered fourteen and won nine. What defeated Kefauver was that though he skillfully used his television popularity to appeal directly to the mass of voters, he never took the time to build a political following; so he lacked a body of dedicated political supporters who would work to turn his personal popularity into greater political advantage. This same lack of a political following helped defeat Senator Edmund Muskie in 1972.

In 1960 the late President Kennedy was wiser. He both built a constituency of professional politicians and younger voters and used his Senate base to dominate television and gain mass support. While it is generally believed that he won his Democratic nomination in the primaries, actually he entered only six of the seventeen possible state primaries; and though he won all of them, only the victories in West Virginia, where he proved his Catholicism no handicap, and Wisconsin, where he beat Humphrey on Humphrey's home turf, greatly affected the campaign. Kennedy used the primaries in 1960 as Roosevelt had in 1932, to demonstrate to the party professionals the existence of strength he had already built up. But again the myth of the "critical primaries" obscured the truth of Kennedy's successful use of massive strength in the invisible primary.

After Kennedy's victory in 1960, the nature of a campaign to gain the presidential nomination stayed pretty much the same for fourteen years, though it is interesting that candidates began officially declaring earlier and earlier. The rules of the Democratic contest did shift slightly from 1968 to 1972 to produce a George McGovern rather than a Hubert Humphrey; but the basic contest remained the same.

Then in 1974 occurred the most radical political change since the creation of direct primaries at the turn of the century, a shift that permeates the entire structure of today's scramble for the presidency. The vast reach of this change is difficult to perceive, and it affects every candidate in ways that still take everyone by surprise.

Briefly, between 1968 and 1974 the number of states holding presidential primaries more than doubled. Now, for the first time, the great majority of convention delegates will be chosen in the state primaries. At the same time the rules for each of the state primaries have become more litigious and complex. By itself this would have been a decisive change in the campaign for the nomination. But there was a second equally important shift. The amount of money that a candidate was allowed to spend to obtain the nomination, which had been unlimited through 1972, shrunk to $12 million—a fraction of what had been usually spent. And the raising of these funds became circumscribed and open to public inspection. No one could contribute more than $1,000 to any candidate, candidates could spend no more than $50,000 on themselves, and the laws against corporate contributions and contributions from bogus committees were effectively tightened. Candidates had to shift their techniques of money raising from the fat-cat few to the relatively well off many, and at the same time publicly account for close to every penny.

The race for the nomination had been made more complex, more tiring, and more costly, and at the same time the amount of funds available for that race had been drastically curtailed and opened to public view. Also the source of political funds had been shifted. Onto this previously unexplored battlefield the 1976 candidates debouched, frantically changing their tactics and strategy to fit modern times—or what they perceived to be modern times.

Historically this 1976 campaign sees the culmination of a trend that began in the early 1900s when the first state presidential primaries were created. Since then the party conventions have gradually been losing their importance as the true locus of the nomination of the presidential candidate. Historically the conventions had held the vital function of choosing presidential candidates for a remarkably long time, since Jackson in 1832. Yet I believe that the last conventions that actually decided on a candidate, in other words where the issue was in doubt up to the vote on the convention floor, were in 1952.

In 1952 in both the Republican and the Democratic conventions it was possible that the candidates who had won the majority of primary delegates—Taft for the Republicans, Kefauver for the Democrats—might gain the nomination over the eventual winners—General Eisenhower and Adlai Stevenson. Since then, in spite of the media efforts to make the conventions exciting, the candidates have always amassed enough votes prior to the convention to make the outcome certain before the convention was convened.

In 1956 the renomination of General Eisenhower was a certainty for the Republicans. While the followers of Governor Averell Harriman of New York might have hoped that ex-President Harry Truman's support would cause a stampede to their man, the figures before the convention showed Adlai Stevenson firmly in the lead. In 1960 both Richard Nixon and Jack Kennedy had the nomination in hand before the conventions, as did Lyndon Johnson and Barry Goldwater four years later. At the convention of 1968 Hubert Humphrey, though he had not entered a single primary, had the majority of the votes through carrying state caucuses. That year Richard Nixon was also a certain winner.

The same was true again of George McGovern and Richard Nixon in 1972. There was action and excitement at the '72 Democratic Convention. Would Mayor Daley be forced out? Would big labor take a walk? Who could the McGovern supporters alienate next? But the convention's purpose was absent. Through victories in caucuses and primaries from state to state, McGovern had gathered the votes to win. Even if all his adversaries had combined to stop him, he still had those votes. The function of choosing a presidential candidate had passed elsewhere.

In 1976 this historic truth that the convention no longer chooses the President has been brutally reinforced. By the time the last three primaries are held in California, Ohio, and New Jersey in late June, the winner will be known. The conventions will still retain some importance in selecting a Vice-President, writing a platform, giving the voters a TV picture of the party. But the nominating function will be over.

In summary, the way the system works today, the candidate who wins the state primaries is assured the nomination, and victory in the state primaries comes from placing first in the invisible primary. The process of history continues: from Electoral College to Congressional Caucus to party convention to state primaries to invisible primary to whatever comes next.

To measure the success of this or that candidate in the invisible primary, and at the same time analyze the primary itself, I judge a candidate's performance on six separate tracks. These are the psychological track, the staff track, the strategy track, the money track, the media track, and the constituency track. Let's take a brief look at each in turn.

The psychological track—how a presidential candidate reacts to the strain and the temptations of the campaign—is his inner test of himself (and in the future, hopefully, of herself). How much does the candidate want the presidency? How much of his private self and belief will be compromised to the public man? To what extent will he abandon family, friends, and other normal joys of life, and how does he handle this isolation? The importance of this track, of not-so-plain-old-fashioned character, has been thoroughly and persistently demonstrated to us by several past Presidents.

The smaller details of a man's inner life *are* important. During his 1972 campaign Senator Edmund Muskie was plagued by his need for at least nine hours' sleep if he was to function effectively and control the ravages of his temper. On the road Senator Henry Jackson often suffers from a chronic postnasal drip that hampers what speaking ability he has. Ronald Reagan needs an afternoon nap if he is to campaign effectively in the evening. All these little bits of detail combine to help or hurt a candidate. To hear candidate Birch Bayh explain to the Young Democrats in St. Louis in August 1975 why he will never be for unconditional amnesty and then the next month say in Springfield, Massachusetts, before a liberal Democratic audience, "I am for unconditional amnesty," is to gain important insight into the strains ambition places on character.

In the invisible primary of 1973–75 the test of the psychological track was to prove decisive for two early Democratic candidates: Senators Edward Kennedy and Walter "Fritz" Mondale. Both withdrew because of the stress of competition on this track, though Kennedy was doing well on four of the other five and Mondale on three.

Strangely, for a man taking such a giant step, Fritz Mondale began to run for the presidency without taking thought or making the decision. The night of Nixon's presidential victory on November 7, 1972, Senator Mondale won his second term. He was standing in the same Minneapolis ballroom where Hubert Humphrey had so fulsomely acknowledged his own defeat by Richard Nixon four years earlier. Now Humphrey was at his side. And Humphrey, as ever unable to be brief when faced by a reporter's notebook or a TV camera, began a speech. "We are seeing," Humphrey intoned for the TV audience, "the beginning of a truly great national career which can take Fritz Mondale to the office which I long sought. . . ."

Over a year of campaigning later, in late 1974—still two years before the first state primary—I talked to Mondale's wife, Joan, about how her husband made the decision to run for the presidency. "I don't think," she says, "that he ever did make the decision to run. Hubert said those nice things about him on television and the invitations started to come in." As will be seen in the examination of Mondale's candidacy, this lack of reflection over the initial decision kept returning to harm his campaign.

The second track on which candidacy in the invisible primary will be judged is the staff track. How good is the candidate's staff, and how does he relate to them? Does he surround himself with second-raters and yes-men? Does he listen? Treat them as equals in moments of crisis? Or is he hungry for the credit and quick to shift the blame? Can he inspire loyalty? Control dissension? In short, will he have the managerial skills and personnel resources he will need when and if he becomes President?

Failure on this track has always hurt Hubert Humphrey in his campaigns.

The paranoia and battles on George McGovern's staff have become the stuff of legend. In the invisible primary of 1973–75 two candidates, quite different in other ways, were generally conceded to have the best staffs: Jackson and Udall. Interestingly, both these men had always used women in positions of executive importance long before this became *de rigueur* on Capitol Hill.

Though the two staffs were organized differently and contained vastly different types of people, what they shared was ability. Jackson had a great advantage in that he was a senator and able to command more staff. As Bill Brock, a Republican senator from Tennessee, not without presidential ambitions himself, remarked: "You've got to feel sorry for Mo Udall, because a House guy just can't compete with this [the large Senate staffs]. What is he going to do? He is not of my party but I love him and I respect him and I know what he is up against. He will be lucky to have one tenth of the staff that is available to any of his senatorial competitors."

For one of the early candidates, Senator Charles Percy of Illinois, the fact that a well-known firm of political consultants was willing to join his staff was of decisive importance in his decision to make the race. Referring to the willingness of Bailey-Deardourff to accept roughly $5,500 a month from him to manage his invisible primary campaign, Percy said: "I was flattered that such a team of professionals—the finest and most knowledgeable political specialists you can find—wanted to devote themselves to my effort."

The third track, strategy, grows out of the first two, a candidate's personality and the strengths of his staff. Precisely *how* does the candidate intend to get through the invisible primary, through the state primaries, through the election, and to the White House? It would be nice to report that most of the decisions and discussions about strategy that occur between a candidate and his staff deal with broad issues of vital effect to all Americans. But of course they don't. They deal with whether to spend more time in Florida or in Illinois.

Nevertheless the strategic track remains an excellent measure of a candidate. Does he actually have a strategy, or is he just Yo-Yo-ing around from invitation to invitation? Is he doing in September what he said he would be doing in May? Does his strategy, as he and his staff see it, conform to reality as you and I see the world? A candidate's strategy also reveals a great deal about the invisible primary, for where he puts his effort reveals the relative importance of the ingredients that bring victory there.

"I've learned something," said Terry Bracy, Udall's administrative assistant and right hand, midway through the invisible primary. "You can't do your job in Congress and run for President."

"I never could have spent so much time campaigning like this when I was governor," said Ronald Reagan, ex-governor of California, during a political swing in late August 1975.

For two of the early Republican starters a strategic miscalculation was to prove devastating to their campaigns. Both Senator Percy and citizen Elliot

Richardson had figured that President Nixon would either serve out his term or come close thereto, and therefore Vice-President Ford would become so enmeshed in Watergate that he would be vulnerable. When Nixon resigned in August 1974 and Ford became President while still clean, they were forced into a painful reevaluation.

"The reality of it [Ford's presidency] loomed larger on the ninth of August than it did in fantasy," explained Joe Farrell, Percy's chief of staff, two weeks after Percy had withdrawn from the invisible primary. A candidate cannot win on strategy alone; but a poor strategy can defeat him.

Tracks four and five in the invisible primary are straightforward: money and media. For all the candidates, the money track was to prove the most difficult and complex. With the fat cats eliminated by the gift limit of $1,000 per candidate imposed by the Campaign Reform Act of 1976, no one was quite certain how to raise the permitted $12 million. The quest became more complex because the new rules ordered the federal government to match $5 million of the candidate's privately raised dollars with public funds if the money raised privately had been gained in certain ways. On the money track there were no performers in the same league as Scoop Jackson and Alabama Governor George Wallace. By October 1975 Jackson had raised $2.3 million and George Wallace $4.2 million, while far in the rear trailed such candidates as Fred Harris, Jimmy Carter, and Terry Sanford.

The efforts of some of the minor candidates to raise the necessary total of $5,000 in amounts of $250 or less in twenty states, thus qualifying for the matching federal funds, became ludicrous. "I'm going to qualify before the governors' conference," ex-Governor Terry Sanford of North Carolina said at a Democratic charter committee meeting in October 1974. At the governors' conference in Hilton Head, South Carolina, in November '74, he told me: "I'll have qualified before the midterm convention." At the midterm convention in Kansas City, on December 7, part of which he missed while trying to raise money, he said: "It's just a matter of weeks, Hadley."

Then in late August '75, at the Young Democrats' convention in St. Louis, his campaign manager, Jean Westwood, said, "Any day now." Sanford was then making a candidate's mandatory pilgrimage to the Soviet Union (the belief that one becomes a foreign affairs expert by jetting from country to country being among the first signs of incipient candidacy in a previously sound mind), yet when the mandatory quarterly financial disclosures occurred on October 10, Sanford was not only still short but was $78,000 in debt.

Track number five, media, is believed by many of the candidates themselves to be the key to the invisible primary. "Our strategy is to stay on the job in the Senate and dominate television that way," said Robert Keefe, Jackson's wily campaign manager. "The public thinks of the election as taking place on television," says I. A. Bud Lewis, head of NBC's election unit, with perhaps as much accuracy as parochial pride. "It's discouraging to introduce legislation and then go home and see Ted Kennedy or Scoop

Jackson comment on it on the six o'clock news," lamented Fritz Mondale during his campaign try.

Contrary to popular opinion, it is not essential that the media love a candidate for him to do well on the media track. Indeed, press fondness for a candidate can be a handicap; the better reporters tend to be deliberately hard on candidates they find appealing. But it *is* necessary for the press to believe that a candidate is serious, that he or she has a chance at either winning or influencing the strategy of the victor. Most of the reporters who cover George Wallace do not espouse his political views. But he receives a great deal of media mention because what he does and says affects the outcome of the battle for the Democratic nomination.

There is, to be sure, a certain confusion of cause and effect here. Consider the case of Van Lingo Wombatt, my favorite imaginary candidate who will surface from time to time in this book. In part whether Van Lingo Wombatt is or is not a serious candidate depends on how much he is mentioned in the press, and reporters and editors play a vital part in deciding whom they will cover. Wombatt becomes a serious candidate by being covered, and after that draws more coverage, and therefore appears even stronger. This paradox forms a key portion of the invisible primary.

The candidacy of Elliot Richardson uniquely demonstrates the importance of the media track. He was a Cabinet officer who had been fired by President Nixon for reasons having to do with Richardson's unyielding conscience. This meant the press considered what he had to say important. Within a period of one month in the fall of 1974, both Richardson and Lloyd Bentsen, the Texas senator and low-keyed, enigmatic millionaire who was driving toward the White House, campaigned for a day in the city of Rochester, New York. Senator Bentsen landed in a private plane with his chief political aide, Ben "the Zapper" Palumbo. He was met by two experienced advance men, one of whom had been in Rochester for two days to coordinate the stop. That all adds up to a lot of cash.

Elliot Richardson came into Rochester on a commercial flight. His visit had been advanced out of Washington on the phone by Richard Mastrangelo, his one-man staff, who stayed at home. Yet Richardson got twice as much TV exposure as Bentsen and three times the newspaper coverage. Why? Because the press believed Richardson to be a serious challenger to Nixon. So Richardson drew with little effort more coverage than all of Bentsen's sweat produced.

It is hard to be precise about just what motion of some magician's wand puts the golden shoes of media acceptance on a candidate's feet. But as long as the magic sandals stay on, and the performance of a candidate before the TV camera or at news conferences helps keep them on, wherever he goes he draws, almost without trying, more publicity than rivals who are working twice as hard and spending twice as much.

The final track on which a candidate competes in the invisible primary is constituency. A constituency is a group of people beneath the candidate and his staff who believe in the candidate enough to work for him and contribute money. The members of the constituency take the candidate's strategy and money and translate these into votes by energizing the mass of eligible voters. In other words a candidate's constituency provides a vital group of activists who will ring the doorbells, make the phone calls, hold parties, give money—all the key expenditures of human energy that move selected portions of the voting mass. The voting mass is politically volatile, shifting from candidate to candidate under bombardment from the media, manipulation by the candidate, or pressure from rival constituencies. A constituency is faithful, often close to fanatic; and if it ever leaves a candidate, it will be with cries of betrayal.

In 1972, for example, Democrat Edmund Muskie had an early mass lead. But he had never established a constituency. So he had trouble finding people to work for him, organize his mass, get it turned out, hold it loyal through the misfortunes and setbacks of the early primaries. Senator McGovern, on the other hand, had a fanatical and hardworking constituency in the antiwar movement. His problem was completely different: To hold the loyalty of his constituency, he had to take positions that were later to turn off the mass. This was the same problem that Senator Barry Goldwater had faced four years earlier. To hold the support of his constituency of young right-wingers, he sounded so extreme he turned off the mass of voters even in his own party.

The problem for a moderate candidate (from Eisenhower through Ford or from Stevenson through Muskie and Jackson) is finding a constituency motivated enough to contribute and work. These two are not always the same. Some constituencies have money to give, others have time. But both, the money and the human energy, are necessary. A candidate may put together several constituencies: for example, a strong defense policy to get a constituency of givers, and a liberal social program to get a constituency of workers. John F. Kennedy brilliantly merged these two constituencies in his invisible and state primary victories.

The problem for all extremist candidates is finding a constituency sophisticated enough to work successfully on moving the mass, and then to hold the loyalty of that constituency without alienating the mass. Historically, from the anti-Masons in the 1830s through Horace Greeley to Goldwater and McGovern, a small constituency can capture a party, but it cannot gain the White House. For both moderate and extremist the constituency must also have leisure time. Every night watchman in America may be for Van Lingo Wombatt, but if they work all night and sleep all day, this won't do Wombatt much good. This is why students and upper-income housewives have traditionally been an important part of a candidate's constituency.

In the 1973–76 invisible primary two candidates, Senator Edward Kennedy and Governor George Wallace, found themselves with constituencies whose real strength was less than it appeared to be. Many of the 17 percent that the early 1974 polls showed favoring George Wallace lacked the education and time to be politically effective. They did not know how to organize, how legally to gain control of the local Democratic party. Also they had to work for their livings and look after their children, so they lacked the free hours to spend in politics, however fervid their support for Wallace.

In the same time period the polls showed Senator Edward Kennedy's popularity at 44 percent. The senator's problem was that much of this support came from first-time voters and from blacks. While both these groups were solidly in his corner, neither traditionally turn out to work for a candidate or have money to contribute. Nor do they even vote in proportion to their numbers. So the senator's staff were fearful that the polls would continually show Kennedy as more popular than his performance in a primary would prove—a circumstance that had proven fatal to Muskie in 1972.

Those, then, are the six tracks on which I propose both to judge the candidates and to explore the largely irrational maelstrom in which they contend. Now it is time to turn to the contest itself, to what has actually been happening between the night of Nixon's election in November 1972 and the February of the New Hampshire primary in 1976. Who were the candidates? What were they doing? How was the invisible primary working?

CHAPTER 2

Kennedy, Richardson, and Other Early Casualties

The number-one Democratic candidate at the time of President Nixon's election in 1972—the start of the invisible primary for 1976—was Senator Edward Kennedy of Massachusetts. No one else appeared his equal in media attention, in poll strength, as a favorite of politicians. Way back in December 1971 the Gallup poll found that more Democrats, 29 percent, preferred Kennedy for President than any other candidate. His closest competitor then was Senator Edmund Muskie with 24 percent, trailed by the just-defeated Democratic presidential candidate,

George McGovern, with a mere 6 percent. By November 1973, 41 percent of the Democrats preferred Kennedy for President. His closest rival had now become Governor George Wallace at a mere 15 percent. Six months later Kennedy had pulled even further ahead. He was number one at 44 percent, followed by Wallace at 17 percent, Jackson at 8 percent, his two earlier rivals, Muskie and McGovern, both back at 7 percent.

It seemed he had merely to stretch forth his hand and the nomination was his. But there was one track on which he raced, the psychological track, in which the senator had serious problems. True, his strengths on some of the other tracks were not as overwhelming as they appeared at first glance, but those deficiencies were minor in comparison to Kennedy's personal problems. For him, the invisible primary was almost entirely a race within himself.

A close personal friend of Kennedy's in Congress, a man who drinks and parties with him, put it this way: "All the other candidates have to go out and look for delegates. He alone has to stay home and prove he wants the job enough to pull himself and his marriage together." Kennedy's performance on the psychological track, being harder to measure than his poll results or his political muscle, was overlooked by many observers. But not by all.

Writing in *New York* magazine in April 1974, Richard Reeves summed up the reasoned arguments in favor of Kennedy's making the race and concluded: "He looks unbeatable for the Democratic nomination, and, conceding that analysis 30 months before an election is like fortune telling, has a very good chance to win it all in November of '76." Reeves, one of the canniest and most thorough of reporters, went on to add: "My head says yes. My gut says no." Wise gut.

Other reporters were convinced that Kennedy had already decided to run. "This man is running for President," said William Honan in his 1971 political biography. Among other little cues Honan noted that on a political swing Teddy wore John F. Kennedy's cuff links. "Now Kennedy," Honan points out, "has become something of a mystic lately, and wearing President Kennedy's cuff links struck me as exactly the sort of thing he would do if he were testing the water for a possible plunge for the Presidency."

Maybe, but knowing the senator's large staff, one could equally well assume that wearing the cuff links was a staff ploy to identify a slightly paunchy playboy with the great days of the past. You take your prejudice and make your assumption.

Senator Kennedy's large staff and his relation to it, the staff track, are a critical part of his brief quest-nonquest for the presidency. How much did the staff control him? How much he the staff? How able were those who worked for him? Kennedy's staff was certainly vast, part of the tremendous advantage all senators enjoy when they run for the presidency. With his seniority Kennedy controlled two subcommittees of the Judiciary Committee: the Administrative Practice and Procedure Subcommittee and the Subcommittee on Refugees and Escapees. Of these two staffs, seven of the twenty-two on the Practices and Procedures Subcommittee actually worked for Senator Kennedy, as did five of the eleven on the Subcommittee on Refugees and Escapees. In this way the senator added another twelve employees to those he could hire with the $498,904 he is authorized for office salaries.

For example, Paul Kirk, chief of Kennedy's campaign staff, worked as a "research assistant" for one committee at $32,000 a year. So for a time did Kennedy's foreign policy speechwriter (at $33,000), his civil rights expert, his Chicano expert, an assistant press secretary, and many mail room employees. Other senators do the same thing. The Washington *Post* calculated Senator Jackson's total staff budget, again accumulated through his chairmanship of committees and subcommittees, at $1,901,970. They found Jackson controlling thirty-two of the forty-two staff members of the Permanent Subcommittee on Investigations and thirty-one of the thirty-eight people on the Interior Committee. Senator Kennedy's Administrative Practices Subcommittee held only one day of hearings in 1974. Certainly Senator Kennedy had a large number of loyal staff members. But how able were they?

The ability and viciousness of Senator Kennedy's staff are twin political myths. And like most myths, the exact details are difficult to pin down. Certainly both press and rival politicians are afraid of Kennedy's staff. On a TV show in Chicago, Senator Walter Mondale, then an invisible primary candidate himself, squirmed and twisted while being questioned on how President Ford's pardon of Richard Nixon was any different from the failure to dig into the truth of Chappaquiddick. Mondale, a former state prosecutor with a strong sense of justice and fair play, finally admitted that he was not "completely satisfied" with Kennedy's Chappaquiddick story. Afterward he sat in his car worrying that Senator Kennedy's staff would learn of his answer and take their revenge.

"A lot of people want Teddy to run because they think politics will be fun again," said Martin Nolan, the Boston *Globe*'s Washington Bureau chief who won a Pulitzer Prize for his story on Ted Kennedy's attempt to make his father's old coat holder, Francis X. Morrissey, a federal judge. "It's not going to be fun. It's going to be ugly."

In talking to the press about Kennedy, politician after politician begins his remarks, "Now, this must never get back to Kennedy or his staff." Pollsters find interviewees reluctant to be critical of the senator for fear of retribution. The members of Kennedy's staff even look rather like those from Nixon's defunct CREEP (the Committee to Reelect the President). Same thin-lipped energy, same tight dark suits and vests, same flat briefcases and uptight ties pulled hard against pinched collars. But then the CREEP people ultimately proved not to be as tough—and certainly not as efficient—as they looked.

Would Senator Kennedy be able to control his people and thwart their ambitions by saying no, if he decided he didn't wish to run? While other candidates might have to make the decision "Yes, I will run," for Kennedy the decision would have to be "No, I will not." If he did nothing, his staff would make certain he became a full-fledged presidential candidate.

In asking questions about the political future, it is important to understand, but not always easy to analyze, which way circumstances are actually driving the politician. In 1955, after President Eisenhower's heart attack, the burning political question was, "Would Eisenhower seek a second term?" Everyone the invalid Eisenhower saw, the White House staff, the Republican leaders, his business friends, were all urging him to run again. The decision Eisenhower had to make was not to say yes, but to say no forcefully. Even when healthy and vigorous, Eisenhower, both as general and as President, had trouble taking a course that went against the recommendations of his staff and peers. Would he do so in his weakened state? Once the question was asked that way, the answer became self-evident.

For Kennedy, like Eisenhower, to remain passive would be to run. The more difficult, active decision was to say no. For if he went out and fought hard, Kennedy certainly had the best chance of gaining the nomination. He had a politically smart staff; and he himself had personality and ability. He was the man to beat. His ambition plus the desire to prove that little brother was as good as the older boys must have yeasted inside him with explosive force. To say no was going to be hard.

Senator Kennedy's staff kept on positioning him to run, leaking information privately that he was ready to go. Indeed the very crassness of this operation called into doubt the efficiency of the staff. Was its vaunted omniscience fact or myth?

On the record, the performance of Ted Kennedy's staff appears at best mediocre. Staff handling of the Chappaquiddick affair left a festering wound. The nomination of Francis X. Morrissey raised the issue of secret cronyism. Then the senator's income tax returns showed fewer gifts to charity even than President Nixon's—a miserly $4,678 out of an income of $451,683, just over .01 percent. Next came the harsh publicity over Kennedy's visit to appear with Governor Wallace of Alabama. Later the staff failed properly to file campaign moneys from a fund-raising party. Were all these the work of a superefficient body? And would a truly efficient staff have allowed itself the luxury of being known as "vicious"—a reputation that has led to another Kennedy weakness: his poor relationship with much of the influential press?

In fact, Kennedy's position with the serious press has never been particularly good, though for a time after the tragedy of his brothers' murders the press treated him with tolerant respect. But there was never the high regard, even admiration, that the President and, later, his brother Robert evoked. Teddy was a Kennedy, he had news value, his staff kept him supplied with good ideas and quotes, he spoke well, and he got lots of ink and TV exposure. But with two or three exceptions the leading reporters remained at a physical and psychological distance. When Teddy Kennedy won his first Senate campaign, *The New York Times* even went so far as to editorialize that his election was "demeaning to the dignity of the Senate and the democratic process."

The two older brothers continually used the press to make Teddy feel inferior. Such quotes as the two famous ones by Joseph Kennedy, Sr.: "Look, I spent a lot of money on that Senate seat. It belongs in the family," and "You boys have what you want . . . now it's Ted's turn," didn't find their way into public print by blabbermouth accident. When *Newsweek* in 1966 ran a cover story on Robert and Ted, Robert refused to pose with his brother on the Capitol steps. Instead he told the magazine to paste a stock photograph of himself beside Teddy on the steps. His press aide insisted that the photographs show him standing slightly higher than Ted. *Newsweek* agreed. More significantly, so did Teddy.

The Chappaquiddick affair, the death at Dyke Bridge, in the summer of 1969 came at a fortunate time for Ted Kennedy as far as media coverage was concerned. The aura of his two martyred brothers still hung over him. Kennedy's story about what had transpired at Chappaquiddick was scoffed at privately, but publicly, it was handled by most of the media with considerable gentleness.

But by 1973, as the invisible primary heated up, that honeymoon was over. Paradoxically part of the reason for the tougher coverage of Teddy by the press was the exceptionally uncritical coverage his brother Jack had received. David Halberstam, *New York Times,* Vietnam Pulitzer Prize winner, spoke for a lot of reporters when he said, "There is a feeling on the part of many of us that we were used by the Kennedy administration." The press was determined never to be taken into camp again, particularly a Kennedy camp. On Teddy's home turf, the Boston *Globe* somewhat timorously moved to tougher coverage. *The New York Times* published a brilliant analysis of the cracks in Kennedy's Chappaquiddick story, "Chappaquiddick Plus Five," by Robert Sherrill, which was serialized around the country.

At the same time, Kennedy's staff was doing nothing to lessen the growing friction between the senator and reporters.

"He has a vast staff who have very little to do so they sit around and figure out ways to screw each other and the press."

"You can't trust a word they say. Paul Kirk [Kennedy's chief political operative] wouldn't tell you if your coat was on fire. And if he did, when you took it off you'd check it; because maybe all he'd want to do is steal your coat."

"He gave me the story; and when the results got out of hand he tried to knock it down by saying I'd got it wrong."

All these are real quotes from major reporters, the so-called heavies of the Washington press.*

Publicly the hardening attitude between Kennedy and the press showed up in many ways. There was *The New York Times Magazine* piece by Sherrill. In the *New Republic*, a bellwether liberal magazine where the senator and his staff might well have expected favorable notice, Walter Pincus, who had worked with both Jack and Robert, wrote in June 1974: ". . . Kennedy has no fixed sense of where he as a person or this country under his or someone else's leadership ought to be going. Priorities are what you get from experts. . . . A disastrous Cambridge meeting earlier this year showed the limits of that approach. . . . It bogged down as the guests (experts) argued among themselves. . . . When the tables were turned and questions asked of Kennedy the meeting fell apart."

The Washington *Post*, in a Sunday feature, was no more charitable: "His Senate career reveals no acquaintance with real world economics, merely the predictable enthusiasm of a wealthy liberal politician for extremely expensive health and welfare measures. . . . Nothing in Senator Kennedy's background, experience or public career visibly equips him to lead America. . . . Jack crossed the tracks, Bobby at least straddled them, but Teddy the rich, spoiled kid brother doesn't travel well in George Wallace territory."

No matter how isolated his staff was holding him, Kennedy must have realized by the fall of 1974 that among the fights he would have to wage to gain the nomination would be one with the media. Not merely editorial attacks—those any candidate can survive—but that kind of skepticism that makes an editor on a dull news day look up from his desk and say, "Let's see who we can find cheating on his campaign financing," and reporters reply, "Right on; let's start with Wombatt."

Further, on the constituency front, the strength of Kennedy's forward position in 1974 was like that of the American front in the Ardennes in December 1944: not as secure as it seemed. That overwhelming 44 percent of the Democrats who preferred Kennedy to any other candidate has to be analyzed. Those same polls that showed Kennedy's impressive lead also

---

*I have some problems about quoting my fellow reporters. In his interesting and highly readable book, *Boys in the Bus,* about press coverage of an actual presidential campaign, Timothy Crouse quotes, with names, private conversations between reporters which he overheard while a fellow reporter. The press most certainly is not a perfect screen through which only "news" passes. It is part of the political process and as such deserves study. But pitfalls open if one runs with both hare and hounds. There are enough problems in reporting the news without reporters having to guard what they say to each other. When I quote members of the press by name in this book, particularly in the chapter on the press, I have had my notebook out and have given due warning they are on the record. In quotes from private conversation, such as those here, I have protected the anonymity of the reporters, as I would the source of any other private comment.

showed that of the remaining 56 percent of the Democrats, some 30 percent-plus would not vote for Kennedy under any circumstances. The average invisible primary candidate is low in the polls early on because people don't know who he is. He is courting his constituency; the mass will begin to move later. Maybe at this time 10 percent of his party are for him, 1 percent against him, and 83 percent wonder if he isn't the astronaut who went to the moon three years ago or the new coach of the Mets. Thus the candidate has a large group of neutrals to whom his supporters can bring their message.

With Kennedy the situation was different. Practically everyone knew who he was. While 44 percent of the Democrats favored him, he had this negative response—or unacceptability quotient (UQ in the trade)—of around 30 percent. This left him with only 26 percent undecided to work on. If he could only convince half of these to vote for him, that would leave 43 percent of the Democrats against him; and that doesn't count Republicans and independents. The polls showed other disturbing signs. Fifty-six percent of the voters thought he had *not* told the truth about Chappaquiddick. Of the 44 percent of the Democrats in his favor, Kennedy had received close to 98 percent of the black vote and 60 percent of the first-time voters, those too young to have taken part in the last election. While both of these groups contribute percentage points to a candidate's poll standing, they have a strong tendency not to vote; and they do not produce the cash and workers necessary to form a constituency.

The polls also showed, though here the evidence is far less conclusive, that Kennedy's efforts to build a coalition among his peers was faltering. His own age group was dividing against him. "All we know about him is he can swim" had become a refrain among his contemporaries. In their 1974 Senate races, both Wayne Owens, running in Utah, and John Glenn, in Ohio, who had made elaborate use of Kennedy in their previous campaigns, now rebuffed his efforts to come into their states. While campaigning with Ab Mikva and Senator Mondale on the North Shore of Lake Michigan, I found that most of the wealthy liberals there, people who normally gave tens of thousands of dollars to the Democratic party, would not contribute or work if Kennedy were the candidate. During a swing through California with Kennedy two weeks later, Chris Lydon of *The New York Times* uncovered the same attitudes.

Up to 1976, weakness on the money track would have been inconsequential to any Kennedy. They and their friends in Massachusetts could finance invisible and state primaries themselves. But under the '76 campaign spending act a candidate and his family could only contribute $50,000 to his own campaign. Even the Rockefellers and the Kennedys now needed money. Teddy had been one of the champions of campaign spending reform. Ironically, he and the other Senate liberals who pushed so hard for its passage were the first to be reined in by the new code. As the current invisible primary progressed, other candidates were to find themselves helped and hurt by the new law in ways practically none of them had foreseen. Probably Kennedy was hurt no *more* than most of the others, but the new difficulty of raising cash was still a factor.

The order of the primaries broke wrong for Kennedy. His greatest strength lay in the industrial states of California and New York; but up until the summer of 1975 both these states planned late primaries. New Hampshire, the first primary, has few blacks; Florida, the second primary, has fewer first-time voters than most states. Indeed, before he dropped from the race, Kennedy's staff had become so concerned over the poor showing they felt he was liable to make in New Hampshire that they had recommended he not enter that primary, their public argument being that he was obviously so strong in New England that to win in New Hampshire would not be a fair test. Again this raises the question, how able is Kennedy's staff? Who could have been expected to believe that a politician would avoid an important race because he could win too easily?

New Hampshire presented a second strategic problem for Kennedy. Mayor Kevin White of Boston, still angry from the secret knife job done on his chances for the vice-presidency by Kennedy in 1972, had concluded on the basis of his private polls he could take Kennedy there. "I'd like you to have been my Vice-President; but there's the son of a bitch that blocked you," said George McGovern to White, nodding his head toward Kennedy on a charter flight during the 1972 campaign. (Was the bungled knife job necessary? Kennedy's staff again?) White was set to run against Kennedy in New Hampshire and savage him. McGovern had been declared the 1972 New Hampshire victor over Muskie by the press, though Muskie got 37 percent of the vote to McGovern's 28 percent. All White had to do was better McGovern's percentage and he would have left Kennedy's reputation as a sure winner in tatters. Even after Mayor White became involved in the Boston busing fight, my own surveys in New Hampshire lead me to believe that White still would have had no trouble bettering the McGovern figures.

After New Hampshire, Kennedy would have had to move on to Florida to face Wallace, Jackson, and Carter on marginally friendly turf. Thus, though his position as the candidate to beat was justified, the political auguries were not as favorable for Ted Kennedy as they appeared on the surface. After all, it is part of conventional political wisdom that the seeming front-runner is always most vulnerable in the media to any slip in the state primaries.

But overtopping all these other problems was the pressure Kennedy experienced on the psychological track. In the first place, how much did the senator want the job of President? He already was the second most powerful man in the United States. Next to the President he could command the most media attention. He could, if he wished, influence the course of history from where he stood already. And at the same time he knew more clearly than most the dark side of such power.

He gets more threatening mail every day than anyone in the United States, after the President. Under the desk of his receptionist and in other selected areas are buttons to summon the secret service and lock the doors of his office so no one can force their way in. No other senator needs these. At home there are the fatherless children of his two brothers. And in his own life public acclaim has not brought personal happiness. In 1962 came the disclosure of his suspension from Harvard for cheating on a Spanish test. In 1964 he endured a near-fatal plane crash and the agony of a broken back. In 1971 reports started circulating that his marriage was breaking up and his wife was under psychiatric treatment. In 1974 these reports were confirmed, when his wife was found to have secretly entered a home for the treatment of psychological disorders and alcoholism.

Chappaquiddick is a festering wound. As long as Kennedy does not seem to be running for President the press leaves the affair pretty much alone. But each time he starts to get serious about trying for the presidency the press reexamines the accident at Dyke Bridge and each time more discrepancies in Kennedy's story turn up. First Robert Sherrill's *New York Times* piece exposed the impossibility of the time sequence of the events in Senator Kennedy's story. Then *Time* magazine discovered that a key car clock on which he based his testimony never existed. *New Times* discovered an earlier statement by the senator to police in which he gave a different story. Other papers got hold of bits and pieces. There is even the possibility that some of his political enemies in Massachusetts might reopen a grand jury investigation.

The political events that help other Democrats have injured him. First Watergate made integrity the most important issue in the public mind. Then Ford's pardon of Nixon agitated the whole question of equal justice. Assuming that Senator Kennedy has not told "the truth, the whole truth, and nothing but the truth" about Chappaquiddick, he is the one candidate who, if he were to run, might not just fail to get the nomination, but might blow apart his entire life as well. He was due to run for the Senate again in 1976. If instead he ran for the presidency and lost—under Massachusetts law he cannot campaign for both—he might be nowhere: without wife, family, power.

Psychologically everything must have seemed to be turning against Kennedy in the spring and summer of 1974. He appeared on CBS *Face the Nation* to talk about his health program and foreign affairs; and the headlines the next morning talked about the inadequacy of his Chappaquiddick answers. He went to Moscow to show he was a world statesman, and the press played up the fact he didn't know how to handle Russian students. He released his taxes after long resistance and they painted the picture of a Scrooge. His son developed leg cancer. His wife, Joan, entered Silver Hill.

In August the press discovered that he had violated the campaign financing law, having failed to file a report on a thousand-dollar-a-plate dinner at his home in McLean, Virginia. There were authoritative reports that if he ran, his marriage might well break up. Several senior Democrats (among them Senate Majority Leader Mike Mansfield and former Postmaster General Lawrence O'Brien) who had been close friends of his brothers and were friends of his, publicly urged him not to run. If Kennedy stayed in the Senate he had power, prestige, influence, good will, the pleasures of family and a good life, for frankly he doesn't work too hard. If he runs he risks quite literally everything—including his life.

On Monday, September 23, 1974, Senator Kennedy found the strength to step aside from the presidential race. "I will not accept the nomination, I will not accept a draft. I will oppose any effort to place my name in nomination in any state or at the national convention. And I will oppose any efforts to promote my candidacy in any other way."

Did he mean it? Was Kennedy really out of the 1976 presidential race? Some supporters and some reporters still didn't believe him. But add up his gains and losses on the psychological track if he were to run. The risks were far greater for him than any other candidate; his rewards far less. "Time and chance happeneth to all men," but I, for one, have never doubted that he meant it.

The second Democratic candidate formally to quit the invisible primary—though like Kennedy he had never officially entered the race—was Senator Walter "Fritz" Mondale of Minnesota. For Mondale, as for Kennedy, the decisive track turned out to be psychological, though by the time he finally dropped out Mondale had not shown the strength of Kennedy on a number of other tracks.

Fritz Mondale entered the invisible primary about as early as possible, the evening of Nixon's reelection, November 7, 1972. That was when Hubert Humphrey stood beside Mondale, who had just been elected to his second Senate term, and told a television audience he thought Mondale would make a great President. Humphrey ended his fulsome endorsement by saying: "If it isn't being too sacrilegious, I don't mind being John the Baptist for Walter Mondale."

Mondale hadn't expected this peal on the Democratic shofar. But as a result invitations to speak began to come in. He found he had the beginnings of a constituency on the liberal left of the Democratic party. "I'd mortgage my house if it would help him," said Joseph Rauh, former ADA chairman. (Is it possible that a liberal is now a man so wealthy he doesn't have a mortgage on his house?) Friends rallied round and offered to help Mondale get organized. He was off and running before he realized what campaigning would entail, his feet moving before he decided to be in the race.

Significantly Mondale could not put his finger on the moment when he decided to try for the presidency. "When did you decide?" I kept pressing him.

"We were talking it over," he answers.

"When?"

"After the last election."

"Can you be more specific?"

"I don't think so."

"Who was 'we'?"

"A bunch of us."

Mind you, he wasn't giving the impression, sitting there in shirt sleeves and puffing a cigar as if it were a seldomly enjoyed sin, that he was ducking questions. His happy round face—reminding one of Orr in *Catch 22*—looked genuinely puzzled and troubled that he couldn't remember, and that the interview wasn't on some safe ground like his energy policy.

"Who was in the bunch?"

"Dick Moe and Mike Berman and myself, I think. [That is, his two aides and himself.] We sat down and said 'Why not?' "

After Mondale withdrew in December, I talked to his wife, Joan, about the personal side of deciding to run for President. We sat before a bare fireplace because the Senator was away campaigning in Minnesota and had forgotten to order wood. "We had him home for a week after he announced he wasn't running for President; and after he drained the air out of the radiators we didn't know what to do with him," said Joan with a laugh.

"I don't think," she said, "that he ever did make the decision to run. Hubert [Humphrey] said those nice things about him on television and the invitations started to come in. . . . We got to travel and went to so many wonderful places. . . . He always talks over major decisions with me and we never talked about his running. I think you're right. The decision never was made."

She paused for a moment, then added: "But he enjoyed campaigning."

"His aides say he'd come back awfully down."

"Sometimes. Sometimes he'd go to bed the whole next day."

On the evidence, I'd say Mondale enjoyed being on the road some of the time, but less and less as the campaign went on.

Privately Mondale used a poignant metaphor to describe how it felt to run week after week in the invisible primary.

"I don't want to be a rent-a-car; that's what I'm becoming in this campaign. You get into me at some airport, whoever wants to, they drive me as fast as they want as far as they want, and then return me to the airport and just forget about me."

The son of a traveling Norwegian Methodist minister (his great-grandfather changed the family name from Mundal to Mondale on friendly advice from an immigration officer), Mondale was brought up strictly, in rural isolation. The result is a character that seems a strange, even uneasy, mixture of conservative habit and cast of mind, combined with liberal beliefs and solutions. Mondale himself is conservative, upright, and unswervingly moral. He brings his children up strictly, likes to hunt and shoot, believes in strong family ties, and is deeply, not just politically, religious. All these are conservative values. As state attorney general he was a strict law-and-order man, cracking down on utilities and ordinary criminals with vigorous impartiality. To hear him talk about the need for alternative life-styles in America and massive aid to starving nations causes one to wonder where his beliefs arise and why.

Mondale's campaign, like the candidate, was full of contradictions: a strange mixture of the haphazard and the totally programmed. Mondale was a planner in rigid control of himself who yet had a campaign without strategy or basic idea. "Except perhaps not to peak too soon," he said with a laugh about a month before he decided to quit the race. "I'm just going around the country drilling for oil, seeing where it gushes up." I reminded Mondale that several months before, late one night on the road, Robert Boyd, the multilingual, poetry-quoting genius who masquerades as the Knight newspaper bureau chief in Washington, had pushed him about what issues he thought were most important to his campaign. Mondale had answered then: "I am not sure I am in a position to give you a definitive answer yet," because he had not had time to do all the research.

That must have been because he was tired (being tired was a continual Mondale problem, probably reflecting the psychological tension induced by his campaign). Mondale said, "I really am an issues man." His face, which habitually wears the look of a surprised owl, assumed the alarming expression of a senator winding up to give you his half-hour "where-I-stand-on-the-issues speech."

I cut in hastily: "Would you be happier running for the presidency as a governor or a senator?"

"Oh, from the Senate. I've learned so much here. . . . I am an issue man. I really don't like administration." He did a Bob Hope double take as the implications of his words that he doesn't like administration hit presidential candidate Mondale. "I mean, I mean, I'm keen on administration, too."

"I really don't think he thought too much about the presidency," says his wife.

Mike Berman, Mondale's close friend and ace political operative, who ran what planned part of the Mondale campaign there was, believes that in the final weeks before his withdrawal Mondale considered more and more the real nature of the presidency, and what being President would do to his way of life.

Of course, what being President would do to his way of life depends on who he is. Albert Eisele, a reporter for the Ridder chain who knows him well, quotes an unnamed senator on Mondale: "[He] is the best politician in the Senate next to Robert Byrd, the biggest self-promoter next to Bill Proxmire . . . and the toughest SOB next to Scoop Jackson." I look hard to find that Mondale; but I don't see him anywhere. He seems to me, to his credit, to be an average politician and rather diffident in self-promotion. In the lavish living room of Margie Benton, in lakeside Chicago, among the questing coveys of millionaires brought together to meet him, Congressman Abner Mikva, who is a shrewd self-promoter and was introducing Mondale, appeared more the presidential candidate than Mondale himself.

And as for tough? He appears a rather vulnerable man, unsure of his beliefs or limits, hiding behind a mask of cold self-containment. Congressman John Blatnik, the battle-scarred senior congressman from Minnesota, who retired in 1974, says of him: "I think he lacks the self-confidence or the guts to stand up and fight when things get really rough."

Mike Berman, who loves the senator, puts it another way. He says that Mondale is an exceptionally private man who likes to keep "almost total control over his own life." He doesn't like people around him who don't know how he thinks; how he works. "One time a speech went from my typewriter, to his desk, to his wastebasket. That was fourteen years ago. We have never brought up that speech subject again."

Continually the picture comes through of an uptight, conservative, very religious man, a former state prosecutor, running on a bunch of loose, liberal programs that are in basic conflict with his life-style. His treatment of his staff is "Lyndon Johnson imperial" rather than "Truman friendly." People have done such balancing acts successfully before. There is no need for the public and private man to be of one weave. His staff like and respect him and are loyal. On the other hand, people reveal themselves in unexpected ways. Like some recurring leitmotif, Mondale, his intimate staff, and his wife stressed to me how tired Mondale got campaigning. "I'm learning to pace myself better," Mondale said toward the end. "If I get an hour's nap around four in the afternoon and in bed by ten thirty, I can recover for the next day." But no campaigning politician gets that. Since Mondale is an attractive, energetic man, how much of his energy went to battle his own anxiety?

"Let's hear a big one for Senator Mondale," screams the loudspeaker system at the Carbondale, Illinois, shopping center. There is no big one. Not even a small one. No response at all. Indeed the parking lot is deserted in the bright noon sun, the asphalt empty beneath the twisting gasoline sign burning energy as it spins against the wind. Inside the restaurant where Mondale is speaking, the couples, some twenty of them, listen dully while they sip their beer. Mondale does not turn people on. He has been campaigning for a year and still only 4 percent of the voters know his name.

In the editorial office of the Chicago *Tribune* Mondale talks about the need for "an open and law-abiding presidency." No viewer of *The Front Page* would recognize the men listening. Respectability has hit the upper reaches of journalism. These bankerlike men smoke expensive cigars and wear white shirts. The editor sits behind a polished, dark, antique desk and behind him are a pair of encased fencing foils. Mondale tells the editors how much his father hated Colonel Robert McCormick, the deceased *Tribune* owner. Then he talks about the need to have compassion and move the country forward.

The senator seems to have trouble finding enough breath to push out the last words of his sentences. On the *Tribune*'s office couch, the head of the reporter from the Washington *Post,* a gung-ho guy who helped nail Spiro Agnew, sinks slowly to his chest. His breathing changes to a soft snore. Out of respect for the integrity of our craft, I nudge him gently awake. Besides, I might need help myself in a few minutes.

In her lakeside living room, Mrs. Benton rises to ask Mondale if he favors income redistribution to aid the poor. Mondale has been briefed that she always asks this question and that a "sock-it-to-the-rich" answer would unlock bank vaults for him. Instead, he gives a thoughtful and straightforward exposition of the problems and difficulties of welfare reform. "I won't stand there in a two-million-dollar house and do a liberal two-step for them," he tells his staff later.

On the media track, Mondale got a divided reception. In May 1973 a gushing profile appeared in the *New Yorker,* eight pages long, mostly lengthy quotes by the senator. The piece began, "Walter Frederick Mondale, a forty-five-year-old Democrat from Minnesota, is an increasingly important member of the United States Senate," and built him up from there with a series of soft questions. "Do you think the Congress is really capable, institutionally, over the long run, of acting effectively . . .?" Not surprisingly Mondale found Congress okay in some 490 words. However, elsewhere the organs of the liberals, who are his natural constituency, muted their enthusiasm. Their themes were usually the same. He has been a good, if not too effective, senator. But he has always been appointed to the jobs he has held, first as attorney general of Minnesota, then to the United States Senate (though he won reelection to both offices in his own right). Can he find the fire within himself to turn people on and stay the course?

In former years the *New Yorker* article by itself would have been tremendously important to Mondale on the money track. Liberals respond to the *New Yorker.* The favorable mention there would have guaranteed several large donations, financed further a more active campaign. But under the new rules where no one person could give more than one thousand dollars to any one candidate, those funds weren't available. To the surprise of all but a few, the first hurt by the new campaign financing laws were the liberal Democrats who had done the most to pass the measure. Middle-of-the-road Republicans and Democrats have many supporters who can give five hundred to one thousand dollars. The conservative Republicans and liberal Democrats had been the two groups relying on the largess of millionaires—the millionaires of the far right giving out of greed; the millionaires of the far left, out of guilt.

Discouraged by the lack of money, political support, media inattention, and by the small size of most of his audiences, Mondale planned to withdraw from the invisible primary in 1973. He told no one but his staff; and they talked him out of the decision. Their argument in effect was: Look, you don't know your strengths yet. As the '74 elections approach, you'll get more invitations to speak, draw bigger crowds, begin to move. You don't really know how effective a campaigner you are yet because you haven't been fully committed. Press the test further. We believe in you. We think you'll become good at campaigning and find it a joy. Mondale said, all right, he'd continue to campaign, see what happened.

The same criticism leveled at Mondale—that he'd had things too easy in politics, never had to face the tough ones—was also charged of his staff. Everyone liked and respected Mike Berman, the Falstaffian leader of Mondale's drive, but they pointed out that though he was an old Hubert Humphrey political operative, he'd left Hubert's disastrous and bloody '68 campaign for President to manage the winning campaign of Wendell Anderson for governor of Minnesota.

"They've never been shit on in a tough fight," a rival politician noted with understandable bias. "Had to turn the nut and kick ass in a losing campaign. That's what makes you or breaks you as a manager."

Convinced by his staff, Mondale went back on the road in 1974—the dinners, the speeches, the cocktail parties, the names: August 17, Dubuque, Iowa; August 19, New York City; September 2, Oakland, California; September 4, Minneapolis; September 7, Great Falls, Montana; September 8, Chicago; September 14, Elk Grove, Illinois; September 16, Phoenix.

Then in the second week of September, Senator Edward M. Kennedy made his Sherman-like statement and withdrew. The press immediately reported that Mondale's campaign was the chief beneficiary. Mondale's staff talked happily about the great benefits now that Kennedy had withdrawn. They pictured their candidate spending hours on the phone taking pledges of support from all over America. "Mondale's '76 Presidential Campaign Gets Lift from Kennedy Withdrawal," headlined *The New York Times* on October 10.

"I'm 99.44 percent sure I'll seek the nomination," Mondale said publicly.

The problem for Mondale was that the shift in support to himself after Kennedy's withdrawal was only a media event. Much of the Kennedy strength—by no means all, but much—had been a press creation. Other parts of that strength like the blacks, first-time voters, and some older labor leaders had been drawn to Senator Kennedy out of memory and the appeal of his life-style, rather than for political convictions. Those groups had no reason to move into the Mondale camp. Nor did the hard-eyed professional politicians, who had joined Kennedy to get in early with a winner, wish to transfer to a man with only a 4 percent favorable recognition factor.

Having created a semi-mythical body of liberal support for Kennedy, the press, with help from Mondale's staff, transferred that nonexistent strength to Mondale. That was all very heady for two weeks; but when Mondale tried to collect from the myth, no one was at home to sign the checks. It was widely reported that the week after Kennedy withdrew, forty thousand dollars came into the Mondale coffers. Mondale's figures filed with the Government Accounting Office show a jump, but nothing like the money coming to

Senators Jackson and Bentsen in the same period. Mondale's staff kept on talking about the Kennedy supporters who were beating the doors to enter the senator's campaign. But they never gave specific names. And sitting in their offices listening, I never heard a barrage of knocks.

In fairness to Mondale, other candidates were also insisting that Kennedy's withdrawal had given their campaigns a shot in the arm. I finally pinned down Terry Bracy, the cuttingly honest thirty-year-old who is one of two masterminds behind the Udall campaign.

"Hadley, stop bugging me," said Bracy. "You know nothing has changed. But the press thinks it's changed so it has changed. What do you want me to do? Tell the press the Kennedy support is a myth they created? You want to kill us? Besides there will be a change. The press is looking for one; so all the candidates will scramble hard and produce one."

Mondale's problem was that he believed the withdrawal of Teddy Kennedy would result in increased support for himself. The other candidates merely talked as if they believed it. When that support didn't arrive, Mondale was upset; they were not.

The next blow to hit Mondale's invisible primary race was New Hampshire. Mondale had planned to build up an organization in New Hampshire so that he could do well in that primary and make a spectacular leap forward, as Gene McCarthy had done in 1968 and George McGovern in 1972. But here Mondale's lack of strategy hurt him. While he was out campaigning more or less without plan, Udall's staff sewed up Mondale's planned liberal constituency in New Hampshire.

The taking of New Hampshire by Udall, a classic piece of invisible primary maneuvering, is worth considering in detail. Terry Bracy, who had worked New Hampshire for Muskie against McGovern in '72, had been impressed with McGovern's magnificent media campaign, orchestrated and designed by Merv Weston, head of Weston Associates and a liberal power in the state. Bracy arranged a trip in April '74 for Udall, the ostensible reason to campaign for Norman d'Amours, the Democrat running for Congress. Weston threw a cocktail party for Udall and invited the deans of the New Hampshire liberal establishment. "We were all favorably impressed," said Weston, though some of the leaders remained on the fence between Udall and Mondale.

Then in September, Mondale's supporters in the teachers' union engineered him a speaking engagement before all the state's Democrats at a fund raiser in Manchester, New Hampshire, on October 5. Mondale said yes, but after Kennedy's withdrawal he ducked out of the New Hampshire engagement because his staff felt he had a better offer from Florida. The Udall people zeroed on New Hampshire and grabbed the speaking date for Udall. Mondale's Florida trip blew up—the mythical Kennedy strength transfer again—and Mondale's staff tried to get the October 5 date back. Mondale and Udall's staff went into negotiation, which is rather like one of the boys from the Saturday night poker game sitting down against Amarillo

Slim. Mondale ended up speaking after Udall and without a proper introduction.

On that fateful Friday evening Udall got up, looked out over the roomful of bored Democrats, and began: "You may think Senator Mondale and I are here because there is a presidential election in 1976. That is not true. We are here to visit museums and the habitat of the purple finch." The audience broke up. Udall went on to tell about the politician back in his state of Arizona who was wooing the votes of the Indians on a reservation. He was promising the moon, new schools, paved roads, hot and cold running water in the tepees, two tepees for every brave and a brave in every tepee. Each promise was greeted by enthusiastic cheers of "Goomwah! Goomwah!" The politician thought he was doing real well till he went down to the corral to accept the gift of a pony and the chief warned him not to step in the goomwah.

Udall slipped in some serious bits about conservation, energy, and the economy and his record on these, but mostly he kept the audience rocking. Then Mondale got up and delivered a head-nodder about his record in the Senate. After the meeting was over, Mondale's staff had him scheduled to leave in a hurry, while Udall stayed around until one in the morning shaking hands and making friends. The next day Marie Carrier, the Democratic National Committeewoman and one of the handful of de facto Democratic leaders in New Hampshire, got on the phone with her other activist friends. They decided to unite behind Udall. It was that simple. And that deadly for Mondale.

In late October Mondale paced his office as he described how unfair it was that a man's fate should be decided in a small state like New Hampshire. It was an atypical state, he complained, small and conservative; why should it play such a large influence in the campaign? His own staff was already recommending that he avoid the New Hampshire primary, much as Kennedy's staff had done.

The second week in November '74 Mondale visited the Soviet Union. This trip supplied the final ingredient in his decision to withdraw. It broke the rhythm of his campaigning, removed him from the grinding bustle and excitement of politics, and let him reflect on how much he wanted the presidency, how much he wanted to lose control over major parts of his life. When he returned from Moscow on November 17, Mondale found the emotional strain of gearing himself up to campaign again nearly intolerable.

The Russian visit may have done more than unravel Mondale's already strained ties to presidential politics. On previous trips to the Soviet Union the Russians had treated Mondale well. Mondale inclines to the belief that the Russians are just like us, only they lace their shoes up a bit differently. This time the Russians, unhappy over Senate pressure to ease the restrictions on the immigration of Jews to Israel, gave Mondale a thorough hosing. Just as Nikita Khrushchev had done to President Kennedy when he thought he detected signs of softness, the top officials of the Soviet Union now showed Mondale just how rough they could be. While his staff say otherwise, friends who saw him right after the trip report him profoundly shaken.

In any event Mondale went through a period of depression on his return. This coincided with the moment at which it became necessary to hire campaign staff. Up to the end of November, Mondale's effort had been run by three men, Mike Berman, Dick Moe, and Sid Johnson. All of them had been with Mondale since his early campaigns for attorney general in Minnesota. He felt he could ask them to help him out early in the invisible primary without imposing great hardships on their lives if he withdrew later. Now it would be necessary to bring others on board, ask them to give up jobs, chances for promotion, money, family, personal life, all in a cause that appeared a long shot at best. In asking people to take such a risk, Mondale felt that he had to reevaluate his own purpose. Could he ask people for a binding commitment when he himself was not sure of his own?

Overshadowing the political and personal issues was the psychological fear that he was losing control over his life. "He felt he was changing," says Johnson. "He didn't like what campaigning was doing to him," says Berman.

The impression that his life was out of control must have been quite frightening as Mondale moved deeper into the campaign. He felt his extremities were beginning to disappear into the political embrace of strangers.

"All the week before, he'd go to bed with his mind made up one way and wake with it decided on the other," said his wife. "We talked it over and over."

"Which way did he seem to be leaning?"

"I couldn't tell."

Mondale called his wife up shortly before noon on Wednesday, November 20, and told her to come down to the Senate because he was going to make an important statement at four P.M. She still wasn't sure which way he was going to decide, "though something in his choice of words made me think he would withdraw."

He surprised his staff also. Sid Johnson had just sold his house in Minnesota and taken an apartment in Washington. He was down at the Democratic governors' conference at Hilton Head, South Carolina, the Monday before the announcement, trying to line up support for Mondale when he got the indication from Berman that withdrawal was possible. I was standing in front of the phone booth door as he came out and assumed he had just learned of a death in his family or had been thrown over by his girl, he looked so white and glazed.

A letter to all the delegates to the Democrats' midterm convention at Kansas City was in the mail, urging them to drop by and meet Mondale. Berman had been talking to an advertising agency in New York about handling the campaign on Monday and was still negotiating with the phone company for office phones on Tuesday.

"I found I did not have the overwhelming desire to be President which is essential for the kind of campaign that is required," said Mondale in his public announcement. ". . . I don't think anyone should be President who is not willing to go through the fire. . . . I admire those with the determination to do what is required to seek the presidency, but I have found I am not among them."

The statement dealt with the race almost exclusively in psychological terms. In it there was practically no mention of politics. Would he have continued running if he had found himself more politically successful? His wife and friends are not sure, but, on the whole, they think not. For Mondale, as for Kennedy, the try for the White House had been primarily an interior voyage.

And what did he do upon leaving the invisible primary? He went ice fishing in the far north of Minnesota in January. Two months later he looked more relaxed and happy than I had seen him in two years.

On the Republican side of the invisible primary the first candidate to both enter and quit the race was another senator, Charles Harting Percy of Illinois. While Nixon was winning his reelection as President, Percy was forging his own landslide reelection as senator, becoming the first Senate candidate in Illinois history to carry all the state's counties. The day after Nixon's and Percy's triumphs, the chief political aide, Annapolis graduate Joe Farrell, who had worked with Admiral Hyman Rickover on the development of the nuclear submarine fleet, began to plan Percy's shot at the presidency. Again, note the time: the morning after the Nixon-Agnew triumph, four years from the next election.

Farrell's first step was one unique to the political world of the mid-seventies. He consulted a campaign management firm, that of Bailey, Deardourff, and Eyre, which specializes in liberal Republican clients and had just helped Percy with his Senate campaign. Back in 1959, when Jack Kennedy reached for the presidency, there were fewer than 10 firms in the country offering campaign management. Today, sixteen years later, there are over 350 public relations firms who list political management as a major activity. This makes these political gunslingers among the fastest growth industries in America. Such firms, both Republican and Democratic, plus a few that will handle either side, are displacing the political boss in politics. Ten years ago the first move of those backing Percy would have been to contact the state committeemen and governors who controlled the convention delegates in key states. Those supporting Eisenhower for President had done just that in 1952, as had those supporting Kennedy in 1960. Now Percy's staff turned to a management firm. Later in the invisible primary when Sargent Shriver entered the race, his staff would make the same initial move, going to a Democratic firm, Matt Reese Associates.

For how long these firms will retain their present importance is an open question. Their services come high; and the Campaign Reform Act of 1976 places such severe limits on political spending that candidates may again have to rely on their own organization whose members can be paid off with political rewards rather than with the now outlawed cash. However, no matter how problematical their future, in 1973–75 they played a vital part.*

Bailey and Deardourff dropped most of their other work and by the end of December had prepared an eight-page brief showing that with proper organization, heavy financing ($11 million), and some luck, Percy was, in that well-known phrase, "a viable political candidate." Immediately after his Senate victory Percy went on vacation to Asia. The evening of his return, December 23, Farrell, Doug Bailey, and John Deardourff gathered at his house and brought him the eight-page outline of his chances. Five days later, after a brief interlude for Christmas, they met in Percy's house again and Percy said "Go."

What had caused him to run for President was, for one thing, the fact that Bailey and Deardourff said he had a chance. Such is the present power of the campaign consultant and the importance of the staff track. "I was flattered that such a team of professionals. . . ."

The other key ingredient in his decision, according to Percy, was that he talked the matter over with close friends like "Milton Eisenhower and Tom Watson [head of IBM]" and they urged him to run.

After this sampling of the electorate and the "go" decision, the next step was strategy and money. The firm of Bailey and Deardourff was hired to produce a master plan by March 1—three years before the first state primary. It came in three weeks early and filled six volumes. On the money track, B & D arranged a meeting of industrialists and financiers believed favorable to the Percy candidacy. This took place on the evening of February 7 at the Chicago home of William Graham, board chairman of Baxter Industries. William Graham is an impressive, slow-moving man in his late sixties, kindly but decisive. He and Percy had been friends for a long time. When Percy moved to Washington, Graham bought his house. Like most of the forty-plus people gathered in his living room, he is a good deal older than Percy.

Those at the meeting, to see Bailey and Deardourff's slide show on how Percy could win, represented a wide spectrum of Republican politics. Robert Galvin, board chairman of Motorola, had been a Goldwater supporter; Max Rabb had worked in the Eisenhower White House; Arthur Watson was appointed ambassador to France by Nixon; Arthur Nielson of the Nielson ratings is enough of a closet Democrat to support liberal Democrats for Congress.

"We were looking," says Graham, "for dedicated people willing to work for a long period of time." Besides cash, what Percy was looking for, without seeming to realize it himself, was his constituency. These older, successful men in Graham's living room were it. They definitely preferred Percy to Rockefeller or Agnew. They use such phrases as: "a question of personal

---

*These firms are examined in detail in Chapter 7.

attraction" . . . "He understands business better" . . . "fiscal conservatism combined with moderation on social issues." Money they definitely had. Time and energy to work was something else.

It is important to remember the political environment in which this February fund raiser took place. Three months before, Nixon and Agnew had carried forty-nine out of fifty states. Watergate was only a Washington *Post* story. Spiro T. Agnew was in Saigon talking to President Nguyen Van Thieu and being hailed by the press for his newfound moderation and substance. In the chambers of the Baltimore grand jury no witness had yet implicated the Vice-President of the United States in kickbacks.

According to the polls, Agnew was the number-one candidate for President of the United States, after the successful rule of Richard Nixon ended in 1976. Wounded by the incompetent moralism of George McGovern, the Democratic party tore at its vitals with a wild roar. Those in the Graham living room assumed they were mounting a campaign against Spiro Agnew in 1976 and that the then Vice-President would have the support of Richard Nixon. The only other visible candidate was that old war-horse, Nelson Rockefeller, who had not yet resigned and therefore faced another chancy campaign for governor of New York.

The meeting agreed that Percy should make the race, and those in the room undertook to raise a substantial portion of the necessary $11 million. Milton Eisenhower wrote a letter asking for money to presumed friends of Percy not in the room. The letter lauded Percy as "reasonable, endowed with vision and courage, compassionate but tough, honest and inspiring credibility. . . ." By the end of 1973, close to $100,000 was raised. Another $150,000 followed over the next year. Percy was off and running.

With his first load of dollars, Senator Percy hired Bailey and Deardourff, at nearly $5,500 a month, to exercise overall direction and control of his campaign. But the firm's six volumes had made a strategic assumption that might well have been fatal even had Percy's campaign succeeded on all other tracks. That decision was that Nixon and Agnew would finish out their term as President and Vice-President.

There were other lesser errors that also would have hurt. For example, their statistical analysis showed that Percy should avoid the two early primaries of New Hampshire and Florida because the Republican voters in those states were too conservative to respond to his appeal. Instead he should concentrate on the Midwest, particularly his home state of Illinois and nearby Wisconsin. Wisconsin was seen as key because of its open primary which permitted Democrats to vote for the Republican candidate and vice versa. Percy had always attracted Democratic voters. But as early as May '74 it became obvious to insiders watching the Democrats fight over the "Mikulski rules," which would govern the Democratic convention in 1976, that open primaries were out. Since the Democrats controlled the Wisconsin legislature, the chances were at least 99 out of 100 that Wisconsin would have a caucus or an ordinary closed primary. When this was told to Percy in June

1974, his jaw dropped perceptibly. "But the plan," he began in refutation. Precisely.

The strategy said: Get known to the press, to local Republican leaders, and build a base among moderate businessmen and other liberal Republicans. So out on the road Percy went, usually with one aide, weekend after weekend and sometimes midweek.

Tuesday, May 14, 1974, two years before the convention, he flies to Pittsburgh from Washington at 6 A.M. A spectacularly lovely day, the Allegheny ridges flow in the spring sun like finger-waves in the hair of some sexy, jolly green giantess. Over lunch in his Pittsburgh hotel room, skimmed milk and fruit salad for Percy—four years of campaigning does things to a man's stomach—he stresses that he thinks the time has come for moderate Republicans and himself. "The GOP is going to be stronger because of Watergate," he says. He adds that he believes 1974 will be a disaster for the GOP; and that that will be a good thing because it will allow new blood to enter the party.

I argue that what happens to parties after shattering defeats is just the opposite. New blood then shuns the party and the extremes take over—who don't really care about victory but want to keep the true faith alight. The Republican party turned right after both the upset defeat of the Dewey-Warren ticket by Truman in 1948 and the close loss to Kennedy in 1960. Similarly the McGovern debacle of 1972 left the Democratic party for a time without a moderate center.

I question Percy about his strategy, his constant reliance on organization and planning. Is it really possible to plan a campaign in minute detail so early? On the surface he agrees that chance plays an important part. He points out that the prayer he says every morning recognizes this: "Trust in the Lord with all thine heart. . . . In all thy ways ask only of him and he shall direct thy paths." But Percy goes on to add that the part chance has played in his life seems always for the best. Organization is important in both business and politics. He put the expanded Bell & Howell together with good organization. Now he is going to reorganize the Republican center to bring victory to the party and himself.

Percy also makes much of his sponsors in his campaign. How Milton Eisenhower is the honorary chairman of his committee. How he checked with Vice-President Ford and President Nixon and they had both urged him to run. He seems oblivious to the fact that Ford and Nixon would need his vote if and when impeachment comes up. What did he expect "good old Jerry" and the embattled President to say? "One move out of you, kid, and we'll cut you off at the diaper." Doesn't he know that John Rhodes, the House minority leader who speaks for Ford, tells reporters privately that the Percy campaign is a joke? What inner agonies drive him to seek the approval of his elders rather than his peers for his campaign?

Percy's rise to wealth and power is almost a Horatio Alger fiction. He was born in Florida on September 27, 1919, the eldest of three children, his family substantial and middle-class. Percy's father, a cashier in a bank, moved his family to Chicago the year after. Until 1930, when Percy was eleven, times were good—pranks, music lessons, Tom Swift books. Then came the stock market crash. The bank in which the elder Percy was an officer failed, and Percy's father drifted from job to job, when he had a job, selling paint, shifting stock, and finally attaining a seven-night-a-week clerking position in a cheap hotel for thirty-five dollars a week, thus ending periods when the family was on relief.

During these hard times it was Percy's mother "who busied herself in everything and who held our family together." In describing his family, Percy again and again returns to this theme of his father's weakness and his mother's strength. From genteel wealth to the edges of poverty; being born small (he is five foot seven); a strong mother and a weak but religious and loving father: almost a textbook example of that psychological kiln that, when the endocrine mixture is right, fires within the individual a hard, constant drive for success.*

With Percy the drive is there and it started early. He is steadfastly ambitious, to use a polite adverb, though like most successful men he can mask this ambition behind a great deal of personal charm. While in high school he held four jobs, stoking furnaces in the early morning, working in the registrar's office during the forenoon, selling newspapers and magazines in the afternoon, and ushering in a movie theater at night. By the time he graduated from the University of Chicago he was, he says, "netting ten thousand dollars a year" supplying food, laundry, fuel, and other such necessities wholesale to the various campus fraternities. "I could hardly afford to quit school."

In high school Charles Percy had taken a fateful step. He entered a Christian Science Sunday School class taught by Joseph McNabb, president of the then minuscule Bell & Howell camera company. The older man and the young boy became friends. A year later Percy asked McNabb one Sunday after church (or wrote McNabb a letter, the story gets told different ways at different times) to take on his father as a mail-room supervisor. The son had saved the father from defeat—an ancient legend, always enacted at some cost.

Percy's rise from summer helper in Bell & Howell's sales department to president of the company at twenty-nine is one of the legendary success

---

*There seems to me a fascinating opportunity for someone to examine the presidential character in terms of the effect their mothers have had upon the Presidents. In traveling with all the putative candidates I was struck by how many of them appeared to have come from mother-dominated households. Percy, Reagan, Mondale, Jackson, and Udall all put their mothers first in conversations about their boyhood. And certainly, in history, Lincoln, Wilson, Franklin Roosevelt, and Nixon spring to mind.

stories of American business. Percy was able; McNabb, the president, pulled for him; the combination worked. McNabb wrote a letter to his Board of Directors, average age over sixty, to be opened after his death, asking that they appoint Percy president. They did. "I have always gotten along better with those older than with my contemporaries," says Percy of himself. Helped by the affluent society and the space age, the young president increased the company's business from $13 million to $160 million in seventeen years.

One of the first actions Percy had to take after becoming president of Bell & Howell was to fire his father—a fact not mentioned in the official biographies and brochures. "The hardest action I have ever had to take," Percy described it to me. His father came to Percy and complained bitterly. Percy gave him a Cadillac and use of a credit card for gas in Charles Percy's name. The father "who because of the depression had never bought more than a dollar's worth of gas in his life" drove down to Florida and back saying "fill-'er-up" and charging the energy to the son. A year later he was dead.

"Everything that has happened to me has been for the best" is one of Percy's constant refrains. Another is: "Let's see if we can't turn this lemon into lemonade."

On September 18, 1966, as Percy's Senate campaign was swinging into its final stretch, Mrs. Percy awoke in their home at 5:15 in the morning, thinking she heard a low moan from her stepdaughter Valerie's room. When she entered the room, she saw a man in a short-sleeved checkered shirt standing over her stepdaughter's bed. The man swung his flashlight beam on Mrs. Percy, pushed by her, and fled out of the house and into the well-known oblivion. Mrs. Percy screamed and woke her husband. The girl had been beaten to death and then stabbed seventeen times. The police came. The murder is still unsolved.

Men and women recover from such things. Still, I am puzzled by Percy's relentless optimism. Perhaps it springs from his deep religious faith, like that of Pope John, who could say, "Any day is a good day to be born, any day is a good day to die." But Pope John knew: "*Sunt lacrimae rerum.*" Percy carries optimism to the point of charade. The final note in my notebook after a three-day swing with him reads: "Campaigning with Candide."

After his lunch in Pittsburgh, Percy is a guest on a television panel show dealing with the problems of nursing homes. Then there is a news conference in one of the ballrooms of the Pittsburgh hotel. The conference is scheduled for early enough in the afternoon to make the local evening newscasts. There are over twenty public relations men from ALCOA and other Pittsburgh industries at the press conference along with ten reporters.

Percy stands behind a lectern, giving short speeches as answers to easily foreseen questions. There are no follow-up questions. Most of the questions are on Watergate and impeachment, but the local TV reporters appear unfamiliar with the intricacies of these subjects. Not a true press conference producing information, the meeting is a media event, giving the candidate free publicity in the invisible primary.

These local press conferences are one of the main reasons the candidates go on the road: to gain exposure on local television. The candidate is seldom questioned effectively; rather his is a show-business performance with awards going to a particular type of short, adept answer that might be labeled "snapback with quickback." The candidate who has time to travel and is reasonably appealing gets seen, while the candidate who elects to stay at his work as governor, mayor, or senator loses out. We have created a new American job classification: Running for President.

Percy uses a completely different voice on television and at press conferences from the one he uses in private, as if he wanted to emphasize the public nature of the occasion. His private voice is soft, slow, and quite convincing. His public voice is lower in register, more nasal, and even slower, as if a tape recording of his ordinary voice is being played at too slow a speed. I sometimes wonder if some machine inside him has jammed. Do the two voices indicate a deep split between the public and private man?

After an evening address to the Economic Club of Pittsburgh, about eight hundred people, 80 percent male, practically all over thirty-five and a good percentage over sixty (Percy failed to turn them on), we jet to Des Moines, Iowa. The brown midwestern earth lies puddled by the previous day's heavy rains, but that day fair-weather cumulous clouds drift past the gold dome of the capitol. Percy is rushing, rushing, rushing, because there is a crucial vote in the Senate on busing the next day, and two days' schedule has been compressed into one so he can make the vote. (Were he a Democrat, and in with the Senate leadership, the vote would be delayed so he could continue with his speaking schedule.) He is also getting rather second-rate billing. At lunch he speaks to fewer than one hundred old people in a room where a month before Nelson Rockefeller had given the word to some six hundred cheering liberal Republicans.

Asked about Percy, several local politicians, state senators, members of the governor's staff, congressional candidates, say: "Well, if Nelson doesn't run . . . maybe." Or, "Rockefeller's worked for the party a long time." Christopher Lydon, the elf-eared sprite who covers national politics for *The New York Times,* and who makes up the national press following Percy this day, rushes to a pay phone to check out more promising political stories in other states.

For Percy the key to the day is a meeting in the downstairs bar of the Wakanda Country Club in Des Moines. Here are gathered thirty men and women who have been selected because they are the liberal GOP leaders in Iowa. To prepare for this meeting Percy takes a shower and changes into a fresh shirt.

The air conditioning makes so much noise that it has to be turned off because it affects Percy's hearing aid and he can't hear the questions. The windows of the room don't open and the place grows shirt-dripping hot. Percy waffles on Watergate, then explains how, as a "businessman who understands government," he saved America millions by having the Army buy coffee commercially. He says, "The Republican party has never been stronger. . . . This recession is our opportunity." He ticks off Republican successes: The war in Vietnam is ended, the isolation of Red China broken, the draft stopped, SALT is a success, there is peace in the Middle East, and Berlin is free. Outside the picture windows, the affluent in golf carts swan around the greens. Percy's audience looks sandbagged. As we rush to leave, I ask several of them if they think the world is as hunky-dory as Percy has described. No one does. Will they work for him? He picks up one or two cards, but most talk about Rockefeller or Richardson.

Flying back to Washington, Percy insists (this is June 1974) that he will stay in the race no matter what Vice-President Ford's fate. "I am definitely committed to the presidential race no matter what happens to Vice-President Ford." He is meeting people and getting names now; and later if the leaders in a state will not back him, he'll be tough—create his own organization and go in and fight.

A month later on July 24 the Supreme Court ordered President Nixon to turn over to the grand jury sixty-four disputed taped transcripts of White House conversations. Nixon debated whether to obey the order. His lawyer, James St. Clair, threatened to resign if he didn't. The President complied. One tape caught Nixon with the smoking gun in his hand—approving the Watergate cover-up three days after the burglary. Three days after the tapes were released the specter of obvious impeachment forced Nixon to resign. On August 8, shortly before noon, he summoned Vice-President Jerry Ford to the White House. The next day the American President was "good old Jerry Ford," who if he does drive down the right side of the Republican road, at least doesn't mount the sidewalk to cream the bystanders.

A week later, before Ford had appointed Nelson Rockefeller, pardoned ex-President Nixon, indeed before he had done anything significant, Percy quit the race. Why?

"The compelling need was no longer there," Percy explained. "The candor, the openness that I wanted in the presidency had been achieved." (He could judge that in seven days?) He finally agreed that neither he nor his staff had faced the problem of Ford becoming President. When saying privately in May and June that he wouldn't decide about his own campaign until the country had had an opportunity to judge Ford, he had assumed that Nixon would serve out his term, or remain in office so long that Ford would be contaminated by Watergate and easy to defeat.

Percy felt his campaign had gone well. He had impressed the party leaders and the media. He had accumulated a card file of seventeen thousand names, all anxious to help.

On my swings around the country or talking to Republicans in Washington I never saw such evidence of Percy strength. Rockefeller and Richardson both seemed to have more of the GOP center and left in their camp than Percy, for all his efforts. As for the names, any politician will get offers of help after a speech. In building the constituency, the quality of the names is more important than sheer numbers.

Percy was not being entirely candid. The reason for his withdrawal from the invisible primary was total failure on one track: money. As soon as Ford became President, Percy's constituency, the fund raisers of the exploratory committee, neither wanted to, nor could, raise the $11 million.

"We told him, no funds," said William Graham. Not that they regretted the $200,000 spent. "All we have done now will be of benefit, if he wants to run for office at some future time." His constituency had enough cash to put a few thousand on a long shot, and when Ford became President to fold without complaint. Once again the problem of energizing the center was that the center lacked the capacity for passionate belief.

Percy's campaign ended because of Watergate. The campaign of the other early-starting Republican, Elliot Richardson, was created by Watergate. In the invisible primary the two men ran a totally different type of race. Percy spent $200,000 and had the power, staff, and prerequisites of his Senate office. Citizen Elliot Richardson, late attorney general of the United States, late secretary of defense, late secretary of health, education, and welfare, late undersecretary of state, former lieutenant governor of Massachusetts, financed himself from his lecture fees, and had a two-person office and no job. Richardson hadn't intended to run for President or be attorney general. In fact, when summoned to Camp David after Nixon's '72 triumph to learn his fate—there were rumors he would be asked to leave the administration because of his constant pressure for welfare reform—"The one job I planned to refuse was attorney general." His preference was "to stay in health, education, and welfare, complete the work started." But he had become too controversial in that job; and Nixon shifted him to secretary of defense.

Then under the dogged probing of the Washington *Post* the "third-rate burglary" of Watergate slowly bubbled bigger into national scandal. On the last day of April, the then attorney general, Richard Kleindienst, resigned because of his "close personal and professional relationship" with some of those being investigated. Less than three months after becoming secretary of defense, Richardson accepted the job he had no intention of taking. "To restore the integrity of Justice itself. . . . 99 and 44/100 percent pure is not now, if it ever was, good enough." He hung in there for half a year: quite a half year, Watergate and Agnew.

In the end President Nixon ordered Richardson to fire Watergate Special Prosecutor Archibald Cox, who was insisting on his right to hear more White House tapes. At the time Richardson had hired Cox, his friend and former law professor, he had pledged publicly before the Senate Judiciary Committee that he would give Cox a free hand. After trying hard to compromise the differences between Cox and the White House, Richardson resigned. In so doing he became a presidential candidate. He also picked up the respect of the press; and since he had always dealt fairly, if somewhat distantly, with reporters, he had established a firm position on the media track.

His resignation and the press conference that followed showed Richardson at his best. The times were passionate, partisan, and confused; Richardson with his intellectual coolness and dramatic act of integrity showed to advantage. He is a lot better at remaining calm in the eye of a storm than in stirring up a storm, a fact at once both his personal strength and his political handicap. Richardson tends to look uptight. He wears conservatively cut, single-breasted gray suits and shirts with high collars held firm and semistarched about his neck by a retaining device—the tight knotted tie cinching the collar even tighter. As he talks informally, he weaves back and forth as if battered by conflicting pressures. He pauses now and again, puts his head to one side as if listening to the echoes of what he has just said, and finding it both brilliant and unsatisfactory at the same time, smiles.

Beneath this controlled Boston exterior is a passionate subsurface. "I always feel I have Italian blood in me," says Richardson. This stream erupts now and then in temper, humor, and, I suspect, private tears (also in some professionally acceptable watercolors). Richardson seems at times perplexed by the buried romantic, which probably accounts for the tight rein on which he holds himself and his opinions. He appears to have stepped out of a late Tintoretto portrait of some leader of the Serene Venetian Republic: patrician, politically calculating, wise past the point of cynicism, but still passionate.

"Honesty is the best policy. It is important to remember that honesty is not enjoined by morality alone but by the benefits it confers on the practitioner. Honest politics are the best politics. Undoubtedly this reason for proper behavior is not quite as good as a genuine moral conversion but the behavior that results is liable to be quite similar." That's quintessential Richardson. Hardly the stuff to cause the troops to leap from the trenches and storm the presidency. Compare this to Senator Birch Bayh explaining he should win the invisible primary because "I can tell a bad man from a good."

Richardson, starting his campaign in the unseen race nine months after Percy, and from his vantage point as a just-retired attorney general, still made the same assumption about Nixon and Ford. "I thought the odds on

Nixon not finishing his term were less than fifty-fifty," said Richardson. He was relaxing while campaigning in Indiana in November '74, the day before the midterm congressional elections—the last day of his own campaign. Richardson felt at the time he resigned that Nixon was innocent of any criminal wrongdoing. "I came slowly to the conclusion over the next three months that there was damaging evidence on the tapes." From the assumption that Nixon would finish his term, Richardson drew the same conclusion as Percy's staff: that Ford would be so tarnished by Watergate as to be defeatable in selected primaries.

So the ex-attorney general set out. He was trying to find "those little random currents of air that successful politicians look for to get up, stay up and get where they want to go." He was also writing a book and delivering a series of lectures to pay his way and cover the office expenses of a secretary and one-man staff, Richard Mastrangelo, who had been with him since his first campaign in Massachusetts. (Does the Italianate subsurface of Richardson account for the number of his close associates who are Italian?)

Even as he entered the invisible primary, Richardson made two decisions, one personal, the other public, as to his degree of commitment. Personally he decided not to say, "Yes, I'm running" because "I wanted to remain my own man . . . not take that psychological step." Too often he felt the decision to run robbed the candidate of all objectivity. He could no longer tell how his campaign was going, whether he should or should not be in the race.

On the psychological track, Richardson was displaying his usual precise caution. All the candidates and their staff talked about this judgmental problem. Most often they cited the example of George McGovern, whom they saw as a prisoner of his staff and his own ego. Seeing the world out of focus through the eyes of admirers, he was unable to master his staff to his will.

The second reason for Richardson's tentativeness about his presidential race was political: "to increase my attractiveness as a candidate." He believed more people would be interested in him as a candidate as long as he was not a candidate. He could also be of more help to those GOP candidates for the House and Senate who asked for his aid, and because he was not a candidate but a crusading ex-attorney general, he would draw a bigger audience on the lecture circuit, which was important both financially and politically. This also says something about how the public regards the pride of presidential candidates who are on the prowl for votes through the political veldt.

Throughout his race, Richardson was very careful never to cross that line he had set for himself and become more of a candidate than he intended. Here are a series of his public responses to probings on whether he was a presidential candidate:

"Mr. Richardson, do you want to be President?"

"The only honest answer I can give is that when I've thought about it, which is not often, I don't honestly think I don't want to be President."

"Do you have any plans to run?"

"No, I don't."

"Well, would you like to run if things broke right?"

"I could be persuaded over my natural reluctance; but this does not mean that I am a candidate."

Richardson was asked to speak often; not as often as he had hoped, but enough to keep him out of Washington three or four days a week. If a wise Republican candidate for the Congress wished to divorce himself from President Nixon without kicking the Republican party in the slats, Richardson as featured speaker at a rally was the ideal way. Richardson had remained a loyal Republican. He obviously had no desire to march forward by the light of bridges burning behind him. He always went out of his way to say he couldn't comment on whether the President should or would be impeached since he had been part of the process. "I think impeachment is a matter on which I cannot afford to indulge in personal feelings. It should be approached on the evidence with as little tinge of partisanship as possible." Only the most ardent Nixon partisan could ask for more. Yet he was the man who refused to fire Archibald Cox, who believed: "No man should be above the law," and "we all should live our lives so we would not be afraid to sell our parrot to the town gossip."

On all his campaign swings Richardson kept himself highly organized. In the three hours between an Indianapolis TV appearance and his flight back to Washington, Mastrangelo had arranged a room so Elliot could finish a chapter in his book. Richardson boasts that one night while secretary of defense, he came back to his house overlooking the Potomac at seven, put on his waders, walked a quarter mile to the river, caught a large bass, saw three blue heron, came home, recorded seeing the heron, showered, shaved, got into a black tie for dinner at the Danish embassy, and was in the car with his wife at precisely eight. Traveling with Richardson, I am both jealous and reminded of the nursery rhyme: "How doth the busy little bee, improve each shining hour."

With the degree of noncandidacy that he had chosen for himself, Richardson did not seek commitments of support when out on the road. He was energizing his constituency for future action but not signing up individual members. Candidates and their staffs differ completely on how to go about obtaining political commitments: "pitch and wait" versus "grab and twist." For example, though Senator Jackson is a tough political operator in the Senate, on the road he and his staff believe that only the names of those who volunteer to work should be taken. To twist arms for a commitment, they feel, merely signs up many people who will later only work halfheartedly or perhaps not at all.

On the other hand, Richardson, like Senator Bentsen, is a convinced "grab and twist." Based on his campaigns for attorney general and lieutenant governor of Massachusetts, he is convinced that after you make your speech you have to force those in the audience you want with you to make a public declaration of support. "The average amateur politician," Richardson holds, "once they have made a public commitment, will stick with you even at some detriment to themselves." (Terror kept me from asking what the average professional politician would do after publicly pledging himself.) But for this noncampaign, while Richardson would accept the names of volunteers who offered to help, he made no arm-twisting grabs.

Richardson claims that he enjoys campaigning, pressing the flesh, meeting different people. Well, maybe. He doesn't exactly radiate bonhomie. Asked for some moments of joy during one year of the invisible primary, he cited a fund raiser in Salem, Massachusetts, where he got to dance with a great many beautiful women in evening dresses. He is a superlative dancer—the Italian in the Brahmin again? Probably Richardson enjoys in the abstract the idea of campaigning as part of his concept of "being of service."

Richardson's eyes were so bad he had to use deception to get himself into the Army, and even then was kept out of the infantry. He ended up as a combat medical officer and speaks with great passion about the "constant heroism" of the men around him in the 4th Infantry Division in the period immediately after D Day as well as his own feelings then. "I was driven to a sustained and extremely concentrated effort to help more. As a medic I knew that nothing I did could ever cause regret. We were picking up the wounded, mostly our own, but the wounded on both sides—pure unalloyed service. And it gave me a keenness of observation and of intellect and a reaction of pure joy I have not experienced before or since."

One has to see Richardson in such moments of passion to appreciate the fuel that drives him toward public office. No man could have survived as he has in Massachusetts politics, the deadliest game in the fifty states, without excellent political sense. But he often seems more a professor who gets his psychological returns out of explaining a fine point to his audience than a politician who enjoys promoting himself for the next higher office. What can one say of a man who describes democracy to a 7 A.M. local TV audience as "not an absolute good. Democracy is a process within which individuals are treated as individually important. Otherwise it's worth little in itself. . . . People accuse me of being overly concerned with process. What they don't see, what is so difficult to explain, is that in a complex society concern for the proper process of government and concern for the individual are one and the same." How lonely citizen Richardson must have been in the Nixon Cabinet!

Successful politician that he was, Elliot Richardson managed to stay airborne on the winds of his Watergate firing for some time. But his lack of political base made him vulnerable on many of the invisible primary tracks, even on media, where he was at his best. Between 1936 and 1972, 90 percent of those rising high enough in public esteem to be considered by the polls as possible presidential candidates have been political officeholders, or else linked to public affairs in some fashion by their job, such as a military officer. Richardson had no job. This handicapped him on the staff and psychological tracks as well as with the media.

Without a political base a man has to be continually careful not to cross that thin dividing line between serious candidate and kook—a line quite a few of the candidates crossed in the period 1972–76. After all, any one of us could call up our local TV stations and newspapers tomorrow and announce that we were running for the presidency. This might disturb our families, but it would not cause much disturbance on the body politic. Constituency, media, and public must perceive the candidacy as reasonable.

For example, in 1964, before either Senator Gene McCarthy or Robert Kennedy had decided to challenge President Lyndon Johnson's Vietnam policies, General James M. Gavin, then chairman of the board of Arthur D. Little, Inc., courageously planned to campaign in New Hampshire as an antiwar candidate. Gavin, because of his past public life and candor on vital issues, enjoyed, like Richardson, a credibility with the press that was close to unparalleled for a private figure. The media were anxious to find someone of stature who opposed the Vietnam War. Yet there were actions Gavin could not take—such as leaving his job to campaign for a month in New Hampshire—that would have come naturally for a political figure.

Running for President, a private individual has to be very careful not to fracture his credibility. And if broken, like Humpty Dumpty's shell, all of Madison Avenue's horses aren't going to be able to put it back together again. ("That Van Lingo Wombatt is nothing but a nut.") Richardson would joke about the strain this need for constant caution caused him, referring to the Doonesbury cartoon which had him refusing to rake the leaves around his house because he is going to look for a job tomorrow. However, his laughter didn't always successfully mask the genuine effects of his problem.

Toward the end of his campaign Richardson felt the batterings of depression. "I don't know where I'm going to live, much less what I am going to do," he said, flying into Indianapolis. ". . . For the first time in my life I am in doubt." He talked about how hard and tiring the work had been. "The crucial and most exhausting moment in any campaign is when the candidate is trying to get his campaign off the ground and that is usually in the preprimary stage."

He also talked in those last weeks a great deal about death and about chance, which he felt had played a crucial part in his life. "I'm trying to live each day as if this very minute were my last. . . . I don't know what it's like to have nothing to do. I mean nothing I have to do." He felt each time that he got onto an airplane that the flight might well end in death. Dropping out of the icy turbulence of the ILS approach to Cincinnati brought into view a large billboard which asked: "Are you ready for Jesus?"

"Hardly reassuring," said Elliot, cinching his seat belt tighter.

Speaking on the political chaos that lack of trust in government creates, he began to repeatedly use a new, and unusual for him, highly personal metaphor. "Have you ever thought to wake in the middle of the night and wonder if the floor between the bed and the door will hold your weight?"

"Have you recently, Elliot?"

No reply, just a slight pause and inclination of the head. As one who now and again wakes in terror not knowing where I am, I sympathize.

In the end his absence of a constituency, plus the chance he so believed in, combined to make the continued Richardson campaign impossible. Once Ford became President and appointed Nelson Rockefeller as Vice-President, Richardson felt that in continuing in the invisible primary he would merely be splitting the liberal Republican vote and so opening the party up to Ronald Reagan. He withdrew. Only for him there was a final irony.

Belatedly realizing that his staff, which had been barely marginal for a Vice-President, was totally inadequate for a President, Gerald Ford called NATO Ambassador Donald Rumsfeld back from Paris to be his chief of staff. The two men had been friends when Rumsfeld had been a Republican congressman from Illinois. Having no place to stay when he first got back to Washington, Rumsfeld moved in with another old friend, Senator Charles Percy. One can only guess what they talked about late at night, two gung-ho midwestern liberal Republicans, either of whom might replace Nelson Rockefeller in '76 as Vice-President. But there was that other guy around, Richardson.

On December 6, Richardson, at his desk working on his book, was called on the phone by Kissinger and offered the post of ambassador to Great Britain. Surprised, Richardson said he would think it over. Four days later the two men met again late at night. Richardson meanwhile had checked around and found that none of the jobs he would have preferred—like being reappointed attorney general—was open to him. So after being reassured by Kissinger that he would have a "substantive effect on policy" and not just sit around and entertain, Richardson took the ambassadorship. He felt that seemed preferable to "marginally trying to keep alive a candidacy."

A year later, as the invisible primary was drawing to its close, Richardson would return to Washington and a new cabinet post. By that time it would be too late to revive what was left of his candidacy. He would, to be sure, remain a Republican vice-presidential possibility, and that could be important for the future. But there was now no hope that history would remember 1976 as the Year of Elliot Richardson.

So two years before the first state primary the invisible primary had begun the task of weeding out candidates in its own peculiar and capricious fashion. Four candidates quite different in skills and political approach, but all with valid reasons to reach for the presidency, had entered the race and then quit. The voters' choice had been narrowed. The nation had hardly noticed. And around the nation other candidates put forth probes or leaped into the fray.

CHAPTER 3

Udall. The New Rules of the Game

"**W**henever I hear myself introduced as 'deeply involved in the Wilderness Act,' I feel as if I'd committed an immoral act in some national park. . . ."

"Mr. Congressman, how do you, as a liberal, win in Goldwater's state of Arizona?"

"Well, there are five or six key elements: good looks, personality, charm, integrity; and my platform: improve your sex life, cure inflation, end the cold war, burn no energy."

Of all the candidates off and running early, at first swift glance none seemed more improbable of success than six-foot-five Congressman Morris "Mo" Udall, the one-eyed individualist from rural Arizona. He was a congressman, not a senator or governor. He was a divorced Mormon from a small western state, in favor of voluntary zero population growth. He had been beaten out for House majority leader in 1970. His major legislative effort, the land-use bill, had recently gone down to defeat. He'd even been captain of the Democratic congressional baseball team for the past eleven years; and in spite of his three famous pitches—the Romney fadeaway,* the credibility sinker, and the Nixon slider ("a sneaky little pitch that comes in inside and low")—the Democrats had always lost. While not quite seeing him as the twice-divorced Arab who is against Sunday bingo and who was nominated after a bitter primary fight—the dream opponent of every New York congressman—most of the press either ignored Udall or wrote him off as an impossibly long shot. In early '74 *The New York Times* thought him "not credible." The night of Teddy Kennedy's withdrawal NBC did not even include him in its roundup of other Democratic candidates. Yet Udall had a number of hidden strengths, when measured by the six criteria of the invisible primary. Particularly in his constituency, Udall had an important base that had been produced both by the changed 1976 rules for presidential selection and by a profound shift of power in Washington.

---

*"The Romney fadeaway starts out on a high trajectory, then appears to change position several times on the way to the plate, and then dives firmly into the turf."

"Had you gone to Washington in the 1920s," Udall explains, "and asked a local bartender or cabdriver—these are the oracles of wisdom in places like Washington—who were the five most important men in town, he might have gotten to Calvin Coolidge around number three, four, or five. The most important man in town was Nicholas Longworth, the speaker of the House."

That was true once; but during the period spanned by the great depression, World War II, and the cold war, power in Washington shifted twice. The first shift was the well-chronicled shift of power away from Congress to the Executive. This occurred not just under Nixon and Lyndon Johnson, but also during the terms of Roosevelt, Truman, and Kennedy. Even the quiescent Eisenhower issued more executive orders in his first month as President than Truman had during his entire term.

Less visible, starting in the early 1900s, another major shift was also in progress: Power passed from the House of Representatives to the Senate. This transfer was quite contrary to the much deferred to but little studied or understood "wishes of the founding fathers." Up to 1912, senators were not even directly elected, being appointed by the governors or state legislatures to look after the state's business in Washington. The great figures of our early years (Madison, Lincoln, John Quincy Adams, and Jackson) came from the House.

Exactly why the shift of power from the House to the Senate happened is not clear. Certainly the six-year term for senators, coupled with the growing importance of seniority for promotion in the House, made the Senate more attractive to able men. Those with ambition, who had the opportunity, tended to try for the Senate rather than wait for the slow grind of seniority to elevate them in the House. At the same time the problems of America, though still simple enough to be solved by generalists, became national rather than local. Increasingly, this placed the scene of action in the Senate more than in the House; and able men gravitate toward the action. As transportation and communication improved, foreign affairs became more important, and traditionally the Senate took the lead on foreign affairs. In any event, the major legislative achievements of the twenties through the fifties all bore the names of famous senators: the Sherman Antitrust Act, the Vandenberg Resolution, the McMahon Act, the Wagner Act, the Taft-Hartley Act.

Then some time in the middle sixties, the power began to shift again, back toward the House. Some people might argue that the shift is neither certain yet, nor significant. After all, are not practically all recent presidential candidates senators? The Kennedys, Johnson, McGovern, McCarthy, Taft, Lodge, Percy, Nixon. Is not the TV tube filled every night with senators bloviating? The national media—TV, wire services, magazines, columnists—focus on senators. But perhaps that might be interpreted as a symptom not of strength, but of irrelevance. Precisely at a time when the problems of America have grown increasingly complex, senators have become generalists and public personalities, mere media figures, images.

In the last ten years members of the House have found that they, with their more narrow areas of expertise, were often better prepared than senators to understand the nation's problems and provide a counterweight to executive power. At the same time, senators now governed by rules more rigid than those of the House, unable to make any substantive contributions to legislation, turned toward investigations. Here senators got national TV exposure and increased their chances both to be reelected and to be considered presidential contenders. But they lost real power. A vicious circle created and fed on itself, where senators did less and less substantive work and more and more media-grabbing investigation. This left the nation's business undone, increased public dissatisfaction with politics, and aided the President's usurpation of real power from Congress. An air of shallowness and cynicism hangs like a miasma over the actions of more and more senators.

And then there was civil rights. The leadership of the Senate in the sixties—Richard Russell, Tom Connally, Russell Long, Sam Ervin, Lister Hill—had all opposed black equality. They had used their considerable power to keep America white. This had created what one respected and leading senator has privately called "a rottenness at the core of the Senate that may take a generation to overcome."

The House members, slowly reforming themselves, knew that the power balance was tilting in their direction, partly through their own efforts, partly by default. Today, the Senate-House conferences where the final legislation is hammered out usually end the way House members want. Yet House members find themselves overlooked and minimized by press and public. They resent it and are looking for ways to emphasize their new power. The Udall candidacy is typical of this House versus Senate struggle.

Congressman Morris Udall started his race with a built-in constituency: important members of the House and their staffs, professionals all of them.

Like so much of politics—perhaps too much—Udall's plunge into the invisible primary took place mostly by chance. Early in May '71 Congressmen Henry S. Reuss and David R. Obey, both of Wisconsin and good friends, were standing together on the floor of the House, having just voted. It is symbolic of the unpremeditated occasion that neither man can recall what the vote was. Reuss, a fiscal expert and more conservative than Obey, in nine months would defeat the aging Wright Patman for chairman of the Banking and Currency Committee of the House, as part of the House "revolution." Obey, a populist and reformer who often has a bird dog called Webster asleep in his outer office, was lamenting the factionalism in the Democratic party and "the increasing possibility of a Kennedy-Jackson shoot-out in which everyone will get hurt." (Before Kennedy's withdrawal Democrats stood around like spectators in an old-fashioned movie melodrama watching the trains hurtle toward each other down the single track but too far away to give warning. All they could do was hope that one or the other engineer would see the smoke in the distance and say, "Ain't that old Eighty-eight?" and hit the brakes.)

"If we could just get someone like Udall to run," said Obey.

"Let's ask him," said Reuss.

They walked over to Udall and asked.

Udall mentioned his great political record: He had been defeated for the House leadership, had endorsed Stevenson, had endorsed Robert Kennedy, had endorsed Muskie, had endorsed a mayor of Tucson who is now an insurance salesman. He suggested they look elsewhere. Finally he agreed that if they could get 10 percent of the House Democrats to ask him to run, he would. Reuss and Obey contacted their friends and within a week were back with a carefully constructed list.

The twenty-nine Democratic congressmen who originally urged Udall to run were not the usual far-out petition signers; they were the middle-management powers of the House, men who were not yet senior enough to chair committees but who ran vital subcommittees. In addition to Reuss and Obey, there were Thomas Ashley of Ohio, James Symington of Missouri, Frank Thompson of New Jersey, Otis Pike and Jack Bingham of New York, Don Edwards of California, Richardson Preyer of North Carolina. In their petition urging Udall to run, the twenty-nine stated: ". . . barely* twenty-six months from convention time the public is presented with a short exclusive list of 'leading contenders.' Almost every name on that list is a U.S. Senator. . . . We think it is important to look in other places including the House. . . . Historically the House—more than any other place—has produced broadly acceptable, unifying leaders. . . ."

Lawrence Hogan, of the House Judiciary Committee, put it more succinctly, commenting on the public acclaim over the committee performance during impeachment hearings: "Everybody is used to seeing those clowns from the Senate on TV. The House operates with real dignity."

"There is great resentment in the House over the way senators' views get priority," says Udall, who always labels the senators running for President as "self-appointed candidates."

With that petition as his launching pad (or cover for his own ambitions, if you prefer), Udall was off and running. Not that his takeoff was marked only by cheers. Udall's struggles to reform the campaign laws, change the power structure of the House, protect the environment, and create a separate postal service had left some badly bruised egos.

House power Wayne Hayes, who had opposed Udall's efforts at campaign spending reform, lashed out: "I have as much chance of being king of England as Udall does of being President. His record in the House is spotty. The post office bill he elbowed through turned out a farce and disaster. As a human being he is a very attractive guy. But as a political strategist he leaves a great deal to be desired."

Bernie Sisk, a senior Democrat from California who has also crossed

---

*Note the word "barely." The petition was written twenty months before the New Hampshire primary, the official start of the presidential race! But the congressmen didn't say "already" or "this early"; they said "barely. . . ."

swords with Udall, believes: "He is trying for a middle-of-the-road image. A working relationship with Middle America. But I have the feeling that some of his positions are not too acceptable there."

Even some of the original twenty-nine who signed the petition urging Udall to run in order to bring more national press attention to the House had inner doubts about Mo's candidacy. One of these supporters, the week of the announcement, fantasized this dialogue between himself and his local political leaders, if he announced his support of Udall:

"Does he have any expertise in foreign policy? Well, no, you couldn't say that. Though he can find the Middle East on a map—if it's a different color. How about economics and inflation? . . . No, he hasn't done much there. . . . Health? . . . No. . . . The plight of the city? . . . Well, no, he hasn't been involved in that either. . . . Then what the hell has he been doing? . . . Well, he's been working hard on land use. . . . Land use, you don't say, now that's a good thing. How's he doing on it? . . . Well, the land-use bill he's been working on for three years just got defeated in the House because of sloppy political handling. . . . Oh. Does this guy have any personal problems? . . . Maybe. He's a one-eyed divorced Mormon with a second wife who doesn't want him to run. . . . You're running this guy, Congressman? What's up? You thinking of retiring?"

But Peter Hart, one of the respected new breed of political pollsters, felt the times were changing faster than realized and that the zeitgeist favored Udall. The public had shifted, he felt, away from respect for the generalist to belief in character and admiration for the expert: If a man could solve problems honestly in one or two areas, he could be trusted to deal with others. Hart thought those launching Udall had more going for them than they realized.

In the beginning as he started out on the road in late May 1974, Udall himself was shy and diffident about his chances. "I wasn't sure anyone would show up for my press conferences."

Arriving in Salt Lake City in July, he opened an evening airport press conference attended by two TV crews, three local reporters, and a gaggle of Democratic officeholders. "It's great to be back in North Panguich again and see all you people. That's where I am, isn't it? . . .

"If you would like to know about my campaign, I can report that neither Fritz or Teddy or Scoop have resigned in my favor. Mayor Daley has yet to call. No corporation has tried to corrupt me—though my wife is thinking of installing a phone in the bathroom so she can talk to reporters.

"In New Hampshire, a wag said that what you presidential hopefuls are doing is kind of like foreplay—going around touching all the erogenous zones in the body politic."

Humor is an integral part of any Udall argument or speech, indeed a basic part of his personality. He uses anecdote and wit to convince people—a technique he learned as a county prosecutor in Arizona—and he admires Lincoln for his conscious political use of the storytelling technique. He keeps two thick dog-eared black notebooks full of stories, cross-indexed for different occasions, to which he is always adding material. His brother Stewart and others who grew up with him in the small town of St. Johns, Arizona, remember him as a ballplayer and leader rather than a wit. Nor do his Army buddies in the Pacific recall the present flood of stories. The technique, like Udall's sophistication on a number of issues, has been learned.

Humor grows out of conflict. The battle in Udall appears to be between his brains and his ambition. "Udall does think, and intellectuals like to talk to him," says Jessica Tuchman, biochemist daughter of historian Barbara Tuchman, who helps to introduce Udall to the "intellectuals"—whoever they are. But while bright, he is also a rambling, small-town plowboy with western gung-ho ambition and outlook. One minute he is the all-out politician going down court full out, the way he used to play professional basketball for glory and the buck; the next minute he is an amused spectator, laughing not at the ambition of the ballplayer, but at the whole silly notion of earning money by stuffing a round bouncing object through a giant's wedding ring.

"We put down our politicians in this country and we make jokes about them. My favorite is about a politician who made a speech before a little group in a small town and ended: 'Them's my views; and if you don't like 'em, well then I'll change 'em.'

"And of course everybody laughs, and it's a cynical story. But seriously, the job of a politician is to find a majority, to build that majority, and to lead people forward together. And if he has to adapt and change his policies to do it, then within the limits of his own honesty and integrity he does this. I made this point to suggest that you are not going to have a democracy if you think that somehow you can put the President or your public officials above politics."

That is basic Udall in technique and outlook. And it was this very technique and outlook that raised the serious questions among his friends as to whether Udall had the stuff to make the race for President. Adlai Stevenson was a delightful man who got a lot of laughs but not many votes.

"Mo has a wonderful, irreverent, and lively mind," says former LBJ White House staff member Harry McPherson, now chairman of the Domestic Affairs Task Force of the Democratic National Committee, "but he takes almost too much of an insouciant view towards politics. Can he incant: 'We must go forward together again,' for the two-hundredth time without laughing?"

"How much does Udall want the presidency?" asks Congressman Jack Bingham. "A man has to be single-minded almost to the point of insanity to run for President."

Udall knows the criticism of himself and faces it. "I am not [Gene] McCarthy," he told a group of college Democrats in Salt Lake City. "I run to win." Later he made the same point in terms of McGovern. "The big difference between me and McGovern: He got beat. I want to win."

Larry King, the Texas writer who knows Udall as well as anybody, believes: "He pokes a little fun at himself because he is self-conscious. But he is a man of real ambition. When he runs he takes himself seriously."

"One of the things we are doing in this early phase of the campaign," said Terry Bracy, Udall's administrative assistant and de facto campaign manager, in May '74, "is finding out how much Morris Udall wants the presidency."

As far as the psychological track is concerned, Udall seems on solid ground. "He always was ambitious," says his elder brother, Stewart, who held the same congressional seat before becoming first JFK's and then LBJ's secretary of the interior. "Anything I wanted to do, he would try and do better. And he usually did, too. He is a better congressman than I was."

The two brothers are close: "as close as Jack and Bobby" is the example they both pick. During World War II when they were separated, they wrote long letters back and forth to each other, mostly about the books they were reading.

Elder brother Stewart rises from behind his desk and ducks and bounces around the room with obvious pride as he demonstrates the head movements his brother used to compensate for having only one eye as a professional basketball player with the Denver Nuggets after the war. "The last time we fought was when he was twelve and I was fourteen. By then, he was as big as I was."

Udall played professional basketball to put himself through law school. One time a fan at court side was riding him unmercifully. Finally the fan yelled: "And what's more you're a lying SOB. No man can play ball with one eye."

Udall wrenched his glass eye from its socket and thrust it at the heckler. "You try seeing with the son of a bitch."

Mo Udall's ambition showed early and remained constant. In high school he captained the basketball team, wrote for the paper, had the lead in the school play, quarterbacked the football team, and marched in the school band at half time. At the University of Arizona he was the first nonfraternity man to be elected student body president. When having just one eye kept him out of the Army, he faked out the test. He put his right hand over his glass eye and read the chart. When the doctor said, "Now the other eye," he dropped his right hand and put his left hand over the glass eye.

Both brothers admit to a great deal of sibling rivalry as they grew up in isolated rural St. Johns, Arizona, on a family farm as part of older, simpler America. "The pace of life in St. Johns was slow and deliberate and allowed parents to let their lives be governed by a tacit children-first policy"—so Stewart has described their boyhood, and also pointed out that there was a sharing of chores and duties that traditionally develops a sense of self. Their small community was pervaded by a sense of trust. One time when the Udalls went to Yellowstone Park for two weeks, on leaving they couldn't find the key to lock their house.

After World War II the brothers practiced law together and in the tradition of ambitious small-towners turned to politics to give their energies broader outlet. Stewart remembers that he ran for Congress because his interests were broad and national, while Mo was interested in the law and ran for judge. Mo remembers that he was set to run for Congress, but his then wife didn't want to go to Washington, so he talked Stewart into running for Congress while he ran for judge. (Sibling rivalry can muss memory.)

In any event Mo got defeated that time for judge. Four years later he was set to run for his retiring father's seat on the state supreme court, when his father died and the Republican governor appointed a Republican Udall, Mo's uncle, to fill the chair. "I couldn't run against my uncle, whom I liked. I resigned myself to being an Arizona lawyer. Then Stewart moved into the Cabinet and I ran successfully for his seat [in 1961]. You can't plan ahead too much in politics."

In 1966 Mo's cousin Dr. Don A. Udall made a survey of the grandchildren of Mo's grandfather, David "King" Udall, the pioneer who settled St. Johns. He wrote: "David Udall's direct descendants in addition to the Washington Udalls include: 8 lawyers, 2 law students, 7 doctors, 2 med students, 4 mayors, 1 city manager, 5 judges, 1 medical school professor, 5 Harvard graduates, and to my knowledge not a single millionaire." They run hard, these Mormon Kennedys.

Their small-town background is important to the brothers and they are proud of their rural roots, but neither Stewart nor Mo glamorizes the past in St. Johns. When Mo was six years old, he and a friend were cutting rope. In some way the rope sprang back, or the friend slipped, and the knife they were using went into Mo's right eye. The only doctor in town was a drunk who treated the eye improperly. Months later Mo's mother began worrying about her son and persuaded his father to take him to an eye doctor while they were on a trip. The doctor found Mo's eye diseased and the optic nerve infected. An immediate operation was necessary if Mo was not to lose the sight in both eyes. The next day the bad eye was removed and the family wrote away to the Denver Optical Company, which sent twenty-four glass eyes in assorted colors and sizes. Mo picked out the one that fit best and looked most like his other eye. Those early eyes broke a lot, he says; but the hand-painted plastic one he has now from Walter Reed is indestructible. Unless you know about it you can't tell the difference, though when Mo gets very tired, the area around the eye gets a little inflamed and he holds a handkerchief up to it from time to time.

In Congress Udall got stuck with a minor committee, Interior and Insular Affairs, because there was water legislation coming up vital to Arizona. Here luck worked for him. That committee handles land use and energy, Udall specialties, suddenly much in the public eye. His land-use bill (defeated by five votes) and his strip mine regulation bill (which passed), while they haven't made his name a household word, have built him a following among planners and environmentalists, another key part of the Udall constituency.

"He has done pretty damn well to move so much legislation," says

Congressman Richard Bolling, Rules Committee power and author of *House out of Order.*

Like all freshman congressmen, Udall bumbled and stumbled trying to learn. From his frustrations came the first political move that set him apart. The next term, to help the newcomers, he organized a school that taught the congressional ropes. Congressman Jack Bingham, a new kid at the time, remembers: "Udall was always available to help me, no matter what my problem or what the time." From this school came a batch of political friends and IOUs, plus his first book, *The Job of the Congressman,* still the Bible for new members.

In 1969 Udall made a more controversial move. He, a relative newcomer with only eight years' seniority, ran for speaker of the House against the incumbent, John McCormack, the seventy-seven-year-old Massachusetts patriarch who had entered Congress when Udall was six. "When I came to Congress," Udall told friends, "Republicans had the old faces. Now it is the other way around." He made the race on principle but, ever the politician, thought he had a respectable eighty-one votes. In the secret ballot he ended up badly beaten, 178 to 58. If being in Congress teaches a man nothing else, as the saying goes, it teaches a man to count.

Two years later Mo Udall made a serious mathematical mistake. He didn't run against Paul Fannin, the former Republican governor of Arizona who was seeking a second Senate term, because he figured Fannin was popular and unbeatable, when in fact Fannin was weak. Instead he chose to continue his work of congressional reform, and ran for the number-two spot in the House, majority leader. By then McCormack had retired—largely because of scandal, but partly because of the pressure from Udall—and Carl Albert, the majority leader, was obviously going to move up to speaker. Udall, along with much of the press, thought he had the votes to take Hale Boggs, the other leading candidate. But two forces tipped the scale against him. His fight against McCormack two years before had offended most of the grizzled seniors of the House and all of the Massachusetts delegation. And Boggs, through his seat on the Ways and Means Committee, could promise junior congressmen choice committee assignments in return for their votes.

"I had it figured wrong, all wrong," Udall said, involuntarily slapping his hand against his thigh at the pain of the remembered defeat. He figured he had 90 to 100 first-ballot votes; Boggs around 70. But Boggs ended up with 95 to Udall's 69. By the second ballot it was all over, 140 to 88—though, Udall adds with a smile, about a hundred congressmen later told him privately: "We were with you to the end, Mo."

Looking back, Udall realizes that he didn't nail down his votes hard enough. He was content with general affirmations of support rather than pressing hard for a specific commitment. This again raises the question: "How tough is Mo?" And in a House of egos, how many enemies has he made as he forced himself forward?

As he began his campaign, Udall not only had his basic constituency of

House professionals, but also a new set of Democratic rules going for him. These rules changed the presidential race even more drastically than the wrench given by the McGovern rules of 1972. By no coincidence the young but seasoned gunslingers of Udall's staff, John Gabusi and Terry Bracy, had written large parts of the '76 rules. They knew their way around inside them, the way McGovern staffers Rick Stearns and Gary Hart understood the '72 rules. Once again, as in '72, most of the press looking in the old places missed the new action. The new rules grew out of old Democratic party battles. The Republicans had to play by these rules also since the Democrats controlled a majority of the state legislatures and could vote their primary rules into law for both parties. In refighting the battles of 1968 and 1972, the Democrats tended to flail at the myths rather than concentrate on how those battles had actually been won. As they were fighting chimeras rather than reality, Democrats often found with pained surprise their fangs were sunk into their own flesh. To understand the 1976 rules and their actual, not their intended effects on Udall and all the candidates, one has first to probe the realities of the last two primary campaigns, particularly 1972.

What precisely has been happening to the Democrats since the mid-1960s? A favorite "game" among reporters covering the squabbles, fights, and massacres among Democrats in the seventies was to try to agree on terms to describe the combatants. The old tags, liberal or conservative, right or left, no longer fit the factions with much precision. For example, the most extreme liberals and conservatives now both believe in limiting the power of the federal government. Distrust of the Soviet Union, while stronger on the right, is no longer confined there—though extreme liberals want a minuscule defense budget. Both extreme liberals and conservatives tend to be more pro-Arab, centerists pro-Israel. Vietnam withdrawal is no longer a touchstone issue. Foreign aid is universally unpopular. Both conservatives and liberals stress local control of programs. (And both tie themselves in knots trying to answer the question: "How is the local control that we want, which we all know is a good thing, different from the local control that Louise Day Hicks wants [or the Black Panthers want], which we all know is a bad thing?" Dead silence and coughs.)

To me the fairest description of the two groups is "realist" and "idealist." The two words are picked with some care. Used together, neither carries a negative load, like calling the two groups sons of bitches and good guys or serious politicians and crazies, or even purists and professionals. To designate the two groups idealists and realists facilitates understanding how there can be a center. There are idealists to whom the thrill of seeing at least part of their program enacted will cause them to compromise; and there are realists with principles who will bend but not break: the old Disraeli argument *fractes non franges* versus *franges non fractes,* with the extreme frangs and fracs hurling grenades at each other.

The curse of the extreme idealist, the purist, is hatred. The curse of the extreme realist, the cynic-pol, is moral corruption. In the end both are destroyed by the imbalance in themselves that leads to their extremism.

For the purist, there is always some bastard in the room, on the committee, inside the party, who must be purged before he destroys everything through compromise. To them, victory only comes by keeping their blessed standard unspotted from the world. In the end the purist finds himself alone, deserted by all but himself, stabbing at fiends. Unconsciously, though supposedly a politician, he has taken as his hero Rainer Rilke's "Cornet," the standard bearer, the ideal of every S.S. trooper:

> In his arms he cradles the standard, as a white unconscious maid. . . . And the troops know their colors are before them and the golden unhelmeted hero who carries their standard. . . . The standard flames alone among the enemy. . . . The golden hero is deep among foes and totally alone. Terror makes a keep about him. . . . He feels eyes on him and knows that his enemy are not only men, they are heathen dogs. And he hurls his horse among them.

On the battlefield such behavior gets you killed; in the committee it pulls the house down.

Were their ostensible hero Thomas Jefferson to appear before a group of purists and intone his famous dictum, "Every difference of opinion is not a difference of principle," they would yell in George McGovern's words to a heckler: "Kiss my ass." And leak to *The New York Times* that shifty Tommy had taken oil money in his last campaign.

The extreme realist, the cynic-pol, finds there is no principle he will not compromise, no commitment important enough to battle over. The act of governing the use of power becomes his end; he feels himself surrounded by idiots who, while hymning his praise, would jeopardize his rule by taking stands. The merest whisper of dissent becomes a hurricane against his soul. Lyndon Johnson bugs Martin Luther King, Jr., Nixon sends the IRS after those on his enemies list. Were Thomas Jefferson to appear before such a one, the cynic-pol would put his arm around Jefferson's shoulder and say, "You're so right, Tom, just go out and explain that to the press. Those bastards don't understand my use of the rack and thumbscrew."

The Democratic party, while largely realist, had always had its idealist wing: William Jennings Bryan at the turn of the century, Henry Wallace in the late forties. Then, in the sixties, the assassinations of three political leaders tore both the party and the idealists apart, for the body politic is torn apart by political assassination the way the human body is destroyed by amputation.

As the nation struggled to find a new life after the murders of President Kennedy, Senator Kennedy, and Martin Luther King, the idealists in the Democratic party split, some trending toward the extreme purist end of the scale, others gathering at the center, while a few, in despair, ended up as cynic-pols. The continuing idealist versus realist struggle and the fractionization of the idealists were both intensified by Vietnam. The intensifying hostility led to a series of vicious intra-Democratic party battles and finally to the nomination and devastating defeat of George McGovern. Battered and bruised in 1973 and 1974, the party created a new set of election rules for 1976 that drastically, though at first invisibly, altered the political landscape.

The most recent battle between idealist and realist started in 1968 when Robert Kennedy fought Gene McCarthy for the Democratic nomination. McCarthy weighed in toward the purist end of the scale. Speaking in January 1968 in Nashua, New Hampshire, before a largely student audience, he was asked: "First, do you want to be President? Second, do you think you will ever be President?" McCarthy paused and gave his serene smile and said slowly, "My answer is: First, no. Second, no."

The audience rose and cheered. When, shortly after McCarthy's win in the 1968 New Hampshire primary, Robert Kennedy, who wanted and intended to be President, entered the race, idealists were forced to choose sides. The Indiana primary, which Kennedy won, caused the final blowup. The extreme idealists felt that Kennedy had won on a law-and-order pitch: "As the former attorney general, I know the importance of tough law enforcement," rather than fighting it out on the Vietnam issue.

Leonard Davis, one of McCarthy's early supporters, describes his own reactions during the campaign:

> Those of us who had been fighting the battle over the years for a political process strategy and for broad-based coalitions to achieve social change came to realize during the last days of the McCarthy campaign that we were part of an elitist, arrogant, exclusive movement. . . . For the purists among us, the 1968 Convention and Mayor Daley's police were final proof that . . . a coalition was both impossible and undesirable. The future lay in a realigned party system with liberal intellectuals, liberated women, activist kids and minorities all under one roof. That roof could be the Democratic Party, which, many resolved, could be captured with the right kind of strategy.*

In the end Hubert Humphrey got the 1968 nomination—that was worth nothing, to put it politely. He had been campaigning in the states that selected their delegates by caucus and through committee. Fifty-nine percent of the delegates to the 1968 convention were selected that way. Hubert Humphrey did not campaign in a single primary. McCarthy and Robert Kennedy divided the primary-selected delegates between them. Not enough for convention victory, even if either one of them had gotten all the delegates from the primary states.

After Hubert Humphrey won the Democratic nomination, big labor, particularly the AFL-CIO, provided the blood, muscle, and sinew of his campaign. They registered 4.6 million voters, distributed 55 million

---

*Lanny J. Davis, *The Emerging Democratic Majority*.

pamphlets, 22 million of which were against George Wallace, rang 72,225 doorbells, and had 94,000 volunteers on Election Day, probably spending around $5 million. To the purists sitting out the election, this made big labor look more like the enemy than the Republicans. Big labor felt the same way about the sideline sitters.

While nominating Hubert Humphrey, the 1968 Democratic Convention also voted to set up a commission to reform the Democratic party. This commission eventually became the McGovern Commission and produced the reforms that radically changed the composition of the delegates to the '72 convention—and altered the Democratic party. A footnote to history should record that this liberal commission was established on a close vote, the winning numbers being supplied by the conservative Missouri delegation, which thought it was voting the other way.

At the time all but the most extreme realists agreed that there was bona fide work for the Commission on Party Structure and Delegate Selection (the McGovern Commission) to perform. In 1968 twenty states had no written rules for the selection of Democratic delegates to the presidential nominating convention, or rules that were so tightly held as to be changeable at the whim of those in control. Merely to get the rules understood, state by state, would drastically change the drive for the presidential nomination. The race would change for *both* parties, since whatever rules the Democratic party adopted, the majority of state legislatures—which were and are controlled by Democrats—would also adopt.

The changes made by the McGovern Commission justify the adjective "sweeping." In 1968 only 3 percent of the delegates to the national convention were under thirty-one, only 13 percent were female, and only 5.5 percent black (this latter figure up from 2 percent in 1964). Four years later, at the 1972 convention, 24 percent of the delegates were under thirty-one, 40 percent were female, and 15 percent were black. Nor were these changes the result of "elitist" reform, as enemies of the McGovern candidacy have charged in hindsight and brought most people to believe. The language agreed to by the McGovern Commission was broad enough so that practically all factions of the party (back then) were happy to comply. In February 1970 every one of the fifty states was in noncompliance of some part of the McGovern Commission's recommendations. By August forty-five states had adopted reform commissions and believed themselves to be in compliance—hardly a record of foot dragging by the majority against an elitist bunch of reforms. This enthusiastic compliance of the states is even more extraordinary because up to then the most the national party had been able to force on the states was a loyalty oath in 1952, pledging delegates to support the Democratic ticket; and that had been fought bitterly.

The pervasive myth has grown that the change in the convention came about because of the language of "quotas"; that delegations were measured against some sociological yardstick to see if the prescribed "quota" of blacks, women, youth, and other minorities were present "in reasonable relationship to their presence in the population in the state." This is said to have occurred even though "mandatory quotas" were outlawed. Both the defeated forces and the McGovern faction have fed this myth, George McGovern himself saying, "The way we got the quota thing through was by not using the word 'quota.' "

But the "quota" myth is only partially correct; and unfortunately that part masks a greater and more important truth—a truth that is radically changing the 1976 rules in the invisible primary. The reason for the change in the composition of the Democratic convention delegates between 1968 and 1972 was that in 1972 the McGovern forces controlled the caucus states. In 1968 the realists, the followers of Hubert Humphrey, had controlled these states, using their victories there to screw the idealists, the followers of Gene McCarthy. In 1972 the idealists, the McGovern forces, controlled those same caucus states, because they understood how the new McGovern rules applied to caucuses. So at the convention, the McGovern forces had the votes. They used these votes to interpret the McGovern Commission language the way they believed it should read. They did to the realists in 1972 what had been done to them in 1968.

The press had focused on the primaries during the 1972 campaign. But the battle wasn't there. The war was fought in the caucus states, whose number had actually increased between 1968 and 1972, up from twenty-three to twenty-four. In using the drastically changed rules to seize these states, the McGovern staff showed its political genius and its human weakness. Joining the McGovern staff in January 1970, master strategist Rick Stearns focused on the caucus states in a thirty-four-page plan of attack. "The open and poorly attended caucuses . . . will favor a candidate with a strongly motivated following. With careful organization a good McGovern showing can be made.

In 1976 the number of caucus states has dropped from twenty-four to sixteen. And everyone understands the rules by which the remaining primary states can be won. The incredible shift in the factors governing presidential selection between 1968 and 1976 lies in the decline of the caucus states and the doubling of the primary states, not in any language change about quotas. This quantum jump in primaries is a quiet revolution; and the noun "revolution" will prove totally applicable.

McGovern's strength in 1972 was in his staff and his constituency, both of them working together in perfect articulation. Any campaign that could take 20 percent of the registered Democrats—the number that preferred McGovern—and less than 30 percent of the primary vote, and parlay that slim base into the Democratic presidential nomination must have done a lot right. At the same time any presidential campaign that could take a 61 percent Lyndon Johnson victory in 1964 and produce eight years later a 60.7 percent Nixon victory must have done a lot wrong. Thirty-three percent of the Democrats who voted in 1972 voted for Nixon over McGovern. Sixty percent of those voting split their ticket in one way or another. And it was not just the split vote that indicated something amiss. Sixty-two million voters stayed away from the polls, many more than the 47.2 million who voted for President Nixon. Only 55.6 percent of those eligible to vote did so, the most miserable turnout since 1948—a drop of 7 percentage points in four years.

McGovern's problem in the general election, quite simply, was that the constituency he had created to bring him the nomination was viewed by the mass as hostile to their interests. One of the major problems of a candidate in the invisible primary is to make certain that his constituency can communicate its strength and convictions positively to the voting mass. Eight years earlier Barry Goldwater had suffered from the same political problem. His constituency, the enthusiastic right wing of the Republican party, turned off the voting mass.

From the beginning, McGovern's strategy, consciously or unconsciously (reports vary), was to recruit his constituency from among students on the elite college campuses. This group is self-starting and highly motivated and contained many who had already worked in Senator McCarthy's campaign. McGovern's constituency, like his staff, was fueled by the opposition to and hatred of the war in Vietnam.

The divisive and poisonous nature of the Vietnamese war in American society has been commented on by all. However, there seems to me an overlooked factor, which for better or worse played an important part in the psychological outlook of the McGovern constituency and led to their harsh use of the political process. This factor was the sociological background of the combat troops in Vietnam. These troops were from the middle and lower middle class, black and white, a group then neglected both by the media and by academia. Both the Vietcong and the American grunt were part of an invisible army. In my three months in Vietnam among combat troops, I ran into only two Ivy League or prestigious West Coast university graduates. MIT, for example, escaped the entire war without a single casualty among its graduates.

The knowledge that other men were dying in their place produced profound feelings of guilt among the highly motivated antiwar students. To justify draft avoidance it became necessary not just to consider Vietnam a stupid error of judgment and national hubris, but rather a lurid combination of national corruption and vicious evil. The guiltier McGovern's constituency felt, the more evil the war became for them; and the more evil the war became, the more extreme became the methods that were justified in opposing it.

A person's whole life-style could be changed to become a form of protest. Polls could be manipulated, lies fed to the press, caucuses packed, and pseudo masses of voters created, because what was being opposed was evil. The Goldwater constituency had felt the same way about "socialists." But the extreme maneuvers justified by both constituencies in the name of their true belief turned off the voting mass.

"The country may not be ready for our candidate." Both the McGovern and the Goldwater constituencies used to use this phrase to describe their candidates. And the voters reacted with the same anger that a man would show toward the parents of a perspective spouse on being told by them that she was too good for him.

By 1974 the idealists of the McGovern camp, their burden of guilt lifted by the end of American involvement in the Vietnamese war, were finding it easier to forget and forgive than the extreme realists in the AFL-CIO. Perhaps winners always find it easier to let bygones be bygones than losers.

McGovern's staff had begun developing strategy and recruiting a constituency in early 1970. By January 18, 1971, when McGovern announced he was an active candidate for the presidency, over a year before the New Hampshire primary, a great deal of groundwork had been laid, including the decision for such an early announcement. With his statement, McGovern got press attention, helping him in his relations with the media, and demonstrated to his constituency his sincerity and candor. He and his staff then traveled extensively in the states they regarded as key—New Hampshire, Wisconsin, and California—energizing his constituency and setting it to work.

Senator Edmund Muskie, the avowed front-runner, was following the more traditional path, campaigning flat-out while maintaining that the invisible primary did not exist. Muskie was also using as his constituency the Democratic organizations around the country, and these turned out to be less loaded with brains and energy than the reform-oriented, antiwar constituency McGovern was building. Muskie waited until a full year after McGovern, January 8, 1972, the month before the New Hampshire primary, to announce his candidacy. This late, overt start, the energy and brilliance of the McGovern staff and constituency, the machinations and slimy deceits of Nixon's CREEP in the "Canuck Letter," plus the Pollyannaish ambition that drove Hubert Humphrey again into the race (and his own lack of stomach for campaigning), all combined to sink the Muskie candidacy.

It is instructive to look at how the McGovern constituency and staff handled the arcane complexities of an early caucus state, Arizona. The Arizona delegate selection process, neither more nor less involuted than many others, worked as follows: First, there was a statewide primary in which Democrats voted for five hundred delegates to a state caucus. Second, this caucus elected the state's twenty-five final delegates to the Democratic National Convention. In the first step, the five hundred delegates ran from thirty different districts, the number of delegates running from each district varying with the population. Also the voters had a varying number of votes, depending on the number of delegates running. Say a district was allowed ten delegates, then each voter had ten votes. In such a district the Muskie people, playing by the old rules, ran a slate of ten delegates. But the McGovern people, who understood the new math, ran a slate of only five—

and told their people to cast two votes for each of the five. Then if Muskie got 100 people to go to the polls, each of his candidates would receive 100 votes. If McGovern only got 51 people to the polls, each of his candidates would receive 102 votes. With a total vote almost double that of McGovern, the Muskie machine would still only pick up half the delegates.

The press and the traditional politicians predicted that Muskie would capture all of Arizona's twenty-five delegates. Muskie had the endorsement of all the state's Democratic officials, including such powerhouses as former Governor Sam Goddard, and Morris Udall, the congressman who in '76 would benefit from the new rules devised because of Muskie's defeat. However, the McGovern staff realized that the Arizona primary system was so constructed that Muskie would have to do everything right to get even 50 percent of the delegates.

Instead, the Muskie organization ran 587 delegates for the 500 places at the convention, guaranteeing a draw-off of needed votes. McGovern's advance man in the state, Rick Sterns, used a computer and came up with thirty as the magic number of people who should use all their cumulative votes for each candidate. Any candidate who could get thirty friends, or members of the McGovern constituency, to give him or her all their cumulative votes would end up a delegate to the state convention.

When the traditional dust that always surrounds a hotly contested election had risen and settled, Muskie had 189 electors at the convention, while new politics masters McGovern and Lindsay had 103 and 108 respectively. Muskie ended with only nine delegates out of twenty-five, Lindsay six, and McGovern five. Only 15 percent of Arizona's registered Democrats had bothered to vote. Of this 15 percent, the majority in the McGovern-Lindsay camp were students. This was the same constituency who would edge McGovern ahead of Hubert Humphrey later in the key California primary. From caucus state to caucus state all during the campaign, the McGovern staff and constituency stitched together victories with minorities, as they had in Arizona, while the press talked about a vast liberal block.

In the primary states, which though less important than the caucus states in determining the 1972 outcome, got far more media attention, the Democratic results were distorted by two factors: the problem of the "clogged center," plus winner-take-all primaries. The "clogged center" comes in a situation where, say, four middle-of-the-road candidates run and each gets 19 percent of the vote. The extremist candidate with 24 percent of the vote in a winner-take-all primary then ends up with all the state's delegates. This happens even though over three quarters of the voters in the state prefer moderate candidates. In '72 a clogged-center primary was Wisconsin. Here McGovern, with 30 percent of the vote, picked up fifty-four out of sixty-seven of the state's delegates, or 80 percent of its presidential convention votes.

With his constituency producing victories in key primary states and his staff and constituency controlling the majority of the caucus states,

McGovern came into the Democratic National Convention with votes enough to challenge successfully delegations hostile to himself. Here the concept of quotas *was* used, particularly to unseat Chicago Mayor Daley's Illinois delegation, so that to this limited extent the myth that McGovern's idealists won by quotas is true. Yet on this minor point, the problem of quotas, the Democratic party was to expend much of its energy in the next four years.

Following the '72 convention, the Democratic National Committee chairwoman, Jean Westwood, appointed a committee to review the rules on the selection of delegates to the national convention, with particular attention to winner-take-all primaries. The committee was also to investigate ways to "continue to broaden the base of the party," a euphemism for the quota problem. As may be expected of a commission appointed by a committee dominated by McGovernites, the committee members were weighted toward the idealist end of the scale. The chairwoman was Barbara Mikulski, a feisty city councilwoman from Baltimore. After the disastrous finish of the '72 campaign, Jean Westwood, whose organizational abilities were also under attack, was replaced by the Democratic National Committee finance chairman, Robert Strauss. Over the next four years Strauss was to prove himself one of the master politicians of the seventies.

Strauss immediately added thirty-five new members to the committee to bring it toward the center; and the committee, now formally called the Commission on Delegate Selection and Party Structure, but known to all as the Mikulski Commission, squabbled on its way. Mikulski fired one Doris Hardesty, the wife of an AFL-CIO staff member. That further divided the already bitter members. The final fight was over whether the rules would go into effect automatically or had to be approved by the national committee, which could also modify them. Here again the wily Strauss had his way, the national committee approving and modifying the final Mikulski draft.

After the 1972 Democratic defeat there was general agreement among idealist and realist that quotas were politically explosive and philosophically wrong. Some of the extreme purists in the black and women's movements continued privately to press for them, but they were a small, even a tiny, minority.

One of the most poignant expressions of antiquota sentiment came from Edward N. Costikyan, a respected reform leader in New York. I am suspicious of lengthy quotations in books but this letter to *New York* magazine says it all so well.

> I used to go to state and national conventions of the Democratic Party. I used to represent my assembly district, the eighth (south) of Manhattan, in New York County Democratic Executive Committee and the Democratic Committee of New York County in state Democratic councils. But, since the so-called McGovern guidelines, which require that the delegates to the national convention reflect the proportion of women, blacks, and younger people in the population at

large, I have lost my constituencies. In those days it did not seem so incongruous for a half-Armenian, half-Swiss Unitarian to represent a district which had few, if any, Swiss, few, if any, Armenians, and few, if any, Unitarians, let alone a county and state with only a handful of any of these exotic types.

For a WASP—a White Armenian Swiss Protestant—those were rather happy political days. I mean, nobody asked me to justify my election as district leader five times in ten years, or my election as county leader twice, in light of my sex, my age, my ancestry, or anything else. . . .

It's all changed. The Democratic National Committee has told us to forget the old-fashioned nonsense that resulted in the voters' selection of a male Armenian-Swiss amateur conductor of oratorios to represent them as a reform district leader and delegate and county leader. Now, the McGovern guidelines tell us, women must be represented by women, blacks by blacks, young by young, and I suppose, rich by rich, poor by poor. And the Democratic National Committee further tells us that unless delegations mirror the color, sex, and age characteristics of the constituency, the non-conforming delegates must justify their election and explain why they are the wrong color, wrong age and wrong sex. . . .

Maybe the Democratic Party will abandon this nonsense before it has lost allegiances of those who do not fit into the neat pigeonholes its sociologist-advisers have invented and its stunned leadership, still shaken by the convulsions that racked the party in the 1968 convention, thoughtlessly adopted. What was wrong with the Democratic Party and its convention in 1968 will not be cured by the invoking of a quota system.

With even reformers feeling this way, "quotas" were thrown out by the Mikulski Commission, and in their stead was set "affirmative action." The states had to take certain rigidly specific steps to assure that minorities and traditionally underrepresented groups were encouraged to participate in the political process. One does not have to be a political genius to realize that he who oversees how the affirmative action rules are enforced is going to control who gets seated at the Democratic Convention in 1976. Mikulski set up and attempted to stack a seventeen-member Compliance Review Commission to monitor affirmative action. But again Strauss fought back, enlarging the commission to twenty-five members, the new members picked by him. The final commission, chaired by Robert Wagner, the wily former mayor of New York, leaned to the realist side of the scale.

Robert Wagner had begun political life as a regular, organization Democrat. In 1961 he joined the reform Democrats and had pulled off the remarkable feat of winning reelection as a reform mayor by running against his own record made as a regular. Any politician able enough to do this could easily handle a twenty-five-member commission. He did. Throughout the period 1974–76, the CRC, as it was known in the trade, met frequently and bitterly and in seeming confusion. But somehow at the end of every weary meeting, Bob Wagner always managed to deliver the CRC for Strauss's realists by one or two votes.

The fight over affirmative action did not affect the race for the Democratic presidential nomination in itself. But the fight over to what lengths affirmative action should be carried was often so bitter that it threatened to blow the Democratic party apart. Should that have ever happened, and several times, as will be seen, it came close, the Democratic nomination could well have become worthless. Democratic candidates in the invisible primary would have had to change their strategy so as virtually to build their own personal party, while the supposedly organized Democrats fought among themselves.

Two other actions taken by the Mikulski Commission and adopted by the national committee directly affected the invisible primary; and the Udall campaign, partly by lucky accident and partly by strategic design, was the first to position itself to benefit from these far-ranging changes. The first of these commission actions was the effort to abolish winner-take-all primaries.

Everyone, the idealist and realist factions, as well as the center, was concerned about the impact of winner-take-all primaries on the presidential selection process. The established practice that a candidate who got 51 percent of the Democratic primary vote in, say, California or Massachusetts should get 100 percent of that state's convention delegates seemed overdue for change—especially when in a four-candidate race he might have won all the delegates with as little as 30 percent of the votes cast. Commission members wanted to produce some mechanism so that minority candidates would get some percentage of the delegates. In this way a middle-of-the-road candidate, or a minority candidate who ran second in a great many states, would do as well as or better than a candidate who only ran overwhelmingly first in just a few states.

The commission's answer was proportional representation (PR), where any candidate getting over 15 percent of the vote in a state (a figure set high to discourage one-issue/lunatic-fringe candidates) would get a portion of the convention delegates equal to his percentage of the vote. This solution solved the problem for those states like California where the candidates and their slate of delegates ran statewide. But some states, like New York or New Hampshire, elected delegates by congressional or state assembly districts. In such states would delegates who had actually won a majority of votes in their district be thrown out and replaced with the losers because in some other district the rival candidate had run up an overwhelming majority? The problem was politically sensitive because many of the states choosing by congressional district were the "good guys," like New York, Florida, and New Hampshire, which in the recent past had elected liberals.

The compromise reached was to give states a choice. They could, as California or Indiana had in the past, run statewide tickets of candidates. In such states proportional representation would come into force, and each successful candidate with over 15 percent of the vote would get his or her percentage of delegates. Or, the fatal choice whose consequences were unforeseen—the pomegranate at Persephone's lips—the states could opt for election of delegates by congressional district, in which event it would be winner-take-all inside each congressional district, the rationale being that a presidential candidate's strength would vary from district to district inside the state. Candidate A would carry district A, which was largely industrial, while candidate B would carry district B, which was largely suburban. So the end result would be much like proportional representation.

But from 1973 to 1976 the totally unforeseen happened: State after state changed, not from winner-take-all to PR, but from winner-take-all to election of delegates by congressional district. There were various reasons for the shift to election by congressional district. In Texas, followers of Senator Lloyd Bentsen feared that, with PR, George Wallace would get a sizable portion of the Texas delegation, while with election by congressional district, Bentsen would get almost all. California politicians felt they could play their historic role as presidential kingmakers better in a district-by-district primary, since one candidate would be more likely to gain a large majority of the delegation.

In every state politicians realized that under proportional representation some "boss" was going to have to select which delegates would go to the convention as part of each victor's percentage. This was going to be a hassle, make enemies, and probably lead to costly lawsuits. But if the election were by congressional district, the decision of the voters—provided "affirmative action" standards had been complied with—would be final. This knowledge, as it began to percolate through the political strata, made election by congressional district look better and better with every passing nanosecond.

The second action the Mikulski Commission took, even more revolutionary, was to make the rules for selecting delegates to the national convention by caucus so complex that any state retaining the caucus system would be in for a long, bitter political and legal fight. The commission members did this without realizing the vast change it would lead to—as if they had split the atom by blowing their noses. Political leaders in the caucus states realized there was no way their states' delegations could escape challenge unless they moved to a primary system. By June 1, 1976, the deadline for change, the number of states holding primaries had jumped from twenty-six to thirty-four. And each had selected election of delegates by congressional district.

This is not what the Mikulski Commission members or Democratic politicians in general thought would happen. But then few understood the effects of any of the rule changes being made in the presidential vote. Alan Baron, director of the Democratic Study Group, a new political activist who had helped draft the rules, said at the time: "I suppose a few more states might switch from the convention [caucus] system to a direct primary as a result of these changes. But I think we've about hit the peak on that."

Dick Moe, Mondale's political operative, said: "It will make it very difficult for candidates to be knocked out of the race." Within a year his man and three others were out.

Both the Bentsen and Kennedy staffs thought the front-runner would be hurt. This didn't stop all the candidates scrambling to be first. Only Bob Keefe, the prescient deputy director of the Democratic National Committee, who was later to head Senator Jackson's campaign, called the turn correctly: "Remember we have never elected a President who has run in more than seven primaries. The next President will have to run in at least twice as many."

Among reformers, the assumption has been since the 1900s that primaries favor insurgents. To adopt a state primary is a blow against bossism. Yet both the 1968 and the 1972 Democratic nomination campaigns had shown that the caucus favored neither boss nor reformer but those who understood the rules. "In 1976 I want to make certain people know the rules," said Chairman Strauss. "In 1972 no one knew what the hell was going on." Not true; in 1972 the idealists knew exactly.

The assumption that primaries favor reform has yet to be tested. When it is, in 1980, it will probably turn out to be another myth. Primaries usually favor the energetic and well organized. If insurgent, then insurgent; if boss, then boss. Indeed, since the average primary is decided by a distinct minority of the voters—at best around 20 percent—the local boss with a handpicked slate, energy, and knowledge of his people would seem to have the advantage. Mr. Organizational Republican, Robert Taft, won more GOP primaries than the phenomenally popular General Eisenhower. But perhaps party fortunes have reached such a low ebb in this media society that there are no longer any able bosses. Or do the new bosses merely sport different names?

At the same time that the Democratic National Committee was adopting the rules that would lead to such a vast increase in direct primaries by congressional district, the Senate and House were passing the Campaign Finance Reform Act. This act limited to $12 million the amount a candidate could spend in the primaries. The same law drastically restricted the amount of money that could be spent inside individual states. In 1972 McGovern had spent $20 million in all the primaries. The late President Kennedy's expenditures before the nomination have been estimated in the same range.

The race had been made longer, tougher, and totally nationwide. At the same time, the candidates' funds had been cut. This vastly increased the importance of the invisible primary because preparation and planning for the augmented state primary circuit became far more important than before.

How did these changes affect Udall? Almost alone among the candidates in the invisible primary, Udall and his staff grasped the new situation and moved to maximize their advantages. Senator Henry M. Jackson and his staff also understood the problem, but their flexibility to adjust to the new rules was more handicapped by past positions and attitudes.

Fund raising remained as important as ever, though it shifted in emphasis. Now, holding down expenses became a vital new area of campaigning. A candidate might be ahead at the halfway mark in the primaries and find he had no money left for California and Ohio. This made the volunteer a critical part of **any** campaign. Further, it put a particular premium on the already trained volunteer who wouldn't make expensive mistakes, run up bills, and need the constant presence of paid staff members to help him out. From the beginning Udall's personal style, his efforts for congressional reform, and his record on the environment and energy made him popular with a constituency that included such volunteers.

Unseen by the press, Udall was picking up a constituency made up of many McGovern-McCarthy-Muskie volunteers who, now older and wiser, were established inside the body politic. Udall's campaign cochairmen, John Gabusi and Terry Bracy, both in their early thirties, had arrived in politics by this road. Supported by an elaborate computerized questionnaire, they sought out volunteers who were self-supporting and experienced. "I assume," Mo Udall said once, "that after a speech any candidate worth anything is going to get a hatful of names. It's *who* they are that is important." By the start of '75 the offices of Jackson, Bentsen, and Rockefeller and Ford were staffed with high-paid professionals, while the office of Mo Udall was staffed with volunteers being paid only expenses.

Furthermore, the growing number of primaries by congressional district made maximum use of Udall's built-in support in the House of Representatives. Instead of having to spend tight funds and staff energy polling and organizing district by district in a state, he could use information and bodies already in being in the offices of key congressmen. At the initial Udall strategy meeting in the congressman's office on November 16, the week before Udall went to New Hampshire to announce his candidacy, the names attending would have meant nothing to all but the most sophisticated professionals in politics and the press. However, they included the best of both the Muskie and the McGovern operations in New Hampshire in '72, as well as a smattering of Humphrey operatives from the '68 campaign. Also present were staffers from key districts in Pennsylvania, New Jersey, California, and Wisconsin—all states with primaries that were strategically important to Udall in terms of both delegates and media.

This combination of knowledgeable volunteers and House support gave Udall an important constituency right at the start of his campaign, which was fortunate, for unlike the other four early Democratic entries—Jackson, Wallace, Carter, and Bentsen—he was broke. By the first month of '75, the candidates had officially filed with the Government Accounting Office, contributions of $1,112,152.53 for Jackson, $927,461.31 for Wallace, $46,723.50 for Carter, $827,300.67 for Bentsen, and only $20,975 for Udall.

In previous years this would have meant the end of his candidacy. But with the restrictions on individual giving and campaign expenditures, the slow start was no longer such a weakness—not that any candidate faced with having money or no money wouldn't respond with Sophie Tucker: "I've been rich and I've been poor and believe me rich is better."

Besides the rules and the seasoned volunteers, other ripples from the '68 and '72 campaigns were aiding Udall, though scarcely visible on the surface. The same series of early state primaries—New Hampshire, Florida, Wisconsin—that had aided McGovern also aided Udall. In New Hampshire his environmental stand plus the astute work of his staff had so locked up the able volunteers in that state a year and a half before the primary that both Mondale and Kennedy believed a New Hampshire win for them impossible. In Florida the environment would again be an issue. And the two congressmen who put together the petition urging him to run were both from Wisconsin. That's the way it looked in '74. In '75 fickle chance turned against Udall. Florida became the battleground for candidates Wallace, Jackson, and Carter which fractured the Udall constituency. While in Wisconsin the machinations of Governor Patrick Lucey to enforce his control over the delegation caused that state's primary to be declared illegal by the courts. Udall had to shift his strategy hastily to Massachusetts where his pragmatic approach to politics turned off many of that state's active purists.

Udall had a constituency, a staff, and a strategy; but he lacked money and was in trouble with the media. He had to convince the Washington press corps that he was that illusive entity, "the viable political candidate." The press, profoundly traditionalist and tending to play follow-the-leader, believed that Presidents rose only from the ranks of senators and maybe governors. Even though Gerald Ford was right before their eyes, it was hard for them to take congressmen seriously: There were so many House members of limited ability.

But the media track wasn't completely blocked. The thoughtful press was concerned that it missed the strength first of Gene McCarthy, then four years later of George McGovern; that it had written off Nixon after his California defeat for governor; and that it had been slow to grasp the dimensions of the Vietnam War. It might be unwise to discount Udall entirely. Also, being human, the press liked to be entertained. With his mix of issues and wit, Udall made good copy or a lively TV show.

As Bob Boyd, the Knight papers' Pulitzer Prize winner, remarked (he was one of the first to sense the strength of Udall): "I know *I* like to be entertained when I listen to a speech. And I can't believe the public is different." Indeed other candidates' staffs objected to some of the early favorable stories about Udall in the *Atlantic,* the *New Republic,* and *New York.* They complained that the liberal press was building up another pet candidate again. "But they'll turn and cut him down to size, just like they did McGovern." With the departure of Kennedy and Mondale from the race, Udall began to receive, at least from the print media, an even greater share of publicity, though the more traditional medium of television continued to think in terms of the show value of Senate names.

Political experts gave the Udall campaign more credence than the press. Shortly before the December midterm convention, Strauss told a group of reporters off the record: "I think Jackson is ahead; perhaps further ahead than anyone realizes. . . . [But] if you go up the creek and look where no one else is going up far enough to look, you will find a surprising amount of talk along the bank for Udall."

"Presidents," observed Udall, "traditionally complain about the agony and the awful burden of their office. But most have spent twenty years on the rubber chicken circuit trying to get that terrible burden put on their back."

As he threw himself into the invisible primary in midsummer of 1974, there was little to distinguish Udall's campaign from that of any senator seeking the nomination. True, Udall always traveled with at most one aide and often by himself; but then most of the senators were then traveling with only one aide, though usually they had another advancing the territory before they arrived.

A two-day three-night Udall swing in July '74 through Denver, Salt Lake City, Phoenix, and White Plains—what senator was then swinging with more frenetic speed?—while it lacked the split-second advance planning of a Rockefeller or Kennedy foray, ran with at least the efficiency of Jackson, Mondale, Percy, or Bentsen. Local political leaders came out to greet Udall at the airport, there were private talks with other political powers in his hotel room, press conferences, radio and TV talk shows and interviews, a list of necessary phone calls to make, and cars always ready.

"As you know," he said to Jean Westwood, former McGovern supporter and Democratic National Committee chairwoman, "I'm here in Salt Lake and heard you were in the hospital. How are you doing?" Before that there was breakfast with Utah's Senator Frank Moss, then a speech to the Salt Lake County Democratic Convention, lunch with the state chairman, a TV show, a radio show with telephoned questions, a talk with the governor, and finally a hotel-room meeting with the younger Democrats and student leaders.

While on the road the campaign functioned as well as that of most other candidates; but to call on Udall's headquarters in the House Office Building anytime in '74 was to realize the advantage of campaigning in the invisible primary from the Senate in terms of office space, staff, and budget. The sign on the floor of the small office in the Longworth Building said, "Udall Legislative Staff." Camped inside the partitioned mini-space, the pulsating disorder appeared more like some frenetic TV director's dream of a campaign headquarters than an actual functioning organization. Piles of yet-to-be-opened mail, constant phones going for the too few people, calendars with three different speaking engagements for the same day and time penciled in with question marks after each.

That was as it should be, reports Terry Bracy, Udall co-manager and veteran of the Muskie and McGovern national campaigns. "The staff should grow out of the candidate, not the other way around. You don't want to get trapped in an organization like McGovern, where you can convince yourself of anything." Bracy, a lean, poor boy from St. Louis, hustling thirty, refers to himself as "young but seasoned." Like FDR's Doc Howe, he and his co-partner John Gabusi are that essential ingredient in any campaign, the twenty-four-hour-a-day man convinced his boss can and should be President. Gabusi was another political veteran with drooping western moustache, who had written parts of the 1976 campaign financing law. At that time he had laid out in his mind the strategy that Udall would have to follow to make full use of the new situation.

In the early days of the campaign Bracy and Gabusi began to think that they had truly seen a possibility and devised a strategy missed by everyone else. "Who is the heavy that planned all this?" Johnny Apple of *The New York Times* asked Bracy in Kansas City at the Democratic mini-convention in December, as he looked at the volunteers and delegates in the Udall hospitality suite.

"I guess us," said Terry, pointing to himself and Gabusi. Apple shook his head in disbelief. "God damn it," said Bracy later. "Gary Hart wasn't a heavy until he became a heavy." (Hart managed McGovern's drive for the nomination in '72 and later became a senator from Colorado.)

In the early days of '74 Bracy and Gabusi were also isolated from the mainstream of Washington political myth because they felt that Teddy Kennedy could be beaten by Udall for the nomination. They believed that Kennedy's strength lay in the two late primaries of California and New York and that he might never reach those primaries politically alive if he were defeated in New Hampshire, Florida, and Wisconsin. They also foresaw the real problems that Kennedy, whose campaigns had largely been self-financed, would have raising money. So they began to put together in the early primary states their organization of younger professionals who would be loyal to Udall whether Kennedy ran or not. Interestingly, this constituency included quite a few who had worked for Robert Kennedy. Even before Peter Hart looked into his crystal poll and saw "Ted Kennedy's peers dividing against him," Bracy and Gabusi had sensed the drift, though they missed the planned presence of Boston Mayor Kevin White as a bitterly anti-Kennedy fourth force in New Hampshire.

On the road, Udall's speaking ability furthered him with his audiences as it had aided him with the media. "We in the House can't afford expensive speechwriters, we have to produce our own words." Udall's clichés had a humorous freshness that made them slide by better than the standard political fare. Speaking in Westchester, New York, before a sophisticated fund-raising audience dancing to the tunes of Peter Duchin, Udall decked out talks about the environment with his own observations. "I burned more fossil fuel coming here to talk to you about the energy crisis than my grandfather in St. Johns, Arizona, burned in his life. . . . A child born in the thirties will see 80 percent of the coal and oil owned by America burned in his lifetime. . . . I can see the President working on his energy message while seated in an air-conditioned office, warmed by an artificial fire, and getting so worked up over the problem, he has to take a dip in his heated swimming pool."

Udall believed at the start of his campaign that the public didn't want specific programs. Those "had done McGovern in." No one could foresee everything that would happen. What the public wanted was a feeling of confidence in the man, that he understood the problems, not that he had all the answers right at that moment.

"You have a sick apple tree. The extreme liberal sees that tree and says: 'Let's cut it down and plant a new one.' The conservative yells: 'Leave that fine old tree alone.' I guess, the Udall position is, 'Let's prune away some of the dead branches because the tree is basically still strong and with help will grow."

His staff was not always enchanted with this approach. "When you get asked about food problems in Latin America you've got to at least show you know they don't raise rice in Peru," remarked Gabusi. But in spite of worries that he was becoming identified as the candidate who told jokes, Udall's old-fashioned speaking ability continued to prove an asset. As late as 1975 Udall still wrote most of his own congressional speeches and newsletters, scratching them out longhand on yellow legal-size pads—not on the backs of old envelopes, as he jokingly tells people who remark on his resemblance to Lincoln.

"I learned the way to convince a jury," Udall says, "was to lay out the other fellow's side of the case better than he could summarize it himself, then knock it down."

Yet, as in physics, for every thrust there is a counterthrust in politics. Udall's extremely personal involvement with his words also created problems for him in the invisible primary.

"How did you sleep?" I asked him on a Saturday morning in 1974 as, after a political breakfast in Salt Lake City, we got into a car at 7:45 and drove off to tape a TV show.

"Not too well. I woke up early, worried about the speech I have to give"—which is fine and makes for a great speech, but how often can a candidate stay awake worrying about a speech? He never got to deliver that speech to the Democratic Convention in Salt Lake City either. As people walked around the half-block-long convention floor wheeling and dealing beneath the spots and the red, white, and blue bunting, the constant buzz of talk and shuffle of feet drowned him out.

"If delegates *can* mill, they *will* mill," said Udall resignedly.

"Many of your friends, and I mean real friends, think your problem may turn out to be your own toughness."

"I talked that over with Muskie," Udall answered. Along with the late Robert F. Kennedy, Muskie, because of his pioneer battles for the environment, is one of Udall's heroes. "We agree, it's a question of balance. One of the reasons I am out here is to find out how much I can take. And getting used to four or five hours' sleep. I would really like to return the presidency to the people. To have a President who could stroll around

Washington. Put on a backpack and walk through the national parks. I think a man who has roots doesn't have to act tough all the time."

He harked back again to the security that growing up in a loving family in a small town had given him, pointing out that the evening of Eisenhower's inaugural, ex-President Harry Truman got on a train and went back to his home in Kansas City, without pomp, ceremony, or yachts. "He knew who he was."

One act of courage all-important in building the Udall constituency was his speech in Tucson in October 1967, against continuing the Vietnam War. This made him one of the first mainstream Democrats to break with President Johnson. For Mo the strain of this break was increased because brother Stewart was in the Johnson Cabinet.

"I have come here tonight to say as plainly and as simply as I can that I was wrong two years ago, and I firmly believe President Johnson's advisers are wrong today."

Style, we have come to realize, is a key ingredient of any political campaign, perhaps because in this day of artificiality, ghostwritten speeches, and trick verbal solutions to complex problems, style still says something about the man. Udall's campaign style is unique, having far more of the forties and fifties about it than the seventies. I am reminded more of campaigning with Harry Truman than with any recent candidate. One might be looking at old newsreels of a thirties campaign rather than a modern precampaign drive. Will such speeches stand up in the later stages of the campaign, or ferment under pressure into raw corn?

When asked in early '74 what he thought his main handicaps were, Udall came up with the following: First, he was in wrong with organized labor, because he had voted for the right-to-work law. The voters of his district were for such a law eight to one, and he felt on that issue he had to represent them. He also felt that campaign reform, which he has pushed in the House, had made him unpopular with some of the party professionals. He was from a small state. He could be attacked as not being familiar with urban problems, though he felt land-use planning included urban problems. And the fact that he was a Mormon could hurt him, too, because the Mormon Church excludes blacks. Then there was his divorce: "though I don't see Betty Ford or Happy Rockefeller bringing it up."

In American political history, Udall has strange heroes for a Democrat: Lincoln and Teddy Roosevelt, both Republicans. Lincoln, the last congressman to become President without holding higher office, seems an almost inevitable choice. He grew up much as Udall, with the same physical size, habits of speech, and political techniques. Udall's knowledge of Lincoln is quite deep—Nicolay and Hay, rather than *Bartlett's Familiar Quotations*. He talked at length on the genesis of the Illinois Election Letter, the one that ends: "What is the Presidency to me if I have no country." Udall remarked that President Nixon, then clinging tenuously to power in the White House, seemed to have turned this sentence backward.

Udall respects Teddy Roosevelt because of his feeling for the land and creation of the national park system. "An ecologist before his time." Udall, who has made his own net worth public ever since he came to Congress, also credits T.R. with being among the first campaign reformers, a politician who tried to take money out of politics.

While the psychological test was not as important for Udall as for Teddy Kennedy or Walter Mondale, he, too, had to consider the effects on himself and his family. In August 1974, after his first swings around the country had convinced him that the idea of running for the presidency was more than some drug-induced vision brewed in the twin limbecks of House machismo and Udall ambition, Mo talked over his campaign with his family. They not only agreed to support him but offered to help in his campaign.

Udall's first marriage had come apart under the pressures of House politics. His second wife, Ella Royston, had worked on the Hill for eight years and understood, even if she didn't always appreciate, the demands of politics. She was frank in her opposition to going out on the rubber chicken circuit herself, preferring to stay at home. She also never hesitated to tell candidate Udall where she thought husband Udall was lacking. "This is a love letter. Now, Tiger, get off my back," he wrote her once in lipstick on their bathroom mirror, after she had complained about how little she heard from him when he was away campaigning. Mo's transition in clothes, from blue jeans and wide belts with turquoise clasps to classy suburban casual, is also her work. "How many times," Ella tells him, "do I have to tell you not to wear the brown belt with the black shoes. . . . How many times do I have to tell you not to wear loafers with a suit."

After a big evening for candidate Udall in Phoenix, when Senator Kennedy shortly after his withdrawal described Udall as "one of the finest congressmen the House has ever had . . . on the launching pad of national leadership," Ella told the elated candidate that her husband "needed a shampoo." Her feelings about being the wife of a presidential candidate are definitely mixed.

The truism that wives of politicians, like the wives of many successful men, lead lonely and frustrating lives is no less true for being trite. The wife who can best immunize a candidate against the deadly virus of galloping self-importance may well be the type of woman who finds the strains of separation and campaigning the most difficult to bear. As one is suspicious of a mother who too joyfully gives up her son to war, so one can doubt a wife who sees no agony in the break in personal contact that campaigning must bring—or, for that matter, covering campaigns.

On November 23, 1974, Udall became the first declared candidate in the 1976 presidential race. Here he was following McGovern's strategy: Announce early, gain a reputation for forthright speaking, reap increased media attention, and openly recruit an activist constituency. But in announcing, Udall was careful to stress his centrist stance. "There is a name for a party that can't get together: Losers."

Ten years before, such an announcement by a congressman without the support of any major political boss or access to big money would have been laughable. But the invisible primary is not won with past tactics. With the political parties breaking down, the number of primaries increasing, and the constraints on funds far more severe, a candidate more than ever has to create his own support through his own constituency. Of the six vital categories—staff, constituency, strategy, finance, media relationship, and self-testing—Udall had significant strength in the first three areas and the last. At the start of 1975 it appeared to me that the final state primary battles in 1976 would be between him and Scoop Jackson. Most other observers doubted my sanity out there on that lonely limb.

The twenty-nine congressmen who first urged Udall to run had applied their political lever at precisely the right place and time. No matter what happened politically to Udall's campaign in '76, members of the House would celebrate their bicentennial with renewed personal and political power.

CHAPTER 4

Jackson. The Problem of Money

With the withdrawal of Senator Edward Kennedy on September 24, 1974, the "acknowledged Democratic front-runner" in the invisible primary became Senator Henry M. Jackson of Washington. "Runner" he certainly was; "front" was more open to question. Though if one were forced to declare an acknowledged front-runner, as distinct from a possible back-walker, any time in late 1974, Jackson would have been the easiest answer to defend.

At the close of 1974 no Democratic candidate could claim as much as 20 percent support from his fellow Democrats. Governor George Wallace came closest with 19 percent; but he was unacceptable to even more Democrats: 29 percent. Perennial candidate Hubert Humphrey was next, with a slim 11 percent favorable; but he made 14 percent of his fellow Democrats sick, a point ahead of George McGovern, who gave 13 percent of his party nausea while appealing to only 6 percent. By this process Jackson became the front-runner with 10 percent of his party leaning toward him and only 3 percent opposed. There was a catch, though—catch 42, 42 being the percentage of voters who had never heard of Scoop Jackson.

Further proof of the uncertainty of Jackson's lead at that time were trial poll heats between President Ford and various Democratic candidates. Here Muskie edged out Jackson. Ford would have defeated Scoop 47 percent to 42 percent, while Muskie would have run a closer race: 45–48 (Gallup), 45–46 (Harris). Further, the Muskie edge came from two areas that were important to any invisible primary constituency, the younger voters and suburban dwellers, political shock troops who could be mobilized for the state primaries.

In the six categories vital in the preprimary race—staff, money, media, strategy, constituency and psychological preparedness—Jackson made an impressive early showing in the first four. His staff of twenty-two paid professionals was led by Robert Keefe, an old-time operator with a new politics understanding of media. Keefe had successfully handled political problems for Indiana Senator Birch Bayh, bringing that pleasant but hardly outstanding senator to national attention through a magnificently organized fight to block the Supreme Court nominations of Nixon candidates Clement Haynsworth and G. Harrold Carswell. A former aide to George Meany, Keefe had most recently been deputy chairman of the Democratic National Committee. He is given to writing little notes to himself which he carries on file cards in his shirt pocket. He is as friendly and as trusted by Democrats of all views as anyone in the party, but like most of the men around Jackson, he has been around for a long time and has a tendency to know those senior to himself rather than those junior.

Jackson's finances were eye-poppingly successful. The senator and his inner circle of friends had reasoned early that financing and cost control would be crucial under the complex provisions of the new campaign financing law. They had laid out a unique funding strategy to meet the law. Their plan was to raise $2 million in units of from $1,000 to $3,000 before January 1, 1975, and of $1,000 afterward, when $1,000 became the individual gift ceiling. This first $2 million would be used to finance a mass mailing which would produce the $5,000 from each of twenty states in amounts of $250 or less necessary to trigger government funding. After that requirement was fulfilled, they would continue to pursue both federal matching funds and private gifts, varying the mix with changes in the law and the results of their direct-mail campaign.

At the close of 1974 Jackson had raised a hefty $1.112 million, which put him ahead of everyone but Wallace, who by then totaled nearly $2 million. But Wallace had started with a small base and raised close to all his cash by direct mail; to plow back much of his funds into the direct-mail operation. Though Jackson's fund raising fell behind schedule in 1975, by the start of '76 he alone among the Democratic candidates had sufficient cash on hand to see him through *all* the primaries.

At the same time, foreseeing that a shortage of cash could be a major

problem in the late primaries where he would have the most support—
Ohio, California, Pennsylvania, and New Jersey—Jackson set up a rigid cost
accounting and reporting system to keep the campaign honest and solvent
until the last ballot at the convention.

Despite his strengths in staff and finance, Jackson still had to overcome
two other major problems. The first and most serious was the lack of any
large constituency, other than the Jewish voters who had been drawn to
Jackson by his unswerving support of Israel and freer immigration for
Soviet Jews.

His second problem was the disastrous lineup of the important early state
primaries—New Hampshire, Wisconsin, and Florida—in all of which
Jackson had severe political competition. In New Hampshire both the active
center followers of Muskie and the more moderate McGovernites had
united behind Udall by the latter part of 1974. The more extreme elements,
which would not have supported Jackson anyway, had coalesced around
Fred Harris's populism and Gene McCarthy's strange vendetta against
imagined past wrongs. The industrial labor unions were unorganized, and
while Jackson might have had a mass in New Hampshire, he had no
constituency who would work and energize his voters to come to the polls.
This was the very problem, only greater, that Muskie had faced four years
before.

Florida held the menace of Wallace in the blue-collar agricultural areas
and of Udall or Carter in the younger, politically volatile suburban areas.
Though Jackson had a strong constituency among Jewish groups and
moderate businessmen, it was hard to see him emerging from Florida with a
clear-cut media-provoking victory. The same held true in Wisconsin, where
three of Udall's early congressional supporters were so sure of their own
reelection that they could spend time and effort organizing for Udall. The
"regular" political organizations in all three states were too fragmented to
supply Jackson with the workers necessary to bring his voters to the polls.
Then in late '75, the political lightning struck. The Republicans,
maneuvering to support Rockefeller, moved the New York primary to
April; next the Democrats in Massachusetts moved their primary to March.
Jackson was strong in both states.

Faced with the new funding limitations and the lack of a constituency from
which to draw volunteers, Jackson and his staff decided early to concentrate
where Jackson was strongest, his home base in the Senate. If Churchill could
say, "I am a child of the House of Commons," Jackson could certainly say, "I
am a teen-ager of the Congress"—twelve years in the House, twenty-one in
the Senate, chairman of the Interior and Insular Affairs Committee, senior
member of the Armed Services Committee and of the Atomic Energy
Committee, chairman of the Permanent Subcommittee on Investigations of
the Government Operations Committee. From any one of these power
bases, but particularly the first and the last, Jackson could conduct
investigations and propose legislation bound to draw headlines.

It is difficult to write objectively about Jackson's performance in the

Senate. To say that he was one of its stars, which is certainly true, is in one context a compliment, in another a put-down—like calling a man a "Mudville Milton" or "the O. J. Simpson of sandbox touch." My own view (prejudice) leads me to blame this ambiguity on the shift of power whereby the Senate had grown legislatively impotent,* and not to fault Jackson for brilliantly exploiting the media opportunities of the upper echo chamber.

"To run for President from the United States Senate." How well Jackson understood all this phrase implied. Day after day his picture was on the front page of the newspapers, his words on the evening and morning TV shows, profiles of him in the leading magazines. His boast was that in 1974 he had spoken in thirty-eight states and missed only 1 percent of the votes in the Senate—which shows how he controlled the Senate. Any time the leadership had wanted to make him look bad they could have waited until he was out of town and then scheduled about thirty quick votes in two days and made him look awful. But no one did that to Scoop—or to any powerful member of the Senate inner club. In July 1974, when Senator Lloyd Bentsen wanted to complete a southern campaign swing, his chief assistant, Lloyd Hackler, was able without too much difficulty to negotiate out of Senate Whip Robert Byrd a week's delay in a vital vote on oil taxes. The club looks after its own.

Jackson's detractors point out that with all his power in the Senate he has accomplished little in the way of important legislation. The trouble with this argument is that no senator is producing important legislation. Most legislation now comes from the Executive, the rest from the House. Senators advance their power by glamorous investigations such as Watergate, the CIA, or the oil companies; or they produce plans to give every motorist all the gas they want at no extra cost, while conserving energy.

Jackson, with a staff of eighty-nine scattered about his office and the committees he controlled, could play this game to perfection. Even his critics conceded that this staff, led by Dorothy Fosdick in foreign affairs, Richard Perle in military policy, and William Van Ness in energy, was the ablest in the Congress. Besides, Jackson could take credit for more legislation than most senators: the original Environmental Protection Act, the Alaska pipeline legislation, amendments to the SALT agreements, and restrictions on trade with the Soviet Union.

Jackson had taken his Senate staff and used it to make himself extremely familiar with the issues he considered vital, and he often knew more about them than other senators and the reporters covering the events. He even knew more than the bureaucrats handling details for the Executive. He used

---

*An all too often forgotten truth of history is that dictatorships do not arise from strong executives, but from weak executives and fustian legislatures. There was never danger that President Nixon would become "Dictator Dick." Against his every move to increase his grasp were arrayed the Congress, the press, the bureaucracy, the courts, all awesome power structures bent on curbing his illegal aggrandizements. But with the present Congress, after, say, eight years of a bumbling and indecisive President who permitted the country to tilt toward destruction, those same power centers that thwarted Nixon could lead the pack in baying for an all-powerful President. Caesar did not seize control. Free-born Romans gave it to him gratefully to escape from foolish counsels and a divided Senate full of wind eaters.

this knowledge much of the time to write legislation or conduct hearings that would draw media attention. To criticize him for this is fair, provided one levels the same charge at every other senator. They all played the game, only Jackson and Teddy Kennedy played it better. When Mondale tried it, he and his staff got the facts wrong and produced a pro-Israel bill that embarrassed other senators and that all the press criticized as uninformed and opportunistic.

Lyndon Johnson took this same type of intense interest in legislation and combined it with his ability to manipulate men, both to pass the legislation he wanted and to make himself rich. Jackson used the same ingredients to build toward the presidency. Certainly wealth per se doesn't interest Jackson. He made his tax returns public reluctantly, believing a man's private life should remain private; but the returns for the past five years showed he had been living on his Senate salary, while giving away his lecture fees to charity. This meant that he gave away 40 percent of what he earned: an act of generosity so rare among his fellow senators that it made many of them bitter.

Much has been written, as a result of Watergate and the fall of Richard Nixon, about the power of the Washington press. Nothing could better illustrate that power than the election by the Washington press of senators, as a class, into the prime contenders for the presidency. Until ex-Senator Harry Truman won the presidency in his own right in 1948—to be followed by Senators Kennedy, Johnson, and Nixon—the last senators to gain the presidency without also having served as governors were Franklin Pierce, Benjamin Harrison, and Warren Harding, hardly historical justification for the present singularity of focus.

Reporters, both newspaper and television, are an intensely competitive group. A great many of the ablest, men on whom their editors rely, are gathered in Washington. On any given day a great deal more "news" happens than can possibly make the papers or TV news shows. A reporter's future, like that of any other marginally protected pieceworker, is tied to what he produces. So to get "space" or "air time," reporters go after men who have proved in the past their worth as news makers. Here senators, with their title, their staffs, their access to what is going on, and their lack of responsibility compared to members of the Executive, have the time and knowledge to be ideal news sources—far more so than members of the House, with their limited areas of expertise. Once a senator becomes known as a news maker, reporters seek him out for information because what he says is news. As more reporters seek him out, the senator becomes more of a news maker, his statements and actions draw more space and air time, more reporters seek him out, and he becomes more of a news maker. The self-reflexive nature of the news takes over, and another career is launched on words.

Given a choice, whose press conference on mental health do you think a reporter would rather cover: that of Senator Edward Kennedy of Massachusetts or Governor Michael Dukakis of Massachusetts? Yet which man has the more direct and judgeable responsibility actually to improve the lot of thousands of people hospitalized with mental illness?

With his excellent staff, his well-funded campaign, his Senate base, his ability to exploit the Washington news focus, and a well-planned strategy, Jackson could have been even further out in front than he was in 1974 and early 1975, except for one final problem. He had divided the Democrats. It wasn't just over Vietnam, where he had remained a hawk long after others had changed their minds; something about the man himself bred division. When Democrats anywhere in the party—Congress, state house, rank and file—talked about Jackson, they chose up sides with a vehemence out of all proportion to the man's words and actions. And the same was true of the press.

Reading the press, it seems there must be two Senator Jacksons: bad Jackson and good Scoop. About all the two seem to have in common is being born in Everett, Washington, to Norwegian parents in 1912, and growing up middle-class poor in a family that was mother-, rather than father-, centered. Jackson describes his mother, who lived to be ninety, as "strong, warm, determined, and stubborn." Both sides agree that Scoop got his nickname not from being a newspaperman, though he had a delivery route as a newsboy, but because his sister thought he resembled a comic strip character called Scoop. Both bad Jackson and good Scoop went to Stanford and the University of Washington where they got a BA and a law degree. They became county prosecutor (as did Mondale and Udall), went on to Congress in 1940 at age twenty-eight, moved up to the Senate in 1952. In 1961, at the age of forty-nine, both married a woman of the same age and name, Helen Hardin, twenty-eight, a Senate secretary and a graduate of Scripps College, who got her MA on Virginia Woolf. Both bad Jackson and good Scoop have two children and drive a 1961 Chevrolet coupe which was bought secondhand in 1965.

At this car the divergence between the two Jacksons begins. The viewers of good Scoop see the car as "straightforward, standard transmission, unaffected, frill-free, hardworking, reliable." But bad Jackson drives a car that is "dull, drab, old-fashioned, and reverse-pretentious." If observers disagree so about a beat-up hunk of metal that just happens to be driven, perhaps on alternate days, by good Scoop or bad Jackson, think of how they fall out over the man himself.

The bad Jackson was vividly portrayed in the *Nation* by Robert Sherrill, whose brilliant reporting on Chappaquiddick helped push Teddy Kennedy into withdrawal:

> The general public is not now and never has been much interested in the junior Senator from the State of Washington. When Henry (Scoop) Jackson bombed in his attempt to win the 1972 Democratic Presidential Nomination, he said it was because the public didn't recognize his name.
>
> For a man who had been in Congress since 1940 and in the Senate

since 1953, who had been chairman of the Senate Interior and Insular Affairs Committee since 1962, and altogether had held assignments on more important committees (including Armed Services and Atomic Energy) than any other member of the Senate, those public relations excuses were themselves a confession of how little he had accomplished and how little leadership he had shown. However, in the last two years he has done what he wasn't able to do in the previous thirty-two: he got a few people to know his name. He has not achieved this, however, by a sudden burst of legislative accomplishments but as an outright gift from the press.

The article portrayed Jackson as a "high class Sam Yorty. . . . Neither his modified racism nor his appeal to the defense aerospace worker force nor his 'I am more Jewish than a Jew' appeal to Jews served him well." Sherrill went on to point out that Jackson is the senator from Boeing, and gave examples of Jackson's headline-grabbing use of his committees to expose nonexistent abuses or problems already documented by the press. Jackson's Interior Committee was accused of having done nothing to meet the energy crisis, or roll back oil prices, or save the independent oil producer or control the industry. The article then turned around and hit Jackson for helping get the Alaska pipeline through, thus hurting the environment; and it listed all the contributions the senator received from big oil in his 1972 presidential drive.

Bad Jackson, to continue, is also a draft dodger, a "kleagle for the Chamber of Commerce kind of racism," who wormed his way into public office smearing adversaries and using the Yellow Peril menace as his chief campaign theme. This racist militaristic nut and friend of millionaires, who has a terrible temper, was the man Nixon wanted as his Secretary of Defense. That fact is true, as is the fact, not mentioned in the article, that Jackson was Robert Kennedy's choice for his brother's vice-presidential running mate.

Other less strident articles about the bad Jackson, that at least credit him with legislative success, appeared in *New York, Atlantic,* and *New Republic.* To quote Stanley Karnow's critique in the latter: "In my opinion Jackson's position on Vietnam highlights his consistency at its most egregious. Like the Bourbons, who never learned nor forgot anything, he continues to believe that he was correct in advocating bigger bombings and faster U.S. troop commitments, and his criticism of Robert McNamara's graduated response doctrine makes the former Defense Secretary sound like a pacifist."

On totally different ground, sometimes equally unconvincing, stands good Scoop. For example, writing in the Minneapolis *Tribune,* contributing editor Geri Jacobs begins:

> Old fashioned virtues have not counted for much in the recent media minded world of American politics. They have been for example no match for the vague but much sought after quality known as charisma. . . .

It is possible, however, that Sen. Henry (Scoop) Jackson, an old hand on Capitol Hill, is out to prove that charisma is not everything, and old fashioned virtues have a place in the modern world after all.

Disciplined and hard working, as unassuming as a next door neighbor, the Senator from Washington has earned his share of news stories over the years. . . .

At a remarkably youthful 62, when others begin to think of retirement, Jackson has reached an apex in his admirable career. Probably no other man or woman in Congress has so powerful —though not uncontroversial—a voice on so many leading issues.

Robert Sherrill had found that "at 62 he [Jackson] is beginning to sag; not badly as yet, but it shows." Obviously two different men. Black and white is seldom an adequate palette for human portraits, even those of presidential candidates. Witness Delaware Senator Willard Saulsbury's description of a contemporary running for President: "I never did see or converse with so weak and imbecile a man; the weakest man I ever knew in high place. If I wanted to paint a despot, a man perfectly regardless of every constitutional right of the people, I would paint the hideous, apelike form of Abraham Lincoln."

Joseph Alsop also sees good Scoop, a man who is "both known and admired by the mass of voters . . . more and more people now see him as the man who had the judgment to be right, and the courage to speak out, when being right was far from fashionable." Joseph Kraft, in *The New York Times Magazine,* described good Scoop campaigning from his Senate base: "Because he knows Congress as few men, and because he is well placed on strategic committees . . . Jackson has been able to gain attention for his views and himself in the press and on television. Repeatedly he has managed to emerge as the key Senator on important legislation."

What is remarkable about Jackson vs. Scoop is that people seize on the same characteristics as a basis for damnation or praise. His friends cite his consistency and yet his flexibility and understanding of politics. His enemies quote Ralph Waldo Emerson about a foolish consistency and at the same time see him as shifty, overready to compromise for political advantage. Supporters cite as an example of this breadth his sponsorship of the Environmental Protection Act, for which he became the only senator to win the John Muir award, and his legislation permitting the Alaska pipeline, with safeguards. They see him as a man who comprehends the realities of both ecology and energy. His enemies cite the same two stands as an example of Jackson's duplicity.

To me the key to Jackson, the elusive element of both his strength and his weakness, and the reason for the animosity he arouses, is the essential boyishness of the man. Jackson often has the spirit and mannerisms of a bouncy ten-year-old; at one moment he can charm and in the next infuriate. This streak of little-boyishness keeps breaking out in him like sunshine (or chicken pox; pick your metaphor). He is unable to keep track of things, always losing notes, suitcases, addresses; his suits are rumpled, his tie never quite straight, his cornucopia pockets full of forgotten junk. There is the sudden grin, not the ear-splitting Eisenhower grin that sent voters racing for the polling booths, but still an appealing boyish smile.

The other side of this coin is the sudden flare of temper. Hughes Air West may be the worst airline in the world, and several passengers were heard to cheer "Right on!" when Jackson lit into the hour-late crew for their sloppy service; but it was hardly the pilot's fault, and Jackson certainly lost the votes of the crew. "I don't think much of you either, Senator," yelled back the pilot. On any five days of campaigning, Jackson is almost certain to let fly at some reporter for an idiotic question. He doesn't suffer fools gladly.

His combative way of speaking also seems boyish. Even when he is trying to be moderate, delivering speeches monochromatic to the point of dullness, the words are strung together as if he was jut-jaw-daring his elders to shut him up.

"This country doesn't have to listen to that tinhorn Colonel Qaddafi." "I look forward to the time we won't have Butz to kick around anymore." "We must behave as if we are in a war, because we are in an economic war." "We need a massive food production program to bring down the Arab oil cartel."

And people react to Jackson's words and stance as they do to precocious boys; they want to either love him or swat him, but they are seldom neutral.

This characteristic of Jackson's may account for his trouble in attracting younger voters. As his campaign began, someone under thirty-five voluntarily and wholeheartedly in his camp was a rarity. Perhaps being closer to childhood, those under thirty—Wordsworth to the contrary—did not find that Jackson's boylike qualities led to the man they wished to follow.

Sometimes it is difficult to know what age group Jackson is addressing. He talks of things that should turn younger voters on: the need to overcome apathy, how in the 1974 Democratic primary in his home state of Washington only 22 percent of the voters turned out, or programs to help the poor, conserve energy even if it means rationing gasoline, help the environment. But his illustrations are out of the past: Senator Arthur Vandenburg and the origins of the Marshall Plan. And those who listen and nod agreement are older people. Those who first endorsed his campaign were also from the past: Senator Sam Ervin, labor leader Sigmund Arywitz, Senator Joe Pastore. How much power could they deliver in the 1976 world?

When he first came to Washington as a congressman in 1940, Jackson was slow to establish himself. I believe he felt he wasn't ready until he had done his homework, had grown up. He says he thinks of himself today as "thirty-five or forty." He added that after swimming in the Senate pool, he then went into the sauna where: "I take the steam at 160 degrees. The boys in the gym tell me that's hotter than any other senator." Then he takes a cold shower. (The boy in training.)

If, at sixty, Jackson thinks of himself as forty, then sixteen years ago at the start of the Kennedy era he would have felt himself under thirty—a young age for a man to be a leader rather than a follower. Also, in marrying late a girl decisively younger than himself, the boy could be signaling his presence to the man.

Jackson's seriousness, one of his salient characteristics, also has a touch of the childlike about it, the wonderment of finding out how things work. His attitude when he finds something wrong is more that of a young man, surprised by evil and determined to root it out, than of a politician accustomed to years of compromise. He is genuinely embarrassed by raw off-color jokes, he is quixotic toward past enemies, forgiving some, feuding with others, and he has a reverence and veneration for the teachers of his youth. He runs through a litany of almost forgotten names around Washington. Chip Bohlen, Frank Nash, Bob Lovett, George Kennan, George Marshall. "The town changed when they left," he says. That it did. And for the worse. But the question is more who will get us through the present seas now they no longer keep the watch.

This boyishness of Jackson's lends credence to the worries, even among some of his friends, about how he will take pressure. Will he use the youthful quality to inspire people, to draw and hold able subordinates, to escape when necessary the killing strain of the presidency? Or will the boy grow petulant amid the continual battles of the modern power world?

"I am not mush" is a phrase Jackson uses often to explain his consistent stand on some issue or his refusal to change his opinions under pressure. The problem is that after the fourth or fifth time I hear this, I also hear the queen in Hamlet say, as the player queen rings changes on her devotion to the player king: "The lady doth protest too much, methinks."

Here is the weakness of the Senate as a proving ground for Presidents. Jackson has, in the words of the cliché, "held high public office" for thirty-four years, and we can only guess at how he takes pressure. After following one of the dark horses, Mayor Kevin White of Boston, for two sleepless days and nights at the height of the Boston busing controversy, I can describe in detail how *he* responds to pressure. He grows strained, combative, irritable, makes mistakes, but never loses control of himself or fails to draw from his subordinates. But no one can say the same of Jackson, Mondale, Muskie, Udall, Kennedy. The Senate—there is no way around the fact—at present provides dangerously little training for the presidency. Indeed by cocooning a man inside an expensive club it may be a handicap.

At least with Jackson one can say that he runs a staff of eighty-six superbly well; that he has shown himself able to get his way skillfully among his peers in the Senate, though he has bruised quite a few as he did so; that badly defeated in his first try for the presidency, he learned from his mistakes. He has passed enough legislation so that one can make generalizations about his attitude in foreign affairs: balance-of-power conservative. And about his stand on domestic issues: New and Fair Deal liberal. But whether he has grace under pressure no one knows.

In addition to his boyishness there are several other themes basic to Jackson's personality, touchstones that he continually rubs as he makes his judgments. There is the many-faceted rock of his Norwegianness and his family.

Jackson's family comes not only from Norway, but from northern Norway: not from the soft southern counties, where the mountains recede and the land slopes toward the Skagerrak, almost an extension of sunny Denmark. Instead, his roots are in that dark troll-haunted land of ice and rock at the edge of the Arctic Circle, where the Eddic giants battle, the winter nights are six months long, and the brief summer is haunted by the nightmare purples of Edvard Munch. Jackson has taken the basic darkness of this land, its pessimism about life and humankind, and combined this brew with the welling optimism of the second-generation immigrant to produce a cluster of contradictions—a dark view of life and a faith in the future. These same contradictions are often found in Irish politicians, particularly of the old school. Perhaps this helps explain why Jackson is the preferred candidate of many such men.

Many commentators have pointed out that Jackson's support of Israel is no mere political ploy, but springs from a deep inner identification, wherein he seems to view the Israelis, like himself, as residents of a small persecuted country. Similarly he identifies with the land and people of the Outer Hebrides, "extraordinary men and women."

Publicly and privately Jackson refers constantly to his family, particularly his mother. "A great woman. No one ever put anything over on her. She lived to be ninety." He sees his family as one that came to America, stood on their own two feet, played by the rules, and made good. "My sister taught for forty-three years in a classroom to help poor kids."

And like the second-generation immigrant of sociological stereotype, Jackson is more American than most Americans, a super-patriot. He feels that those like himself and his family who have worked hard, who helped themselves, who served America, who have been charitable, deserve the rewards. Hence his hostility toward both the oil companies and the affluent young. He sees both as trying to manipulate themselves into power without having paid their dues. Thus he can be short-tempered and abrupt with both left-wing students and oil company presidents without expressing any contradictions in his personality.

Finally, Jackson's legal training is important to him. Not in making him neutral—he is seldom if ever that—but in the way he thinks. No matter what his initial prejudices, he will chew at both sides of a major question; not for the abstract interplay of idea against idea, but to find out all the effects of various courses of action on the country and himself. He doesn't go so far as President Johnson, who once defined a "good idea" to his White House staff as one that "gets off its ass and goes out in the street and uses its elbows for Lyndon Johnson." But by the time Jackson takes a stand, he is certain as he can be of all the practical effects of his action, including its political possibilities. Sometimes he may be proven wrong. Senator Russell Long of Louisiana, a brilliant Senate tactician, blocked his efforts to roll back oil company profits: and certainly Jackson's 1972 presidential campaign was a disastrous joke. But Jackson gains his way a surprisingly high percentage of the time.

In the early days of the invisible primary, Jackson's campaign had two major goals: to neutralize the hostility of the Democratic left, and to find some sort of constituency in the party's center. After McGovern's defeat in 1972, a great many of the Democratic left said, with both heat and conviction, that they would walk out of the party if Jackson were ever the presidential nominee. Jackson knew he could never gain these people's support, but his aim was to become what they call in New York clubhouses, "a guy we can live-wid."

Jackson campaigned in 1974 for Congressman Robert Drinan of Massachusetts and Allard Lowenstein of New York, both early and outspoken critics of the Vietnam War. "I had to convince the Jews on Long Island that Allard was all right on Israel," Jackson remarked with a laugh. How would these leaders of the left, whom he had helped politically, be able to walk out of a convention that had chosen him its candidate? Instead of seeing bad Jackson—the Vietnam hawk, the author of a constitutional amendment to prevent busing, and the supporter of the SST—could they not focus on good Scoop, early foe of Senator Joseph McCarthy, enemy of the oil companies, author of the Environmental Protection Act, and early supporter of civil rights legislation?

Another consequence of Jackson's opening to the left was that it pushed the other candidate of the Democratic party's right, Senator Lloyd Bentsen of Texas, further right. Jackson and Bentsen were both maneuvering in the media (though Bentsen's campaign staff seemed only intermittently to realize this) to gain the safe left center position. Similarly, Mondale and Udall had maneuvered from the left for the right-center position. When Udall gained that place, he contributed to the pressure that forced Mondale to drop out, leaving the extreme liberals desperately searching for someone else and ending up with Fred Harris, the former senator from Oklahoma. As Jackson moved to the left, Bentsen did not react fast enough. So Bentsen was left on the right, the candidate of the conservative business Democrats (as distinct, I guess, from being right on the left, the position of Fred Harris, the poor man's populist).

Some notes on Jackson campaigning in late 1974, quick watercolors of the politician in action in the invisible primary:

San Diego, California, campaigning for congressional aspirant Colleen O'Connor, former McGovern organizer, who has had Jane Fonda helping her in the district. Ms. O'Connor, a pert, minute-sized firecracker of energy who is a history professor at San Diego State (the locus of American political power shifting towards academia again), is concerned that the defense workers in her district, alarmed by her antimilitarism, will all vote Republican. Jackson has been called and is here to slay that dragon before three hundred breakfast-eaters, mostly from labor and the academic community: "Colleen and I will work together in Washington to keep America strong." In return Colleen introduces Jackson as "the man the oil companies fear most. The man President Ford fears most. The next President of the United States. Senator Henry M. Jackson." That's not an opening to the left; that's a gap you could hurl an armored division through.

The usual rush afterward for the airplane. Jackson carries his own suit bag. He pauses as we load into two cars for a quick bag count. He is always pausing to count the bags, fearful that we will lose one. Before the week is out we do lose one, the only time he doesn't count. One final press of the flesh with the local people, jump in the cars. The lead driver takes the wrong turn to the airport; running we just make the plane. Mike Casey, the ulcer-thin, weskited advance man, gulps two stomach pacifiers. Jackson sits down and begins talking about transfer of payments, oil company profits, the Italian banking situation, Democratic party rules, and Kissinger's failure to hold together the Atlantic alliance. It is not yet 9:30 in the morning. Jackson has flown in from Seattle with his devoted shadow, Brian Corcoran, a phlegmatic nonworrier with the moves and size of a bruised pro-football tackle.

Norwalk, California, eight stops later; it's dark now. Speech and press conference at a precinct headquarters in an abandoned barbershop next to a garage. Jackson enters, skirting pools of oil. He looks a bit drawn beneath the neon lights as he holds a press conference and gives his pep talk. Gets short with a reporter who presses him for a complex answer on wage and price controls. 12316 Firestone Blvd., say the gold letters on the window. The trucks roar by, drowning out Jackson's words.

Norwalk's mayor, Bob White, running for Congress, a big ex-first baseman swaying back and forth on plowboy feet. "I didn't go to school just to eat my lunch; I'll figure out how to save the economy if I get to Congress." White is broke. He held a hundred-dollar-plate dinner to raise funds, didn't sell a single ticket: "So help me, God, I'll never go through that again if I run for President."

"Honest, hon," says one of our two drivers to his wife over the phone. "I can't get home. I'm driving Senator Jackson. Naw, not from the state. The guy from Oregon."

What are we doing here? We are running for President by trying to energize the center. Middle, middle, middle, everywhere we go. But are we energizing or piddling? Political systems and weather systems are the opposite. In weather the energy is at the storm's center, in politics on the fringes.

Eleven P.M. A late-night problem. Hy Raskin, the financial genius of Adlai

Stevenson's campaigns, stops by our motel. Someone has just held a bogus fund raiser for Jackson. Invitations were sent out to meet Jackson and Edmund Brown, without either's knowledge, on the future governor's letterhead. Naturally neither Jackson nor Brown sees any of the cash raised. Nor do the party-goers see the promised greats. Now people are mad. What should be done?

Next day, Saturday, 8 A.M., another breakfast, another candidate for Congress, Jackson bothered by postnasal drip. The rabbi begins the invocation: "Forty years ago I was in Auschwitz condemned to die. Twenty years ago I was in Soviet Germany condemned to a spiritual death, unable to practice my religion. . . . People asked me, will you travel on the Sabbath to this breakfast? I am proud to travel on the Sabbath to bless such a man as this." Jackson looks embarrassed; crowd is hushed. Jackson introduces Jerry Voorhees, who used to represent this district. Voorhees was the first Nixon victim, smeared as a Red in Nixon's first campaign for Congress, the start of his march to the top and down again. Once more Jackson is surrounded by old men, particularly from big labor, who smoke cigars and nod agreement with Jackson's serious speech. Jackson leaves his notes on the lectern and we have to race back. We're running late at 9 A.M. "People always want you to do too much," Jackson says. "But if you don't do too much, you disappoint the people."

Jackson runs late because he is an avid flesh presser, enjoys meeting people. He draws from the repeated contacts as Eisenhower did and Udall does, building up his energy through them as an actor draws energy from an audience. Other politicians like Muskie or Mondale are depleted by constant human contact and have to rest in the middle of the day. For such politicians campaigning is so without joy that it becomes almost an unbearable ordeal.

Today we campaign in a light twin-engined airplane, a De Havilland Dove, chartered by the California State Democratic Committee. There are some enthusiastic and well-organized stops, some funny and confused stops, some plain sad.

Oxinard is a sad stop: a middle-of-the-day speech in Dianne Arbus land delivered from the back of a flatbed trailer in a parking lot at the intersection of a two-lane and an eight-lane highway. Jackson mounts the trailer on a rickety ladder casually balanced by a guy smoking pot. The local advance man makes the mistake of telling me there will be three hundred listeners. There are twenty-one, all fat and in tight, garish clothes. As Jackson yells into the faulty loudspeaker system over the hot-rod roar, a little old lady in (so help me God) tennis sneakers, limps by on the superhighway in the breakdown lane, pulling behind her a shopping cart four bags full. She never turns or pauses. Brown smog drifts overhead. I stop an old-timer whose face seems to have some connection with the land. He tells me that before the Korean War this area was all orange groves and he used to work in them. Now it's tire stores, bungalows, Chicken Delights, used car lots, and gas stations.

Scoop obviously a bit unnerved. Quotes David Rockefeller on the deepening depression, calling him "hardly a Republican." Then ends his speech slamming his fist dramatically into his palm, as he leans forward to yell: "And if you want more of this mess, vote Democratic!"

Nine P.M., last stop of the day, a fund raiser for congressional aspirant Norman Mineta (he made it), at the home of Mr. and Mrs. Richard Levin. This was to be the penultimate stop, the final stop being the Kiwanis October Fest. But the Kiwanis have been caught using nonunion labor to draw the beer. So we scrub the Kiwanis. Too bad. I had looked forward to festing. The Levin house is perched high on a hill overlooking miles and miles of urban sprawl electrically beautiful in the dark. Guard dogs, swimming pool cleaned by ultrasonics. Two of the token blacks get drunk and ask never-ending questions while the moneyed guests look embarrassed. I feel I am surrounded in California by people playing roles, typecasting themselves into various parts they think will be good for them, rather than trusting, however painful, the more rewarding oddities within themselves.

Next morning Jackson tries to breakfast alone in the hotel dining room. But the California chapter of NOW is meeting there; and the women cluster around his table urging him to support more money for an all-female Olympics. When they leave, Jackson discusses the efficacy of cod-liver oil for colds. Both our mothers believed in that magic potion. We agree it probably helped us, though we remember the awful taste halfway up the throat as we burped the oil back up while running to school. Another check of bags. Rush for another plane to hit Nevada, Arizona, New Mexico, Wyoming, and Utah in two days. In case you've forgotten, the nominating convention is still over two years off.

Las Vegas, helping Harry Reid, born in a one-room cabin in Searchlight, Nevada, run for the Senate. Reid has his own mobile TV studio which tapes his speeches and press releases. These are then given to TV stations throughout Nevada, which run them as news and so save money by not having to hire reporters. Reid is shiny-faced young and surrounded by aides who keep tellin' him he is "doin' fine, jes fine." They admonish each other endlessly:

"How you doin'?"
"How you doin'?"
"Keep on truckin'."
"Yeah, keep on truckin'."

A jowled old-timer called "Judge" beckons with index finger from a back room of the Dunes Hotel. Reid says, "Yes, sir," jumps up, and goes to him.

Jackson makes a TV spot endorsing Reid. He stands on a patch of grass in back of the Dunes Hotel, looking boyish and small as he squints into the sun. The sunlight floods everything with desert glare. Jackson warns Americans of dark days ahead: oil shortages, inflation. In the distance the golf balls float through the air. Reid's aides stop three golf carts driven by fat old men from coming between Jackson and the camera. Overhead the jets turn to final and extend their wheels bringing in jumbo loads of tourists to gamble. At the fund-raising lunch where all you want to drink is free, Jackson is unable to get a glass of skimmed milk.

After lunch Jackson and an old friend of his, Jerry Mack, a former part-owner of the Riviera Hotel, sit in Mack's suite on the twenty-second floor of the Dunes among the artificial grapes and reproductions of Louis IV furniture and talk finances. Mack, seated on top of the TV console and swinging his legs, explains how he is going to sell his tankers before he comes to work for Scoop so there can be no question of conflict of interest.

Scoop explains the mechanics of getting four thousand people in twenty states to each give $250 to comply with the new campaign law; also the need for seed money in units of $1,000 to finance his direct-mail fund appeal. Together the two friends run over a list of names, while Corcoran takes notes. Who will raise what money where, chair what committees, contact what groups? Jackson says he believes the new stricter financing laws give him an advantage because givers on the far left, like Stewart Mott, know only how to give their own money, which they can no longer do, not how to raise cash from others.

In order to understand better why Jackson believes he is so strong on the money track, we shall have to pause and take a closer look at the new rules of this intricate, vitally important business of campaign financing. Politics and money are as American as betting on horses. George Washington's enemies attacked him for buying votes through his awarding of Army contracts. Abigail Adams, then wife of ex-President John Adams, wrote a hard letter to President Thomas Jefferson about his use of patronage to achieve reelection, and received back a carefully soft answer. In the 1860s James Buchanan was called as a profligate spendthrift because he spent $25,000 to become President, about $150,000 in today's dollars.

The selection of delegates to the nominating convention by direct primaries, introduced in the early 1900s, sharply increased the cost of gaining the presidency. In 1912 Theodore Roosevelt spent $611,118 prior to the convention; his rival, William Howard Taft, $499,527. On the Democratic side that year Woodrow Wilson spent $219,104 to secure the nomination; his chief rival, Judson Harmon, $150,496. After the spurt connected with the primaries, the price of the presidency stabilized for a time. Between 1912 and 1945 the cost per voter of gaining the presidency averaged out at around twenty cents. Then, after World War II, came another jump. By 1960 candidates were spending twenty-nine cents per voter; by 1964 thirty-five cents; 1968 sixty cents; and the 1972 costs are estimated at a dollar a voter.

Another measure of the increased cost of presidential campaigns is the decreased value of what the fat cat receives for his buck. Back in 1959 a

$1,000 contribution to the Democrats bought a membership in the "President's Club," special tickets to the convention and the inaugural ball, plus an invitation to a party where the donor could meet the President. At the convention hall was a special suite where "club" members could chitchat with each other. By 1967 a $1,000 contribution to President Johnson's campaign bought the fat cat merely membership in the President's Club and a presidential party invitation. By 1969 $1,000 to Richard Nixon got the cat a membership in "R.N. Associates" and an invitation to a party where he might meet a Cabinet member. By 1971 the $1,000 was only worth a gold-plated R. N. tie pin and a form letter from the President. Talk about double-digit inflation!

Before the campaign reform law of 1972 a candidate's expenditures in the invisible and state primaries were hard to estimate. Including the goods and services contributed by friends and pro-Eisenhower organizations, General Eisenhower probably spent between $5 and $8 million, Jack Kennedy around $10 million. By 1968, when some disclosure practices had been enacted, Senator Gene McCarthy was found to have spent $11 million in his drive to secure the Democratic nomination. Richard Nixon spent roughly the same on his Republican campaign.

Both Democratic and Republican candidates rely on wealthy donors for their seed money, though since Woodrow Wilson's time the liberal Democrats have attacked "Wall Street" publicly while taking the money secretly. Cleveland Dodge gave the Wilson campaign $51,000; Cyrus A. McCormick gave $12,500, as did Henry Morgenthau, Sr. In 1968 most of Gene McCarthy's money came from the wealthy few: Jack J. Dreyfus, the mutual fund king, around $500,000; Steward Mott, the General Motors heir, $210,000; and about thirty other bankers and Wall Street brokers, plus some in industry and with inherited money, contributed $100,000 apiece.

Easy come, easy go. The finances of the McCarthy campaign were confusion compounded. Two groups of McCarthy advisers battled over the money. One group, led by McCarthy's brother-in-law, Stephen Quigley, and Howard Stein, one of Dreyfus's business partners, wanted to use the money primarily for radio and television commercials. The other group, led by Blair Clark, McCarthy's campaign manager, and Arnold Hiatt, wanted to keep the candidate "pure" and use the money for a grass-roots organization.

Blair Clark set up a "Clergyman for McCarthy" account in the Freedom National Bank in Harlem for the grass-roots cause. Arnold Hiatt had people who opened the mail at McCarthy headquarters and took out the checks and put them in his dummy account. Similarly, Stein and Quigley had three or four dummy accounts between them. When money is passed around like that, a great deal of it just disappears.

In 1972 the McGovern forces spent $20 million to gain the nomination. In New Hampshire, for example, they dropped $150,000 on media alone. The tab for this $150,000 was picked up by two men, Miles Reuben, a West Coast millionaire, and Stewart Mott. How this money would be spent was decided when Joe Grandmaison, McGovern's fiery New Hampshire manager, cornered Reuben in an empty campaign office outside of Manchester and slugged him into agreement. Overall, in 1972, the liberal Republican Ripon Society estimates that Richard Nixon was raising between $50 and $70 million. One assumes this boodle was divided up with the same layerlike efficiency that percolated most of Watergate.

Ever since the 1900s Congress has from time to time tried to get some type of handle on presidential campaign spending. However, at least until the 1940s, a heavy majority in both House and Senate felt that primaries and caucuses were state affairs and that regulation of them should be left to the states. In particular they believed presidential nominations could only be regulated through a constitutional amendment. The Corrupt Practices Act of 1925, one of the first modern attempts to control the flow of money into politics, specifically excluded from regulation spending for any federal or state nomination. Finally, in 1947 the Taft-Hartley Act brought under mild federal regulation primaries and caucuses for state and federal office; but still the selection of presidential delegates was specifically excluded from any form of control.

In 1966 President Johnson sent Congress a special message that urged tightening the law on contribution disclosures and formulating rules for all nominations, including that for President. These suggestions formed the basis for what finally became, in 1972, the Federal Election Campaign Act, the first major election reform in seventy-four years. The act established public accounting procedures for presidential elections from the opening of a campaign until the final vote. It also made corporate contributions illegal. Its main provisions for enforcement were in its disclosure section, the so-called sunshine section, under which most gifts had to be publicly reported. This is the law that during the Watergate scandal sent illegal contributors to jail and forced others to pay heavy fines.

Then, in 1973, came Watergate. Under voter pressure to clean up politics, particularly presidential politics, Congress reluctantly responded with the most sweeping reform legislation in American history—the Campaign Reform Act of 1974. As we have already noted, this act, which became law in November of 1974 but did not go into effect until January 1, 1975, totally altered the invisible and state primaries.

First, this law restricted the amount an individual could give a candidate in any one race to $1,000, period. Then it limited how much candidates could spend to secure the presidential nomination to $10 million with an extra $2 million allowed for fund raising. That was less than any successful candidate had spent since 1954. In addition, the law restricted, based on a per capita formula, how much a candidate could spend inside each state. For example, the limit for all spending by a candidate inside New Hampshire is $200,000, more than $10,000 under what McGovern spent in 1972 in that state. A special commission and some rigorous reporting procedures were established to enforce the new regulations. Of additional interest, a $50,000 limit was placed on what a candidate or a family could contribute to his own campaign: a move that placed the Rockefellers and Kennedys more on a par with other candidates.

The second major change made by the act was the creation of a system whereby, after taking certain actions, a candidate would receive matching federal funds to help finance his presidential campaign. On the surface, what the candidate and his staff had to do looked simple. In practice, getting federal funds proved a complex operation. The organizational strength necessary to grab the federal money proved beyond the resources of some candidates' staffs.

To gain the funds, a candidate had first to raise $100,000 in amounts of not more than $250 per person in twenty different states. The amount that could be contributed from any one state was limited to $5,000. After the candidate had raised this initial amount in this manner, the federal government would start to match every further gift up to $250 per gift. (For example, for a $7 private gift the candidate got an additional $7 in federal money; for a $700 gift the candidate received only $250 in matching federal funds.) The maximum amount the federal government would contribute to a campaign was set at $4.5 million.

As might be expected, the act was pushed and hauled through Congress by the liberals in both parties and battled by the conservatives, particularly the Republicans. "An evil bill . . . so bad and so biased it could be called a one-party bill," said House Minority Leader John Rhodes. While the fight over the bill was in progress, writer John Margolis described the battle in the Sunday *New York Times:* "Nor does it seem to be an accident that most of the public financing friends are liberals, its foes conservative. Behind every political process is a likely political result and the likely result of equal campaign spending is a plus for liberals."

When the bill became law, the liberals slowly began to discover what a look at the history of campaign financing would have told them: The chief beneficiaries were Republicans and right-of-center Democrats. The chief losers: liberal Democrats.

The reason is that both Republicans on the far right and Democrats on the far left relied for funds on what in the political trade is known as "ideological money" or, less politely, "bucks for bullshit." This is particularly true of left-wing Democrats who have a few extremely rich supporters who can give them several hundred thousand dollars but not many middle-income supporters who can give $100 to $1,000. Up until June 1972, George McGovern was actually getting more large gifts than President Nixon. On the other hand, not only do centrist Democrats and moderate Republicans have access to big money but, more important now, their supporters include many people who can give in the $100-to-$1,000 range.

In summary, the reform act financially benefits candidates with a large number of moderately wealthy supporters who are well organized. Hurt are candidates with a few very wealthy supporters and large numbers of lower-income supporters: specifically, the Wallace right and the McGovern left.

Political professionals and other experts caught on to what was happening with varying degrees of speed. Senator Percy was still protesting the bill as unfair to Republicans, though admitting it was necessary, as he folded his tent. Since large sections of the bill have been written by Udall's campaign co-manager, John Gabusi, Udall's campaign plan to rely largely on volunteers had been laid well in advance, though Udall's staff seriously underestimated the difficulty in meeting the matching federal fund requirements. Walter Skallerup, the comptroller of Senator Jackson's campaign—a melancholy Dane with a wry sense of humor and independent cast of mind—had figured out the effects of the bill while it was still in conference. Jackson and his staff then geared up a detailed campaign to raise the necessary public and private funds early, hoping they would be free to do nothing but go after delegates by late 1975.

Senator Lloyd Bentsen, who had made a fortune buying and selling insurance companies, remarked as we talked about the bill just before it was signed: "I wonder when the press will figure out what that bill does. I won't have any trouble with funds as a result of that bill." On the other hand, one week later Joe Rauh, former head of the Americans for Democratic Action, was gloating that "the bill really tags the GOP." When how it tagged liberals was explained, he replied, "It can't do what you say."

Shortly after the law took effect, Senator Gene McCarthy, whose 1968 campaign had relied so heavily on major gifts from wealthy liberals, joined forces with James Buckley, conservative senator from New York, in a lawsuit to have the act declared unconstitutional. Obviously, by then they had figured out what the law did and were proving once again Arthur Koestler's dictum that the yogi and the commissar are mirror images of each other. Many of the minor candidates and much of the press didn't fully understand the law until late in 1975. The press kept on waiting for a dark horse candidate to appear. But in the past, dark horses had been able to get $400,000 or $500,000 worth of oats out of five or six loaded citizens, or even from their own family. With that hay the darkest horse can buy a little TV time and rent a Lear jet. But to get $500,000 from five hundred people at $1,000 a head, one had to be a horse of a different color, to push a straw metaphor too far.

None of the candidates would admit to being hurt by the Campaign Reform Law, though they all thought the other fellow probably would be. This is understandable. Consider the reaction to a candidate who told reporters: "Frankly, with the bullshit I hand out, there is no way I can make the White House on my own merits. I was counting on that fat-cat money to zing me in."

Most of the impartial criticism of the law came not over the details of financing the presidential races, but over the head start it gave incumbents in the House and Senate races. In fact, opponents of the measure called it, with certain justification, "the Incumbency Protection Act." However, one section directly affecting the invisible primary worries many, including myself. This is the requirement that all gifts of $100 or over must be disclosed publicly. I don't think a person buys much influence for $100. And the presidential candidate—or House or Senate candidate for that matter—who can be corrupted by a century note has other major problems. At the same time, ordering disclosure of such minor gifts comes close to forcing a man to disclose his vote. I can think of a great many organizations, including some for which I have worked—and some communities where I have lived—where employees who might have wanted very much to contribute from $100 to $500 to certain candidates would be dissuaded for fear of their senior's reaction. Traditionally, since World War II, gifts of $1,000 or over have been thought of as major gifts. To make the point of disclosure closer to $1,000 or even set it at $1,000 would seem to assure political purity while not providing such a threat to political participation by the less well off.

When the Campaign Reform Act took effect on the first day of 1975, the American political situation became one of classic irony. One part of the United States political process, the Democratic party, had written a new set of rules. These rules, though this was not the intent of their writers, multiplied the number of primaries a candidate had to enter and at the same time greatly increased the expense of each primary by forcing them to be held on a district-by-district basis. While the Democratic party was thus engaged in greatly increasing—without meaning to—the amount of money a candidate had to spend to become President, the Congress, another part of the political process controlled by Democrats, was drastically cutting back the amount of funds a candidate could spend, and at the same time making it vastly more difficult for him to raise any funds.

That is why the end result of these conflicting reforms made even more important the invisible primary. No longer could a candidate hope to gain the nomination by first entering a small number of primaries with limited funds provided by a few wealthy backers. Nor could he use a good showing in these primaries to raise more funds quickly from wealthy donors to continue his campaign. The battlefield had widened, the resources available had shrunk. So the caliber of staff, the devotion of the constituency, and the early accumulation of money had become more important. And all these are determined largely before the state primaries begin.

Faced with the new complexity, plus the spending limitations and the $1,000 limit on individual gifts, Jackson and his inner financial staff devised a strategy to raise funds early, and at the same time take full advantage of the matching federal funds.

Jackson's staff contained a great deal of financial as well as political expertise. Walter Skallerup had untangled funding problems in the past for both Jackson and Adlai Stevenson. Richard Kline, the chief fund raiser, a pleasing, fortyish, Doral-smoking man, had been the financial boss of the Muskie campaign. The treasurer, C. Peter McColough, was a former board chairman of Xerox and recent treasurer of the Democratic National Committee.

The obvious way, these men believed, to raise $5,000 in each of twenty states in amounts of $250 or less was by direct mail. The problem of direct mail is the horrendous start-up cost of developing a list that will produce cash fast. Subscription and membership lists from various magazines and organizations have to be purchased or pirated. The *New Yorker, Bulletin of Atomic Scientists, Harper's, Atlantic,* and *New Republic* are favorites with liberal fund raisers. Then there are large organizations like the Red Cross, the American Legion, the major unions, state granges, religious organizations, and the mailing lists of friendly politicians. All these have to be compiled, sample mailings sent out, the returns codified and analyzed by computer. This takes both time and money.

After McGovern's defeat, a major battle developed over whether McGovern or the Democratic National Committee would keep the computer tapes of 1972 contributors. The committee won, but at the cost of much hard feeling. To head off such a battle in 1976, Democratic National Committee Chairman Robert Strauss made the committee's lists available to any presidential candidate who asked.

To put the bite on the little man by direct mail for political contributions has not been easy in the past, and it appears to be getting even harder. Too many politicians, causes, charities, citizens' lobbies, have been back to the same wells again and again and again. Howard K. Samuels, a Democratic aspirant for New York governor in 1974, sent out 200,000 computerized letters to what he thought was a highly selected group of sure givers, at a cost of $49,521. He got back a little under $15,000, for a net loss of over $34,000. In trying to pay for the midterm convention in Kansas City, Democratic Chairman Strauss sent out a mailing to all the delegates to the national convention of 1972 that had mandated the midterm '74 miniconvention. He didn't get back enough to pay for the mailing's postage. In fact he did better from a mailing to names selected at random from phone books. At the start of 1975, various political and lobbying organizations that use mailing lists were all complaining that funds were tighter than ever before.

George Wallace, who had funded his '72 and was funding his '76 drive largely by direct mail, had raised some $2 million by 1975. But of this only $200,000 was keeping money; the rest had been plowed back into the direct-mail operation. Senator Lloyd Bentsen, raising money in units of $1,000, had netted as much as Wallace in just two trips to mythic Texas. Morris Dees, the direct money wizard who handled George McGovern's mail drive in 1972 and who, along with Governor Wallace's Richard Viguerie, is considered the best in politics, once remarked: "If you gave me $100,000 for direct mail, and we kept plowing back the proceeds to expand the list of donors—which is what you have to do—it would be a year and a half to two years before you could hope to get back the $5 million you want for a primary campaign."

The Jackson strategy to beat that time lag was to raise $2 million in contributions of $1,000 in late '74 and early '75, and then turn a large part of this seed money over to Morris Dees, who had been hired to produce another $5 million. The $5 million produced by direct mail would then trigger off the matching $4.5 million from the federal government. Most of this was to be done by late '75. From then on, Jackson could devote his full time to reaching voters. By the start of '75, the financial experts had in fact raised close to $1.2 million, much of it in $3,000 units, the limit Jackson had placed on contributions before the official 1975 start of the Campaign Reform Act.

By far the largest portion of this money came from wealthy Jews attracted to Jackson because of his friendship for Israel and his actions in trying to force the Soviet Union to permit more Jews to immigrate. A series of dinners was held around the country in November, December, and January, concentrating on Florida and California. Under the 1974 act, the names of all contributors are public and the records indicated that Jackson's Jewish constituency was giving generously.

While funds were shrinking, and expensive primaries multiplying, inflation also was prodding up the cost of politics. Radio and television time is the largest and most important item in the budget of almost all preconvention candidates. In 1960 candidates spent $14 million to purchase broadcast time. In 1968 that figure had orbited—the verb is inadequate—to $40 million. By 1970, which was an *off-presidential* year, the figure was $50 million. And these figures represent only the dollars used to buy time. Production costs were also rising. In 1960 a half-hour political film could be produced for $30,000. Today, the identical production would cost $100,000. The same escalation of costs is seen in polling. The relatively crude polls that Jack Kennedy took in 1960 in such states as West Virginia cost him in the neighborhood of $15,000. To poll the state today would cost $25,000.

"Getting and spending we lay waste our powers," wrote William Wordsworth. With the getting much tougher and the costs higher, the obvious way not to waste money power is rigid controls on spending. But this also presents problems. As Walter Skallerup remarked, he could set up a computer operation that would keep track of every penny in the Jackson campaign and let the candidate know his financial picture every day. The only trouble was such a complex computer operation would bankrupt the campaign.

Traditionally, campaign money hasn't been accounted for too closely. A couple of floors down on another elevator shaft there's always a back room no one talks about, in which are a couple of guys with large rolls of tens for the boys. (Anything over ten and the nosy feds may have track of the serial numbers.) It looked like hard cheese for the boys in '75 and '76. "They want bids on who will supply the liquor," said an aghast Bentsen staffer of his campaign higher-ups, while trying to provision his man's hospitality suite in Kansas City. "Don't they know from nothing?" They knew all right. But they could count scarce dollars, too.

Similarly, the fund-raising dinner may be becoming, praise to God, a thing of the past. The $50- or $100-a-plate dinner where $20 went to the cost of the food and booze was a professionally sound method of raising funds when there was no limit on the amount a candidate could take in or a citizen contribute. But now every dollar raised counts in a candidate's ceiling. Who wants to raise $10,000 at a $50-a-plate dinner when $4,000, 40 percent of the take, goes for dinner expenses that count against the candidate's total but achieve no political effect?

In the past the political money, in addition to media exposure, has largely been spent to buy human brains and energy. With media costs rising, the obvious area of campaign restraint is in the purchase of human energy. The volunteer, a vital part of past campaigns, may now be all-important. Since the close of World War II, volunteers have traditionally come from three areas: the party professionals, the labor unions, and citizens' organizations created for the campaign. A great deal has been written about the decline of the political party in America. David Broder's *The Party's Over* and the Ripon Society's *Jaws of Victory* are particularly perceptive and free of sociological jargon. I tend to emphasize the growth of the American Bureaucracy—federal, state, local, and industrial—in contributing to the decline of the party. If there is no personal economic advantage in being an active Democrat or Republican, why will the average person waste time getting involved in party affairs? But whatever the reasons for its decline, in both the invisible and the state primaries, the party can no longer provide adequate volunteer help. Senator Muskie found this out painfully in 1972. He had endorsements from party leaders galore but few followers out working for him on the streets. By 1974, campaigning for governor of New York, Hugh Carey found it more effective to run against the party as an Independent than to receive organized Democratic support.

Nor are the hired guns of labor, particularly the AFL-CIO's COPE, effective any longer. In November 1974 the AFL-CIO launched a statewide drive in California to turn out members to pack the caucuses selecting delegates to the Democratic midterm convention. Out of a membership of 1.7 million, less than 4,000 showed. The complex reasons behind the decline of big labor's political wallop have not been explored as fully as the fading of America's political parties. Undoubtedly the shifting age of the work force, its increased social mobility, its greater education, its new freedom to pursue leisure-time activities and increased worker security, all play a part. While labor can still turn out a number of bodies, their record in nominating the candidates endorsed by their union leaders has been poor in the last few presidential campaigns.

To be effective a volunteer must invest sizable amounts of his or her time. To have such a gift of time to spend on politics, and be willing to give it, requires a special motivation and position in society. Volunteers must have the economic freedom to leave whatever they are doing and work for the candidate instead. In addition, the person must be able to work within an organization and be persuasive. There are three large pools of such people with time and persuasive skills from which the candidate can draw his constituency: the upper-middle-class housewife, located primarily in the suburbs or major cities; college students, including the affluent just graduated; and the middle-aged retired.

In the past, a presidential candidate had to spend an inordinate amount of time doing his rain dance for fat cats. He also had to tailor a certain number of his issues and programs to appeal to the big money, right or left. Now he has to spend that time and do that tailoring to appeal to the volunteer fat groups. Both Senators George McGovern and Gene McCarthy invested much time and effort in mobilizing the wealthy college student and recent graduate to work for them. And it seems to me they were suspect by the mass of voters for just this reason, even as the voters were formerly suspicious of a candidate too obviously tied to big money.

Yet, with the stringent limits on campaign getting and spending now in force, volunteer appeal may become the sine qua non of the early stages of a presidential campaign. The problem again is to energize and form a constituency without turning off the mass. Senator Percy tried to tap the energies of the recently retired in his campaign before he folded his tent; but he met with, at best, limited success. Udall was going after the sophisticated second-time-around volunteer, someone largely self-motivating, who had worked in a previous campaign. Kennedy's constituency, which he hadn't moved to exploit, had lain with the younger students and the first-time voters. No one in this invisible primary was out pitching heavily to the affluent upper-class woman, but then there is some question as to just how much leisure this class has. John Kenneth Galbraith has reasoned well that except for the tiny minority who have servants, "the menial role of the woman becomes more arduous the higher the family income." Still, that tiny minority, augmented by those who could afford temporary help, would be an effective organizational force. Adlai Stevenson made excellent use of such a constituency in his 1956 primary victories.

With the financing starting to pay off, the Jackson staff, headed by Bob Keefe, with Kline as chief fund raiser and Bill Brawley, a longtime Jackson worker, as strategist, opened their search for delegates in a renovated row house two blocks north of the Capitol. The headquarters, while not plush, were certainly pleasant. The house was painted a fresh lime green, the front door had a polished brass plaque saying "Jackson Planning Committee." The walls were papered with a green and white abstract floral design, the desks Scandinavian modern, the coffee better than merely drinkable. The staff were liberally supplied with electric typewriters, Xerox machines, and phones, campaign items in short supply elsewhere. The monthly rent was $1,950.

Since fund raising was the initial name of the game, the country was broken down into five regions with a high-powered chairman appointed for each. It was the hope of Kline and McColough to raise 85 percent of the allowable $10 million before New Hampshire. If they raised more than that, fine. Starting in early January with a 1,500-person $250-a-plate dinner at Los Angeles, which, of course, more than met the $5,000 quota from that state, a series of dinners were planned around the country, one every ten days. The initial funds were invested in the direct-mail campaign, as planned, and sample mailings went out. In addition, the staff went to work drawing up budget projections on ways to spend the money—for example, how best to get Jackson past the early primaries, where he was weak, so that he could exploit his presumed strength in the industrial states of Ohio, Pennsylvania, New Jersey, and parts of California, all with late primaries.

Jackson meanwhile went ahead with the strategy of being conspicuously on the job in the Senate, demonstrating what he called "the charisma of competence" on "issues that are bugging people every day." With television time so expensive, he concentrated on gaining free media time by making news. In the early part of 1975 this strategy was successful. Jackson appeared on the cover of *Time*, was on TV and radio on both energy and economic issues and even on the subject of Cambodia. On Cambodia, he proposed that Senate Majority Leader Mike Mansfield be sent to negotiate with the Cambodian rebel leaders as a special emissary of President Ford. His staff stressed the theme that Jackson was "Mr. Competence," pointing out that in 1973 he spoke in twenty-seven states, yet voted in 594 out of 596 Senate roll calls.

But the problem remained: How would all this money and media activity transform itself into primary votes? The Jackson staff was frank to admit that their man lacked a broad constituency. He had the Jews and that was just about it. Big labor had turned sour on him, partially as a result of his moves to the left, partially as a result of his refusal to do their bidding on restrictive trade legislation. The youth constituency was turned off by his long pro-Vietnamese war stand and by matters of style. Everyone remembered what had happened when Muskie relied on the Democratic state organizations for politically effective cadres. So Jackson's staff of able old-timers fell back, or relied on, the ancient idea that "politics is people." They knew a lot of the people. Not just the old-timers, but the new effective ones also. If enough of those people could be convinced that Jackson, with his funds and organization, was the man with the best chance of winning, Jackson would have created his own constituency.

Finally, on February 6, 1975, with everything in place, Jackson dropped the other shoe and formally declared his candidacy. Like everything else in his campaign, the announcement was carefully planned. It was made in a five-minute pretaped broadcast and shown just before 11 P.M., after the CBS movie. Research had indicated that the most voters per dollar would be delivered in that time slot. The five-minute documentary was produced by film expert David Wolper and cost $23,000, including air time. To cut the cost down and provide authenticity, Jackson had announced, with Wolper's cameras rolling, at a dinner in California three weeks before that he was declaring himself a presidential candidate. But then he had hastily added that this was an announcement he hoped to make shortly. Thus Wolper was able to film, in advance of the statement, Jackson making his presidential bid to a large crowd that reacted favorably. With such strategy, professionalism, and cost accounting, would the campaign take off?

There is a short, low-key story by Stephen Benet, "The Curfew Tolls," that illustrates in fable the need to be not just at the right place, but at the right time. Having to vacation for his health in the South of France in 1788, an enlightened English nobleman is forced by the boredom of the small-town resort to listen to the dreams of a retired French major on how he would fight battles and reshape the modern world. The major, tremendously well read, is not without energy and charm, but totally without relevance to the calm and peaceful world in which they both live. The Englishman finds the egotistical French ex-officer strangely powerful and, while appealing as a man, often frightening. In the last paragraph the reader learns that the name of this "odd fellow" is Napoleon Bonaparte; but born not in 1769, when the flux of revolution gave opportunity for driving, driven men; but in 1737, when his energies beat in vain against the confines of a peaceful world.

Similarly, in George Dangerfield's masterpiece, *The Strange Death of Liberal England,* published in 1935, Winston Churchill is dismissed in these words:

> Brilliant and capable as he [Churchill] undoubtedly was, . . . his most radical gestures were ruined by the fact that he was a Marlborough, that he was quite incapable of identifying himself with the public for whom he seemed to cherish a sort of genial disdain. By nature flamboyant, insolent in his bearing, impatient in his mind, and Tory in his deepest convictions, he was a curious person to be found holding a responsible position in the Liberal Party, and few men could have been more distrusted, and taken a more curious pleasure in being distrusted.

To succeed, a leader must be a man for his time; the politics of the past will not entice voters any more than the politics of the future. It seemed, throughout the invisible primary, as if Scoop Jackson, who almost became John F. Kennedy's Vice-President, was, for all his skill, playing to perfection the politics of the past. Yet, at any moment a new oil embargo, a new Arab-Israeli war, or some Russian intransigence, or even a worsening depression, could make Jackson seem, not a holdover, but a consistent man of the present. Time and chance happeneth to all men.

CHAPTER 5

The Democrats: Explosion Deferred

Shortly after six in the evening, December 7, 1974, the 2,038 delegates to the Democratic midterm convention in Kansas City successfully avoided their own Pearl Harbor. By voice vote they roared through a semantic change in their complex rules and so prevented a threatened walkout by some blacks and their supporters. More than this, the change actually left the vast majority of the delegates reasonably happy. By closing their midterm convention without tearing themselves apart, the Democratic party guaranteed that the candidate the national convention crowned in '76 would not carry off a meaningless prize as McGovern had in '72 and Hubert Humphrey in '68. Winning the Democratic invisible primary would have meaning. But until the final tense moments at Kansas City, while delegates milled on the floor and leaders dealt backstage, no one could be sure.

With the fading of Lyndon Johnson's power in 1967, the Democratic party seemed not only ready to tear itself apart, but often exultant at the prospect. In 1968 the regulars shafted the reformers at the presidential convention, and the reformers retaliated by causing the defeat of Hubert Humphrey. At the 1972 convention the reformers shafted the regulars right back; and the regulars retaliated by helping bury George McGovern. After the '72 debacle many were totally certain that at its next convention some portion of the party would bolt. In fact the donkey might tear itself apart with both front and back splitting—as had happened in 1948 when the left walked out with Henry Wallace and the right with states' rightist Strom Thurmond.

Republicans also have schizoid tendencies, as they demonstrated with the nomination of Barry Goldwater. The extreme idealists in that party, secretly swigging their Old Hoover, still believe that rugged individualism is an adequate answer to the increasingly complex problems of a postindustrial society. Once President Ford had elected to keep a toehold in the twentieth century and nominated Nelson Rockefeller to be his Vice-President, the Goldwater-Reagan purists began their predictable stirrings. But they lacked the numbers and outside power bases in academia and the media of the doctrinaire McGovern purists. Besides, in the frigid wind off the Watergate those Republicans remaining in public office tended to cling together for warmth. Like the Conservatives in Great Britain, the Republicans are rather pragmatic; less interested in abstract ideas than the Democrats. Note I say *rather* pragmatic. Any party that can produce the fratricidal warfare of William Howard Taft versus Theodore Roosevelt, Robert A. Taft versus General Eisenhower, and Nelson Rockefeller versus Barry Goldwater isn't as dully victory-oriented as its admirers and detractors often believe.

That December at their midterm convention in Kansas City there was nothing the Democrats could do that would increase their party's chances for victory in 1976. But there was a great deal that they might do that would diminish those chances. Why, then, were they meeting in 1974, midway between two presidential conventions?

Because the '72 convention that nominated George McGovern had mandated that such a convention be held. Those in charge of the '72 convention dreamed of a strong, European-type political party, with a body of doctrine that was to be enforced upon its members. They established a Charter Commission to write such a doctrine and ordered that a midterm convention be held to ratify that charter. The Democratic Planning Group's newsletter, the organ of the mobilized idealists, explained: "We should be telling the elected officials what to do, rather than vice versa."

The Charter Commission was to write the rules that would govern the Democratic party *after* 1976. In addition to this prestigious body, the '72 convention created another lesser commission to draw up rules for delegate selection *through* 1976. This was the so-called Mikulski Commission. Thus, for two years, the Democrats had *two* committees simultaneously battling over rules. Since, by and large, the regular-realists—with their focus on winning elections—didn't give a damn about language and rules, the energy and attendance on both these commissions normally came from the reformer-idealists whose adrenaline flowed from debate over abstractions and distinctions.

For example, in October 1974, when the Democrats were in the stretch drive to elect a House of Representatives that could override President Ford's vetoes, a group of extreme idealists led by Miles Reuben and Margery Benton raised some seventy thousand dollars. This money did not go to help congressional candidates win close races. It went to Alan Baron, an energetic and manipulative purist, to help elect delegates to the midterm convention who would be in favor of a strong central party. Since at that moment the Democratic party was broke, the decision to use those funds that way probably gained the Republicans five seats. And certainly gained the idealists about forty seats at the midterm convention.

The 167-member Charter Commission, carefully balanced between reformers and regulars, met five times before the midterm convention. All of the meetings except the last two were harmonious. That's because less than half the members bothered to show up and very little was done. After several sessions debating the rules that would govern its meetings and how it would proceed, the Charter Commission began, as its sponsors had intended, to consider rules that would make the Democratic party more like a European party. These included detailed definitions of who was or was not a Democrat, charging all party members dues, creating a compliance commission to judge who was or was not a Democrat, and writing platforms that all Democrats would be pledged to support.

These reforms died soon, and not just from the opposition of party regulars and states'-rights Democrats. The reformers faced a basic philosophical division within themselves. On the one hand, they wanted a strong central party whose decisions would be binding on the local parties. On the other, they were against "bosses" and believed that almost anyone should have the right to run as a Democrat for public office. They were trying to be both American populists and European social democrats at the same time. That these two beliefs are in part basically contradictory didn't prevent most reformers from holding both at once; but the inconsistency did put a dent in their arguments. Arnold Weiss, one of the leaders of the NDC (New Democratic Coalition or November Doesn't Count, depending on your bias) who fought for a strong, binding charter, was asked:

"Would you vote in a primary for a candidate designated a Democrat even though he supported a platform you disagreed with?"

"We're so bright, we'd write the platform."

"But if you didn't?" I pressed him as he loped from caucus to caucus.

"Shit, I don't know."

With the idealists intellectually divided and the realists not wanting a strong charter, the question in the commission quickly came down to: In what limited degree would the national party control the state parties? But within this narrow compass there was plenty of room for battle between reformers and regulars, idealists and realists, purists and cynic-pols, right and left. And playing an important part was the history of who had been on what side in the bloody battles that began in 1966.

"Everyone in the Democratic party today is bearing his own special brand of paranoia," said John Gilligan, the lame-duck governor of Ohio, by defeat set free to utter those truths on camera that other Democratic leaders are forced to mumble *in camera.* "Every single comma in the proposed charter is important to somebody." That was where the potential danger to the Democrats lay—not just at the midterm convention but at every meeting where the Charter was discussed. The words themselves might appear unimportant, but key groups in the party had over the years loaded every syllable and phrase with complex emotional freight. The AFL-CIO, the Women's Political Caucus, the black caucus, the Latin caucus, the New Democratic Coalition, the Democratic Study Group, the state chairmen, the governors, the Congress—all fought for their language, their power.

To understand the bitterness, the battle, and the victory at Kansas City, one had to have been at the Democratic governors' conference at Hilton Head, North Carolina, in November 1974; to understand that, one had to have been at the Charter Committee meeting in mid-August; to understand that, one had to have been at the National Committee meeting in mid-March; and so on and so on, through deadly battles over bitter trivialities all the way back to 1968, the war between Gene McCarthy, Robert Kennedy, and Hubert Humphrey in which real blood flowed.

At every meeting the extremists on both sides, purists versus cynic-pols, tried to turn the clock back to 1972 or 1968, respectively, when "they" were firmly in control. A disinterested observer might point out that both '68 and '72 had been Democratic disasters, that both Hubert Humphrey and George McGovern had received from the triumphant hands of their followers crowns of horror as burningly destructive as those garments woven by Medea for an erring husband. "We have already compromised too much," the extremists in both camps would shout back.

Nor were the battles merely over the soul of the Democratic party. The power centers backing this or that phrasing were not monolithic themselves, but faced their own internal battles. The fight over the Democratic party's future was also a war over big labor's future, who would succeed George Meany, who would control the Black Caucus, the Women's Caucus, and the power of the Democratic Study Group inside the Congress.

The words over which the Democrats battled for three bitter days at Kansas City—"mandatory quotas," "all party affairs," "affirmative action," "burden of proof"—while unimportant themselves, had become, like Gettysburg or Waterloo, significant terrain over which coalitions of great power fought for control of a nation's future. "Never in the history of human boredom have so many traveled so far to be stirred by such matters of immeasurable triviality," intoned Congressman Jim Wright of Texas. "America is full of unmet needs and we appear to be tearing ourselves apart over esoteric language," Governor Wendell Anderson of Minnesota warned.

Both men overlooked the human truth that as many have died for words as for territory. In Nicea in A.D. 325 the delegates to that conference had fought for two months over the spelling of just one word. Was God "homoousian" or "homoiousian"? Yet over that little "i" the churches of the East and West had divided for a hundred years; and in other guises the battle would continue for many more—armies raised, heretics burned, towns leveled. Scholars still debate whether Meletius of Antioch, the supposedly neutral chairman, had stacked the conference against the "i"; or the part played by Cyril of Jerusalem (known variously as St. Cyril or Cyril the Shifty, depending on which parchment you read) in engineering the final compromise. While to compare the Democratic Charter with the Nicean Creed would shame blasphemy, the problems at Nicea and Kansas City were the same—people using words as instruments of power, or trying to.

Most of the Democratic candidates for President, indeed most leading Democratic politicians, stayed as far away from the fight over their Charter's wording as possible. They reasoned that if the party blew up, it would be damaging enough merely to be a Democrat, without having been somewhere near the center of the explosion. Terry Sanford, ex-governor of North Carolina and now president of Duke University, a minor candidate, was involved as chairman of the Charter Commission, a position he fondly believed would elevate him to the White House in some miraculous fashion. Sanford, a gray-haired imposing figure of a man, easily pushed around, was the candidate of a small group of younger voters, but practically no one else. He suffered fatally from Wallace disease: a dire political malady peculiar to southern candidates who can be easily defeated by George Wallace in their home state. Sanford had been shellacked by Wallace in 1972.

The major candidate involved, partially against his will, was Senator Henry Jackson. The chief spokesman for the realist-regulars (as distinct from the idealist-regulars) on the Charter Commission was Jackson's close friend and political ally, Congressman Thomas Foley of Washington. (Foley represents one of the problems in trying to place political labels on today's politicians. In summer and fall of 1974 when he was involved with the Charter Commission he was identified in *The New York Times* and the Washington *Post* as a "regular" or "member of the conservative wing." Three months later, in early 1975, when Foley won control of the House Agriculture Committee as part of the modernization of the Congress, he was hailed by the media as "a reformer" and a "member of the liberal caucus.") On the commission, Foley was identified with the conservatives and with Jackson; and this linked Jackson's name, and therefore his fate, with the battles on the commission. Further, Jackson was at that time allied with COPE, the political arm of the AFL-CIO. After McGovern's 1972 defeat, COPE and Jackson had joined to oust McGovern's choice as head of the Democratic National Committee, Chairwoman Jean Westwood, an energetic and inefficient causist, and replaced her with the committee's finance chairman, Robert Strauss.

From the beginning Strauss appeared to the idealists in the Democratic party, particularly those on the liberal side, in the Erich von Stroheim role of "the man you love to hate." He is an unabashed wheeler-dealer from Texas, who wears a sapphire pinkie ring, monogrammed shirts, and likes to drink, gamble, and tell "good-ole-boy" stories. He remains a friend of John Connally's, Texas's former conservative Democratic governor who left the Democrats to join the Nixon Cabinet and organize Democrats for Nixon. He calls women "gals," and is full of down-home flimflam, as distinct from the sociological kind currently in vogue.

"Bein' chairman of the Democratic party is 'bout like makin' love to a gorilla. You don't quit when you're tired, you quit when the gorilla's tired." That's a long way from Aristotle—that politics is the science of life, or seems that way. Liberals even look on the fact that Strauss was born poor and Jewish as part of some plot, probably engineered with stolen votes in Houston, to try to elicit sympathy for himself where none is deserved.

Finally, Strauss hates ideology. To the question "Who is a Democrat?" which the idealist needs twelve single-spaced pages to answer, Strauss replies: "Anyone who calls himself one." Strauss uses the word "professor" as Harry Truman used the word "Harvard," as a humorous pejorative. (Or, as they used to say on the New York *Herald Tribune,* "Yale is a four-letter word.") "Bunch of ranchers in Wyomin' had trouble with these coyotes destroyin' their sheep. So they brought in this bunch of professors to solve the problem. The professors' solution, and they charged plenty for it, was to castrate the coyotes. 'But professor,' said one of the ranchers, 'them coyotes ain't loving our sheep; they're killin' 'em.' "

Did the hostility of the liberals and conservative unions bother Strauss? "Ah got no more pride than a twenty-dollar whore. . . . The only description of myself I ever saw that totally satisfied me was the letter my mother wrote me when I graduated from high school. And I guess I could have improved on that some."

The fifty-two-year-old Strauss adds: ". . . I'm a success. I was a success as a lawyer. I was a success as a businessman. I've been a success as a politician. . . . I've never had a friend quit me or a client leave me. . . . I've never lost touch with my children. I've been a success in thirty-three years of marriage and I'm a success as a father. If you want a loser in 1976 go back and get the other crowd. If you want a loser you picked the wrong son of a bitch. I'm a winner."

By the time he had been in office a year, the idealists of both the right and the left were after Strauss. The basic complaint of both groups was that Strauss had no principles but always tacked with the wind. "Slippery," "double-crosser," "order of the jackal with palms," "congenital liar," and "bullshit Bob" were some of the milder epithets coming from both right and left. As the idealists on both sides fulminated against Strauss, and he gave it right back to them, I was reminded of that basic division between humans chronicled by Shakespeare's Caesar:

> *Let me have men about me that are fat,*
> *Sleek-headed men, and such as sleep o' nights:*
> *Yond Cassius has a lean and hungry look;*
> *He thinks too much: such men are dangerous. . . .*
>   *he loves no plays,*
> *as thou dost, Antony; he hears no music.*

Strauss loves to play; the music of the dice or of the ice cube or of a racing horse's hoof can rouse him from the deepest lethargy. He is sleek, steeped in the soft blue plush of his chauffeured limousine with his tailored pin-striped suit, his suntan, his tight loafers, and combed-back silver hair. He is loud. His favorite means of communication is the exaggeration, the put-on. He could easily be typecast as a caricature of the self-satisfied *arriviste.*

But beneath this surface, and much of it is surface—with friends he has little Texas accent—lurks incredible complexity. What else explains the eighteen-hour days spent at the thankless chairman's job? What does Strauss want that he couldn't have more easily and safely as a political leader in

Texas, including the Cabinet and the Senate? All day and most of the night Strauss pads through life with a ravenous hunger for something. But lean he is not.

"Do you have any trouble sleeping at night, Mr. Chairman?"

"What the hell for?"

Politicians, like actors, accomplish much of their purpose by assigning themselves roles: Mr. Law and Order, the Vigilant Idealist, Friend of the Little Man, Watchdog of the Family Farm, the Cool Cat from the Mean Street, Never Forget the Home Folks, and so, endlessly, on. Strauss did not fight back against those who accused him of lack of principle. Rather, he took the epithets and shrewdly built them into the part in which he had cast himself—the highly successful, if a trifle shady, broker, the man who would do anything to please a client. "There's not a principled bone in my body."

Such remarks masked the fact that while Strauss may not have had principles, he certainly had an objective—not to let any dispute blow up the Democratic party. Again, this can be called unprincipled or Holmesian, depending on the point of view. As he battled the purists, left and right, issuing press releases, packing committees, doling out funds, pressing the flesh, arm twisting, exhorting, begging, Strauss tried to hold together a shaky coalition of moderate realists at the center of the Democratic party. He did this largely alone. Most Democratic officeholders felt safest at the greatest remove possible from the party-splitting squabbles.

Did the Democratic party have a center that would hold? This question was not a semantic quibble, an abstract intellectual inquiry, or even a test of the gargantuan energies of Robert Strauss. Until the outcome of the midterm convention in Kansas City, the breakup of the Democratic party before the 1976 presidential election was a strong possibility. The wag who said, "The resignation of Nixon has destroyed one of America's major political parties, the Democrats," was dishing out truth with a smile. Without Dick Nixon to kick around, the flailing boots of the Democrats could easily cripple each other. Political parties in the past have discovered that they lacked the common ideology and purpose to keep going after disastrous defeats. The Whigs, both British and American, have disappeared; so have the Federalists. The survival of the British Liberal party is in doubt. The birth and death of French political parties is a subject of farce, at least for Anglo-Saxons. What evidence was there that the famous Roosevelt coalition of labor, liberals, big-city bosses, and southern conversatives would hold after the battering of '68 and '72. Or that groups equally powerful and alive could be merged into the old party—particularly with the extreme idealists on all sides bent on destroying the fragile Democratic unity in the name of their own ideological purity?

In 1972, as he gathered the shattered pieces and tried to force, coax, cajole, flimflam, lure, reason, persuade, kick them back together, Strauss had to fight on two fronts—the dread *zwei-frontenkrieg* that Prussian strategists always inveigh against as suicidal and then end up fighting. Front I was the Mikulski Commission, producing the delegate selection rules for the midterm convention in 1974 and the national presidential convention in 1976. Front II was the Charter Commission itself, where the new rules, which would be approved in 1974 and go into effect after 1976, were being written. At times the two battles merged into one. Many of the issues had to be fought out for both '74 and '76 and afterward. The delegates selected by the Mikulski rules would approve or disapprove whatever the Charter Commission wrought. On both fronts Strauss fought: first, to control the two commissions writing the rules, in which he was only partially successful; second, to control the committees interpreting what the rules of the commissions said. In this he was almost always successful. He had modernized Boss Tweed's famous dictum, "I don't care who does the electing as long as I do the nominating," into "Ah don't care who does the rule writin' as long as Ah do the rule interpretin'."

On both commissions the major word battleground became the phrase "affirmative action in all party affairs." Basically this was the old quota fight with a new twist. Everyone had agreed that quotas were bad philosophically and morally; but there was also agreement that certain minorities needed help. "Theoretically, everyone including myself is against quotas," said Basil Paterson, the New York politician who, as deputy chairman of the Democratic National Committee, had proved himself a master negotiator for the black realists. "But look what's happened to us. In the real world minorities still need some kind of help." In that real world blacks had had 15 percent of the delegates at the convention that nominated George McGovern in 1972, and only 9 percent of the delegates to the midterm convention, elected under "affirmative action." They had obviously given up something.

Behind the rhetoric against quotas were some hard facts of political life affecting both liberals and conservatives. Quotas were found to cut both ways. In the District of Columbia, white regular delegates challenged the McGovernite blacks (who controlled the delegation) on the grounds that conservatives had been unfairly excluded while white liberal Tom Uncles (whites who mumble yaasah, yaasah, when a black militant coughs) had won the places. (Strauss finessed that, too. A committee found no "historical" pattern of discrimination.) Also, quotas favored the most militant. Even if a person was unpopular and ran a botched campaign, he or she could threaten and yell loud enough to gain admission to the delegation under some quota or other, because that was easier than fighting a challenge. Finally, quotas forced politicians to remove popular delegates who had won a majority of the vote and replace them with unpopular loudmouths, all in the name of sociological jargon—a high-risk operation.

Quotas were thrown out by both the Charter and the Mikulski Commissions, and the phrase "affirmative action" was substituted. Affirmative action was what a candidate had to take to bring minorities onto his delegation. He had to beat the highways and byways for blacks, young people, and women to run. Being a Democratic document, the exact nature of the steps a candidate or state chairman had to take to achieve affirmative action was spelled out in vast detail. But still there remained the problem that what to one would appear to be unflagging zeal in the pursuit of minority participation would appear to another as mere limp-wristed tokenism.

This battle was no theoretical exercise. The shape of the Democratic party would be determined both by its charter and by the man it selected as presidential candidate in 1976. The convention delegates would determine both of these. The interpretation of the affirmative action rules would determine the delegate mix.

The first and decisive challenge to the new affirmative action rules, the success or failure of which would determine the face of both the midterm convention in 1974 and the presidential nominating convention in 1976, came almost totally unnoticed, in July 1974, at Harrisburg, Pennsylvania. There, thirty Democrats, all but lost in the vast red and gold pseudo-plush of the Penn Harris Motel ballroom, gathered to squabble for seven hours over how vigorously Harvey Thiemann, Pennsylvania Governor Milton Shapp's handpicked Democratic state chairman, had pushed his affirmative-action program. There was no argument that Thiemann had such a program or that the Democratic National Committee had approved it. But had Thiemann then enforced it fully?

The action was typically Democratic. It began an hour late. It was confused, complicated, bitter, and the vital national questions were woven through with complex local feuds. For example: The chief witness against Thiemann was Ann Jordan, head of his affirmative-action committee, but an ally of his political rival, C. Delores Tucker, a live wire who just happened to be in California on the day of the challenge. In effect, Ms. Jordan was indicting herself for failure in an effort to get Thiemann. However, while Thiemann hadn't sabotaged affirmative action, he hadn't made straight the highways in its path, either. He had a speakers' bureau, but no one from it had ever spoken. He had a master list of one hundred black leaders to contact, but three of them were several years dead. On the other hand, he had spent forty thousand dollars and much time on registering new voters.

The result of all this effort was that 184 Pennsylvania Democrats filed to be one of the 77 who would have the privilege of paying their way to Kansas City in December to argue with their fellow Democrats over obscure words that would undoubtedly be changed later. Of these 184, 51 were women, of whom 32 were elected (42 percent). Six were blacks, of whom 3 were elected (4 percent).

Trying to decide whether Thiemann's enthusiasm came up to standard were four members of the executive committee of the national committee selected by—you guessed it—Chairman Robert Strauss. They were aided by Dr. Mark Siegel, Strauss's expert in delegate selection, a sociologist who can quote E. E. Schnattschneider the way Republican lawyers quote obscure court cases. (If an excess of lawyers is the curse of the Republican party, an excess of sociologists is the curse of the Democratic party—another bellwether of the shift in power in America to academia?)

The five harassed Solomons had to render a verdict that would satisfy a majority of the national committee and enough of the protesters to head off a lawsuit without tearing apart the Pennsylvania Democrats and hurting Governor Shapp's chances of reelection. The fact finders promulgated, and the national committee endorsed, the Harrisburg formulas. This ruling, which determined the middle-of-the-road liberal composition of the midterm convention, would be vital in the invisible primary. It would determine all delegate selection for 1976.

Under the Harrisburg formulas, quotas are, in effect, moved further down the line. A delegation can end up all white, all black, all male, all female, all Polish, and still not be successfully challenged, provided that blacks, youth, women, Indians, etc., had all filed to run in proportion to their presence in the Democratic electorate. In other words, who was elected no longer mattered; but who had made the race was all-important. Though idealists on both sides found this ruling objectionable, another example of Strauss's lack of principle and his deviousness, it was accepted with silent relief by a decisive majority. The battle then shifted from interpretation of the Mikulski rules to the Charter Commission.

On the Charter Commission, the last three words of "affirmative action in all party affairs," rather than the first two, provided the battleground. Did "all party affairs" mean that each time a deputy sheriff, school board member, or dog catcher was up for election, the whole complex process of affirmative action had to go into effect? And if a state failed in just one school district, would that throw out its whole delegation to the presidential convention? "Yes," shouted the liberal purists. On the other side, the cynic-pols insisted that all party affairs meant only the election of delegates to the national presidential convention and the National Committee. Here the battle was the ancient one: How much control would the national party have over the various state parties.

At the March meeting of the Charter Commission the liberal idealists had been firmly in control and passed a number of charter articles, including a broad definition of all party affairs that caused the regular idealists and some regular realists to shriek. As the noise grew, Strauss pointedly suggested to the regulars that the best way to change the language was to show up for the next Charter Commission meeting in Kansas City in August. After all, he had carefully structured the 167-member commission so that if everyone attended, the realists would have a 20-vote majority.

But some of the regulars were not going to be able to make the Charter Commission meeting in August in Kansas City. So Strauss polled the Executive Committee of the Democratic National Committee by mail and got agreement that those who resigned from the Charter Commission could designate their own replacements. The idealists soon figured out that this meant they would be outvoted at the August meeting. Led by Congressman

Donald Fraser of Minnesota, they unlimbered for bureaucratic battle. Fraser, a winsome, romantic, little Quixote, had been one of the three or four prime movers behind the creation of the Charter Commission. He dogtrots concerned and happy through life behind a briefcase almost as big as he is; and fervently argues that he can create the Kingdom of God on earth through the Democratic party with the aid of complex rules.

Now Fraser and his allies sent telegrams to Strauss claiming that the mail poll of the Executive Committee was illegal and demanding that the Executive Committee meet and vote in person. That's what they demanded; but Fraser's strategy was to have their telegrams arrive at the National Committee so late that there would be no time to call the Executive Committee into session before the Charter Commission met on Saturday. This meant the Charter Commission meeting would be invalid and the March language would stand going into the midterm convention.

But when the first telegram arrived on Wednesday, Strauss figured out the idealists' game plan and hastily called a meeting of the Executive Committee for Friday. From all around the country harassed members flew in to vote. The question was, would enough members make it so that a quorum would be present. In a desperate and unsuccessful effort to keep a quorum from being present, Fraser and his idealists now boycotted the meeting they had sent telegrams demanding be held. Both sides issued press releases accusing the other of double-dealing. In such a happy atmosphere of internecine knifing, this frolic by grown men who believed themselves capable of governing the country was transported to the Muehlebach Hotel in Kansas City.

"What is going to happen?" I asked purist Robert Dryfoos as the liberal caucus broke up in Kansas City.

"We are going to tear this party apart on the front page of *The New York Times*."

"You can't do that. The *Times* doesn't have anyone here. Their political reporters are covering Ford's search for a Vice-President."

"That can't be true," he wailed, and the liberals caucused again. (It's not if you win or lose, it's how you caucus.)

The first fight on Friday was over the order in which the articles of the Charter would be taken up by the Charter Commission. The realists wanted to take up the tough ones first. The idealists wanted to take up the articles in their numerical order, which would bring up the tough ones last, at the meeting's end. "I remember what the Communists used to do to us at the end of a meeting when everyone had gone home," said Evelyn Dubrow, the brilliant tactician for the Garment Workers' Union and member of the Charter Commission. But those battles with the Communists inside the union were back in the thirties; now this was 1974 and these were fellow Democrats. So many of the Charter Commission members were like old grads trying to recapture some mythic youthful victory. We don't learn from our past; we ritualistically repeat it in ignorant passion.

All Saturday and half of Sunday the 150 members present at the commission meeting battled on. The hotel contributed by not cleaning up the room Saturday night so that by Sunday the Gadarene swine would have felt at home among the Coke cans, the cigarette ashes, the cigar butts, and the stale smell of tired ideas. The idealists continued to attack Strauss for using the power of the party machinery to pack the commission. This was ironic, since what they wanted was a strong central party where the machinery would do just that—but such quibbles of logic never deter debate when Democrats gather in the name of unity. Every time a hassle threatened to tear the commission apart there was a caucus call. Labor met outside the men's room, the blacks met in the press room, the white liberals in a banquet room, the regulars in another banquet room, the state chairmen around the cigarette machine. All these caucuses were closed to the press, naturally. Nonsense is best transmuted into "our firm position as a matter of principle" in private.

Outside there was a tornado watch, and the air over Kansas City became mysteriously still and oily as if aerated with bacon grease. Inside it became obvious that the idealists of big labor had control over this particular meeting, and that the realists probably did not have enough votes to prevent the idealists on the right from rewriting the Charter in such a way that the idealists on the left would walk out. The first test vote came over an amendment that would deny the presidential candidate of the Democratic party the right to pick his own campaign chairman. (I know it's unbelievable, but that's what the extreme idealists on both sides wanted so that "their" party would remain pure no matter who the candidate might be.) After this there was more caucusing and maneuvering while black purists and Tom Uncles tried to smear as antiblack those who wanted to limit "all party affairs," and the limiters tried to smear as pro-quota crazies those who wanted a broad interpretation.

Finally the all-party affairs issue was compromised by agreeing to present four different choices to the miniconvention in Kansas City in December. So, instead of 160 Democrats battling in semiprivate, 2,038 could fight on network TV. By then, tempers were so high a walkout was inevitable. It finally came over a minor motion introduced by Doris Hardesty, a substitute delegate. She was the same woman whose firing by Barbara Mikulski had almost broken up the Mikulski Commission. (The memory of the donkey for past wrongs is nearly absolute.) The motion made, the blacks and some white liberals walked out. The Charter Commission had been destroyed. The odds looked good that the Democratic party would suffer the same fate at its midterm convention in December. But first the Democratic governors had to meet at Hilton Head, South Carolina.

Hilton Head is a small island off the coast of South Carolina amongst whose pines have been inserted a series of expensive, tacky condominiums, bungalows, and hotels, cleverly designed to look like windowed coffins—the whole effect being that of a shoddily constructed army base for almost-millionaires. Here, on November 18, the Democratic governors gathered to do a little socializing, get to meet thier newly elected members, and lambaste the Republicans. Instead, for the two full days they did almost nothing but talk and maneuver over "affirmative action in all party affairs," Article 10 of the proposed Democratic party Charter.

There were also a few minor hurdles as the governors' conference began. The newly elected Democratic governors complained because they had all been seated with their backs to the TV cameras. Governor Jerry Apodaca of New Mexico was furious because his name hadn't been spelled right. He calmed down a little when Governor Wendell Anderson of Minnesota pointed out that his *state* hadn't been spelled right. Then they began the word battle.

The prospect of having four separate affirmative-action sections presented to the convention for choice was so horrifying that everyone looked for a compromise. Strauss and the state chairmen had worked up language that Strauss had forced down the throat of Charter Commission Chairman Terry Sanford. Now Sanford assured the disbelieving governors that everything would be all right at Kansas City, that the Charter takes "the forward thrust of the middle ground." Strauss watched Sanford like a recent Texas millionaire eyeing his first oyster. He knew he was going to have to swallow the son of a bitch and that it wouldn't hurt him, but he'd rather it weren't there.

Before Strauss could set the requisite number of balls in motion to get the governors to support his compromise language on Article 10, John Gilligan, the lame-duck governor of Ohio, came up with his own. Having just been defeated for reelection, he was free to be courageous.

Gilligan's compromise was a substitution—for Article 10 of the Charter, the affirmative-action section, which would take effect after 1976, he would instead insert the language on affirmative action already agreed to by the Mikulski Commission for 1974 and 1976. The beauty of this compromise was not that the Mikulski language was any better or worse than that in the proposed Charter, but that the Mikulski words had been battled over for two years and finally been agreed to, unhappily, by all sections of the party. After some debate the governors, from Apodaca to Wallace, bought the Gilligan compromise. "My strategy was to build a coalition of the center," said the governor. "And let the crazies of the left and the crazies of the right take it or leave it."

"You've cut my balls off," said Strauss to Gilligan over a martini at lunch. "I've saved your ass."

Convinced or not, Strauss set out to lobby for the Gilligan compromise. In this he was following the well-known political rule that a man makes fewer waves battling for someone else's idea than for his own. Strauss and Gilligan held a unity press conference during which, every time Gilligan tried to walk away from the trained TV cameras, Strauss grabbed him by the coattails and pulled him back. Then Strauss got on the phone and tried to sell the compromise to the idealist-regulars and big labor. Basil Paterson, vice-chairman of the Democratic party, went out to try to sell the blacks. Alan Baron pledged support of the idealist-liberals. Don Fowler, the loping six-foot-two state chairman from South Carolina, and Charlie Reilly, the five-foot bouncing state chairman from Rhode Island, a powerful political combo known as "the kangaroo and the lightning bug," went out to sell politicians.

On this fragile note of temporary unity the Democrats assembled four weeks later for the midterm convention in Kansas City, Missouri. Or most of them assembled there. The New York delegation hadn't paid its dues, and as a result was billeted across the river in Kansas in a grungy motel that must have been closer to their state capitol in Albany than to the convention hall in Missouri.

Such a flocking of Democrats excited the mating instincts in every presidential candidate of even the vaguest potential. They all came, with their separate strategies, staffs, and gimmicks, hoping in some way or other to light a fire among the delegates. Many of those same delegates (the percentage was endlessly debated) would return in two years as members of the national presidential convention.

Scoop Jackson came well financed and highly organized, with two trailers, fifty volunteers, ten paid workers, and a complex strategy of identifying key delegation leaders in the first two days and then meeting with them in small groups in his two trailers, which huddled together like mating worms in the basement of the convention hall. He also gave out large numbers of Washington State Delicious apples. Congressman Morris Udall was there with eighty volunteers, six paid workers, three rented tables, and a small hospitality room. He gave away Udall buttons without a union bug on them. His strategy was to obtain the names of as many future volunteers for his constituency as possible. Anyone interested got a long, complex computer form to fill out so their skills could be retrieved in the future.

George Wallace was there, working his old magic among his supporters from his wheelchair. Ex-Governor Jimmy Carter came, working the delegations and flashing his smile. By the time the convention was over he had achieved the status of a full-fledged-question-ducker candidate. A full-fledged-question-ducker candidate is one serious enough not to be a joke, but such an impossible long shot that if a politician mentions his name the endorsement will have no meaning; and the real candidates won't get mad.

"Who do you favor for the presidency, Mayor Daley?"

"We ought to look at a lot of candidates like Sargent Shriver and that Governor Carter." Translation: I haven't made my commitment yet.

Populist candidates Gene McCarthy and Fred Harris avoided and condemned the convention as tainted by illegitimate power.

Of all those arriving candidates, none made a greater impact on the delegates than the enigmatic Texas millionaire Senator Lloyd Bentsen.

Friday night, after the opening day of the convention, he threw a gigantic cocktail party to which every delegate, alternate, visiting VIP, and all the press were invited—some four thousand people. Since Bentsen's campaign strategy was to portray himself as a moderate, thoughtful, middle-of-the-road, non-Texas wheeler-dealer candidate, the effect on the delegates of a mammoth party may not have reinforced his planned image. Indeed, having decided to throw the party, Bentsen's staff had to spend a great deal of time discounting reports of its cost. They claimed the party cost only $10,000. Outside catering experts estimated at least $35,000. And for what? To prove to delegates he was a fiscally conservative moderate?

The whole Bentsen campaign appeared as flush with contradictions as with money. He had made his initial moves in Massachusetts in such a way that he angered Boston's politically powerful Mayor Kevin White. In New Hampshire he was listing as among his committed early supporters politicians who had already declared for Udall. At a political rally in Rochester, held astride two counties, he forgot to include politicians from the second county. He continually tried to move to the center, yet his staff scheduled for him—and he attended—a California luncheon given by the most conservative financial interests in the state: Ford dealer Holmes Tuttle, Dart Industries head Justin Dart, and oil baron Jack Wrather—all Ronald Reagan supporters. Now came the giant, lavish Kansas City party. All this raised and reraised the basic question: Who and what was Lloyd Bentsen? Why was he running for the presidency?

This might be an appropriate place to examine some of these questions for ourselves. Indeed, it might be refreshing to take momentary leave of the squabbling Democrats in Kansas City and look briefly at the ambiguous campaign of Lloyd Bentsen.

One can spend a long time with Bentsen and still not know much about him, as several men and women who have known him since childhood admit. He is the handsome son of a self-made Texas millionaire. After serving six undistinguished years as a thoughtfully conservative congressman right after World War II, Bentsen retired in 1954 to make his own fortune in the money business, insurance and banking. But like many canny Texans, Bentsen kept up his political ties while gaining wealth. In 1970 he upset liberal Senator Ralph Yarborough in a bitter primary campaign, then went on to win the general election. His reputation as a sound, middle-of-the-road conservative, plus his political skills, almost instantly made him a member of the inner club that runs the Senate. He voted against the big oil companies and in favor of the independents, who can be pretty big themselves. He was against the Trident submarine because the construction program was inefficient. He is bright; even his enemies grant that. He grasps the essence of an issue, and its political implications, thoroughly and fast. He graduated from the University of Texas Law School at twenty-one. He had a good war record as a pilot.

His brooding, hawklike face, made longer and thinner by the

close-trimmed sideburns, makes him seem more at home in the board room than among voters and politicians. He is a dull, flat speaker given to such gems as: ". . . proper audit practices may be the area of solution to the swollen federal bureaucracy." At times he shows a real awareness of American problems. "We are not going to live better than our grandparents. . . . We have reached the point where to get a little bigger slice of the pie you have to take from someone else." He has a wife and three children who have followed him into business. That's about it on the tangibles. On the intangibles he seems an instinctively impatient, programmed man who displays great outward patience, with all the tensions and complexities that that contradiction implies.

The part of Texas Bentsen comes from is important—"the Valley," a newly wealthy area stretching inland from the Gulf Coast port of Brownsville, which after World War I became fabulously rich through irrigation. Bentsen's father arrived in the Valley early, as the first canals were being dug right after that war, and realized there was more money to be made in selling land than farming it. The senator's father and uncle went into business for themselves, starting on the proverbial American shoestring. The day he married his wife, Bentsen's father says he had $1.50 period. In the 1960s, when they more or less retired, the two brothers ended up with fortunes estimated at around $50 million each. A man does not make that kind of money in the real estate business and leave no one but friends. The Bentsens had their share of lawsuits from disgruntled buyers, the most famous of which was settled in favor of the purchasers, though without any finding of wrongdoing on the part of the Bentsens. They are a tough, aggressive family. A picture in the valley's local newspaper shows the elder Bentsen, at the age of seventy-five, standing beside the skin of a ten-foot rattlesnake he had captured with his bare hands.

Lloyd, Jr., the present senator and candidate, went to local schools in the Valley where he won prizes in declamation, a gift that unfortunately, like Sir Lancelot's vision, has deserted him. Schoolmates remember him as shy, but not reserved. "He smiled a lot, but not with his eyes," a remark that still applies. Pushing himself constantly, Bentsen graduated from high school at fifteen, entered the University of Texas Law School while still an undergraduate at that university, graduated from law school at twenty-four, enlisting immediately in the air force. While in training in New York, Bentsen reencountered another displaced Texan, a Conover model, Beryl Ann (B.A.) Longino of Lufkin, at a cocktail party. They walked out of the party together, borrowed a car, and drove up to Pittsfield, Massachusetts, to go skiing. Before Bentsen went overseas a year later, the wartime romance had jelled into a successful marriage. Bentsen went to Europe as a B-24 pilot, and Mrs. Bentsen, who had been an orphan since she was six, went back to the Valley to live with her new in-laws.

In 1946, at the age of twenty-six, Bentsen ran for Congress. The local congressman, in poor health and not relishing a fight against a well-financed war hero, bowed out. Bentsen won handily over his other three opponents. In his six years in Congress, Bentsen's record was undistinguished and conservative. He was in favor of changing the law so that "spies and traitors" could be fired from civil service, "without all the costly litigation now involved in due process." A month after the start of the Korean War he delivered his famous "nuke the gook" speech which he and his staff fervently wish people would forget.

"I propose our Commander in Chief, the President of the United States, advise the commander of the North Korean armies to withdraw his troops to the north side of the 38th parallel within one week, or use that week to evacuate a named list of principal North Korean cities which would be subject to atomic attack by our air force. . . ." The North Koreans deserved this treatment because they "brutally murder . . . American boys. . . ." "[And] the atom bomb awaits those who would violate the peace of free men."

There was a great deal of such thought, to dignify the mental process involved, among air force brass at that time, and some of Bentsen's old flying buddies on duty at the Pentagon persuaded him to make the speech. Usually he is and was much more cautious. On the other side of the ledger, it should be recorded that he was one of the two Texas congressmen in 1949 who voted to repeal the poll tax. But that was an exception. The year 1952 found him as part of the conservative group in Texas that refused to support Adlai Stevenson because of Stevenson's belief that the so-called "tidelands oil" belonged to the federal government and not the states.

Dissatisfied with the slow pace of the House, Bentsen retired from Congress after three terms and with his family money set up the Consolidated American Life Insurance Company with assets of close to $7 million. This company split, bought, sold, consolidated, and did those other complex, pirouetting wonders that holding companies do. When Bentsen unloaded it, upon winning his Senate seat in 1970, it was worth $30 million. Bentsen put his assets in a blind trust and estimates his net worth at around $2.3 million, a minuscule figure that causes fellow millionaire Texans to roll on the floor in spasms of laughter whenever they hear it.

Meanwhile Bentsen kept his hands on the levers of Texas politics, particularly that most potent of all levers, cash. He was Houston finance chairman for the Kennedy-Johnson ticket in 1960, raising more money there than all the rest of Texas combined. In 1964 conservative Bentsen was set to run against the incumbent liberal Ralph Yarborough for the Senate. But Lyndon Johnson, who didn't want an internecine Democratic battle in his home state while he was running for the presidency, talked him out of making the race. This decision to collect IOUs and wait six years seems to me to be profoundly Bentsen. Six years is a long time in today's America. Politicians, by and large, are impatient, present-oriented men. They have to be: Voters are too volatile, the future too uncertain. But Bentsen is different. With his cold self-control, he can plan and wait. As a result, when he moved against Yarborough in 1970, he had all the Texas power centers behind him:

Lyndon Johnson, Governor John Connally, and the state boss, now national committee chairman, Robert Strauss. He had their computer lists, their money, their friends, their top aides. And Yarborough made the fatal mistake of underestimating him, neglecting the home folks, starting late.

The campaign was dirty, even by Texas standards. Bentsen's TV commercials depicted Yarborough as against prayers in school, a friend of crazies, Weathermen, and the Vietcong. A standard Yarborough speech was reported in the *Texas Monthly,* which was friendly to his campaign, as "a purplish diatribe on wetback exploiting, land defrauding, slaveholding and other heinous everyday activities of the family Bentsen. . . . He usually sought to portray him [Lloyd, Jr.] as a kind of combination Boss Tweed and Alfred Krupp, with possible genetic deficiencies to boot." Bentsen won with 53 percent of the vote and went on easily to defeat the Republican George Bush. Arriving in the Senate in 1970, he took care to move away from the extreme right, join the inner club, and become a hand-tooled moderate conservative.

Bentsen also showed his shrewd political sense by moving to work with former Yarborough supporters. But when the Big Thicket Wilderness area in East Texas finally became a national park, Bentsen successfully opposed naming any part of the park after Yarborough, though Yarborough had made creation of the park one of his many lifelong battles.

Once again, when a man moves into the Senate there is usually no way to judge his executive abilities—whether he will turn out to have the gifted touch of a Truman or the talent for disaster of a Harding. But one of the ways a man can be judged is on his staff. Bentsen's Senate staff was headed by Lloyd Hackler, a Lyndon Johnson White House political operative, the sort of master politician who gives politics a good name. If Prince Lucifer should ever consider rejoining his former party, he would probably first hire this former Oklahoma Marine with the humor of Ring Lardner and the brains of a Disraeli. But it wasn't Lucifer that hired Hackler away from Bentsen in the middle of the invisible primary; it was the American Retail Association. "Just one of those jobs a man couldn't turn down," say other members of the Bentsen staff. Maybe. It's impossible to imagine the chief advisers of any other serious candidates leaving as the battle got hot.

But apparently Bentsen has trouble building loyalty in a staff. He listens to them; they respect his judgment; "But we always seem to be at a distance," says one. "He is unencumbered by people, ideas, anything," says another. He is monumentally cold. The only time I've ever seen him catch fire is when he is describing airplanes. He has a love of mechanics and flying, and when he talks of that, bursts of energy flash through. But at other times he seems almost purely a man of image. One can no more tell beneath his reserve what he truly believes than one can distinquish the true face of a model beneath elaborate makeup.

This can be both an advantage and a disadvantage. His supporters admire his coolness, call him Cool-Hand Lloyd. His poised caution contrasts with the passions of Jackson. Shakespeare praised those people

> *Who, moving others, are themselves as stone,*
> *Unmoved, cold, and to temptation slow;*
> *They rightly do inherit heaven's graces*
> *And husband nature's riches from expense.* . . .

But how will we take the measure of a man who leaves such minute portions of himself behind for us to judge?

With the departure of Lloyd Hackler, the management of the Bentsen campaign devolved totally upon Ben Palumbo, a thirty-six-year-old former New Jersey politician and assistant dean of the Woodrow Wilson School. In February 1973 (note again the early date), while sitting in an audience in Bergen County, New Jersey, listening to Lloyd Bentsen, this seemingly rational political scientist from Rutgers had a vision—or so Palumbo says. That vision included a revitalized and competent Democratic party in which business and labor lay down together, the White House and Congress were solidly Democratic, the party united, and a moderate businessman led them: Senator Lloyd Bentsen, the Texas unifier. And the John the Baptist in the Wilderness, howling the truth at unbelieving followers of Jackson and McGovern, would be himself, Ben "the Zapper" Palumbo.

It is hard to argue with visions, particularly well-financed ones, however ephemeral they seem to outsiders. Bentsen's office for the invisible primary was one any Washington law firm would have been proud to display. Bentsen rented a whole building on northeast C Street, a few blocks from his Senate office, sixteen hundred square feet, four offices upstairs, four offices down, and a large reception area. The paint is virgin-white fresh, the bay window downstairs has three hanging plants, there are lots of black leather chairs, modern desks, and the latest office machines. And there is Palumbo seated on a modern tan couch before a fireplace, expounding campaign strategy. Even an unbeliever must credit the vision with a certain amount of flesh.

It was also quite probable that Lloyd Bentsen and Ben Palumbo had different visions. That having gotten so far by patience and brains, Senator Bentsen had realized that the office of Vice-President was an almost sure stepping-stone to the White House. A man bright enough to reason this far could take the next step and understand that the odds favored the next Democratic presidential candidate coming from the "liberal" wing of the party. But such a candidate might need some conservative delegate votes to put him over the top, and a moderate conservative as his running mate. And then, after eight years, in 1984, the moderate conservative would become President. Not many politicians plan their life with so much calculation. But Lloyd Bentsen seems to be different.

There is no way to do other than guess at this. For if this is Bentsen's strategy, the merest admission of it would destroy that strategy. Bentsen insists he is running for the presidency. Palumbo insists he is running for the presidency. And Lloyd Hackler? He rocks back and forth on those big plowboy feet and just grins you to death. Now, further suppose that Bentsen and Hackler started out together sharing the highly sophisticated and rational Bentsen vision. And then Bentsen moved over and began to share the Palumbo vision that he could actually become President—it's happened before—would Hackler remain? If Vice-President Bentsen, at the age of sixty, is the Democratic candidate for President in 1984, he will have expanded the invisible primary by eight years.

As they began whatever campaign it was they began, the initial strategy of Bentsen, Hackler, and Palumbo was to get Bentsen accepted by the politicians and the national media as a credible candidate and to raise the necessary seed money in 1974. The initial money came easily. In November 1973, a "Fall Evening with the Bentsens" held in Houston raised $365,000. By the start of 1975, Bentsen had raised $827,300. Then, like Jackson, he started on a direct-mail campaign to raise the $5,000 (in amounts of $250 or less from twenty states) that would trigger future federal financing.

Palumbo had good contacts among the eastern political bosses, and the necessary speaking invitations began to flow in. The bosses had projects for which they needed federal funds. Senator Bentsen of the Senate Finance Committee listened. The national press, again reacting to the mystique of a senator running for the presidency, weighed in with respectful, if not always admiring, attention. *The New York Times,* the Boston *Globe,* Evans and Novak, CBS and NBC, regularly mentioned Bentsen as an able possible candidate.

By the time the Democrats had gathered in Kansas City for their midterm convention on December 16, 1974, Bentsen was up there with the rest of the front-runners. Indeed some in the press ranked him just behind Jackson. Friday, the first full day of the convention, his hospitality suite was open and the sauce laid out by 10 A.M. Amazingly enough, considering this was a political gathering, no one was boozing it up. Indeed, there was no one in the hospitality room but a guy with a gym bag, ripping off a couple of bottles of seven-year-old Scotch. Around the corner Ben Palumbo, in a chaotic office of constantly ringing phones, was denying rumors about the cost of the Bentsen cocktail party. "No. No, no barbecued beef. No, no canapés flown out from Neiman-Marcus; just a little booze and potato chips. I don't even known if there'll be sandwiches. Jesus Christ, how do these rumors get started."

"Is it true that Fanny Fox, the Argentine Firecracker, is going to swing from a chandelier?"

"Go away. Shut up."

Palumbo, like all the key Bentsen aides, is wearing a little black box on his belt that goes beep-beep to summon him to the phone. So many are going off in the crowded room that people can't hear each other. No one can find the stapler, the press has been issued the secret appointment schedule for the staff, there is a misspelling in one of the Bentsen signs, a deal with labor is coming apart. Hackler, in Washington, is trying to locate Alex Barkin, head of AFL-CIO political action arm in Kansas City to straighten out the matter. Palumbo leaves this confusion to check the Bentsen trailer in the basement of the Kansas City Auditorium. (Jackson has two trailers but the Bentsen staff insist their single one is a superior model.)

As Palumbo heads through the lobby of the Muehlebach Hotel, he runs into Barkin. He draws Barkin aside and begins to talk politics. Off goes his beep-beep. Palumbo lets go of Barkin and races for a phone. It's someone testing to see if his beep-beep is working. "Goddamm it, it's working. Cut that shit." Palumbo chases after Barkin and catches him just about to enter the elevator for his suite. He grabs Barkin's arm. The beep-beep goes off again. Palumbo falls back. Barkin and Udall's labor representative enter the elevator. Palumbo answers the phone. "No, it's not going to be the most expensive party in campaign history. No. Hell, no. Listen . . ."

An aide comes up and asks, "Where is Bentsen going to go when he first arrives?" The question is lost in the confusion. Palumbo gets back on course for the trailer. As we meet more Bentsen staffers, I run into gunslingers who recently, when they worked for others, have told me the one candidate they couldn't see was Bentsen. Cash buys people. We arrive at the trailer. It is indeed very ornate; but no one seems to quite know what it will be used for. Palumbo's beep-beep goes off again. This time it's about the case price of beer for the party. The air conditioning in the trailer is making a strange noise.

Another aide demonstrates the excellence of the trailer, how it can even produce ice water for delegates. He presses a button for ice water. A tube is hooked up wrong and liquid waste squirts out of the trailer over a passing delegate. While undoubtedly the secret ambition of all presidential hopefuls at Kansas City is to cover as many delegates as possible with this stuff, Bentsen alone has had the audacity and managerial insight to spray it from his hospitality trailer.

Friday morning in Kansas City, Bentsen begins his day at the two-hundred-person VIP breakfast thrown by Strauss. The other presidential candidates are also there, except for Mo Udall who is out meeting with the caucusing state delegations rather than backslapping with the other VIPs. Poor presidential candidate ex-governor of Georgia, Jimmy Carter—no one comes to sit down beside him at the VIP breakfast. Imagine that, a presidential candidate no one wants to bother to sit beside. Finally, alone with his daughter, he digs into the grapefruit. Bentsen leaves after the grapefruit and picture-taking to have a second breakfast with the Texas delegation, then moves on to the economic panel where the Democrats get together to whomp the Republicans. He and Jackson vie for the day's dullest speech but are outpaced by an economist who proves brilliantly that a

Harvard professor can make even a presidential candidate sound interesting.

All the candidates must sit on one or another of the issue panels all morning to prove they are broad-gauge men, not just vote hustlers. Jackson makes the mistake of sticking with the economics panel for most of the afternoon also. Young liberals who don't like him get up and attack his war record, and his Vietnam positions, while the other candidates are racing from state delegation to state delegation making friends. The idealists are very pleased with the issue panels. They believe they forced them down Strauss's throat. Actually Strauss looked forward to a day of dull panels as giving him room to maneuver between the Executive Committee meeting on Thursday and the convention votes Saturday.

At lunch, Bentsen addresses an overflow group of businessmen and other Democratic heavies at the Kansas City Club. The audience is 80 percent male, 70 percent over forty-five, and close to 50 percent cigar smokers. There is a profound aura of self-satisfied fatness. Bentsen is excellent with this group, serious, forceful, yet almost diffident. But, again, his staff. Twice during serious moments in his speech their beep-beeps go off. And he is trailed by not one but two staff photographers taking pictures of this (historic?) occasion. They pop their cameras in his face as he tries to make serious points.

Back to the cars to drive to two more motels, meet two more delegations, Kansas and Illinois. At Illinois the delegates mill about the buffet table in the center of the room. Bentsen praises Chicago Mayor Daley as a "man of integrity, ability, who has the confidence and is the fighting heart of a great city." The next day, at Strauss's urging, Daley supplies the key votes to get a liberal measure passed to prevent a party split. In 1972 his delegation was denied their seats by the McGovernites. Such is the measure of change, by both sides, in the Democratic party. And the key has been the rules of delegate selection, carefully fought through committee after committee by the crafty Strauss.

After Illinois, Bentsen spends an hour taping a local TV talk show that won't be aired until late Sunday after the convention is over. He unveils a new slogan: "Bentsen, he dreams dreams but he doesn't chase rainbows." Next, another TV talk show; this one runs live while all the delegates are inside the convention hall voting. He's lucky to have that spuming trailer going for him.

When Bentsen finally took the public relations plunge in the caucus room of the Old Senate Office Building and became a declared candidate in mid-February 1975, the national media all called him: "the most conservative of the declared Democratic contenders." Since Bentsen's strategy had been to move centerward of Jackson, this, too, represented a failure on his part. The Bentsen campaign often appeared like the war in

Vietnam. The general sat calm and collected in his air-conditioned bunker; but outside the battles didn't go as planned.

While the presidential aspirants were doing, with varying degrees of success, their thing, back at the convention Strauss and other realist leaders, right and left, were still battling to hold the Democrats together. By then the party really didn't want to blaze up and explode, but there lurked fire in the ashes of its old battles that could burst into flame beneath the right wind. There was a great deal of wind at the convention, not all from politicians. The press, particularly television, finds it much easier and more rewarding in terms of space and air time to cover fights and disasters rather than complex craft and obscure success. "Let's you and him fight" is the reporters' gonfalon. There stands your favorite TV newsman, facing the camera full square, microphone in hand, the smoke all around him. Boom! Crash! Kapowie! "Here I am before the ruins of Donkey Plaza, and with me is delegate Ted Wisloki, who just lost his wife and half his baloney sandwich when the roof fell in. Tell me, Ted . . ." Enough reporters looking for that story can create it.

Once the midterm convention started, the expected began to happen. The Gilligan compromise to use the Mikulski language for Article 10 of the Charter was officially adopted by the Executive Committee. Then various power groups began flexing their muscles, trying to change this or that word their way, nudge themselves a little closer to control of the 1976 presidential convention. The initiative for further change came from the more radical members of the black caucus and then was picked up by some of the women's groups and liberal labor unions. Once these had united, they had enough clout to loosen the Mikulski language: to make it somewhat easier to challenge delegations. They didn't have the votes to make this change on the floor. An exhausted Strauss, his face gray, his weight up ten pounds, with his allies in the governors' conference, the mayors' conference, the state chairmen, the congressional leadership could still have forced the Gilligan compromise down their throat, as some urged. But a 60-40 victory, with perhaps 10 percent of the idealists walking out, would leave behind little of the Democratic party. The left had enough power to force further off-stage concessions. Without which, said Strauss, "Ah might even lose thirty-five percent of mah Texas delegation."

Since the thirties there has been a political saw: "Reformers don't know how to win, regulars how to lose." In his private air-conditioned room back of the podium beneath the stands of the convention hall, Strauss, that most regular of regulars, reconfirmed the rule. Tearing bits of paper out of his notebook, rolling them into balls and chewing them, he refused to press for "victory." Rather he gave up a comma here, a word there. Like a football team in a preventive defense, he was willing to give up small yardage of Charter language to prevent the long bomb of a party-splitting walkout.

Afterward some of the idealists claimed they had the votes to force more radical language down Strauss's throat; they said that they had been the ones who held off and did not split the party. Not so. The really close vote came over whether the party would hold another expensive (Kansas City cost the bankrupt Democrats $500,000), potentially explosive midterm convention in four years. The idealists badly wanted this as part of another effort to write strict rules for a centralized party. Strauss defeated this motion 968 to 851. If he had the strength to convince a group of Democrats talking, politicking, and drinking free booze that they didn't want to have this subsidized good time all over again in four years, he had the votes to do anything he wanted, within reason.

On the convention floor each delegation had two phones: one white, one red. The white phone was for making outgoing calls. The red phone had a red light on top and beneath a sign that read: "Red light indicates a one-way call from podium. Answer alert phone. Listen for message." When the message came, it came with a soft Texas drawl. And the majority listened.

For the record, the last symbolic fight over language, at least for the month of December 1974, was over Article 10, Section 6: where the burden of proof would lie if a state delegation was challenged for discrimination. In the original Mikulski language, the burden lay with the outsiders, the challengers. The new language shifted it slightly toward the insiders, the challenged. Did the change have actual meaning? "I think I know as much about the Charter as anyone else," said Mark Siegel, Strauss's Charter and delegate expert. "And I am not sure what we did." Certainly the change had extreme political importance.

The fifty-eight words of the final compromise were credited to Governor Reuben Askew of Florida, who produced them late Saturday afternoon at a meeting of the leaders between the governors' caucus and the black caucus in Strauss's hideaway behind the podium. Outside, in the convention itself, the delegates milled about in a three-hour recess while their leaders battled to arrive at some set of words over which no one, or hardly anyone, would walk out. The history of the fifty-eight words is as labyrinthine as a Roman catacomb. They were first written by Victor Gotbaum, executive director of the New York District of the American Federation of State, County, and Municipal Employees, a politically active, liberal union. Gotbaum tried out the words on several moderate members of the black and women's caucuses, then passed them on to Jerry Wurf, leader of his parent union. Wurf checked the language out some more, then passed the words to an ally of his, Glenn Watts, leader of the Communications Workers. Watts gave them to Strauss, who cleared them with the congressional leadership and with the kangaroo and the lightning bug—Fowler and Reilly—for the state chairmen, among others, and then got them to Askew late Saturday afternoon. Askew tried them out on a few governors, including John Gilligan, who had been working hard to save his compromise, then gave them to the black negotiators. The blacks took the words back to their own and the women's caucus. This routing says much of what there is to say about present power alignments inside the Democratic party.

Finally the various caucuses and state delegations had to decide whether to accept the compromise. In the women's caucus, Barbara Mikulski and Congresswoman Bella Abzug pushed and shoved for the microphone. Abzug wanted to walk out rather than accept the compromise. Mikulski, yesterday's radical, fought for the compromise and her language. The women's caucus accepted the compromise. In the black caucus, extreme radicals thought so little of the compromise that they moved to strike out Section 7, which allowed cochairpersons of different sexes. "Sister," a delegate shouted at Congresswoman Yvonne B. Burke, who had been among the Charter Commission's more effective members, "you've got to choose. Are you a woman; or are you black?"—as concise a phrasing of the dilemma of being both quota and person as ever made. The antiwomen move was overwhelmingly defeated, and the black caucus accepted the compromise.

Though the old-line AFL-CIO unions either defiantly refused to accept the compromise or released their delegates to vote as they chose, they refrained from "taking a walk." From his trailer headquarters beneath the convention, Senator Scoop Jackson's staff put out a press release in favor of the compromise. Congressman Morris Udall issued a favorable statement. Mayor Daley agreed to go out on the convention floor and work for the compromise. "What's the word from the lightnin' bug and the kangaroo?" yelled a Tennessee delegate looking for guidance. That duo was in favor of the compromise, having slipped in a countermove of their own, by which the key phrase "all party affairs" was to be defined in the bylaws later.*

And who would control the committee that was to do the defining? From his private room back of the podium a bone-weary Texas voice could be heard to say: "Ah will, your great and good friend. . . ." And two months later he did.

So in little bits and swirls and pieces all about the Kansas City convention hall, the Democratic party found it had, at least for a moment, a center. The location of this new Democratic center followed a basic law of physics: When a larger and a smaller mass come together, they are both displaced, but the greater—here the moderate-realist center—is displaced the least. The Democratic center moved left. Mayor Daley and his delegation, which was not only overwhelmingly white and male but seemed mostly shorter than Daley, fought and voted for legislation they would have spurned as "radical" two years before. And was cheered in return.

But even more, the "left" moved right, to become part of that sociological River Jordan, the "mainstream." McGovern's former campaign manager,

---

*In March the lightning bug and the kangaroo were to pull a little nifty of their own when Don Fowler, with Reilly as his manager, won the chairmanship of the state chairmen, defeating incumbent Robert Vance, who had the support of both McGovernite and Wallaceite idealists. Another example of the yogis and commissars joining forces, albeit unsuccessfully here, to try to clean out those objectionable, impure politicians.

Gary Hart, was at the convention as a United States senator who had won election by opposing gun control. Warren Beatty, a far-out McGovern delegate in '72 who back then wore blue jeans and long hair, now sported a three-piece suit and hair slightly shorter than the new Bob Haldeman. John Gabusi, another former McGovernite, with moustache trimmed and necktie in place, well, around his neck, was Udall's co-manager. The old rhetoric was occasionally heard and cheered, just as Republicans still whoop it up for Goldwater. But the new reality spoke louder. After six schizophrenic years the Democratic party had, with the much self-advertised help of Robert Strauss, refound itself.

Since in 1975–76 candidates and politics were going to be more important than ideology, and since the memories of Vietnam were fading, there seemed every chance that the new center would hold. "I am a winner," said Strauss after the convention. "I am a winner." If he hadn't played the stereotyped Texan quite so loudly, he might have gotten more of the credit he deserved. He would have liked that. But then if he hadn't been the effervescent boastful political genius (it's not too strong a noun) that he is, there might not have been much for which to take credit.

CHAPTER 6

Ford, Reagan, and Today's Voters

"**S**ome are born great, some achieve greatness, and some have greatness thrust upon them." I find it hard to spend any time with President or quondam Vice-President Gerald Ford without seeing the cross-gartered and hopelessly hoaxed Malvolio preen across the stage. This is not a judgment against Ford, who does not preen, dresses conservatively, and is much better built than your average Malvolio. Merely it is a reminder that after taking into account the flow of history, the current of events, the effects of genetics, and the schemes of the great, we can never fully account for the wayward tides of fortune.

Nowhere do those tides swirl more murkily than about the vice-presidency. Presidential nominee John F. Kennedy and his brother Robert had wanted Scoop Jackson on the ticket as the vice-presidential candidate. But John Kennedy and his advisers decided that politically they needed Lyndon Johnson to carry the South. Kennedy, Nixon, and George Wallace split the South, while the Kennedy-Johnson ticket lost the entire West, so the strategy was, at best, dubious. But the effect on Lyndon Johnson and Henry Jackson (and you and me) was total.

President Roosevelt had wanted to run with Henry Wallace again, but was blocked by the "bosses," and so chose Senator Harry Truman as a compromise.

When Spiro Agnew finally took the advice of his lawyers and accepted retirement rather than face the strong possibility of prison, ex-Democrat and former Treasury Secretary John Connally of Texas was Nixon's first and only choice for Vice-President. "I like John Connally," Nixon told his friends and advisers privately. "He knows what he wants and he goes for it."

"I think in Connally Nixon saw someone who dared to be openly what he [Nixon] dreamed of secretly," one of these advisers explained later.

Charming, powerful "Big John" Connally wanted the presidency. He had left the Democratic party in 1971 and hitched his lone star to that of Richard Nixon, becoming a fund raiser extraordinary and leading the "Democrats for Nixon" in the 1972 campaign. He regretted this later. "I don't know why I left the Democratic party," he told Senator Percy, standing on the porch of the home he'd built himself in Jamaica, looking out over the well-tended golf course of the Tryall Club to the bright blue Caribbean. "I'm not comfortable around Republicans. They don't even tell the same type of jokes I do." In the dark hours of his life when Connally, on trial for perjury, sat in the courtroom not knowing if the jury would find him guilty or innocent, it was his Democratic friends who came to his defense. Yet he had come touch-close to the presidency. "The ablest man I know," said Nixon. "A man I admire."

But Nixon's choice of Connally faced vehement opposition from those senior councilors who still remained at the White House, principally Melvin Laird, Bryce Harlow, and William E. Timmons. The first fear of these men, in those days when Watergate was still a Washington *Post* exclusive, was that the open and zealous Connally would take the play away from their more reclusive and harassed President, that John Connally would end up running the Nixon administration. "John Connally has his accelerator screwed down to the floor all the time," says Bryce Harlow. "There just is no way he could have played number two."

The second concern of these men, as they remember it later, was that the scandals just below the surface of the administration might erupt and get the President in trouble with Congress. If so, it made no sense to nominate Connally as Vice-President, a move that would generate extreme hostility in both parties in Congress. The Democrats regarded Connally as an apostate, the Republicans as a parvenu. Moreover, as a conservative secretary of the treasury, Connally had angered many liberals. Was there any point in asking for a congressional battle right after Agnew's departure and with the remote possibility that Congress might try to investigate Watergate?

Melvin Laird began to orchestrate a complex political choreography against Connally. One after another, powerful anti-Connally groups met with the President: members of the Republican leadership, old friends of Nixon's from the House, powerful Democratic senators who often voted with the Republicans, other Democratic politicians against Connally, business leaders who didn't like Connally's economic policies. Nixon, more aware of his Watergate problems than his anti-Connally advisers, got the message. Reluctantly he scrubbed his favorite. After that it was easy. Good old Jerry Ford was the first choice of some and the second choice of almost everyone, including President Nixon himself.

Having decided to drop Connally and nominate House Minority Leader Gerald Ford, President Nixon then went through the type of bogus charade that even his admirers find distasteful. Though his decision was set, he made a great show of consulting various groups inside the Republican party and within the Congress as to who should be his Vice-President. Insiders later revealed the deception, but at the time the sham was cleverly concealed. Your intrepid author admits to being fooled. I touted myself off Jerry Ford and unwisely wagered five dollars, at 3 to 1, on George "Poppy" Bush, ex-Texas congressman, ex-U.N. ambassador, and then chairman of the Republican National Committee. And all because of an offhand remark by Senate Minority Leader Hugh Scott (R-Pa.), whose Houdini-like ability to pull the rug out from under himself with his own tongue had in some manner slipped my mind. So much for my omniscience.

The puppet dance being over, President Nixon called Gerald Ford on Ford's daughter's unlisted number, thereby giving rise to the telephone story that reporters traveling with the Vice-President heard on an average of once a day: " 'Please call me back on the other line, Mr. President, I want my wife to hear this.' . . . Fortunately he didn't change his mind." The President asked General Alexander Haig, who had replaced Halderman as White House chief of staff, to arrange a public announcement party. Haig concocted a strange mixture of high school prom and Graustarkian reception. The air force strings played Muzak while before the Cabinet, ambassadors, and congressional leaders the President pulled Jerry Ford, who had decided to retire from Congress, out of a decent obscurity and into history.

This charade was to have an important aftereffect. When, nine months later, President Gerald Ford had to choose his own Vice-President, he determined that his selection process, in contrast to Nixon's, would be completely aboveboard. He would consult with the Republican leaders and legislators by sealed poll and then make up his mind. And so he did. But the press had so soured on both the White House and the phony process by which Ford had been selected that they regarded Ford's efforts to reach some consensus with extreme suspicion.

Before he became Vice-President, Ford had to hurdle the 25th Amendment passed by the Congress on July 6, 1965, and finally ratified on February 23, 1967. Indeed, without that amendment, passed with the succession of both Harry Truman and Lyndon Johnson in mind, Carl Albert, the diminutive speaker of the House, a crafty, silent, sixty-seven-year-old Democrat from rural Oklahoma, would today be President of the United States.

As Nixon's advisers had foreseen, Ford had no trouble passing the scrutiny of Congress. In this he was helped by some reckless charges against him that embarrassed into support some on the borderline of opposition. The Senate Rules Committee voted to confirm him unanimously, and the full Senate voted 92 yeas, 3 nays, and 5 abstentions. The House Judiciary followed with 29 yeas, 8 nays, and 1 present, and the full House, 387 yeas to 35 nays. Not even close, though Vice-President Ford would, when tired and pressed, recite rapidly the names of the eight Judiciary Committee members who voted against him with unusual, for him, bitterness.

With his official swearing in as Vice-President on December 6, 1973, Gerald Ford entered an office whose main importance in today's America is that it commands media attention. The Washington orientation of the press, particularly television, has transformed the vice-presidency from what Roosevelt's first Vice-President, John Garner, called a "warm bucket of spit" into a bully-pulpit second only to the presidency. What the Vice-President does is a media event, and that makes it news. Not a major media event like a triple Mafia killing, an air crash, or the actions of a President. But right up there with tornadoes, nontitle prizefights, and film-star divorces. The Vice-President is always available, if he so chooses, to make news. He has even less to do than a senator, yet holds the symbol of office to give importance and legitimacy to his words and actions. While few would agree with me—I believe that television and the invisible primary come close to assuring the progression of the Vice-President to presidential candidate—even as the secretary of state usually became the strongest presidential candidate in the Republic's early days. Hopefully, in the future, a President will delegate to the Vice-President duties and functions on which the man (or woman) can be judged; now we have only his press and television performance.

The average candidate in the invisible primary flies by commercial aircraft with one staff member and perhaps two persons from the press. The Vice-President's air force plane leaves from Andrews Air Force Base, flown by air force pilots on his own schedule. Secret service men guard him and attract crowds. Staff members handle his and the press's luggage and television equipment. Before he opens his mouth he is a quantum jump ahead of what other candidates can afford.

Fifteen members of the press wait for Vice-President Ford in the VIP lounge at Andrews Air Force Base. A blond sergeant serves us coffee as we watch on the lounge's TV set the House Judiciary Committee debate impeachment. Today we are all traveling by Convair, a two-engine piston plane. As

Vice-President, Ford has traveled in a converted cargo plane without windows, an army transport whose roof leaked, and a navy transport without toilets. Yet he has kept the press beside him and touched political bases in distant parts of the country no other candidate could have reached in the same time.

The press, plus Ford's personal staff of three, plus twenty secret service, plus four air force guards will be cramped in the Convair. But we are all traveling with him. This much press, plus the expensive network TV equipment stowed in the Convair's belly, almost guarantees by rigid economic law that the trip will somewhere be recorded as news. Indeed the next morning Vice-President Ford is—eat your heart out, Jackson, Udall, Bentsen, Mondale, Richardson, Reagan, Wallace—on the *Today* show.

Vice-President Ford's first stop is Muncie, Indiana. Magic Muncie, fabled as Middletown in the pioneering sociological studies of class in America by Robert Lynd. At the Muncie airport, set in fields of fat green beans, are about one hundred people happy to see their Vice-President. No one hassles. The hand-carried signs say "Welcome to Muncie" and "Welcome to our next President." The temperature is in the mid-eighties; overhead in the haze a blue police helicopter circles. We drive, a ten-car motorcade and the press bus (oh, to be an invisible primary candidate followed by enough press to need a bus), to a local high school, a modern chunky building of red brick. The brick construction would have made the school expensive but pleased the building trades unions. The building is also windowless, perhaps in deference to the ageless belief of students that schools are prisons.

The purpose of this portion of Ford's trip is to aid the reelection campaign of Congressman Harold Dennis, one of President Nixon's staunch defenders on the House Judiciary Committee. The local experts tell us that the district is probably two to one against impeachment, that some twelve hundred people will turn out to eat Colonel Sanders' chicken in the high school auditorium, at $50 to $100 a head. From this the Dennis campaign will net $25,000. (Dennis, who won, will record expenditures of $79,840 in his campaign. A candidate for President in 1976 will only be allowed to spend $52,407 in the same district in the Indiana primary. But no one asks that sort of question on this night. And if we did, no one would know the answer—let alone whether the answer should cause joy, concern, or a bit of both.)

Vice-President Ford wears his uniform, a single-breasted, wide-lapeled suit of moderate hue with three-button cuffs, two wide flap pockets on the right side of his jacket, one on the left, blue shirt with narrow button-down collar, and a moderate striped tie of red, white, and blue theme. Ford, as he admits cheerfully, doesn't pay much attention to his clothes. Shortly after becoming Vice-President he showed up at the office with a tie in which little blue screws were inserted inside little white "U's." He was surprised when a reporter pointed out the implications of what he had around his neck.

Ford's indifference about clothes extends to furniture. When his wife was having difficulty furnishing the Vice-President's mansion on Massachusetts Avenue, she was explaining her problems to him one night when Gerald Ford got up and began to walk away.

"You are not listening," she said.

"Oh, I'm listening all right," he answered, and kept walking out of the room.

Now in a high school classroom we hold another fake press conference in which the local press ask the questions on everyone's mind for the one-thousandth time, while the candidate pretends they are brand-new and he must struggle to answer because he has never heard them before. Hearing any candidate deliver the same answers or the same speech more than one hundred times makes you bored, and some candidates' stock answers make you sick. Ford's answers belong to the bored classification. Press conference over, there is a quick cavalcade to a local country club to meet the hundred-dollar givers. Then back to the high school auditorium for the speeches.

My notes record and the schedule handed out in Washington before the trip confirms that at this time one Paul Boltz—he is not otherwise identified—is to take one minute to introduce Indiana Governor Otis R. Bowen. Instead Mr. Boltz sees fit to introduce thirty-one distinguished local Republicans, the vast majority of whom are physically present though cannily hidden. Further, this Boltz makes the most basic mistake of not asking that the applause be held until all the VIPs have been introduced. As a result, by my watch, each presentation consumes an average of one minute and forty-two seconds. A total of fifty-two minutes and forty-two seconds to begin the one-minute introduction of the governor which then went on for another seven minutes. Unfortunately this is not even close to a record for one-minute introductions.*

Ford's speech touches the usual political bases. He mentions the excellence of Congressman Dennis and his "tremendous legal argument" while defending President Nixon on television. He mentions the excellence of Nixon. "There is only one leader in the world today in which other countries have trust: President Nixon . . . I can say from the bottom of my heart that the President of the United States is innocent. He is right." That's the part that makes the *Today* show the next morning.

The next afternoon in Chicago, where Ford addresses a group of businessmen assembled by the Commerce Department, he is asked by the press about this statement.

---

*The only record of this kind that it was my certain good fortune to attend was in 1954 at a prayer clambake in Maine with President Eisenhower. The signal for Eisenhower's arrival was erroneously given early and two elderly ladies began to play "Hail to the Chief" on a pair of harps. They had been playing for several minutes before I realized I might be in the presence of a historic occasion and began to count. Even so my count reached 143 before Eisenhower entered and they could shift to "Oh, say can you see." I am confident this represents the all-time record for "Hail to the Chief" on two harps at a prayer clambake.

"I meant right in the sense that he was innocent," says Ford. "I used that figuratively."

Why did he go so far at this time?

"I just said in more emphatic terms what I have been saying before."

That night at a large fifteen-hundred-seat banquet for Republicans at which Ford is the principal speaker I ask Representative Les Arends, the retiring Republican whip of the House, how he feels about Nixon and impeachment. Arends, an extremely conservative Republican from the Chicago suburbs, says he thinks Nixon is wrong. He adds he now doesn't know how he will vote on impeachment. Yet Arends is listed on all the form charts as certain to be for the President. Will Ford be the boy on the burning deck?

The next day in Canton, Ohio, another conservative district, Ford again delivers a hard-charging defense of the President. The area's Republican Congressman, Ralph S. Regula, describes his constituents as "content and quiet." I ask him privately if he will vote pro-Nixon. "Look, Ford got appointed. I got to get reelected. I'm going for impeachment." Arends and Regula are two conservative Republicans. I realize Nixon is through.

Ten days later, on August 8, Ford is called to the White House from his office across the street in the Executive Office Building. There he learns from President Nixon, whose defense has just been flattened by the final revelations on the subpoenaed tapes, that he is about to become President. For Ford the elevation comes not a moment too soon. With each week the Vice-President has been growing increasingly strident in his defense of the President, tying himself more tightly to the apron strings of his benefactor. Had President Nixon stonewalled just a few months longer—not necessarily to the bitter end, but merely two angry months longer—the Republican party and the country would have divided more each day. Ford would probably have moved by then so far into the Nixon camp that no recovery toward the center would have been possible. The wily Rockefeller would not have agreed to serve as his vice-presidential partner. A discredited Ford would be part of Nixon's Watergate cover-up.

As it was, Nixon's resignation came while the Vice-President was still able to zigzag. In one speech he would urge the President to release the tapes, "the quicker the better," or to "respond affirmatively to all requests for tapes and documents." In the next he would say, "The President's attitude is proper," or he would attack the hearings as "partisan . . . a travesty" and claim that they were doing "real harm to the country," that the President "deserves much better. . . . You can't vote against the President." But the zigs urging the White House to be "forthcoming" were growing fainter, while the zags stridently defending President Nixon to the end were becoming louder and more hard-nosed. The Vice-President was rapidly losing the respect of the press, the Congress, and liberal Republicans to become instead Nixon's puppet.

But Ford's luck, something President Ford believes in, held to the end. For him, Nixon resigned in time. As Ford raised his right hand on August 9 he entered the presidency still his own man. He did not officially enter the invisible primary that day. He then still insisted he had no intention of running for President on his own.

Three days later the new President entered the steaming hot chamber of the House to address a joint session of Congress and the nation, to prolonged applause from both Democrats and Republicans. The applause appeared longer and heavier than anyone had expected. It seemed to arise not so much for the new President as from a feeling of profound relief. The miserable Watergate drama was over, the country was still intact, "good old Jerry" was President, the fat weskited world could go on. During his speech Ford drew the loudest applause when he promised not to bug, pry, or commit crimes—cheers for a President of the United States who was promising not to break the law.

The presidency of Gerald Ford lies outside the scope of this book. More has been written about him and his actions than about any other candidate in the invisible primary. Still he must be judged by the same six criteria applied to other candidates. The first of these is the candidate's psychological reaction to the tests of driving for the presidency. In Ford's case, this means the test of being President.

Also it is important to note again the obvious truth that being President gives a man an enormous lead in the invisible primary. Indeed we automatically assume that if a President wishes he will be able to engineer his renomination by his party. True, Lyndon Johnson stepped down. But most observers believe, correctly I feel, that had he chosen to fight he could have gained the nomination. If he could anoint Hubert Humphrey, his surrogate, what would the Texas tornado have been able to accomplish for himself?

The new "reforms" beneath which primaries have proliferated have, if anything, made it easier for a President to succeed himself. Now that the new rules of the game are understood by everyone, a primary appears to have increased the power of the Executive and the party machine, rather than diminished it, though the conventional wisdom continues to hold otherwise. The party organization has the personnel, the lists of voters, the local knowledge, and the access to money. Even a President of moderate ability should be able to control a majority of his party's state organizations. Where he doesn't, he has the overwhelming advantage of practically unlimited media exposure—all of it free. At the same time, his challengers must comply with a more complex campaign law and increasingly limited funds. We may have forced the President to spend more time working on politics, rather than governing the country—hardly the intent of the reformers; but in no way have we dropped his advantage.

That television has increased the power of the presidency through the President's unique free access to that medium is coin of common knowledge. But the obverse of that coin is often hidden. As the reliance of voters, particularly younger voters, on TV for their political information has increased (40 percent of the electorate makes its voting decisions on the basis of the tube), the political party has declined as a source of political information. Even if all the GOP leadership had desired and conspired to dump President Ford, they would have found this more difficult to accomplish in 1976 than at any time past. There wasn't that much power left in the party. They could bad-mouth the President to a few regulars, but Ford could appear on television sending in the marines. Party leaders relied on the President to raise their funds. Ford did that and then raised more for himself besides. The regulars had been powerful because they controlled whom the party built up or tore down. The new men of power were those who controlled access to the tube. Ronald Reagan, Ford's chief challenger, was more a television man than a party man.

The exact nature of our future first TV President is, mercifully, still veiled, whether he or she will resemble John Wayne or Cher Bono. But television is a medium of energy, action, and motion; and these Ford has to an extraordinary degree. All during his minority leadership in the House he had been away most weekends helping out fellow Republicans. Now that same energy was let loose to help himself. Practically every weekend he was away from the White House politicking somewhere. He flew back from a grueling six-day European NATO meeting and rose at eight the next morning, while the press and his staff slumped exhausted in bed, to deliver a speech at West Point. Week after week he surged on, doing what came naturally, what he had done all his life in politics; only now it made national news. On becoming President, Gerald Ford moved from being the strongest candidate on the Republican side of the invisible primary to the 90 percent certain winner.

President Nixon, who quite unintentionally, and even against his will, had done so much for retiring House Minority Leader Gerald Ford, left behind in Ford's White House the explosive problem of citizen Nixon's future. Here politics and the personality of the new President all mixed together. To the total surprise of "informed Washington," President Ford pardoned ex-President Nixon completely and almost immediately. The Congress and the press, partisan and slightly paranoid from Watergate and Vietnam, looked for political reasons. They should rather have examined the psychological makeup of the new President.

Why had Vice-President Gerald Ford become increasingly strident in his defense of President Nixon? What had the Vice-President been thinking as he logged those countless miles of travel—thirty-eight states, over 100,000 miles—and heard himself over and over called "the next President"? Or very often, by wish fulfillment or Freudian slip, "the President" or "our President"? Who and what is Gerald Ford, about whom so many have speculated?

To me the most important of several major keys to President Ford is found in his story about his real father coming into the lunch counter where Ford was working as a seventeen-year-old high school senior. Ford had, so he says, learned just that year that he was adopted (or the year before, he tells the story different ways). There had been hints when he was younger, but he had never paid attention to them. Ford stresses that the hurt of seeing his real father, Leslie King, was very great. "I thought, here I was earning two dollars a week and trying to get enough school, my stepfather was having difficult times, and here was my real father obviously doing quite well. . . ." Yet the real father never helped him. His stepfather always helped. Over and over Ford stresses how close he and his stepfather were. How surprised he was to learn that he was adopted, that this man, Leslie King, had abandoned his mother and himself.

I believe that this sense of loyalty Ford has, of being a team player, of being committed to hard work, springs from his continuing desire to repay his stepfather, Gerald Ford, Sr., to be worthy of that man's loyalty to himself.

While, for a politician, Ford is pleasantly unambitious, he didn't become football captain at Michigan or work his way through Yale Law School or move up to his position of Republican leadership in the House by benignly sitting on his duff. As people cried, "There goes the next President" or "our President," he must have heard with both pleasure and alarm: pleasure that he had succeeded; alarm that he was betraying Nixon, another foster father. When finally he sat in the Oval Office as President, he knew who had placed him there. Gerald Ford, Jr., could no more be disloyal to foster father Richard Nixon than he could loaf through life and betray the standards of stepfather Gerald Ford, Sr. Ford's hope that Nixon would have a better life on leaving the White House was genuine.

The Nixon pardon flowed from Ford's deepest emotions, not from any reasoned analysis of the political situation. And politically the results were disastrous. After the pardon, Ford's rating dropped sensationally in the polls, and the House Judiciary Committee, swollen with televised righteousness, called him to account.

Ford's life has been loyalty. When Eisenhower was President, he went down the line for Ike. In those days of the 1950s, he was known as a moderately liberal Republican. Coming to Congress under the wing of Senator Arthur Vandenberg, also of Grand Rapids, Ford supported the Marshall Plan, something few conservative midwestern Republicans were doing. (My grandfather, a conservative Grand Rapids Republican, thought Senator Vandenberg and Congressman Ford had taken leave of their senses.) Ford has been loyal to his constituents, loyal to the House of Representatives, to old friends, and finally to President Nixon. His admiration of President Truman is quite genuine, predating his sudden rise to the vice-presidency. Truman was his leader when he was in the House during the Korean War. Ford's character is all of a piece.

In any discussion of Ford, the question of his brains immediately arises. Lyndon Johnson's famous remark that Ford couldn't walk and chew gum at the same time is quoted ad nauseam. Actually, what Johnson said was that Ford couldn't walk and chew *bubble* gum at the same time. It's the little touches, like the knocking at the gate in *Macbeth,* that mark the master. Just as often quoted in riposte to Lyndon Johnson is Ford's record at Yale Law School. He finished in the top third of his class, getting mostly B's with a smattering of A's, and coaching the Yale freshman football team on the side. The members of his class with whom I've talked remember him as reasonably bright. At that time the Yale Law School was split between America Firsters (extreme isolationists) and those who favored increased aid to the Allies. The future President joined neither group, too busy working and coaching for politics.

When Ford was at Michigan and Yale Law, there was a general assumption among men (and among those women of that generation lucky enough to attend college) that book learning and ideas were something one studied in school. When one left school, one left ideas behind and entered the real world. In that world, experience taught. That ideas and experience form a gestalt, continually checking and reinforcing each other, is an outlook that is still only beginning to come into popularity. Too often America still divides into those who get information from books and the media and those who get it firsthand. And both groups look down on each other, to each other's loss and the political benefit of George Wallace and his heirs. Ford, a member of this generation, seems to have put abstract ideas resolutely behind him once he quit school. He relies entirely on his experience, which has, since the navy, been Republican, midwestern, and conservative. This, plus a certain Boy Scout solidness, causes reporters, most of whom are idea and book people, to rate him stupider than he is.

I include myself among those who so rated him. During the Korean War, as *Newsweek*'s defense correspondent, I used to breakfast occasionally with the Chowder and Marching Society, a group of young, moderately liberal Republican House members, of whom Ford was a member. I kept in touch with some of them, the ones I figured as comers, who would be good sources as they, and (I hoped) I, moved up the ladder of life. Alas, I figured good old Jerry didn't have the mental stuff to make it. As the late Stewart Alsop once remarked, "As I grow older I realize that most of the world's problems aren't solved by brains, but by attributes like trust, kindness, and loyalty." He was right. The man with the highest IQ, among either the victorious prosecutors or the vanquished defendants, at the Nuremberg war crimes trials was Hermann Göring.

Charles Goodell, the former liberal Republican senator from New York and a close friend of Ford's, calls him: "a solid, inertial guy. . . . He is not fast on his feet, but he is an intelligent, hardworking guy. . . . He is genuinely naïve and has no instinct for power. . . ." Everyone stresses what a "good guy" Ford is.

On becoming President, Ford had the presidential seal removed from the backs of all the chairs in the Oval Office. He also replaced the President's chair at the Cabinet table, which President Nixon had made much larger than the other chairs, with one the same size as the rest. Photographs show that former President Nixon still wears the presidential seal on his jacket in retirement in San Clemente. Senator Teddy Kennedy attended an antiwar rally wearing his brother's Commander in Chief jacket. Jefferson rode his own horse to Madison's inaugural. Some people know who they are.

Still the unexamined life is a life not worth living. One could wish that Ford, like Truman, had done enough reading to put the enormous questions of our time in some other context besides a game of football. His decisions might not be any better, or even any different, but they would have a reassuring depth and at least the smell of present agony.

Ford shares one final trait with so many of the other candidates in the invisible primary. When he talks about loyalty and goodness, he often mentions his stepfather. But when he talks about the things that shaped him as a boy—energy, drive, stick-to-itiveness—he mentions his mother. As with the other candidates and so many of our Presidents, he grew up in a family where the mother, not the father, provided the hard edge of ambition and drive.

For any President to be successful, not only must he have ability, but he also must be a man for his particular time. It is as hard to imagine the voters electing John F. Kennedy at the close of World War II as it is to visualize the presidency of General Eisenhower at the height of the great depression. As President Ford and the other candidates sought votes, to whom were they talking? Each candidate was convinced he could best represent the electorate. But who really was out there, making that sea of faces and outstretched hands?

Three times in the two-hundred-year short history of America our political structure has disintegrated.* The first of these was the breakup of the Jeffersonian Republican party into Whigs and Democrats, the latter led by Andrew Jackson. At the same time the congressional caucus system of choosing Presidents broke down beneath the new political pressures. A political realignment was forged between the middle Atlantic and the border states that almost led to war.

The second political upheaval, the passing of the Whigs and the rise of the present Republican party, did lead to Civil War: 364,511 dead, 281,881 wounded. With some retuning during the presidency of William McKinley, the Civil War Republican alliance of industrial East with western and midwestern interests dominated politics into the late 1920s. During that time both the black and the ethnic voter were solidly in the Republican fold.

By the election of 1928, the political processes of our democracy were again close to breakdown. In that election 50 percent of those eligible to vote did not do so. Though statistics from earlier days are imperfect, it would appear that such voter dissatisfaction had not occurred since the Civil War.

---

*Many historians cite five periods of disintegration and realignment. They add the Federalist breakup under Jefferson's presidency and the political realignment under McKinley to the shifts under Presidents Jackson, Lincoln, and Franklin Roosevelt.

We were in our third great political crisis. With the coming of the Roosevelt revolution and the New Deal, another major realignment of the political parties began. As citizens found that these new structures satisfied their physical and ideological needs, the number of nonvoters slowly began to drop, reaching a low of 37 percent in the watershed year of 1960. Since then the number of nonvoters has again surged upward. In 1972, 67 percent of those who could vote did not vote. And that figure cannot be blamed entirely on the dismal choice between presidential candidates, for in the off-year election of 1974, the number of nonvoters remained close to the same (63 percent).

Once again, as in the periods just prior to the Jackson presidency, the Civil War, and the New Deal, parties, politics, and particularly politicians were becoming an anathema to a *majority* of Americans. In 1976 a majority of Americans of voting age, 58 percent, are not registered to vote. Fifty-five percent of those under thirty-five have never voted. By 1980, if the trend continues, over 60 percent of those Americans eligible to vote will *never* have voted. And how many of the remaining 40 percent will make the effort to reach the polls that election year? Can our democracy sustain itself on such a slender chord of plugged-in people? Is not a new and possibly violent realignment of the political process at hand?*

While the decline in the percentage of voters is serious for all America, for President Ford and his fellow Republicans the vanishing of the Republican party is catastrophic. Only 18 percent of the American people identified themselves as Republicans in 1974. When this statistic is broken down further by age, the future of the present Republican party seems even more doubtful. The largest group of those calling themselves Republicans, 31 percent, were age sixty-five or older. Only 11 percent of those under thirty-five thought of themselves as Republicans. Parties, like Robert the Bruce, have bounced back from such a nadir. But on what regional or philosophic base would the revised and revived GOP build?

"Who needs to be burdened by the weight of the Republican label?" challenges conservative strategist Kevin Philips from the right.

"I could probably run seven percentage points higher without the Republican label," agonizes liberal Republican Senator William Brock of Tennessee.

"I sell things," says Wallace fund raiser Richard Viguerie. "And you can't sell the term 'Republican.' "

While the outlook for Democrats is not as dark as for Republicans, the donkey has scant cause for braying. Less than a majority, 42 percent, of Americans think of themselves as Democrats, a mere 2 percentage points above the 40 percent who classify themselves as independents. Back in 1964, 51 percent of the voters called themselves Democrats. As with the

---

*For the sources of the statistics in this section, as well as my gratitude to those who compiled them and guided me through their intricacies, please see the Introduction.

Republicans, the majority of the Democrats are older voters who came into the political system with FDR and Truman. Fifty-one percent of those between the ages of fifty-five and sixty-five consider themselves Democrats. Only 34 percent of those between seventeen and twenty-four consider themselves Democrats. In this same age group, 12 percent call themselves Republicans while a whopping 55 percent say they are independent of both political parties.

Even those twin pillars of Democratic strength—blacks and union members—are leaving the Democratic party. In 1965, 80 percent of all blacks called themselves Democrats; now the figure is 60 percent. Union Democrats outnumber union independents by a bare three points: 47 percent Democratic, 44 percent independent. Again the fall-off is among the younger voters. Analysis of the 1968 election shows it was the union members under thirty-five who voted for Wallace. Their parents flirted with the idea for a while, then came back to the Democrats and Hubert Humphrey.

Why the dramatic rise in the numbers of independents and nonvoters? What is happening to the American political party? Who will vote in the state primaries?

In the past the American political party has had important economic, information, and status functions. The party provided jobs. Not just to the low end of the economic scale and in the form of relief for recently arrived immigrants, but also in the form of high-status government jobs that were only open to members of the "in" party. These economic functions have mostly passed. The welfare bureaucracy decides who gets how much relief. Merit examinations and seniority systems allocate the fat jobs that represent getting ahead in most of government today. At the same time, being active in party affairs no longer confers, as it did through most of the sixties, automatic status on an individual. Indeed the tag "staunch party member" calls to mind a person worming his or her way forward through graft or wire-pulling, rather than ascending by merit.

> *The hall of fame is very large*
> *And all its portals full.*
> *Some enter through the door marked push,*
> *More through the door marked pull.*

Most important for the invisible primary, people no longer get their information on how to vote from their political parties. Nor do the parties provide the candidates with facts about how the people feel. The party structure no longer transmits political information up or down. Until well into the fifties, the word from local and state party leaders, conventions, party meetings, rallies, parades, and mailings were vital ingredients in a person's decision how to vote, particularly in a primary. Now the media, particularly television, has taken over this function. Even insiders choose this or that candidate on the basis of polls and press reports , rather than as the result of subtile vibrations of the party network. And the candidates, to gain insight on how the voters feel, resort to polls rather than information from ward leaders and other front-line party officials.

Perhaps the parties might be saved if one or the other of them were strongly identified with an emerging social issue. But the great issues of the seventies—energy, busing, bureaucratic bumble, the environment's decay, honesty in government, crime, federal versus local control—all of these cut across party lines rather than reinforce them. Philosophy no longer defines the two parties. The voters don't need the party: 52 percent of them don't want party labels on the ballot. Inevitably, candidates are beginning to build their own organizations independent of the two traditional parties.

To be blunt, the independent voters have one large, sad trait in common: they don't vote. Only 15 percent of the independents voted in 1974 as distinct from 60 percent of those who classify themselves as Republican or Democrat. The independent voter is tuned out and turned off.

As the pollsters interpret the statistics, the following seems to be happening. Prior to 1960, as Americans became eligible to vote at eighteen or twenty-one, they started out as independents. Then, sometime in the next three to five years, their attitudes coalesced and they joined the Republicans or Democrats. Since 1960 those who began as independents have stayed independent. At the same time about 10 percent of those who were already Democrats or Republicans have left their party to join the independents. More Republicans have quit their party than Democrats.

Visualize all those eligible to vote as inside a great tube. At the right of the tube are the older voters. They are committed to a political party; and they are also those most likely to vote. At the other end, the younger end, are the new independent voters. They are also the voters who usually don't vote. As the older voters die and the younger nonvoting independents keep pushing into the other end of the tube, the American democracy gradually fills with those who have never voted: 60 percent, as we have noted, by 1980.

Up until 1968 the independents were regarded as one group. They were seen as people who had consciously chosen independence. They were believed to be a little bit better off, a little bit better educated, a little bit younger, a little more upward mobile than average. With '68 and the rise of George Wallace, this profile of the independents began to be questioned. Pollsters now postulate two groups of independents: the traditional group, just mentioned, and a second group at the top of the lower middle class. These latter have finished high school or attended college, they hold skilled artisan or other such blue-collar jobs or lower white-collar jobs, they live in the old city neighborhoods or newer subdivisions, they make a little more than most of their neighbors—around thirteen thousand-plus a year—and the average family has two children. Like the first group, they, too, are a bit more upward mobile than most of their neighbors. What both groups appear to have in common is a sense of threat. The system is not working for them. They are putting out more but not receiving more. However, the threats that the two groups identify are often different.

The second group of independents is often referred to as "ethnics." But the voters in this group are not independent because they are "ethnics." The fact of their ethnocentricity—Irish-American, Italian-American, Jewish-American—happens to coincide with their place in the social scale. Their independence and nonvoting is a socioeconomic phenomenon, rather than a function of ethnic status. This second group of independents is largely composed of those who, before 1960, would have voted Democratic. The first group is largely composed of those who, before 1960, would have been Republican. This is why it is so hard to form an Independent party. Except for their upward mobility and youth—the older independents are now pushing forty—the two groups so far have little in common besides their independence.

Many conservative writers and commentators, generalizing from early studies of the independents, believe that the group as a whole is right wing, and so they predict a new conservative majority. I find no evidence for this. The number of those who call themselves conservative seems to have remained constant since 1960, at around 40 percent of the electorate. In some years the percentage of conservatives is up slightly, in others, down. But the questions asked have been different enough in the various years to make comparisons suspect. Robert Teeter, whose work on this subject has been particularly prescient, holds that people vary so much about how they feel from issue to issue that the self-designated labels they give themselves—"liberal" or "conservative"—cannot be applied with much accuracy to predict their voting behavior.

For my part, I feel that since the older voters outvote the younger voters by almost two to one, and since older voters tend to be more conservative, the nonvoting independents will probably turn out to be more "liberal" than the present voting electorate. Further, among today's *nonvoters,* one-third call themselves "liberal," one-third call themselves "conservative," one-third don't know. Among today's *voters,* one-third call themselves "liberal" but almost half (48 percent) call themselves "conservative." Again I find the terms "liberal" and "conservative" of diminishing value in classifying 1976 political actions. (Is a person who favors local rather than federal control over highway siting and spending a liberal or a conservative?)

While the rise of the independents has been a result rather than a cause of party breakdown, there is a ripple effect. In primaries and general elections, candidates need the independent vote. This causes them to take stands close enough to their party to hold on to votes from party loyalists, but far enough away to gain the independents. Indeed, to be a Democrat but run against the Democratic "bosses" appears the ideal political stance of the mid-seventies. Research has recently identified a key group of voters I call "splitter hit men." Though aligned with one political party, these voters invariably vote for at least one member of the opposition party to prove their psychological independence. In a close election, a candidate may sabotage the rest of his party's ticket if he tries to be the one for whom the splitter hit man votes. Again, for better or worse, the party suffers.

Teeter points out that his studies show the electorate aren't just turned off by political parties and politics; they are turned off by everything big. The nonvoters are without allegiance. They regard their work as a bore, their company as a paycheck, their union as a pain in the neck that, like the government, puts a crimp in their pay envelopes and hassles them with rules. Their church they used once to get married and will use again when they die. They belong to no clubs, fraternal organizations, or veterans' groups. They spend their spare time before television or doing things with their families. When they go out, it's with small groups of friends, but they still remain basically alone. They wish to escape the complex world and so tune themselves out from the information and horror that bombards them. In this process they block out much they need to know for their survival. And since they are us, for our survival.

The pollsters' statistics document the rise of this gloomy story of paradoxical American quiescence and dissatisfaction. In 1964, not the best year for Americans, 76 percent of the voters thought you could trust the government most of the time. Today 32 percent believe this. In '64, 68 percent of us thought those in government knew what they were doing. Today less than half of us (47 percent) believe this. In '64, only 28 percent of us thought *most* of the people in government were crooks. By 1974, that percentage had risen to where 49.3 percent of us thought *most* of those in government were crooks. In 1966, 37 percent of us believed that what we thought didn't count for much. Today 61 percent of us believe this.

Following the 1974 election, pollster Pat Caddell asked those who actually voted—that mere 37 percent of those eligible to vote—"Do you think your vote changed anything?" Only a third thought their vote had mattered. Caddell's report continues: "If we were to extrapolate this figure for the whole electorate, assuming those who didn't vote all in the negative category, we would have about 12 percent of the electorate indicating confidence in the basic efficacy in the political process." Since I find the nonvoters quiescent rather than negative, I'm not prepared to go this far. But I'm not throwing my hat in the air with joy over Caddell's figures, either.

Looking at America, the voters of today echo King Lear: "We have seen the best of our times. Machinations, hollowness, treachery, and all ruinous disorders follow us disquietly to our graves." Since 1959, those of voting age have been asked to rank how they felt about America on a scale of 1 to 10. One represents hellish; 10 represents heavenly. In 1959 America's present was ranked toward the better end of the scale at 6.7. At the same time, our future was rated positively golden at 7.4. Now our present has fallen below mid-scale toward a sere and yellow 4.3. We still believe our future will be better than our present, but we grade it only 5.9 today.

Increasingly, American voters support actions outside the political system to change things. Forty-three percent of those eligible to vote approve of setting up vigilantes if the police "don't stop crime." Forty percent approve of disrupting legislatures to get their taxes lowered. Support for such "violent" solutions is greatest among young middle- and upper-middle-class Americans who don't vote. Those approving such solutions are largely under thirty-five, earning fourteen thousand or better, have more than a high school education, live in the Northeast or heavily industrialized states, and classify themselves as "liberals."

Putting a number of factors together, pollsters have come up with a dissatisfaction index. Recently this index has been rising rapidly. From 1966 to 1970 the number of Americans who were ranked as dissatisfied increased only 13 points, from 29 percent of us to 42 percent of us. From 1970 to 1975 the increase was 30 points as the numbers of us dissatisfied jumped to 72 percent. And the sharpest rise has come since 1974. The bright colors in which we used to paint the American dream have been wiped from the pallet of our belief.

Yet along with this darkness and alienation, paradoxically, a flag-waving faith in America remains. Eighty-seven percent of us believe ours the greatest country in the world. The reasons most often given include: our freedoms, our justice, our democracy, and the quality of our life. We do not perceive our system or our ideals as rotten; but we do so perceive our leaders.

It is as if a town had had the greatest baseball team in the nation for a number of years. Then a new group of players arrived, and the team lost game after game. After several seasons of finishing at the bottom of the league, the townspeople quit going to the local ball park or following the fortunes of the club. They reviled the players. But if you asked them what the greatest sport in the world was, the vast majority of them would still say baseball.

Will the fans return to the old team and the old ball park? Will the nonvoters—the 62 percent of us in 1972—vote again? He who reaches the nonvoters, wrote the social scientist E. E. Schattschneider in the fifties, "will control the country for a generation." Now it looks more likely for several generations.

The conventional wisdom beneath which we basked for many years held that nonvoting was a function of ignorance and discrimination. But in the past twenty years education and political knowledge have increased, registration and voting have become much easier, and at the same time nonvoting has risen dramatically. For a majority of Americans nonvoting has become a purposeful act—their way of saying to hell, not with the system, but with those scrambling for their vote. "Send them a message," cried the followers of George Wallace. It's the nonvoter, whether he calls himself a Democrat, Republican, or independent, who is sending the message.

There is yet another new class of nonvoters: those who take the trouble to register and then don't vote. In 1972, 13 percent of those who took the trouble to register failed to vote. By 1974 this percentage had risen to 25 percent, or 18 percent of the total voting-age population.* Details on the nonvoters are difficult to come by because those polled tend to claim they have voted even if they haven't. Follow-up checks and questions to correct this also indicate that about 10 percent more of the "liars" claim to have voted Democratic than Republican—about the only statistic in this grim picture that can give a Republican any cause to smile.

The nonvoters, like the independent voters, appear to divide into two groups. (This is not surprising, since the nonvoter and the independents share many of the same characteristics, including not voting.) At the lower end of the economic scale is the nonvoter making four thousand a year or less, most often from the South and with a good probability of being black. This southern nonvoter is joined by his or her northern counterpart: a white, under-thirty-five, making ten thousand a year or less, with at most an eleventh-grade education and living in a city in the mid-Atlantic states.

At the higher end of the economic scale, accounting for 21 percent of the nonvoters, is the white college graduate making thirteen thousand a year or over. If he is under thirty-five, he is more likely to be a nonvoter if he has graduated from college than if he is merely a high school graduate. (Yet college graduates wonder why hardworking high school graduates cheer when George Wallace talks about taking a "tire iron" to the "intelligentsee.") This type of nonvoter regards politics as another spectator sport to be watched on the tube. He understands the sport, he often knows more about what is going on than the voter; but he doesn't care which team wins. If he does vote, it will be more likely because he is against one team rather than for the other. The number of such nonvoters is growing, though their actions cannot be justified on the grounds that their votes couldn't have made a difference. In 1974 nine Senate races were decided by less than 5 percentage points. The New Hampshire race was declared a draw.

The nonvoter, while younger and slightly more liberal than the voter, is no revolutionary. His main wish is for the government to stop hassling him and give him more for his taxes. He may be slightly more likely than a voter to favor a third party which will "change all politicians," but only about 30 percent of the nonvoters seriously favor such a course. Legitimacy is important to the nonvoters at both ends of the economic scale. They believe in leaders, father figures, gurus. In their doubt, quietude, and occasional anger, they want a man from the past who represents the old values but who looks, moves, and speaks in modern style. "Liberal" and "conservative" mean nothing to them. Less than 1 percent list ideology as important in their lives.

The age we live in is often said to mark the end of ideology. It seems to me rather the end of the old ideologies: liberalism, capitalism, socialism,

*The 1974 election broke down as follows: Of those eligible to vote 44 percent didn't bother to register; of those who registered 25 percent didn't go to the polls; of those who finally voted 66 percent didn't think their vote made any difference.

communism. These aren't working and the voters have found this out, though the politicians and academicians keep telling them otherwise. But sometime a common thread will again be found to tie together a number of the world's paramount discontents. In the strands of this thread will be woven new answers and new ideologies. Meanwhile, we live with the vague suspicion that democrats solve problems by throwing words at them, liberals solve problems by throwing money at them, socialists solve problems by throwing bureaucrats at them, revolutionaries solve problems by throwing bullets at them, and conservatives don't see any problems. They all have failed.

With fewer people voting—and those that do increasingly turned off and discouraged—a candidate has great difficulty in choosing whom to target in the invisible primary. Who are his potential supporters? Is he reaching them? Will they vote in the actual primary? What will bring them to the polls?

Forecasting how people will vote in a primary is the most difficult part of the pollster's mix of science and art, and perhaps also the most important of their present frontiers. For primary victory, while seemingly not as influential as the general election, may actually be the key to the political process. Just as in a political debate, the votes on whether to table or to amend have more importance than the final tally for or against.

Three problems confront the pollster as he tries to determine where a candidate's support will lie in a primary. First, the sample is minuscule. Primaries are decided by about 30 percent of the registered party members, about 10 percent of the total electorate. Just finding that 10 percent is hard, let alone screening them for voters, nonvoters, and those in between. Second, one of the best measures of whether a person will vote is party loyalty. In a primary this factor is negated. Third, the primary vote is an against-vote and therefore very volatile, with effects hard to predict.

A fascinating instance of this third point was the vote for Senator Gene McCarthy against Lyndon Johnson in the 1968 New Hampshire presidential primary. McCarthy "won" with 47 percent of the vote, gaining almost all of New Hampshire's delegates. This was interpreted by everyone as a vote against the President, and particularly as a vote against the Vietnam War. But after the primary, the University of Michigan's research center polled those who had voted for McCarthy. They found that three out of five of those voting for McCarthy had voted against Johnson because they believed he wasn't fighting the Vietnam War hard enough. Gene McCarthy's antiwar vote was actually a hawk vote to expand the war. How was a poor pollster to predict that?

Faced with such problems, the pollster and the candidate are liable to just assume that those who vote in primaries are the same as those who vote in general elections, older white-collar whites with better than average incomes and education, suburbanites rather than central city dwellers: a salesperson, a professional, a skilled artisan. There is a gut feeling on the part of pollsters that those who vote in primaries may be more issue-oriented, more "programmatic," than those who vote in general elections. There is speculation that parts of the independent voter group may be more apt to vote in the primaries than in the general election. There are also indicators that the primary voter may be different in the South, where the one-party structure of many states made the primary more important, than in the middle Atlantic states and the Northeast. But here polling is pushing its own frontiers.

As President Ford moved to lead this complex, politically volatile muster of America, his first major act was to pick a Vice-President. Even before he became President, informed speculation—whatever that is—had begun ranking candidates. My notes show that on June 5, two months before Ford's ascension, I strained and plucked the first insubstantial straw off the wind. My notes read that "John Rhodes, Republican leader in the House and Ford's close friend, said at lunch: 'Rocky is looking better and better to the conservatives all the time.' Rocky was at a big fund raiser in Arizona a couple of months ago and drew fine. They have forgiven him. (Perhaps because they no longer feel him a threat.) Rhodes said it was quite possible that Goldwater would endorse Rocky. Does Dusty speak for Jerry?" (I get objectionably chummy in my notes.)

On August 7, the day before Ford learned Nixon would resign, the first trial elephant thundered out of the Republican thickets. Behind the beast's tail was observed the oval face of that wily GOP mahout, Melvin Laird, former secretary of defense and White House counselor; the man who had persuaded President Nixon to take Ford rather than Connally as Vice-President. "Ford and Rockefeller will form a winning combination for the Republican party," Laird said. A carefully articulated and rehearsed background chorus chanted amen.

Laird had taken care to prepare the ground with Nelson Rockefeller, the retired governor of New York. He reached Rockefeller at his home in Tarrytown, New York, as the future Vice-President was about to leave for Seal Harbor, Maine. Rockefeller thanked Laird but said, "I am genuinely in my own mind divided about the job." Rockefeller then tried to persuade Laird to take the post. Laird got the feeling that Rockefeller would accept the vice-presidency now, though he had turned it down before, and set about skillfully to prod the elephant in Nelson's direction. Rockefeller went up to Maine and had all his phone numbers changed.

"I really wasn't sure," he recalled afterward. "I wanted nothing to do with it [seeking the nomination]. . . . I was torn inside by what to do." Friends who spent time walking the beach in Maine with him during that period confirm that Rockefeller's memory is accurate.

"You had a paradox," said one guest at the house. "It was not an easy thing for him to do. Though it was always a sure thing that he would do it."

On one side was the ambition, the lure of power, the desire to get one more shot at the country's problems. On the other a feeling of completeness, of content, and a lack of desire, as another friend put it, "to stir up that poisonous brew of 1964 [the campaign against Goldwater] again."

As Rockefeller pondered in Maine, other names were put forward right and left: Elliot Richardson, Ronald Reagan, NATO ambassador and former Congressman Donald Rumsfeld, Barry Goldwater, and GOP National Committee Chairman George "Poppy" Bush. Following the well-known political axiom that you can't beat somebody with nobody, the right wing of the Republican party quickly coalesced around George Bush. Barry Goldwater, John Tower of Texas, conservative congressmen from North Carolina and Oklahoma, all pushed Bush. The left and left-center rallied around Rockefeller.

Mindful of the odor of chicanery surrounding Nixon's choice of Ford for Vice-President, President Ford now began a genuine search. All Republican senators and House members were asked to submit to the White House in sealed envelopes their candidates and thoughts. Other Republicans around the country were polled. Speculation grew. Ford remained sphinxlike.

This was a basic test of Ford. Not whether he was liberal or conservative, but how strong a man was he? Was he sure enough of himself to accept as his Vice-President a powerful man who might on occasion disagree with him? How did the man in the Grand Rapids double knits, who had worked his way through high school, college, and law school and represented a slightly right-of-center midwestern district, see the fabulous multimillionaire, four-time governor of New York?

In fact, Ford saw a very different Rockefeller from the image presented in the press. The press, with a few exceptions, was describing a Rockefeller of time past. We portrayed a tough, aggressive man with an energy quotient to rival St. Vitus and Sisyphus, an eye for the ladies surpassing even John F. Kennedy, a man who continually thrust himself forward to be number one. In the mid-fifties and sixties Rockefeller certainly was many of these things and took pride in so being. "Khrushchev told me I would beat Governor Harriman because I am tougher than Averell Harriman," he reported to friends proudly. But by 1975 that image of a driving, aggressive Rockefeller was importantly askew. He didn't even call people "fellah" anymore.

The change in Rockefeller, from the man who challenged Goldwater in 1964 to the retired governor who accepted the vice-presidency in 1974, is not political but personal. Men don't often change much for reasons of polity. They may get worn out by the use and pressure of power, become hard, drained, or closed. But the changes in politicians tend to be like those in the rest of us, set in motion by drives from our private rather than our public lives. Between 1964 and 1974 two such major changes had occurred in Nelson Rockefeller. He had grown old. He had become happy.

In 1964 Rockefeller was fifty-seven. When chosen as Vice-President, he was sixty-seven. Those who are in, or close to, the same time period know what this means. At fifty-seven, to a man of outsized energies and used to success, the world can still seem a devourable oyster—at least on good days.

At sixty-seven, only the insane are still unaware that man's reach exceeds his grasp.

"He's grown old."

"He's changed, you know, you can see that, he's older."

"It's hard to believe, but he is old now."

Three of those who have served him longest and most intimately use the same words when talking of Rockefeller today. Yet the myth of the legendary energy dies hard. John Osborn, the perceptive White House correspondent of the *New Republic* interviewing Rockefeller late in the afternoon of a strenuous day after he'd been in office a few months, recorded his surprise at observing that Rockefeller looked tired.

In addition to being older, Rockefeller had also become content in his personal life. There are two ways to look at Nelson Aldrich Rockefeller's 1963 courtship and marriage of Margaretta Fitler Murphy, then the wife of a virologist working for the Rockefeller Institute. One can believe that Nelson was so confident that he could have everything he wanted that he thought he could have both the presidency and another man's wife. Times were changing. Adlai Stevenson had been divorced. After all, God had not seen fit to lift the kingship from David over the little matter of Uriah the Hittite's untimely demise.

If Rockefeller believed life would flow serenely on while he divorced Mary Todhunter Clark, his wife of thirty-one years, and wed Happy Murphy, he was profoundly wrong. Gossip and bitter jokes mushroomed everywhere. Dr. Murphy sued. So many newsmen trekked to Philadelphia to dig into Happy Murphy's family background that the Philadelphia newspapers had to close their morgues to outsiders. Rockefeller lost the Republican California primary and therefore the presidential nomination to Barry Goldwater by .03 percent. Happy was visibly pregnant at the time. There can be no doubt that without his divorce he would have carried the state and gained the Republican nomination. His chances of beating Lyndon Johnson in 1964 were marginal, but he would have been well positioned in 1968 to regain the nomination and take on the Vietnam-battered Democrats.

The second way to look at Rockefeller's 1963 marriage is to view it as a carefully weighed personal commitment: a decision to place the happiness of the private man above the ambitions of the public figure. This, too, can be a form of arrogance. Men who have sweated up from the bottom of success's ladder have a tendency to castrate their private selves to prevent the inner man from ever threatening the grip of the public figure on the upper rungs. This is also known as commitment and is judged—or was until recently—to be a "good thing." Yet so is a sense of balance between private happiness and public ambition.

(A digression for a story: During the night of Eisenhower's first inauguration I was the news magazine pool man for following the newly minted President. Through some error on the part of the secret service, which I did nothing to correct, I ended up not in the pool area at the back of the District of Columbia Armory, but in the President's box in the third row. Those in the box who knew me, Cabot Lodge and Sherman Adams, seemed a bit surprised; but life was easier back then and they said nothing. Directly in front of me, two rows lower, stood the Vice-President and Mrs. Nixon, waving to the crowd. Their moment of triumph. Nixon waved and smiled. Mrs. Nixon waved and glowed.

(President Eisenhower entered the armory. The band, after a quick "Ruffles and Flourishes," broke into the National Anthem. Mrs. Nixon, along with the majority of the celebrants in the hall, didn't hear the music. Richard Nixon reached around behind his wife and grabbed her in that soft roll of flesh that comes down beneath the corset and pinched hard.

("Shut up. Turn around. It's the National Anthem," he hissed at his beloved in his hour of triumph. Nothing that he has done since, including some impressive triumphs in foreign affairs, has decreased my distrust of a man whose public posture so overbalanced his private person.)

Whether his marriage to Happy Murphy arose from arrogance or commitment, by that act Nelson Rockefeller decisively changed his life. The Republican crown and quite probably the presidency were denied him. He ran again for governor in 1966 and won. But having proved his political power in 1966, in 1968 he was a most reluctant candidate for the Republican nomination.

I watched him closely during that campaign as he tried to make up his mind whether to run. Ferdinand the Bull beneath his cork tree was a seething hive of activity compared to Rockefeller as the time for decision approached. He wanted to be home with his new wife and family, not out on the road. It was that simple. His private life was so full of satisfactions that the pull of public commitment had weakened. I don't mean to overdo this. His political juices still flowed: when shoved, he shoved back; and, of course, in the end he sort of ran. But he would no longer accept the eclipse of the private man behind the sun of public success.

"It seemed to me, Mr. Vice-President, watching you in 1968, that you were genuinely doubtful about running for President, of two minds?"

"It would be fair to say I was divided in my own mind then."

This older, contented man was the person President Ford was considering as his Vice-President. And if the press hadn't yet sensed the change in him, perhaps they also overlooked the fact that even in Rockefeller's younger days he had been more willing and able to play number two than is generally recognized. Rockefeller put in two years as number two in the Department of Health, Education, and Welfare under Oveta Culp Hobby without making a single public wave. When what he wanted to do for health care and welfare proved too liberal and expensive for the aged standpatters in the Eisenhower Cabinet, Nelson was quietly transferred to special assistant for security affairs. Again he was on the liberal, expensive side of the famous "massive retaliation debate." He advocated spending money to build flexible forces, a position President Kennedy was later to espouse and turn into government policy. When he lost this battle, he found himself eased out of power. He retired silently, as he had from the Truman Administration in 1945.

This is not to say that Rockefeller wouldn't still have preferred to be number one, the President and not the Vice-President, if the cards had fallen that way. But since he was dealt the vice-presidency, so be it. He had reached a point where he was no longer consumed by a single ambition. When Laird's phone call came, he was chairman of his Commission on Critical Choices, financed at $3.4 million—$1 million from himself and $1 million from his brother Laurance. Rockefeller had created this commission, as an aide put it, "to keep his options open."

"If you hadn't become Vice-President, would you have run for the presidency in 1976?"

He paused, took off his thick-rimmed glasses, then put them back on. "David Lawrence [founder of *U.S. News*] once told me that men don't make events, events make men. Now I don't quite believe that. It's more like a wave and a surfboard. You have to get the wave. But it's your own skill that keeps you balancing on the board and moving." I guessed that meant probably not; but maybe.

Now, in the third week of August 1974, as Ford made up his mind, two political events pushed the trend toward Rockefeller. First, the ancient rivalry between Greek and Turk, bloody and bitter since prehistory, exploded on the divided island of Cyprus. War in the Mediterranean threatened. The Greek Government fell, the Turks mobilized, NATO fragmented, our ambassador was murdered. Ford himself says publicly that international affairs is not his strong point. He likes to listen to experts, and Nelson Rockefeller is the acknowledged elected Republican foreign policy expert. The Cyprus crisis also meant that Henry Kissinger, long a Rockefeller partisan, was constantly in and out of the Oval Office.

The second event was domestic. The love affair between big labor and the Democratic party blew up publicly at a hearing of the Democratic Charter Commission. Labor charged the party with favoring the draft-dodger and shirker at the expense of the patriot and worker. Republicans had hoped for some time to break the solid labor-Democratic front. (The idea isn't that impossible: until the time of Franklin Roosevelt, parts of the labor vote had been Republican since the Civil War.) Rockefeller probably had better relations with labor than any other Republican. During the depression he had insisted that only union men be hired on the Rockefeller Center construction site. He had had labor support in four successful drives for governor. The labor-Democratic battle, like the war in Cyprus, occurred at the ideal moment to help Rockefeller's cause.

So, from the candidates submitted to him, President Ford chose the most powerful and controversial, Nelson Rockefeller, as Vice-President. The results were immediate and predictable. *Time* and *Newsweek* felt they were witnesses at the second coming. "Only rarely since the days of John Adams and Thomas Jefferson has a man with the stature of Nelson Rockefeller risen to the U.S. Vice-Presidency," said *Time,* with its accustomed editorial restraint.

"Nelson is not corrupt, he is corrupting. He doesn't take bribes, he offers them," said the *Village Voice,* with its accustomed editorial restraint.

One is reminded of 1930s music critics listening to a new Mahler symphony. They are totally divided over what's going on, but they are all reacting to a work of size.

Rockefeller's record brilliantly spotlights the advantage to Americans of selecting governors rather than senators as presidential candidates. The public personality of Nelson Rockefeller stands revealed to a degree senators and congressmen can easily avoid. The state university system, Attica, the Urban Renewal Agency, the Albany Mall, welfare reform, controversial drug laws, fall-out shelters, vetoing an antiabortion bill, his record as an administrator—all these are there for a citizen or the press to react to.

Like the press, the Congress reacted violently both ways. The public confirmation hearings were longer and harsher than anyone, including Rockefeller and his staff, had anticipated. The final votes, 90 to 7 in the Senate and 287 to 128 in the House, in no way reflect the hard questioning in the Senate Rules Committee or the bitter cross-examination in the House Judiciary Committee. For a time, while Congress was doing what it does best, taking a recess, and the House committee was leaking secret raw FBI reports on Rockefeller to the press, the nomination appeared in danger.

The explosive issue was a series of gifts Rockefeller had made to aides and members of his administration: $50,000 to Henry Kissinger, $100,000 to William Ronan, $86,000 to one Judson Morhouse, a former Republican state chairman of New York who had been convicted of bribery in the granting of liquor licenses and later pardoned by Rockefeller. Rockefeller insisted he had made the gifts to enable top talent to serve him and his New York administration and to reward individuals for their service to the nation. However, the gift to Morhouse was suspect because Morhouse had never named his accomplices. The $86,000 could have been a reward for silence. The hearings found that Rockefeller had never strayed over the bounds of legality; but one could see places where a powerful man, guided by expensive legal talent, had cantered along the fence.

From Rockefeller's point of view he was fortunate that the Senate, jealous of the publicity the House had gotten with its Watergate impeachment hearings, moved to question him first. Rockefeller had more rapport with the senators. They were men of power themselves, knew the rules of the game, and lacked the populist fervor of several members of the House Judiciary Committee. The Senate Democrats in effect set the ground rules for both Houses: Be thorough, damage Rockefeller enough so that they had ammunition to use if a Ford-Rockefeller ticket ran against a Democrat in 1976; but let the President choose his own man. The House was not so polite, but in essence followed the Senate's lead.

A great deal has been made in parts of Congress and the press that Ford and Rockefeller are the first two nonelected Vice-Presidents, that this "nonelection" somehow sullies their mandate to govern. This seems to me a misleading half-truth. No Vice-President since the early days of the Republic and the advent of the congressional caucus system has been chosen by the people. Vice-Presidents are chosen by the bosses and the President-elect, usually under intense pressures of time and when everyone is exhausted. George McGovern—dead tired; plagued by a divided staff; with his first choice, Mayor Kevin White of Boston, vetoed by a jealous Kennedy and a purist Massachusetts delegation—was racing against a 3 P.M. deadline on the afternoon he bombed with Thomas Eagleton. If Eisenhower or Kennedy had faced the prospect that Richard Nixon or Lyndon Johnson would have had to go through the same questioning as Rockefeller and Ford, they might well have picked other Vice-Presidents.

Nevertheless, the 25th Amendment worked; the representatives of the people investigated and passed two candidates for Vice-President. For Rockefeller the ordeal had been debilitating. As he picked up his bags in his Fifty-fourth Street office in New York City to leave for Washington and his swearing in, well-wishers congratulated him. "Big deal," said Nelson.

But Rockefeller's despondency was brief. Within a few weeks he was enjoying the vice-presidency. When Rockefeller traveled as Vice-President, he traveled in the style to which he was accustomed. Whereas the atmosphere about Vice-President Ford's planes is relaxed and easygoing, everything on a trip with Rockefeller seems slightly larger than life. One has the impression of myriads of people offstage, handling the lighting, whispering cues, or preparing position papers. Traveling to New York to deliver a political speech in July '75, he effortlessly makes the front page of the *Times* and the Washington *Post* as well as the evening news on all three networks. Even the President has trouble topping that.

At lunch, where he picked up a three-thousand-dollar tab for four hundred Republican leaders, he was surrounded by roughly forty reporters and TV crewmen as he walked toward the door after his speech. That evening he made it clear he didn't want anyone campaigning for him for Vice-President. "Whatever others may do there will be no effort on my part to put the slightest constraints on his [Ford's] complete freedom [to choose anyone for Vice-President]." The press played this straight, remarking puzzledly about Rockefeller's new humility. "Unusually deferential" was *The New York Times*'s phrase.

What they failed to realize was that Rockefeller had just read a lengthy brief by his lawyers on the new Campaign Financing Act. "This campaign spending act, it's got to be the greatest thing for lawyers," he said. By taking himself out of the race for Vice-President, a decision he would make formal in November, Rockefeller removed himself from many of the provisions and restraints of the Campaign Financing Act. He was thus in a far better position to help Ford and other Republicans, and incidentally himself, than if he were campaigning for Vice-President. At sixty-eight Nelson Rockefeller is still capable of fancy footwork.

The capacity crowd in the Waldorf ballroom gave Nelson an ovation. But like the statistical makeup of the Republican party, everyone in the audience looked old and a bit tired. They seemed conscious that the Republican tide was passing from New York. At the head table on the dais was Clay Maitland, chairman of the Young Republicans. He was thirty-two.

When President Ford appointed Rockefeller and Rockefeller went out on the banquet circuit, it became inevitable that there would be people on the right who would raise aloft the standard of Republican purity. They might not be willing to challenge Ford, but they would take dead aim at Nelson Rockefeller. Were he to move right of Attila the Hun—and in September on a southern swing to court George Wallace he wasn't far from there—he would still be unacceptable to the purists. In 1975 the chief gonfalonier of Republican purity was Ronald Reagan. "I was a Democrat, a New Deal Democrat, until 1962. I became a Republican not because the parties were alike; but precisely because there was a difference. . . . A political party cannot be all things to all people. It must represent certain fundamental beliefs which must not be compromised to political expediency simply to swell its numbers."

Hear the purple purity warble its woodnotes wild. Nader and Reagan, Wallace and McGovern: you can interchange chunks of what they say without violating the sense of their speeches. Those who appeal to the passions of the electorate's alienated extremes use many of the same code phrases. Not politics but certainty makes strange bedfellows.

Reagan's problem, as he swung down the highways and byways of the invisible primary, was whom to campaign against. To attack Ford marked him as a party splitter and spoilsport. Time after time he vehemently rejected the idea of himself as a third-party candidate: "Third parties usually end up electing those they were formed to keep out." But, as with Edward Kennedy's withdrawal statement, the press refused to take him at his word.

Following Ronald Reagan around in mid '75, one wondered continually: "What is this man doing?" Asked about whether Ford had the nomination sewed up, Reagan would talk about how "the future of the GOP would be better served with an open primary." Then two questions later he would say that he himself had no strategy to capture the nomination. "Nothing of that sort has ever come into my mind."

As for running against Rockefeller, how was he reasonably to do that? he would ask. A man runs in primaries for presidential delegates, not vice-presidential delegates. Would he run against Ford in just a couple of districts in a couple of states to show his strength? Would he run a separate slate of delegates pledged to Ford for President and himself for Vice-President? None of this made political sense.

Would he accept the vice-presidency if Ford offered it to him? he was asked. "Every day of my life I hope that doesn't happen." In politics that's certainly not a no; but it isn't a subtle way of saying "gimmie" either.

"I think Rockefeller is bored with the vice-presidential job," he told a few friends in June '75. Reagan's observation perhaps said more about himself and the vice-presidency than about Rockefeller. Consider further that Reagan turned down the certainty of the GOP nomination for senator to run for the seat now held by John Tunney—a seat the experts regard as up for grabs. "After being governor, he just couldn't see being in the Senate," said aide and close friend Mike Deaver. While the vice-presidency is a more prestigious job than senator, Reagan's refusal to make the Senate race is a good indication of how the ex-governor, at sixty-four, feels about the strains, hassles, and intrusions of political life.

As with Nelson Rockefeller, so with Ronald Reagan: Age is a vital factor in their future political actions. The vice-presidency has become newly important because Vice-Presidents nowadays often become their party's candidates for President. Before Richard Nixon and Hubert Humphrey, no Vice-President had become a presidential candidate (except through death of the President) since Martin Van Buren. But all that has changed. Before his forced retirement Spiro Agnew was considered the man to beat for the 1976 Republican nomination. Even Sargent Shriver is a serious—if remote—choice as Democratic candidate. In selecting a Vice-President, particularly a young, active Vice-President, a political party is also choosing a potential future presidential candidate.

Ronald Reagan is sixty-four. Did he want an active but boring job that will give him the opportunity to run for President when he was sixty-nine? Paradoxically, Rockefeller's age could have helped him remain on the ticket. The very fact that he will be seventy-two in 1980 and too old to run for President might have kept other ambitious middle-agers from rebelling. For whoever started the rebellion would probably have opened for someone else the vice-presidential prize, with its four years of exposure and head start in 1980.

"Scratch an actor and you find an actor," Broadway producer David Merrick once remarked in exasperation. In the invisible primary Reagan seemed to me to be playing a role inherited in large measure from what he calls "my previous occupation." This is not to put down acting; merely to remark that a man brings his former life with him into politics. Former labor leaders, lawyers, businessmen, professors, actors, politicians, doctors, generals, approach their political roles in differing ways. Ronald Reagan, ex-actor, approaches politics as a media performance, particularly a radio and TV performance. Ironically Reagan may be the new politics personified, the first post-Gutenberg politician, to use McLuhan's jargon.

Reagan's trips around the country, to a greater degree than the swings of other politicians, are media events, rather than political events. *Newsweek* refers to his trips as "frenetic, driving" and the Washington *Post* as "break-neck pace." Actually his trips seemed rather relaxed compared to those of Vice-President Ford, Scoop Jackson, or Mo Udall.

"I want to make the people in this country aware," says Reagan. "Aware" is the key. He sees himself as motivating people by speaking to them in groups and by appearing at press conferences and on television. Absent from

Reagan's trips are those continuous meetings with possible supporters and contributors that fill in the interstices of the average candidate's schedule. Reagan's typical day includes a morning press conference, a luncheon reception, a luncheon speech, a move to another location, an evening or afternoon meeting, another reception, another press conference, and an evening speech. There are days he does more; days he does less.

This is not slacking. It's lengthy and obviously tiring for a sixty-four-year-old man. But it's not the back-breaking pace of the committed candidate either. Missing are the two breakfasts, the local radio talk shows, the local TV panel shows, the street corner and shopping center rallies, the coffee fund raisers going on until late at night, the hotel room handshakes with political activists.

Reagan's staff usually manages to save him some free time each afternoon, two or three hours when he can read the newspapers or even nap. His day is usually ended by 11 P.M. In between the weeks on the road are weeks of rest at his ranch outside of Santa Barbara. During the entire month of August he had no speaking trips; "his vacation month," said his staff. His advance schedule for September 1975 showed most of his trips were nonpolitical, and again, they are only scheduled for every other week. On the road Reagan gets better press attention than any other swinger in the invisible primary except the President and Vice-President. But his whole operation lacks the single-minded, pulsating drive of a grab at the presidency.

Traveling, Reagan gets celebrity treatment, recognition in airports, hotel lobbies, streets. Off-duty policemen recruited by Reagan's skilled advance team protect his movements. How much of this positive response is for Reagan the film star and how much for Reagan the politician is hard to measure. He isn't treated quite the same way as other politicians. They get handshakes, wishes of support, requests to "wait a minute" and be photographed. But Reagan gets all these requests for autographs from everyone: food processors, cab drivers, stewardesses, mechanics, the wealthy at receptions. His progress is a personal illustration of the breakup of traditional party ties in today's America.

I have the feeling—it can be nothing more substantial than that—based on the quality of the crowd reception he receives, that Reagan is treated as a figure from the past as much as a present candidate. "There goes the famous actor who made governor" is the attitude toward him; at least as much as "there goes the actor-governor who may run for President." We Americans, rootless as we have always been, value age and legitimacy far more than we profess. Reagan has moved into the senior statesman category, receiving that type of treatment we give to those removed from the fray. How much of that aura will carry over now that he has become an active candidate for President is hard to measure.

Reagan's inner staff, most of whom have been with him some time and have a relaxed, if somewhat distant, relationship with him, were ambivalent about his running for the presidency. He is excellently staffed and advanced by a team of at least three or four people working out of the public relations firm of Deaver and Hannaford, a firm formed by former members of his staff when governor. But after eight years of public life (and one on the road) with their possible candidate, they, too, were divided about their role in '76. They miss their homes, their wives, their children. Mike Deaver, the general manager of Reagan's advance, was against Reagan running in 1968. He felt Reagan had little chance and would merely damage his credibility as governor by running. Did he think Reagan will run seriously this time? "Some days I think yes, some days I think no."

Deaver and the rest of the staff made little effort to stay behind, get names, keep contributor and volunteer lists. "We get about one thousand letters a week because of the radio programs," said Deaver as late as July 1975. "I suppose I should put them on tape. But we haven't done that yet." They didn't doubt the rightness of Reagan's cause or his strength. But they questioned whether running against Ford would be the best way for the conservative cause, for him, or for them.

Just by being on the road, by preaching his message of conservative Republicanism, or "constitutionalism" as Reagan prefers, Reagan was able to channel the Republican party more into his own image and close certain options to Ford. "I have advocated that Ford take an adversary position with the Congress," says Reagan. ". . . We can take steps to ease the suffering of some who will be hurt more than others. But if we turn from fighting inflation and adopt a program only to fight recession, we are on the road to disaster."

Again the restrictions of the campaign financing law came into play. On a week-long swing through the District of Columbia, New York, Pennsylvania, Indiana, and Texas, Reagan often used corporate or other private aircraft. This would have been illegal or subject to spending limitations if he had already been a declared candidate. His trips have been largely self-financed by his appearance fees or paid for out of the revenues of his radio program. As a candidate he would have been subject to the fifty thousand dollars on such self-financing.

To spread the word, Reagan had what reporters following him call "the Speech." When asked why he didn't change "the Speech," he answered that when you have something that's good and people respond to, why change it? Actually "the Speech" was three separate speeches, and he could take parts of each one and intermingle it with the others, depending on his audience. He usually did this the day of the speech, writing the key words to various parts of the comingled speeches in capitals on 5 by 8 cards and then proceeding extemporaneously.

The speech contained the famous one-liners: "I think Adam and Eve must have been Russians. They had no roof over their heads, only a fig leaf to wear, and nothing but an apple to eat, and thought they were in paradise." . . . "We will have a society in which everything that isn't compulsory will be prohibited." . . . "Recently the government spent $249,000 to study the

'Demography of Happiness.' They found that young people are happier than old people, people who earn more are happier than people who earn less, and that well people are happier than sick people—$249,000 to find out it's better to be young, rich, and healthy than old, poor, and sick."

In between the one-liners and the personal stories were masses of statistics. The governor thinks in statistical terms, polls, economic indices, numbers of experts hired, of welfare cases reduced, of dollars saved, recommendations made, laws passed, blacks appointed, tax dollars refunded, and taxes reduced.

The statistics, the one-liners, the personal stories, reveal both Reagan's strengths and limitations as a politician. He can take a mass of facts or an issue and explain them to people in simple, moving terms. He can test his own feelings about an issue, make up his mind, and move. But he himself is unhappy around complex ideas, among those shades of gray in which so many of our current problems—it seems to me—present themselves. No Hamlet he. The native hue of his resolution is not faintly disturbed by any pale cast of thought. He is not anti-intellectual in the sense that George Wallace is, full of rage against the intellectual establishment. It is impossible to think of Reagan deliberately mispronouncing "intelligentsia," as George Wallace does, to enrage an audience; or to tell a story about hitting people with a tire iron. But Reagan is *non*intellectual.

One should hastily add that the records of the Kennedy Administration show that many of the proclaimed "intellectuals" were pretty nonintellectual also. As this chapter shows, I, too, am fascinated by statistics as indices of change. Still, after what Defense Secretary Robert McNamara did to us in Vietnam with statistics, a wise man wants to know something more about problems than numbers.*

How came Ronald Reagan, actor, New Deal Democrat, college strike organizer, union leader, to the bastions of the right? "He was very quiet and could go on for hours all by himself playing," says his brother Neil, recalling the young Ronald growing up poor in Tampico, Illinois, Chicago, and finally Dixon, Iowa. Like that of so many of the other presidential candidates and past Presidents, the Reagan family was dominated by the mother. "Ask Reagan about his father and he starts talking about his mother," a friend said. Working his way up slowly—"My father never made more than fifty dollars a week in his whole life," says Reagan—the elder Reagan finally owned a shoe store in Dixon, a small town on the Iowa border. Wiped out by the depression, Reagan's father became, because of his strong Democratic party connections, a relief distributor for the WPA. Reagan, like Jerry Ford,

---

*I often wonder if those on the Kennedy National Security Council who authorized the Bay of Pigs Cuban invasion realized that Thomas Jefferson had thought of invading Cuba. Jefferson was undeniably a great man, but his reasons for wanting to invade Cuba sound pretty silly now. President Buchanan was in favor of invading Cuba also. His reasons sound even sillier. They both held back.

played football and worked his way through college, Eureka College outside of Peoria, Illinois. He was a lifeguard. He recalls he saved seventy-seven people from drowning—that passion for statistics again.

At college, Reagan led a strike to restore some of the courses being cut back because of the depression. Reagan describes the strike as "orderly." The students kept up with their work; they just didn't attend classes. The college gave in and the cut courses were restored. College also gave Reagan an interest in radio and his first success as an actor. In a play contest at Northwestern he drew praise for his performance as a shepherd strangled to death in Edna St. Vincent Millay's *Aria da Capo*.

Out of college Reagan went to work as a sports announcer for station WOC, "The World of Chiropractic," at Des Moines, Iowa. He started at ten dollars a game, finally worked up to seventy-five a week as the station grew and "Dutch" Reagan became known. That was a mammoth salary for depression-torn Iowa. In 1937 Ronald Reagan got one of those breaks that supposedly only occur in Horatio Alger stories or press agent legends. In California to broadcast spring training with the Chicago Cubs, he got friends to arrange a screen test at Warner Brothers. The test was so successful that he was signed to a contract. He even got to keep his own name.

Actors who go into politics, whether they be John Wayne, Jane Fonda, or Ronald Reagan, find their films judged by their politics. Reagan made some good films and some bad films, much like any other star. There is, for example, *King's Row*, in which Reagan, a small-town playboy, comes out of anesthetic to discover both his legs have been cut off at the pockets by a sadistic doctor whose daughter Reagan has been screwing. "Where's the rest of me?" he asks, in what he and many critics feel was his best moment on film. There was also *Bedtime for Bonzo*, in which he was upstaged by a chimp. The war hit right after *King's Row*, when Reagan might have begun to break into the superstar class. By the time he got out of the service (he made training films during the war) the public was looking for new faces and he himself was being drawn into politics.

When did the New Deal Democrat become a Republican? The answer is hard to find. When asked, Reagan cites three factors. First, there was his fight against Communists inside the Hollywood unions in the late forties and early fifties. He felt then that most of his liberal friends were blind to the danger of Red infiltration and hypocritical in their judgments. Second, his experience of socialism as it applied to the British film industry when he was making *The Hasty Heart* in England in 1949. Finally, his exposure to American problems when he was on the lecture circuit for General Electric as host of the General Electric Theater in the late fifties.

But these answers seem to skirt the core of his change. After World War II, Reagan joined a number of slightly left unions and organizations and immediately began to try to change them. That made him an activist—at that time a Democratic political activist. He campaigned for Helen Gahagan Douglas against Richard Nixon in 1950. Previously, in 1948, he had been one of ten leading Democrats who, along with Congressman James Roosevelt, had signed a telegram to NATO Commander in Chief General Dwight Eisenhower, urging Eisenhower to run for President as a Democrat. In 1952 he campaigned as a Democrat for Republican Congressman Alphonzo Bell of Los Angeles, though many of Bell's supporters urged him to drop Reagan as too "radical." By the time General Electric sent him around the country in 1957 they must have known that even though Reagan was still registered as a Democrat (he didn't change to Republican until 1962), his views were not too different from those of company management.

Perhaps Reagan himself, who is not a particularly introspective man, is not certain when or why he changed. He just woke up one time, like Paul on the road to Damascus, a convert. Then, like so many converts, he became the true believer, more Catholic than the Pope, ever ready to defend the doctrine of pure Republicanism and free enterprise.

Ronald Reagan became governor of California in 1966, winning by close to a million votes. As he had been in 1937, when he landed his first screen part, he was lucky. The opposition Democrats were divided over Lyndon Johnson and the Vietnam War. Governor Pat Brown, who had beaten national political figures William Knowland and Richard Nixon for governor, couldn't believe that the ex-actor would give him any trouble. Reagan was also skillful. He and his staff, paced by Spencer-Roberts, another of the new PR firms that specialize in politics, skillfully played on California's historic distrust of politicians and on the media appeal of Ronald Reagan—"citizen-politician." The businessmen who financed Reagan's bid, led by Holmes Tuttle, the largest used-car dealer in the country, were well organized and generous. Reagan used television brilliantly, attacking Governor Brown on subjects where the polls showed him weakest, law and order, campus militancy.

In his perceptive and evenhanded book on Reagan's politics and governorship, *Ronnie and Jesse*, reporter Lou Cannon succinctly states the great paradox of Ronald Reagan the politician: "The ex-actor from Illinois had mastered the political vocation because he refused to think of himself in political terms."

Reagan's strength is both that simple and that unusual. Reagan will talk about how he learned politics in negotiating for the unions with the studios. "It's settled in the men's room. After about three days of negotiating you get the feeling things are ready to move. I'd get up, or one of them would get up, and we'd find ourselves standing beside each other in the men's room and one of us would say, 'Now, what's really important to you guys?' " But he sees himself as an amateur, almost a prophet, just passing through the political world to persuade people to do what is right.

This nonpolitical view of himself, which is psychologically quite genuine, enables him to accomplish feats in politics that, in a politician, would cause gasps of disbelief. They cause gasps of rage in his enemies. "He is a good guy ingenue," says Democratic Congressman John Burton, youngest of the

Burton brothers who control California Democratic politics. "He has a touch of paranoia and lives in make-believe. He goes around supported by more bodyguards than Carter has pills. He's not so tough. Look at the people he picks on, the aged, the blind, the young, those who can't fight back." Burton was speaking before the two California assassination attempts.

Reagan was astute enough politically, as governor, both to pledge himself "to cut, squeeze, and trim" and to put through a tax increase of close to $1 billion; then successfully to take credit for both. What's more, through skillful use of television he managed to leave the Democrats with the blame for raising the income taxes, while he got the credit for lowering property taxes. All this while appearing as a citizen in politics rather than a politician. No wonder his opponents climb the walls.

I'm baffled as to how he achieves this political-yet-nonpolitical stance. I find several times in the notes I wrote as I tromped after him through five states, "He doesn't look like a politician." I know that statements of effect on me don't help the reader much. What they need are the facts that produced the effect. But I couldn't pin down the facts. Reagan's ties are more square and more precisely knotted; his clothes are more his own than the Main Street double-breasted or casual worn by the average candidate. His hair is more in place; his gait more measured. But that just scratches the surface; there is something deeper.

Reagan does not seem to be out after people's votes. Out after their adulation, yes, their respect, yes; but their votes, no. He wants to move people and change their ideas. Before the TV camera or on the rostrum he puts out to deliver the conservative message with personality, wit, and eloquence. But in the political receiving line or with local politicians he is tense and rather reserved. His hands wiggle, clench and unclench, his smile is more contrived than natural. What he likes about campaigning are the public appearances rather than the private contact. This makes him appear closer to the touring celebrity than the campaigning politician.

Except in small groups where he feels at home, Reagan remains a performer before an audience. He doesn't relax and make that effort to seem one of the boys that is common coin among politicians. We are back with Cannon's insight that Reagan "refuses to think of himself in political terms." This includes thinking of himself as a campaigning politician even when he may be on the presidential campaign trail. However, this doesn't prevent him from playing the game of politics with great skill. In fact it aids him; just as Republicans can make concessions to Communists and Democrats can grind labor unions. Everyone knows they wouldn't do such a thing.

Like Mondale or Muskie, Reagan is a man who needs time by himself to survive as a person. His passion for getting home by six when he was governor caused both derisive comment and criticism. On the road his average day contains several hours when he can be by himself. This shows a wise pacing of his energies, but would be a genuine handicap in the final drive in the invisible primary.

Candidates deeply committed to their campaign love to talk politics. Jackson, Udall, Ford, even Rockefeller, come alive as they talk that mix of programs and people whose proper proportions lead to the governance of America. They'll talk about their homes and families also. But missing are those fond details, recollections of joy, a lift of voice, that indicate where a person gets his or her major returns from life. This vocal surge of excitement the candidates show when talking politics. Not Ronald Reagan. He comes alive when he talks about building his home in the mountains himself. Or tracking down rustlers: in this case rustling field mice that had made nests in the walls of his new house. He describes with laughter trying to keep his wife's attention occupied elsewhere while he removed a nest of field mice from their bedroom closet.

Some feel that this love of home and wife is a put-on, part of the role he consciously plays, a cloud of cutsie-pooh cuttlefish ink behind which he swims his predetermined political course. While actors tend to act out everything, if his feeling of family peace is mostly fake, I'm fooled. He seems far more to me like a retired man who is having a good time relaxing than an active politician. He is keeping his hand in, to be sure; he touches bases with old friends. When the polls finally seemed to show he had an excellent chance of winning, he was persuaded to move. But all along he conveyed the impression of enjoying himself too much to be eager to get back in the rat race. Indeed, after the announcement of his candidacy, he retired to his ranch for two weeks.

Testing Ronald Reagan's performance on the six tracks on which one runs in the invisible primary, we find that Ronald Reagan has track one, psychological commitment, firmly in hand. Despite his formal candidacy, he is suspicious about running, understands both the pressures on himself and what it will mean to split the Republican party or create a third party.

On the staff track, Reagan doesn't have a political staff. He has a few political operatives and old friends around him, but they lack the cohesion and organization of a true staff. Most of the committee urging him to run and later planning his campaign had other jobs, like Senator Paul Laxalt. Financing wasn't started until August 1975. Reagan has a constituency, the conservative Republicans, but he has not been tapping that constituency for staff, funds, or volunteer energy. He probably has another constituency in the blue-collar workers who feel alienated but distrust the violence and racist rhetoric of George Wallace. But he appears to lack plans to mobilize this group.

Strategy? He has no long-range political strategy as to which primaries to enter, where to look for funds, what issues to use to broaden the base of his support. He was going to enter the early primaries, then see what came next.

Funds? He'd started late and his performance was about average. The track on which Reagan spurts is media. He is a colorful institution. The press, in its desire to be fair to right and left, grants him a great deal of coverage. He exploits this media opportunity, not just with skill but with brilliance. He is a masterly TV candidate. By 1980, if we have direct-mail registration, a national primary, and other "reforms" now being hawked in the name of liberalism, to do well on TV may be enough to gain the nomination. Today a candidate has to do more. Reagan does not seem to have started early enough, or to be committed enough, to beat out Ford. Had he run harder in the invisible primary, he might have achieved the starring roll. If he gains that stardom subsequently, during the state primaries or at convention itself, he will have performed a minor political miracle. And I will be the first to admit my surprise.

In politics, as in warfare, the best defense is a strong offense. On becoming President, Ford said publicly in August 1974 that he didn't think he would ever run on his own for a full term. Two weeks later President Ford was saying through his press secretary, Ron Nessen, that he "probably" would run for a full term in 1976. In November, on his one-hundredth day in office, President Ford finally made it certain, saying he "definitely" would run for President in 1976.

No wild celebrants raced through the streets of America cheering the news that Ford's helmet was in the ring. With the pardoning of President Nixon and the decline in the economy, the President's popularity had slumped badly. In August 1974, 71 percent of the American public had thought Ford was doing a good job. Three months later only 43 percent approved his conduct in office, 39 percent disapproved, and 18 percent were undecided. From the right and the left of the Republican party, particularly from the right, came a chorus of criticism. "Mr. Ford," said Congressman Robert E. Bauman, a middle-aged shellback from rural Maryland and founder of the Young Americans for Freedom, ". . . has frittered away potential national support by adopting policies of amnesty for draft-dodgers and deserters, the biggest budget deficit in peacetime history, relentless pushing of détente, and a succession of presidential appointments culminating in the elevation to the high office of Vice-President of the single most unacceptable nominee one might contemplate—Nelson Rockefeller."

Having announced he was going to run, Ford didn't immediately do anything else. He seemed to be reasoning from his experience as a Grand Rapids congressman, when all he had to do was announce he was going to run again, visit some with the home folks; and the Republican organization would reelect him.

Asked about a campaign organization, the President said he thought he would run his campaign through the Republican National Committee. He wanted, he said, to avoid anything that looked like Nixon's private army, the Committee to Reelect the President (CREEP), whose arrogant excess had led to Watergate. He seemed oblivious to the fact that in any intraparty challenge to himself, the Republican National Committee was going to have to stay neutral, at least officially. And, further, the Campaign Financing Act had made it impossible for either national committee to run anyone's invisible primary campaign.

While Ford sat, his popularity dropped, and Ronald Reagan crisscrossed the land, gaining converts to his gospel of purity. By March 1975 only 37 percent of the voters thought Ford was doing a good job as President. Fifty-five percent thought he didn't understand foreign affairs, and 86 percent thought he couldn't manage the economy. The Republican congressional dinner, a major annual fund-raising event, which this year featured President Ford, raised less money than the year before at the height of Watergate. Ronald Reagan climbed to within 8 points of Ford as the Republicans' first choice: Ford preferred by 31 percent, Reagan by 23 percent, others or not sure, 45 percent.

Still, the ability of any challenger to wrest his party's nomination from an incumbent President remains highly doubtful. President Truman stepped aside in 1952, after his surprise defeat by Senator Estes Kefauver in the New Hampshire presidential primary. In 1968 Lyndon Johnson stepped down in part because of Gene McCarthy's strong showing against him in the same state in 1968. (Incidentally, neither President had gone into New Hampshire to campaign.) Yet both these Presidents retained the political strength to gain the nomination for their chosen successors: Adlai Stevenson in 1952, Hubert H. Humphrey in 1968.

I believe this same strength would have given both men the power to grasp the nomination for themselves. And that unless he made a series of horrendous blunders Ford had such power. Even Calvin Coolidge, hardly the hottest political property in history, made it into the White House on his own. He entered seventeen primaries and lost only two: South Dakota and Wisconsin, the Wisconsin loss being to Senator Robert "Fighting Bob" La Follette, the state's pride and native son. Ford may have problems, but he is no Coolidge and he has the power of the modern presidency at his right hand and the TV cameras at his left.

What made Ford change his mind and decide to run? His friends give two sets of answers. From those that know him least well, though they may claim to be insiders, comes "Jerry's a team player."

"He knows what would happen if he dropped out," said a White House staffer. "He doesn't want the party to fly apart, I guess," said a member of Congress.

Those closer to the President put more emphasis on Ford's ambition. Not just that "he enjoys being President," as Ron Nessen, his press secretary, stressed; but a harder, tougher attitude. "He wants to prove he can do it." Under his easygoing good humor, "good old Jerry" is also a man of pride and ambition. The football captain, the man who worked his way through law school, became minority leader in the House, is competing again. All those jokes about the only reason he was doing such a good job was because they'd taken the chewing gum off *Air Force One*. These got to him. If he could get himself elected President of the United States against long odds in an overwhelmingly Democratic country, that would show them. So President Ford decided to run.

In May 1975 the Cambodian Communists got Ford's campaign off the ground. They seized the American freighter *Mayagüez* in international waters. Ford sent in the marines to rescue the crew. The marines botched the job badly, but the Cambodians let the crew go anyway and Ford's popularity took an 11 point upward jump to 51 percent approval of his performance as President. This was the second highest monthly jump ever recorded by the Gallup poll, though the climb seemed more to measure the volatility of the electorate than the ability of the President. More important for Ford, he pulled far ahead of Ronald Reagan as his party's choice: 40 percent to 17 percent. Even among Republicans classifying themselves as conservatives, Ford led Reagan better than two to one.

At the same time, the President and his advisers were discovering the Campaign Financing Law. There was no possible way legally to run their campaign through the Republican National Committee. One of the law's major provisions required that each candidate have a separate committee which would collect all funds, disperse all funds, and keep public records. Ford, like any other candidate, had to create such a committee as soon as he had spent or collected one thousand dollars. The staff soon realized that the fact of his being President made it more difficult for Ford to comply with the new law than for other candidates. When Jackson or Reagan or Udall traveled, they bought themselves and an aide a plane ticket. When President Ford campaigned, the secret service and the code room personnel and the military aides went with him. Who paid for them? The taxpayers or the Campaign Committee?

What happened if the President went on a purely nonpolitical trip to give a speech at West Point, or dedicate a dam, or meet with the governors, and was asked political questions by the reporters covering the trip? Did that make a fraction of the trip a campaign trip? And if the President went to a GOP rally to raise money for the local Republican party, but not for himself, who paid for that trip—the GOP National Committee or the Ford Committee? "Compliance with this law is more difficult for the President than for any other candidate," said White House aide Richard Cheney.

Ford's political advisers, Donald Rumsfeld and Richard Cheney, talked the matter over with the President. Rockefeller's staff studied the law and the Vice-President waded in with advice. All agreed that Ford had to create his own separate committee, just like other candidates. Since any challenge to Ford would most likely come from the Republican right, the manager of his campaign should have the type of conservative credentials that could head off or blunt such a challenge. Not surprisingly, everyone's first choice for this job was the old elephant driver himself, mahout Melvin Laird.

Laird said no thanks—hard. He insisted he had to stay with *Reader's Digest,* enjoy private life, and make money. Thus Ford found what the other candidates already had run up against: With money tight it was hard to find people. Before, big names could take leave from their corporations while holding on to their stock options and deferred payments. That was now illegal. And with a $10 million overall spending limitation there was no money to throw around on fancy salaries.

The next choice was Dean Burch, a conservative lawyer from Arizona. Burch had been one of Nixon's lawyers during the final days of impeachment, at one point branding the House Judiciary Committee as "a black spot on jurisprudence." He had also managed the Republican National Committee during the unsuccessful presidential campaign of his friend Barry Goldwater. Both these positions gave him impeccable conservative credentials. Burch didn't want the job either, but agreed to head up an interim committee to manage the nomination, file the necessary papers to make the campaign legal, and search for a genuine campaign manager.

Dean Burch called his committee together just once. Several of its members learned they were on it when they read their names in the newspapers. It was that kind of committee. At its only meeting in Burch's office, all present agreed that Ford needed a campaign committee quick and that they didn't want to head such a committee. They also agreed they needed a lawyer right away. The first week in June, President Ford, Dean Burch, and Donald Rumsfeld got together in the President's Oval Office and went over a list of names on a yellow legal-size pad. The choice of that meeting for campaign manager was Howard Hollis "Bo" Callaway. Callaway is a genial, outgoing Southerner with a conservative record as a congressman who had run unsuccessfully as Republican candidate for governor of Georgia. He was then secretary of the army, where he had done a surprisingly good job—surprising because he is generally regarded as a genial lightweight—in getting both the army and the public to accept the volunteer army. Callaway had close ties to Republican conservatives and, importantly, was rich enough to pay his own way as campaign manager.

Burch sounded out Callaway, who said, "yes." On Friday, June 13, Callaway slipped into the Oval Office for a brief talk with President Ford. They shook hands on the job. Dean Burch let out a sigh of relief and found office space for the Ford Committee on the floor beneath his own offices: six small rooms with the door always open (compared to the six floors and heavy security that Nixon's CREEP had boasted). Ford and Callaway talked over campaign strategy the next day on the flight of *Air Force One* to Fort Benning, Georgia, for an infantry demonstration. On the following Wednesday the appointment became official. President Ford now had the nucleus of a campaign organization: Bo Callaway making $42,500 and two staffers making $25,000 and $8,400.

"The first thing this headquarters needs now is a good lawyer," said Bo Callaway, sounding the universal theme of both Democrats and Republicans as they faced not just the voters but the new clean money act.

Deliberately, to emphasize the difference between CREEP in '72 and the Ford Committee in '76, Callaway was in shirt sleeves when he greeted the press at a coffee and pastry opening for Ford's small suite of offices. He stressed that the pictures of Ford on the walls of the six sparsely furnished rooms had been bought from the government. That's how picayune honest politics had become four years after Watergate. Callaway also caused a press furor by stressing that "the Rockefeller and Ford campaigns are not one and the same. . . . I have no direct responsibility for the nomination of Nelson Rockefeller. . . . Ford and Rockefeller are not a team for reelection. . . . [I am asking] will you vote for Ford for President, period."

Some interpreted this as a deliberate strategy to free Rockefeller, as a noncampaigner, from the rigors of the Campaign Financing Law. "I'm not running for anything. Who ever heard of a man running for Vice-President?" said Rockefeller. But in his first few weeks as campaign manager, Callaway pushed Rockefeller a little too far out on the plank, and Rockefeller supporters began to shove back. The Vice-President and Callaway had a reconciliation breakfast in which Callaway claimed he'd been misquoted and Rockefeller reiterated he wasn't running for anything. In the light of subsequent events, Callaway's efforts to dissociate the Ford and Rockefeller campaigns now appears to have been something of an omen.

The question among Republican politicians was how truly separate from the White House Bo Callaway's Ford Committee would be. Even before the committee started, Rumsfeld, Cheney (his deputy), and Burch had been making calls around the country soliciting and sometimes pressuring local Republican leaders to support Ford. Callaway was seen as being more politically astute and relaxed than the White House staff. Left to himself, he would probably ease off the pressure and make more converts in the end. But would he be allowed this much freedom? White House aides stressed that Callaway was in effect another staff member, that he would report to the President through Rumsfeld. And Rumsfeld was hard-nosed about his politics, particularly about heading off Ronald Reagan at the pass.

As presidential politics picked up in September 1975, Gerald Ford had drawn away from the other Republican hopefuls on all six tracks of the invisible primary. Psychologically he was happy in his job, healthily aggressive and self-assured. His always powerful competitive instinct was up and there was nothing tentative about his campaign.

With his Campaign Committee he had broadened the base of his staff, bringing in conservatives there to work with the more liberal members of the White House staff: Rumsfeld, Cheney, Hartmann, and Seidman. His strategy was simply the age-old presidential ploy of being a successful President and letting others do most of the campaigning. To this Ford was adding campaign swings of his own to meet people, just as he had done as a congressman. The money had started to come in. His constituency was the center and slightly right-of-center professionals and amateurs in the

Republican party. These the Campaign Committee were starting to mobilize. He was dominating the media, particularly television, effortlessly.

On Friday, October 15, 1948, in Grace Episcopal Church in downtown Grand Rapids, Jerry and Betty Ford were married. Ford's mother noted with horror that though Jerry had changed into his best suit, a gray pinstripe, he was still wearing the dusty brown shoes in which he'd been campaigning that morning. Friday night and Saturday morning the newlyweds had to themselves. Saturday afternoon Jerry took Betty to a Michigan football game. (For those who like auguries, Michigan defeated Northwestern 28–0.) Saturday night they attended a Republican reception in Owosso, Michigan. On Sunday Ford was back in his district campaigning. Gerald Ford has been running like that ever since. Only now national television was picking him up as he did so, making him, for better or worse, a household figure.

CHAPTER 7

Reports, Pollsters, and Gunslingers

The late Robert Kennedy believed that two minutes on one of the evening network TV shows advanced his presidential hopes more than a front-page story in every newspaper in the land. In the invisible primary every candidate pants for TV news time like a lost Foreign Legionnaire for an oasis. Candidates don't mind newspaper publicity, but when they talk privately about the media, they talk television almost exclusively.

"It's terribly frustrating," said Senator Walter Mondale, during his shot at a candidacy, "to labor over a bill, introduce it, and then see Kennedy or Jackson discussing it on the evening TV news."

"Our strategy," said Robert Keefe, Jackson's campaign chief, "is to campaign from the Senate, maximize TV exposure."

"One of Bayh's great strengths is he is known favorably to so many TV newsmen," explained one of Senator Birch Bayh's staff.

"TV is screwing us, *screwing us,* because Mo isn't a senator," said Terry Bracy, codirector of Morris Udall's campaign.

Getting nominated means winning primaries. Winning primaries means contacting people. In the invisible primary a candidate positions himself to contact the maximum possible number of people with his message. Since the decline of the party, the party machinery is no longer adequate for this task, though it's still some help. The best present method of reaching voters and boosting one's standing in the polls is through television. For a candidate the most effective television, in terms of cost and impact, is not paid advertisements or paid programs, but free mention on TV news or talk shows.

How does an unknown candidate get on TV news? When asked this question, television reporters and news executives have an unfortunate tendency to sound like executives of General Motors or Exxon—neither good guys nor bad guys, merely identifying their own welfare with that of the country. "Television covers the news. You don't want to restrict that." That's not a satisfactory answer, but one must grant members of the press cause for partial paranoia, after the verbal bludgeonings, wiretaps, and economic pressure visited on them by the Nixon administration. (Not that previous presidencies were simon-pure. The first time I was warned by friends that an illegal wiretap had been placed on my home phone was during the Truman administration.)

To decide which candidate should get time on the air or space in a newspaper means deciding which candidate is making "news." And that brings up one of the most difficult, dirty, unanswerable questions any thoughtful news man or woman ever faces: "What is news?" News is, says Webster, "a report of a recent event." Possibly, but the last time you caught a cold did you see it on CBS? Webster's second definition lets the cat out of the bag: "any matter regarded as interesting to newspaper readers or news broadcast audiences."

News is what sells newspapers or draws audiences. And the judgment of what does that—and what audience one wants to reach—is made by reporters and editors. While hopefully this judgment is based on long experience tempered by thought, it still is highly subjective. "News is what an editor puts in a newspaper or out over the air." No more sophisticated definition will hold up under argument.

In 1948, before the Korean War, there were only twelve reporters assigned to the Pentagon beat, as against some two-hundred-plus credited to the State Department. Since America was never going to fight a war again, what the military did was not "news." Science reporting is even newer. As late as the fifties, only a few newspapers and no TV networks had specially trained people working full-time on this beat. The great Russian wheat sale scandals were uncovered by a small local paper because none of the major news organizations thought agriculture "news." Serious sociological reporting is just beginning in the press. Such examples of the subjective, cultural, and historical nature of news are legion.

If the nature of news is in part subjective, how does a reporter, editor, or executive decide which candidate is producing news?*

"I am always asking my people," says Walter Cronkite, "why do we have this candidate or that candidate on and not someone else? Are we looking in the right places?"

David Broder, the uncrowned "dean" of political reporters, writes in *Newsweek:*

> There's nothing inherent in the work of the Senate that qualifies a member for the Presidency, and much that may inhibit him. Yet the accessibility of senators to television cameras and the fixation of the press on that chamber has helped keep any state or local government officials from being nominated by a major party for President since 1952. . . . unless we of the press open our eyes to the leadership being exerted in local and state government today, we may blind voters. . . .

William Small, the aggressive network boss of CBS news, sees the Washington focus of television as being around for some time to come. Small, who looks like the member of a small freewheeling law firm that handles teamster negotiations, points out that since the TV outlets are in Washington and the able reporters are in Washington, the news is going to come out of Washington. If this worries him, he doesn't show it.

How would a candidate outside of Washington get on the air? Small says that there are several ways: Perhaps the candidate might have an extraordinary thesis that CBS would hear about, or he might get shot, or he might attack someone or be attacked, or he might devise "some cockamamey feature" that gets him on the news, or, like Ronald Reagan, he might already be a media personality with news clout.

I asked Martin Agronsky, who used to run *Face the Nation* when Small was Washington Bureau chief of CBS, how a candidate got on that program.

"That's a ridiculous question, Hadley," he replied. "Candidates get on television just like they get into your newspaper [the New York *Herald Tribune*], by making news."

"Yes, but what we decide to cover also becomes news." Silence. "Could you just describe the process?"

"I'd be walking down the corridors of Congress and see my sources," Agronsky began. He then went on to describe how he and Small would have a conference, decide who would be on *Face the Nation,* and that was that.

---

*An interesting, gossipy, and admittedly biased (pro-George McGovern) view of how the press makes up its mind on who is where in the presidential race can be found in the opening chapters of Timothy Crouse's *The Boys on the Bus*.

Off the record, others connected with *Face the Nation* describe a somewhat different process. There are two news divisions in CBS: Public Affairs and News. As in most organizations, the two divisions sometimes fight. *Face the Nation* used to be under Public Affairs. Then William Small got the program placed under himself in News in return for giving up Space (that is, the subject of space). This was considered a major corporate triumph on Small's part, as *Face the Nation* was strong while Space was on the way out. As a result of the victory, *Face the Nation* had to stay close to the news so it couldn't be grabbed back by Public Affairs. Every Monday morning those connected with the show measured the number of column inches in *The New York Times* and the Washington *Post* relating to what was said on their show. If they got more inches than their NBC rival *Meet the Press*, jubilation. If not, despair. They knew the New York management was reading the two papers in New York on Monday and comparing.

To make news in the Monday papers, *Face the Nation* is forced to stay close to events. It is also at the mercy of the unscrupulous leaker and his press secretary. "Put my candidate, Van Lingo Wombatt, on *Face* and he'll name six Communist governors and denounce the CIA for murdering Kennedy." During the week, pressure on the program builds, after its number one and two choices have said no. Lacking news experience themselves, those connected with the show search through *The New York Times* and Washington *Post* for story ideas.

"It's entirely a reactive thing," said one of the show's producers. "We are looking for those mentions we can cut out and paste in a scrapbook." On the fact sheet ABC sends out about their news talk show *Issues and Answers*, those past programs on which the guests have made enough news to appear on the front pages of Monday's Washington *Post* or *New York Times* are marked by an asterisk.

As so often happens when two network news shows are compared, the NBC program, *Meet the Press*, runs itself on a more long-range view of the news. Lawrence Spivak, the show's host and creator, came out of magazine reporting; he was editor of the *American Mercury* in the thirties, and feels a strong responsibility to do more than just cover "news." Back in 1946 Spivak had Senator Theodore Bilbo of Mississippi on *Meet the Press*, then a radio program. Bilbo boasted of his membership in the Ku Klux Klan on the air, and extolled the Klan as a great organization. Spivak says that got him thinking: "Supposing we had an Adolf Hitler in America, should I have him on the show?" While Spivak is confident that in the end TV will expose and destroy a demagogue, he is not sure how long the process takes. A man could get elected to the presidency before the destruction through exposure had time to work.

Spivak was also upset at the way the late Senator Joseph McCarthy was able to dominate both the print and broadcast media with his false charges. Trapped in its unexamined definition of "news," the press had no way to protect itself from the senator's manipulations. Interestingly enough, in interviews, Spivak was the only broadcast journalist/executive to mention Joseph McCarthy. Yet McCarthy's ability to jerk the press around like a Yo-Yo brought on the first serious post-World War II examination by the press of their standards of objectivity and news.

With his more philosophical view of news and television, plus ownership of his own program, Spivak's guest list has been broader than those of his rivals. There has been more of a mix of diplomats, businessmen, foreign visitors, though Spivak remains a canny enough showman to keep a close eye on the ratings.

Consider, for example, one question of concern for the invisible primary: the media of attractiveness of senators versus the attractiveness of governors. Between 1964 and 1974 *Face the Nation* had senators on 172 times; *Meet the Press* only 116. Not surprisingly, for governors the statistics are reversed. *Meet the Press* had governors on 74 times; *Face the Nation* a mere 26. Since, as has been pointed out, governors don't make "news" the way senators do, this figure represents a deliberate effort on the part of *Meet the Press* to get outside of Washington.

Yet the overall decline of the number of governors appearing on *Face the Nation* and *Meet the Press* over the years pinpoints the increased Washington focus of television news. In 1964 *Face the Nation* had governors on 5 times, senators 15. In 1973 the program had on 26 senators and did not interview a single governor all year! With its conscious effort to look beyond Washington, the drop-off is less on NBC's *Meet the Press*, but still significant. In 1965 governors appeared 10 times, senators 9 times. In 1973 governors appeared 7 times, senators 11 times.

Anyone who watches network television news day after day soon comes to realize that the similarities between the NBC and CBS news shows are more evident than their differences. Nevertheless, the competition between them is intense. With the sincerity of a Defense Department spokesman chronicling victory in Vietnam, both networks cite statistics to prove their competitive edge and excellence. The news coverage at ABC, on the other hand, appears to be something that network would gladly drop if only the federal government would let them.

At the present time within the news trade, NBC is given the edge over CBS for both its morning and its evening news. CBS has the old Edward R. Murrow reputation and a few veterans of craft and competence such as Walter Cronkite and Charles Collingwood. However, it is NBC that has beaten the bushes and recruited a stable of young, talented reporters, some of them from CBS, and given these men a bit more freedom to search for news on their own. As a result, NBC seems more ready to break away from the purely reactive format of TV news coverage. More reporters have time to do their own legwork and their own checking.

Furthermore, NBC is seen as more willing to admit its errors and human imperfections than CBS. As the thoughtful press examines its own power position after Watergate, those willing to criticize themselves gain prestige at the expense of those standing pat. Much of the press is unhappily aware that however right dear Brutus may have been to stab the incipient tyrant Julius Caesar, he is remembered in history without love—considered more a murderer of a friend than a savior of democracy.

For example, both CBS and NBC in the summer of 1975 carried charges on their morning news shows that Alexander Butterfield, the man who first revealed that President Nixon was taping all his conversations, was a CIA "spy" in the White House. These charges were made on the basis of one report from a retired colonel, and neither network checked with Butterfield. When the charges proved false, NBC had the grace to admit that pressure to be first had affected their judgment. "In a situation like this," said NBC's Ford Rowan, "my thought is to get it on the air and see if it flies." But Daniel Schorr of CBS stoutly insisted there was no competitive pressure to get the Butterfield allegations on the air first. (Anyone who believes that can be expected to have soot on his face on Christmas morning from looking up the chimney for Santa.)

Richard Wald, chief of NBC's network news, believes that no candidate in the invisible primary is going to get much network mention on television. And they haven't. The candidates' hope is local television, thus the continual jittering around the country by contestants to attract the camera crews of local stations. Wald also sees the economics of entertainment television, actors' salaries, rerun limitations, and crew costs making news more economically attractive to local stations and networks. As the networks put out more and more news to their affiliates to run or not as they choose, and the affiliates feed back more news to the networks, there will be more air time available for all news; and this will mean more air time available for all candidates.

Still, for some time to come, to get on network television, or even local television, the first thing a candidate must do is go to Washington. It's that simple and that profound a change in our national life. Had George Wallace chosen to run for the Senate from Alabama in 1972, instead of seeking another term as governor, I believe he would now be close to doubling his standings in the polls through television exposure alone. Television is the oxygen of a candidate's public life.

I. A. "Bud" Lewis, the sad-eyed, troubled man who handles NBC's election unit, points out that, for the public, the whole election process is becoming a television process. Politics takes place not in the real world but on the tube. People don't go down to their local political headquarters to get the election results. They stay home, or go to a friend's house and watch TV. In both primary and national elections the campaigns and the decisions take place psychologically inside a TV studio. The networks are deluged with requests to get inside their studio election night. Even events like the ballroom gathering of the candidates' supporters are by now largely staged to take place for television. The people who attend have often been ordered there, or lured there, so the TV audience can see them. Otherwise they, too, would probably be at home learning the outcome of their labors on television like the rest of us—candidates included.

"It's despicable what they [the candidates] will do to get on television," says NBC's Edwin Newman, an old-time journalist of precision and wit. "Particularly their use of polls. A man's popularity should be about the last thing we want to know about him." The Scylla and Charybdis between which the candidate finds himself crushed is that for his standing in the polls to rise, he has to get on television. Yet to get a greater amount of TV time, his standing in the polls has to rise.

Here we turn a corner and face another paradox. The public gets its information about the candidates from television; but television decides which candidates to cover on the basis of wire service reports and stories in the Washington *Post* and *The New York Times* and, to some extent, *Time* and *Newsweek*. Walter De Vries asked Americans: If you get differing versions of the same story from the various media, which would you tend to believe? Forty-six percent answered television, while only 26 percent picked newspapers and 6 percent radio. Interestingly enough, Democrats and liberals believe television, while Republicans and conservatives believe newspapers. Moderates doubt all media. Twenty-eight percent of those calling themselves moderates don't believe any of the press.

With its complex equipment and its advanced deadlines on the processing of film and tape, television news is forced to be primarily reactive. The producers decide the night before, or at the beginning of a workday, what stories they should cover. Then they position their reporters to get that story, often agreeing between networks to share the cost of expensive equipment and crews. The journalists themselves are not out looking for stories to the same extent as the reporters in the major print media. With some honorable exceptions such as George Herman, Roger Mudd, Douglas Kiker, William Monroe, William Plant, or Fred Graham, to mention some random names, few TV reporters have had journalistic experience in developing complex, fresh material. And even those that do are kept in close rein by their editors so as not to miss the daily story—much as newspaper reporters were twenty years ago.

TV is also handicapped by lack of time in which to explain stories. Written out, the entire content of a network's evening half-hour news would not fill the front page of the Washington *Post*. This is not to knock television's ability to cover visual history—an inauguration or a space shot—but merely to emphasize its problems in evaluating candidates in the invisible primary.

There are exceptions, but generally the eyes and ears of the TV press are the reporters of the print media, or the daybook compilers of the wire services. This is particularly true in areas where there are major papers. Out in the countryside and suburbs it often seems to me that extremely astute political reporting is being done by television. The TV reporters are paid more than print journalists, and in their hometowns, have at least equal professional prestige. Ability follows pay and prestige, though these men, too, suffer from being held quite closely to visually exciting events and the breaking news story.

Richard Wald, the forty-five-year-old former newspaper editor and reporter who heads NBC news, stresses the importance of a candidate getting into "the national talk circle." As a network executive lunches or dines, do his friends ask him, "Why are we looking at that twerp on the tube?" Or are they enthusiastic?

"Jackson was getting on the air every night, till we put a stop to it," says William Small. Why stop it? Because he was no longer making news? Jackson's strategy had been to run for the presidency from the Senate, to gain points in the invisible primary by dominating the evening TV news. The decision not to air Jackson frustrated this strategy. I should add I agree with the decision; but I'd have a hard time justifying it on any other basis than the hoary shibboleth of judgment.

Edwin Newman also stresses the importance of the "talk circle." He points out that the producers and news executives from the various networks have lunch at the same places, vacation in the same areas, read the same newspapers and magazines. If a candidate's name keeps on coming up in these places, he is in the talk circle. This is where an astute press secretary can contribute much to a candidate. He can't sell his man to TV reporters and editors outright, but with skill he can lever him into the talk circles. Editors think, as Newman puts it: "Yeah, we ought to have that guy on." Then the candidate will be on, and then more reporters will want to cover him, and then his polls will start to rise, and then the whole process will be legitimate.

I asked Wald, a tough and charming man who, with brutal insight, once described my job on the *Herald Tribune* as "to improve the paper without changing it," if he could identify for me any of the loci of this magic talk circle. My hope was that you, reader, and even I, could then slip inside this charmed circumference and learn: "who loses and who wins; who's in, who's out." But Wald's reply was vague. Perhaps if I had offered to pay for the lunch.

The papers most widely read in the talk circles are *The New York Times* and the Washington *Post*. It's not that the political reporters on these papers, good as they are, are any abler than those on many other papers. It's just that other newspapers aren't read by the network executives with any regularity. So Robert Boyd of the Knight Newspapers, Andrew Glass of the Cox Newspapers, Peter Lisagor of the Chicago *Daily News*, Jack Germond of the Gannett Chain, and Alan Otten of *The Wall Street Journal* can't do the candidate as much good as David Broder or Jules Witcover of the Washington *Post* and Johnny Apple or Christopher Lydon of *The New York Times*.

The New York Times used to be the competition to beat in national political reporting. It wasn't news if it hadn't made the *Times*. A series of high-powered *Times* editors had the cash and the prestige to hire the best up-and-coming reporters away from other newspapers. "Six reporters and a gentleman from the *Times* are covering this story," was a standard thirties journalistic jest. And the humor was tinged with envy. "The *Times* has a man at every rat hole, but we have a rat at every manhole," was the *Herald Tribune*'s brave but tremulous cry in an ultimately lost cause. The *Times* had two reporters covering presidential candidate George McGovern; and they both rated a seat on the prestige plane with the candidate.

But like the powerful empires of old, the *Times* has recently divided internally into a number of warring satrapies: Editorial, Sunday, Daily, National, City, etc. Chris Argyris, a Harvard Graduate School of Education professor whose specialty is improving communications inside ailing corporations, spent three years at the *Times* trying to bring about change; finally he gave up. Then the news magazine *More*, devoted to critiquing the press, got hold of some of Argyris's reports. Their depressing tenor was summed up by one senior *Times* editor, who said: "You know you've become a full member of this organization when you genuinely believe that few changes are possible and that it is necessary to hold such a belief in order to remain sane."

The *Times,* which in print always pushes for a freer flow of information from the government, hit Argyris with seventy pages of changes and deletions when he presented to the *Times* editors the book he had written about their organization. "I never before felt such personal pressure on me not to publish the results of a study," said the professor.

In his three years at the *Times* Argyris could point to one accomplishment. He got publisher Sulzberger and his top editors together to discuss, face to face, the function of the page opposite the editorial page (the Op-Ed page). The editors had been staging power plays behind each other's backs over that page for four years. In thirty minutes they solved their problems.

More and Argyris see trying days ahead for the *Times.* Argyris found *Times* editors "projected their 'bad' behavior onto the world and attacked it wherever it was 'reasonable' to do so." *More* notes that the *Times* has long been hostile to "the suggestions of outsiders" while "*Times* executives themselves feel powerless to effect change." These internal battles have had a stultifying effect on the *Times*' news coverage. Editors are too busy covering their tails to shift to newer views of news or political philosophy. The paper's news coverage has grown both shriller and more predictably conventional at the same time. Hemmed in by restrictions imposed by editors protecting their fiefdoms, a number of the paper's abler reporters have gone elsewhere.

At the same time, the Washington *Post* had been broadening and expanding its concepts of new coverage. Questions of style change and news emphasis that might literally take several years of debate at the *Times* are decided at the *Post* in the course of several weeks. Now it is the *Post* that is picking up able reporters from other newspapers, including snaffling the then-dissatisfied David Broder from the *Times* itself. As I traveled around the country for this book, I was surprised by how often during the last four years I found that the Washington *Post* rather than the *Times* had become the second newspaper for those involved locally in politics. Also, how often local newspaper editors were choosing stories syndicated by the Washington *Post* news service, rather than those from *The New York Times* service, to portray national political events for their readers.

The *Post* is also more ready to admit its occasional errors. Along with the Louisville *Courier Journal,* the *Post* has designated an editor as internal ombudsman. This editor covers the working of the newspaper and prints articles critical to the paper, based either on his own investigations or on readers' complaints. The ombudsman's work is placed prominently in the feature news sections of the paper. *The New York Times* has turned down the idea of an ombudsman as too threatening to the power of its senior editors.

Still the *Times,* with its tradition of broad coverage, has a tremendous influence on popular opinion as to who is where in the invisible primary. To be recognized by the *Times* is to become that modern political approximation of medieval sainthood, the "viable candidate." With access to the *Times,* gained via the columns of Johnny Apple and Chris Lydon, entrants in the invisible primary maneuver with one eye constantly on both men.

Since Jack Sprat and his wife, it is hard to conceive of a more unlikely pair of reporting mates than Chris Lydon and Johnny Apple. (No one calls Apple "John"—for the sufficient reason that his name is Raymond Walter Apple.) Apple is chubby, Lydon is thin; Apple is loud and sure, Lydon is soft and tentative; Apple is a protégé of Managing Editor Abe Rosenthal, Lydon of Editor James "Scotty" Reston. Apple has longish hair and a studied sloppiness ("You should be ashamed, wearing your hair like that," a proverbial little old lady told him recently as he bounced down the streets of Rochester). Lydon has shortish hair, is well groomed and professorially tweedy. Apple is Princeton and *The Wall Street Journal;* Lydon is Yale and the Boston *Globe.* Apple is prompt and likes the good life. The pixie-eared Lydon is always slightly late (he races down the endless corridors of airport after airport, yelling, "Hold it, hold it"). Apple's heroes are winners with a superb organization. Lydon's heroes are blue-eyed Irishmen with political savvy.

Yet they are similar in that they are both profoundly *Times.* Both are always worried about getting their facts right, always trying to be first, always alert for inside information, traveling continually to see things firsthand, yet stopping short, or being stopped short by their editors, of taking the last step that transforms great reporting, which they do well, into breath-catching insight and event.

In Timothy Crouse's *Boys on the Bus,* Crouse, who apparently doesn't like Apple, quotes an unnamed "fellow reporter" on Apple: "He is classically the reporter that the *Times* would have invented. He asks just the questions that they want asked and not one more; he doesn't probe too deeply; and if he ever started to doubt what he was doing he would tell them about those doubts. He is not like that deliberately to please the *Times.* It's just the way he is."

Though this shaft is aimed at Apple, it seems to me to fall more on the *Times*—indeed, on American newspapers as a whole, minus the much noted but little honored, honorable exceptions. There is always another question that can be asked—in the news, in self-examination, in fiction. There is always the final choked-out answer that reveals more than the teller wishes and often more than the questioner or reader can stand—the frightening chaos of the post-Heisenberg world. A reporter soon learns where his questions should stop. Even that multilingual philosopher who bitches by quoting Dante, Robert Boyd, the Knight Newspapers Pulitzer Prize winner who uncovered Tom Eagleton's lies, knows there is a limit to what he can ask.

Apple's knowledge is prodigious. For each election of the last six years, Peter Hart, a sophisticated, modern political pollster, has polled the "experts" a month before the election to see how their predictions stand up. Johnny Apple is the only two-time money winner, he placed second twice. In '74 he called all but one of the Senate races. I, who picked losing Democrats Harry Reid and Wayne Owens over Republicans Paul Laxalt and Calvin Rampton in Nevada and Utah, can only tip my hat.

For all its excellence the *Times* keeps its reporters on a tight, traditionalist rein. Take its front page political story on George Wallace, datelined May 22, 1975. This story culminates two months of investigative work by Christopher Lydon. It is, to be forthright, one of the best political stories I have ever read. And the story didn't just float in over the transom because Lydon worked for the *Times*—a pleasant something that often happens to reporters on powerful newspapers. Lydon laboriously pieced together how George Wallace raised his money. His story detailed how Richard A. Viguerie, who heads a conservative direct-mail fund-raising firm, advanced Wallace the cash to cover the beginning costs of Wallace's direct-mail fund raising; and then advanced further funds to continue its operation. If all the money advanced by Viguerie had to be paid back immediately, Wallace's whole fund-raising operation might even show a loss. The article raised profound questions as to whether Wallace has broken the Federal Campaign Law. The law forbids corporate contributions and all individual contributions over one thousand dollars. Do Viguerie's advances to Wallace fall in this category? Viguerie and Wallace aides said that the money was merely a bookkeeping device, representing delayed payments of bills; just as you don't pay your credit card charges until the next month.

The *Times*, to its credit, let the story run, giving it over two-thirds of page 16. But where did the story start? At the bottom of page 1, a mere two columns, under an italic headline of the mild sort usually reserved for a feature about unusually gifted chimpanzees. Nowhere in the headline or opening paragraphs of the story were there hints of Wallace's legal problem. Other less traditional papers would have led or off-led the front page with the Wallace story. And their headline would have mentioned the governor's legal problems. When editors exercise such caution, reporters learn to be conservative in their questions and public judgments.

Such an old-fashioned bias toward the nature of news works against any candidate making it in the *Times* without traditional credentials. This in turn throws a conservative cast over the whole vital process. Jack Kennedy renewed the practice of running for the presidency while in the Senate, after the sorry state in which that play had been left by Harding. Senators are now *in* at the *Times*. So are governors, though no governor has been a candidate since 1952, and the present work load on governors makes it impossible for them to put in the four years of constant travel now required for nomination by the proliferation of state primaries. The idea that ex-governors or members of the House might run for President, or maybe ex-mayors, or cabinet officers, the *Times* finds almost too fantastical to contemplate. The *Times* editors are not entirely wrong in this; many of the flowering presidential candidates in the hot summer of 1975 were ridiculous blooms. But to admit candidates to their columns, to get a person into the talk circles and onto television, the *Times* still uses filters designed in 1950.

The Washington *Post* is a newspaper in flux, scrambling to keep the number-one position it attained with its uncovering of the Watergate scandal. Its political reporters are allowed much more freedom than those at the *Times*. And the editors rely on the news judgments of their reporters to a greater extent. "The candidates are mad at me," said David Broder, flying back from a relatively obscure Democratic bloodletting in June 1974, "because I won't let the paper start covering them yet." It is unlikely that a reporter on the *Times* could make such a statement. Along with their freedom the Washington *Post* expects a great degree of depth from its reporters. All three of the *Post*'s top political reporters have written books of political worth. Lou Cannon, who covers Republicans, has *Ronnie and Jesse: A Political Odyssey*, a detailed study of gubernatorial politics in California, laid out philosophically to show the unexpected effects of political reform. Jules Witcover, who sees plots to keep him uninformed everywhere and who helped unmask Vice-President Agnew, wrote *A Heartbeat Away*. David Broder's *The Party's Over* is a thoughtful, detailed examination of shriveled political responsibility in today's America.

David Broder is important not just because of his position as chief political writer for the *Post* but also because the rest of the media takes what he writes extremely seriously. Not that other reporters take their cue from him. That's an insult to a group of able individualists working under the great pressures of a deadline.

(Never make light of the difficulties of a deadline; just try to get the damn names spelled right under pressure. When a group of terrorists shot up Blair House, where President Truman was then living while the White House across the street was being repaired, the reporters covering Truman gathered in the operating room corridor of the hospital where the wounded terrorists were being treated. We were waiting for the word as to who the terrorists were. A hospital spokesman came out of the door at the end of the corridor and told us that the men were Puerto Rican Nationalists. "What's your name," yelled the reporters on deadline. They had to attribute this information to someone. The man mumbled something like *Zbyjzipopospi*.

"You go back inside that door," yelled the legendary Merriman Smith. "And get someone called Jones to come out and give us these facts.")

But if Dave Broder writes something one way, and a reporter and his editor see it another, they will question their own judgment first. If Broder were to decide that one of the most likely presidential candidates was a frozen fish-stick salesman from the Bayou country of Louisiana, the *Post*'s editors would front-page his story out of respect for his judgment. And on other papers reporters would reach for their airlines timetables. After all, at the height of papal cynicism and corruption in the seventeenth century, the College of Cardinals, instead of a Medici or a Borgia, picked an obscure hermit who claimed to have been stigmatized. Now if Broder says this fish-stick seller . . . He has that kind of power.

The son of a reasonably prosperous dentist in suburban Chicago, the forty-six-year-old Broder grew up in a family where politics were constantly discussed at the dinner table. He ran the campus newspaper at the University of Chicago, which he attended shortly after World War II. He has been a journalist ever since. The discipline that goes into his prose, which is an eighteenth-century delight, can be seen in his body, which manages to stay trim and thin through the rigors of continuous travel. He exudes the humorous, childlike quality of so many of the best reporters. He is the bright kid at the back of the classroom so far ahead in his lessons that he can peer out the window, dreaming of ideal worlds. He is also the kid who was always willing to help someone slower, not out of notice-me show-offness, but out of the sheer delight in sharing knowledge.

Lest I seem to go overboard, let me add that Broder and I disagree about the invisible primary. With his strong sense of order, Broder likes things to remain in their proper place. It is his belief that the Gwirtzman rule still holds: "Nothing that happens before New Hampshire has any meaning." This rule was formed by Robert Gwirtzman, an aide to Robert Kennedy. After I had questioned the aforementioned Gwirtzman about his rule, he inadvertently drove off with my coat and suitcase in an airport taxi. When I finally ran him down, he returned the suitcase but forgot the coat. The next day, generously trying to deliver the coat, he got lost in the woods. And when in return for his courtesy I dropped him back at the main road, he started to hitchhike in the wrong direction. Still, if Broder believes Gwirtzman is the expert to watch . . .

To court Apple, Lydon, Broder, and others, the candidates and their staffs go through intricate mating dances. Lunches with the candidates in their offices, tidbits about the campaigns saved for each reporter exclusively; breakfast appearances with groups of reporters that either include the top correspondents of the *Times* and the *Post* or their friends; approaches to them through third parties to plant ideas in disguise. ("Send the money in small bills," quipped Roger Mudd to McGovern's press secretary, Richard Dougherty, during one such luncheon in early '74.) Later in the campaign, if he gets that far, the candidate must be careful not to turn the majority of the press against him by playing favorites to the few. But in the opening days, when only the few cover him, he must save what little he has for the *Times*, the *Post*, and the news magazines, again, not so much to get coverage for its own sake, but because mention leads to TV time.

The print media, important as they are, are not the only means by which the candidate gets more television time. Another is by increasing his standings in the Gallup and Harris polls. Here again the self-reflexive nature of news is perfectly illustrated: to get on the air, a candidate must increase his standing in the polls, but to increase his standing in the polls, he must get on the air. Once the magic hoop starts to roll, it's like perpetual motion; but what about the early days when pollsters don't even ask the voters to rate our provincial heroes and dark horse candidates, the Van Lingo Wombatts of this world?

How does the Gallup organization, the oldest of the polltakers and the one most usually looked at first by editors and reporters, decide whom to ask the voters about? Charles W. Roll, a roly-poly, genial Princetonian in charge of political polling for the Gallup organization, worries continually about leaving out someone and so being sued, charged with bias by the press, or getting called up before Congress. As a result, "we put practically anyone on who has ever been mentioned for President." In the spring of 1975 the 5 by 8 card that the Gallup organization hands out to the fifteen hundred scientifically selected individuals it polls to determine presidential preference contained, for Democrats, thirty-four names, listed alphabetically. (Oh, to be Aardvark rather than Wallace.)

Name number 25 is Ralph Nader. Roll doesn't believe that a private person like Nader has a chance or that he should be on the poll; but the Gallup organization got so many phone calls about his not being on their list that they felt it prudent to include his name. Basically the Gallup executives sit down and decide what names are "on television and in the news" and include them in the poll. Since the members of the Gallup organization are in Princeton, New Jersey, in a pleasant frame house just off the main street, what they read, again, is the *Times*, the Washington *Post*, the news weeklies, and *The Wall Street Journal*. So with polls as with television, the starting blocks for a candidate are largely the two major newspapers. Roll, who is quite shrewd behind his narrow tie sprinkled with red beer steins, realizes the irony of using news to decide which candidates to poll about, when the poll results are themselves news. But he sees no way out of this circle.

Except for Nader and possibly Julian Bond, the Gallup names are from the mainstream of American politics. Seven governors, seventeen senators, two ex-governors, two ex-senators, one congressman, one mayor, one ex-mayor, and one Kennedy relative. Pity the poor candidate trying to move out from a ruck like that. Note also that the list does not include some of those names the newer pollsters use when they try to glean sociological information about America. Such polls would indicate the first choice of the vast majority of Americans for President is Walter Cronkite; the second, Billy Graham.

There is a great deal of mistrust and anger directed at the pollsters, particularly at the two old-timers who do the syndicated newspaper predictions, Gallup and Harris. Bills have been introduced in Congress to restrict political polling and even to make it illegal. How can anyone predict the preferences of a nation of this size and complexity on a mere fifteen hundred interviews? The answer lies in what pollsters call the "screen"—making sure that the sample used is typical of America as a whole. Thus all pollsters are now finding it increasingly difficult to "screen for Republicans." There are so few Republicans out there that a pollster has to interview a large sample of voters to be sure that he has talked to a significant number of Republicans.

There are two methods of sample selection. The first, the quota system, involves constructing a sample that is like the population of the United States—so many people over sixty-five, so many under twenty-one, so many women, so many blacks, and so on. There are various problems with this method. An interviewer may interview only twenty-year-olds, for example, for his under-twenty-ones, or he may unconsciously select certain types of women to interview and neglect others. There is no way statistically to check the sample. Past errors in quota sampling led to such bloopers as the predictions that Dewey would defeat Truman and that Labor would defeat the Conservatives in Britain in 1970.

Since these disasters, and with the refinement of statistical techniques, the method most widely used today is the probability sample. A pollster asks questions at random across America in areas of varying population density and allows the law of averages to make the sample representative. A complex series of statistical equations are used to indicate the size of the sample that must be obtained to reduce possible polling error to negligible proportions. Note here that error depends on sample size rather than on the size of the population. If one drinks a martini to make sure the mixture is right before serving them to six people, it is not necessary to drink ten martinis before serving them to sixty people. By and large, pollsters use samples of from fifteen hundred to eighteen hundred people when determining American attitudes. This, they believe, reduces the possibility of polling error to around plus or minus 3 percent.

The pollster's real problem is not with the size of the sample but with the quality of the screen. A pollster must be certain that areas of all sizes are included, that those who are not at home the first time are interviewed on follow-up interviews, that those who live in corner houses aren't counted more than those who live in apartments, that migrants get in somehow, that the answers of those groups less likely to talk are given proper weight to make them equal to the chatter of the voluble. It is this sophisticated process of balancing and screening that leads to the possibility of error and charges of cooked data. For example, college-educated people are more inclined to answer poll questions than those who did not finish high school. Therefore a sample must be statistically tuned not to down-play the fewer answers of the high school dropouts.

Two other areas open to error and abuse are the wording of the questions asked by pollsters and the order in which they appear. Obviously, "Did tricky Dick steal the 1974 election?" will bring a different percentage of responses than "In view of the nature of politics do you feel President Richard M. Nixon's overwhelming majority was the result of unprecedented political manipulation?" The order of questions will also swing the results. If a pollee is asked, "Has the rise in crime made you more afraid?" "Should the government do more to control inflation?" "Has increased unemployment hurt you?" "What sort of job do you think the President is doing?" our leader isn't going to come out as well as if the last question had been asked first.

Since in presidential politics anything that can be manipulated will be manipulated, candidates try to jimmy the poll results in various ways. The most common of these is to overinflate the popularity of another candidate and underplay your own. Then no matter if you are beaten by 55 percent, you can point out the candidate didn't get the 60 percent he had expected. This happened in New Hampshire in 1972. A Boston *Globe* poll using rather unsophisticated questions was taken early in January 1972. It showed Muskie with a 65 percent lead. Muskie's own polls never put him at more than 50 percent. But McGovern's staff cleverly stuck Muskie with the need to gain 65 percent of the New Hampshire vote in order to be considered a winner. So Muskie lost even though he came in first, with 48 percent of the vote to McGovern's 33 percent.

Conversely a candidate whose private polls show him well in the lead can down-play that lead. In West Virginia, in 1960, Kennedy talked about being lucky to get 40 percent of the vote against Hubert Humphrey, when his polls showed he had close to a 60 percent lead. Thus when Kennedy gathered 60 percent of the vote on election night, the press made his win seem even bigger.

A more direct form of poll manipulation occurs when the candidates schedule events that will affect the percentage points themselves. In 1968, when running against Nelson Rockefeller, Richard Nixon learned that the Gallup interviews for the before-the-convention poll standings were to take place on July 20 through 23. Nixon strategists timed ex-President Eisenhower's endorsement of Nixon to be announced just before that period and Nixon took a five-point spurt in the poll.

One of the most sensitive secrets of any pollster is where his representative polling districts are. If a candidate could find the fifteen hundred people who are to be interviewed, he could direct TV programs at them, have special mailings sent to them, even meet some of them. In the late 1960s and early 1970s candidates won by packing the party caucuses. In the late 1970s a modern candidate may try to lever the polls. If a candidate knew with some precision even a few of the geographic areas in which the interviews were to be conducted, his staff could jump his standing significantly. "Polls show Van Lingo Wombatt surging in the Midwest." Broder's at the door, Apple's on the phone, a man from the Milk Fund has left a brown paper bag, the *Today* show is tomorrow, Wombatt is in orbit.

In the last ten years a gaggle of highly sophisticated new pollsters has been born. They employ advanced techniques of screening and questioning and have a sociologically complex view of the electorate. These organizations now form a vital link in the invisible primary, filling another part of the void left by the erosion of the political party. They send political information back up the ladder. The pollsters, not the party workers at the precinct level, now tell the candidate what the voters think and feel. And by their ability to fill this function, the pollsters contribute still more to the breakup of the party. Now television brings information about the candidate to the voters, and the polls bring information about the voters back to the candidate.

In the 1890s Tammany Hall leaders would station party workers at bridges and key intersections about New York to ask people their choice of candidates for public office, and Tammany leaders would even rotate workers from location to location in order to make sure the count was honest. From such humble origins the modern science of polling arose. The first political candidate to use modern polling methods was probably Mrs. Alex Miller, in her successful 1932 campaign to become the first woman secretary of state in Iowa. Or so George Gallup believes. He persuaded Mrs. Miller, his mother-in-law, to use the polling techniques he had developed to help magazine sales (something he had done while still working on his Ph.D.). In the 1940s President Roosevelt commissioned Professor Hadley Cantril of Princeton to poll how the public felt about the war in Europe. Nowadays candidates tend to suspect that the information they get from party sources may be "biased." They prefer to run their own polls. And reporters, the next link in the chain, tend to be more impressed with poll results than the assessments of party regulars and other activists.

The head of a modern polling firm has to be half hustler, half scientist. Too much of the scientist and he loses business to some other aggressive young man hauling himself up success's ladder with sales psychology and statistics. Too much of the salesman and his reputation slides as his statistics begin to cook in favor of his personal beliefs and the desires of his clients. In 1974 one of the better-respected small firms that polls for Democrats overestimated the level of one of its clients, a senate candidate, by 16 percent one month before the election. No favor to the client, who went low-key to preserve his lead and lost.

Typical of the new firms are Hart Research, headed by Peter Hart in Washington, D.C., a firm that polls exclusively for Democrats (though it refused to poll for George Wallace), and Market Opinion Research in Detroit, whose political division is headed by Robert Teeter and polls exclusively for Republicans. The statistics produced by both men are respected by both government and academic pollsters: "classy" is the adjective most often applied to their work. In 1976 Hart is handling seventeen statewide races, the limit he feels his organization can cover, while Teeter has the Republican national polling task.

What do these firms do? To quote Teeter's brochure about Market Opinion Research:

> We apply a variety of innovative forms of multivariate analysis to the problems of campaigns. . . . Generally, our questionnaires cover

issues awareness and perception of candidates and current voting intentions. The primary analysis breaks each question by past voting behavior, geographic regions, current voting intentions, various demographic groups, and by media use habits. . . . [We] identify . . . target groups based on demographic and behavioral variables, budget planning and selection of media. The goal is to optimize the allocation of campaign personnel and economic resources.

In more Madison Avenue style (its offices are on that controversial thoroughfare), Tully Plesser's Cambridge Opinion Studies, which polls for both Democrats and Republicans, hits the hopeful candidate right between the eyes:

Here are [some] applications of voter attitude survey research that have proved actionable. . . . (1) Critical estimates of how large the voter turnout will be and who will vote. (2) Evaluations of public concern with national, regional and local issues. (3) "Leverage" issue identification: Evaluations of relative influence of specific issues on the voting behavior of specific target voter groups. . . . (4) Comparisons of voter attitudes toward specific candidate characteristics vs. profiles of the "ideal" candidate. (5) Indications of specific weaknesses in the personal profiles or political postures of opposing candidates. . . .

"I own New Hampshire," says Plesser modestly. His claim is that as a result of past campaigns he has all the voters in that state on file, with the habits and secret fears of many of them recorded in lengthy interviews. Even discounting what he says by 50 percent—considering that Plesser, a pleasant, youthful hustler, came into polling from advertising—the importance of what he has to offer the aspiring candidate is obvious.

"Basically we tell the candidate what's out there," says Peter Hart. "Then it's up to him to position himself on the issue. There's no magic in polling. Though we do try to structure the candidate so that he will be perceived favorably by those who don't already know him. . . . The American people have become cynical about their leaders only because their leaders have become cynical about dealing with the people. They have offered oversimplified answers and avoided hard choices."

Hart dresses with the same stylish mixture of modern and conservative with which he covers issues or strokes a ball in tennis. The son of a Berkeley English professor, he drifted into polling by accident after he graduated from Bowdoin, because a friend got him a job with Lou Harris. In the 1968 election he traveled around the country for the Harris organization, helping CBS with their election coverage. From there he went to the Democratic National Committee as a pollster. He got back into independent polling for Quayle, then switched to Harris again, and finally decided he could have more impact on the political process by going into business for himself. He delights in testing out on the voters offbeat theories of his own. In early 1974 he ran a trial heat of Henry Kissinger against Teddy Kennedy. To his surprise Kissinger won hands down. This caused Hart to be among the first to ask some shrewd questions about the locus of Kennedy's poll strength, which turned out to rest in important measure on the black and very young—groups that traditionally do not vote.

This analysis of a candidate's "base constituency" is for Hart the name of the game in the invisible primary, far more important than measuring a candidate's strength. Early in the race mere popularity is almost entirely a function of name recognition. What is important to the candidate is who is for him, and how he can build on this constituency. Also critical is the candidate's "U.Q." ("Unacceptability Quotient"), those who will not vote for him under any circumstances. Again, unfortunately for Kennedy, his U.Q. was highest among older whites with a high school education or better, a group that usually votes heavily.

Suppose a candidate stands at 20 percent. This may mean that he isn't very well known but those that have heard of him like what they have heard. Or it may mean that he is in solid with one group, but everyone knows him and 80 percent can't stand the bastard. In both examples the candidate stands at 20 percent favorable, but their political futures are totally different. Going further, suppose that in a primary, candidate A stands at 35 percent and our hero, Van Lingo Wombatt, at only 30 percent. Candidate A is the favorite of the young, the blacks, those with some college. Wombatt is the favorite of those over forty-five who are white and are either high school or college graduates. Bet on Wombatt to win hands down because his supporters are more than twice as likely to vote in primaries than candidate A's. Note that if the pollster is forecasting an election result rather than merely measuring popularity, he must use "screeners" to correct such imbalances.

Robert Teeter, on the other side of the political fence from Peter Hart, uses the same cautious words about polling: "I'm tired of candidates who want me to tell them their program . . . who look for some magic leverage issue. I tell them we have this little airplane that flies five hundred feet over the ground and learns what everyone is secretly thinking. That we'll win it for him. The candidate should have his beliefs."

Teeter is continually forced to disillusion Republican hopefuls who believe that the slogan "I will bring business efficiency to government" turns people on. It turns them off. Teeter is also suspicious of pollsters who claim they can locate some magic issue, tie their candidate to it, and send him whizzing through to the finish. He defines politics as the application of human energy to problems. The pollster's art is in identifying the issues that generate energy, locate the people who respond to such issues, and permit the candidate to observe himself and his opponent through the eyes of these people.

Robert Teeter is in the American tradition of small-town boys (he graduated from Albion College) who came to the big city (Detroit) to make good. A thirty-five-year-old energy hound, bouncing around in drip-dry suits, he finishes other people's sentences for them in his rush to tap his own wellspring of ideas. He got into polling through politics, working for George Romney in the early 1960s and becoming convinced that no one knew enough about the electorate to campaign effectively. "Republican strategy in Michigan was to work like hell in the country and pray for rain in Detroit election day."

In 1967 he went to work for Market Opinion Research in Detroit, then largely an industrial pollster, soon becoming head of its political division. In 1972 he did the Nixon campaign polling, on the results of which were based the devastating anti-McGovern TV advertisements. A founder of the Environmental Protection Agency, he has great stories of sneaking environmentally necessary actions past the White House staff by inventing phony political benefits for Nixon.

As he sits at lunch in downtown Detroit, people wander over to his table, or arrange to stand beside him in the men's room to talk about judgeships and the pulling power of this or that candidate for lieutenant governor. Or his lunch will be interrupted by a call from Governor Christopher Bond of Missouri who wants to check out the language of a statement he is being asked to sign. Thus he moves through a series of vignettes, each demonstrating how thoroughly the modern pollster has displaced the old-fashioned political boss.

Some pollsters, notably Pat Caddell of Cambridge Survey Research, see the electorate as moving steadily left. Reasoning from the same basic data, theoreticians like Kevin Phillips believe the voter is growing more conservative. Hart, Teeter, and, to an extent, De Vries at Duke see the electorate as neither right nor left, radical nor conservative, but quiescent and potentially volatile. It is turned off, rather than questing after new gods. Basically, voters would rather improve the old ways to make them work again, than move rapidly elsewhere. They await a leader, but a leader with modern style. Understanding this, a young astute operator, like thirty-year-old Senator Gary Hart of Colorado or thirty-six-year-old Governor Jerry Brown of California, can move in from the left by taking up a life-style and certain issues that appeal to the previously turned-off younger voter, while at the same time using enough of the old rhetoric to hold the older voters. Or, *mutatis mutandis,* the leader can be older and move in from the right, like Republican Governor William Milliken of Michigan, fifty-three years old, also taking up the young life-style but keeping the older political issues.

Because they have a unique political specialty, the pollsters have not been hit as hard as other practitioners of the new political arts by the drying up of campaign funds occasioned by the new campaign financing law. Media consultants, film makers, total campaign managers, all are cutting back their offices. But pollsters still flourish, along with direct-mail specialists whose ability to raise large funds across the nation in small amounts is suddenly in great demand. It would appear that faced with a shortage of funds, candidates may cut back on paid advertising, or banks of phones, or planned management, but not on information about the voter.

As with the pollsters, so with the campaign managers—until recently. Up until 1973 and the passage of the new finance law, the campaign management firms, or gunslingers as they are known in the political trade, were one of America's most spectacular growth industries. In 1957, when reporters and political scientists first began to notice the rise of political management firms, there were some forty public relations firms offering campaign management in addition to their other types of business. By 1973 around 350 firms, with several thousand employees, offered political consultative services in addition to their other business. More important, about 100 firms did nothing but work on politics for profit.

The late 1960s were the golden days for gunslingers. In 1970 David Garth, a talented, stormy media expert who hires out to both Republicans and Democrats, managed the losing congressional campaign of multimillionaire Democratic hopeful, Richard Ottinger. Shortly after the campaign, Garth's wife was seen luxuriously furred at a Broadway opening.

"What is that glorious coat?" asked a friend.

"It's an Ottinger," replied Mrs. Garth.

The first firm to offer professional campaign management, it is generally agreed, was the California public relations firm of Whitaker and Baxter in the 1930s. The fact that the firm was Californian is important. For California is the first state in which the traditional functions of the party broke down. In the years following 1910, the reform movement of Hiram Johnson laid hands on the corrupt party system of California and reformed the parties out of practical existence. Jobs were placed in civil service, the initiative and referendum were adopted, and cross voting in primaries legalized. With the party done away with, up rose a public relations firm that handled politics for cash.

Critics of the campaign management firms frequently accuse them of causing the breakup of the political party by usurping their services. The California genesis of such firms appears to show that the party breakup came first, though undoubtedly the presence of the firms contributed to the fragmentation. Also, even before the rapid growth of the firms, many candidates insisted on building their own personal organizations. The Kennedys were always suspicious of the party politicians. "Never trust the locals," said Robert F. Kennedy. Later, the Kennedys would be equally suspicious of the hired gunslingers, those they called "in business for themselves." They wanted an organization of people loyal to them, whose payoffs would be from that loyalty, rather than from dollars or the party.

I personally question the widespread theory that the campaign management firms have made indecent profits. While the living's been good, none of the firms have offices that can compare with those of a small commercial advertising agency or law firm. I suspect many of the practitioners are in it for money, yes, but also for ideas, fun, and power. It is like writing for a newspaper or news magazine: If one's major interest is money and one has writing talent, there are higher paid places to string words together.

In any event the campaign management firms are now in financial trouble. And not just from the new campaign financing law. The skills these firms possess—skills that the individuals in them had learned by painful trial and error—are now general knowledge, and the candidate's own staff can use them and put them into action. Matt Reese, the continually dieting giant who broke into politics helping to deliver West Virginia to JFK in 1960 and now runs his own shrinking campaign management firm, points out: "Some guy who graduates from journalism school today knows more about election politics than Larry O'Brien, the old master, did when he went on the road for Kennedy in '59."

There are books on being an advance man, selling media, handling the press, shooting commercials, organizing neighborhoods. Theodore White has held the mirror up to a whole level of political activity largely unrecognized and unreported before. Back in 1959 pollsters weren't sure how to separate voters and nonvoters, media experts didn't know how to buy by selected markets, and the practitioners of direct mail hadn't built up those all-pervasive lists. Now these subjects are taught in college. The older experts who first made it with Kennedy or Reagan find themselves under pressure from the young hustlers who made it with McGovern and Christopher Bond.

"I was sitting in my office thinking my campaign was hopeless," says Jack Roderick, champion of controlled growth, now the reform mayor of Anchorage, Alaska, "and this long-haired, slightly far-out guy from California I'd never met before walks in the door and says, 'I can make you mayor.' He turned out to be a genius. He got my campaign really moving. The day after the election we shook hands and he left." With such free-lancers, what future has the professional?

Typical of this diffusion of knowledge is TV know-how. The first political management firms to get hot were the television specialists back in the fifties. These firms dealt largely in the paid aspects of the media: advertisements and campaign films. But they also advised a candidate on his news appearances and the staging of news events. Robert D. Squier, Joseph Napolitan, Charles Guggenheim, David Garth, all formed firms that specialized in the then new medium. Now it would seem that the era when the candidate who dominated television dominated the election is passing. Not that television is becoming less important, but now all candidates understand and use it as a matter of course. Up till 1970 if Van Lingo Wombatt mounted a good TV campaign he would be devastating, because Wombatt would be up against a candidate who hadn't yet mastered the tube. Now everyone is on television.

The result, of course, is a kind of canceling out. In the 1972 presidential campaign the Democrats spent half as much again on paid television commercials as the Republicans—though myth has it otherwise. Those extra

Democratic dollars bought zero results. In the 1972 Florida presidential primary, John Lindsay's TV blitz, well produced and orchestrated by David Garth, produced no better than a weak fifth place for the New York mayor. Occasionally the TV experts still have a success—Garth with Hugh Carey in the New York Democratic gubernatorial primary in '74, and John Deardouff with James Rhodes's campaign for governor of Ohio that same year—but, the hope of a candidate's dominating television becomes more remote with each passing year.

In addition to those consultants and consultant firms that specialize in television, there are other campaign firms which purvey particular talents. Morris Dees and Richard Viguerie are the direct-mail stars of the left and right respectively. They have—or know where to find—the computer tape lists of hundreds of thousands of names that produce cash and contact for their candidate. If you subscribe to a magazine, have a driver's license, belong to a church or fraternal organization, a union, a citizens' lobby, a management group, or have a credit card, you are on a list and have gotten mail from these men. Richard Viguerie, George Wallace's wizard of tactics and computer, sent out 50 million pieces of mail in a single year of the invisible primary, 1975.

"The trouble with politicians is that they're impressed with seeing themselves on television," said Viguerie. "Letters, they're a one-time thing and they don't make any noise; but they get people elected. . . . Wallace will have communicated with maybe 20 million people out there by his mailings. . . . Direct mail can be devastatingly effective. . . . It's a lot more effective than radio or television. It's also a lot more expensive."

Morris Dees, the philosophical civil rights activist who made a fortune as a direct-mail salesman in his twenties, in 1972 took 3 million of George McGovern's fat-cat dollars and raised 20 million by direct mail.

"There are only two mail donating segments of our society," says Dees, "the right fringe and the left fringe."

"I have the best collection of conservative names in the country, 2 million on 170 lists," says Viguerie. Viguerie got into direct mail himself because he was frustrated by the ineffective way conservative causes were soliciting money. A quiet man, with an open "plowboy" presence, he built up his computer banks from such diverse sources as lists of Republican contributors, the Air Line Pilots Association, *Football Digest,* Stern's nurseries, boat owners, and *Motor Age* subscribers.

Some other firms or individuals with particular specialties are Oldfield Dukes and Yancy Martin, who specialize in black attitudes; Spencer-Roberts, who work the West Coast for Republicans; and F. Clifton White Associates, who handle conservative candidates and train businessmen to deal with political problems. In addition to the older established firms, practically every university and college town has its own set of enterprising Ph.D.s in the social sciences with a business card and know-how from past campaigns ready to help a candidate for devotion or money.

Not all campaign management firms are specialists. A few go so far as to offer the total management of campaigns, from running the candidate's office to deciding the strategy to manning the phone banks to making the TV commercials. Perhaps the best known of these on the Republican side is Bailey, Deardourff, the organization that sparked the abortive Percy campaign; and on the Democratic side, Matt Reese Associates.

In addition to their experience and political skills, such firms bring a candidate important tangential benefits. A famous firm can legitimize an unknown candidate. David Garth Associates did this for Hugh Carey in the New York governor's race. The firm solves the candidate's bookkeeping problems. A senator running for President has to be careful not to finance his campaign staff out of his office payroll, lest he violate statutes about contributing to his own campaign. If the firm and its employees run his campaign, that problem is solved. The firm usually doesn't want anything from the campaign but money. In today's holier-than-thou atmosphere when politics is suspect, old-fashioned payoffs of ambassadorships, jobs, referrals, and favors are out; but money is still okay. Many candidates lack executive skills. They have a hard time dealing with volunteers, making decisions, firing and hiring people. The professional firm removes this burden from the candidate—at least till he gets to the White House.

I hold in both my hands with awe, reverence, and some skepticism the ten-pound book that contains the "Bayh Presidential Plan/1971," developed by Matt Reese Associates. The chapter headings are indicative of the scope of the plan: "Phase 1, Leadership, Workshop, Research, Media; Phase 2, Talking, Listening, Go-Day, State Hq, Country Orgs, Core Campaign, Bayh Partisans, Mail Day, New Hampshire, Wisconsin," etc., etc., etc. All the essentials of a campaign are present. On reading it the adjectives that spring to mind are detailed and professional; also the imperative: caveat emptor.

The first paragraph of the ten pounds describes accurately and with literary gusto the fouled-up state of Democratic politics in 1971. Having baited the line, the second paragraph sets the hook:

"Meanwhile Birch Bayh, having made himself a national figure in the Supreme Court Challenges, has established himself as a credible potential contender with his personal appeal and efficient personal organization. But in terms of measurable progress towards winning the nomination, Bayh has been unable to break the interlocking barriers of lack of name recognition and lack of media coverage." The introduction then outlines a strategy for Bayh much like that effectively followed by McGovern. It correctly identifies Edmund Muskie's weaknesses and recommends concentrating on the New Hampshire, Florida, and Wisconsin primaries. Recognizing that "most primary victories are media-selected," the introduction concludes that "[this] strategy is the one that can break the name/media circle of Birch Bayh."

After the broad strategic outline, the campaign plan gets down to tactical and technical details. There is to be a region room, much like a Pentagon war room, where staff members on regional desks process requests from their states. There is to be a national newsletter, coordinated "fly-ins" during announcement week, six Watts lines for the war room, roughly $41,000 per state for polling, a computer program for identifying and recording the hard-core primary voters in key states, and funds for several direct mailings to those voters.

The trademark of a successful Reese campaign is, in Matt's words, "constant, repetitive contact to get the voter to the polls—one-to-one contact. Most campaigns are decided by people who really don't give a rat's ass how they vote. They've got to be motivated for your candidate and then gotten to the polls."

Reese's expertise is the telephone campaign. First his organization polls and examines voting lists precinct by precinct to find the areas where those most likely to vote for his candidate live. His organization starts contacting voters in those precincts, moving on to the less likely precincts if time and money permit. Voters are contacted from banks of telephones. Matt Reese estimates his phones have reached 9 million voters during the fifteen-year life of his firm. The average skilled phone volunteer or paid professional can make fifteen phone calls per hour and the phones are manned for twelve hours a day. Reese reaches between 150,000 to 250,000 voters by phone in a statewide campaign, depending on state size. "If you want to run a phone campaign, no one can do it like Matt Reese," admits a rival. Reese himself is concerned that phone campaigns are so expensive. In Texas in 1970, he had 150 phones going in the closing weeks of the campaign. "I'm pricing myself out of the market."

After the voter is contacted on the phone, the phoner fills out a computer form on the contact and the voter automatically gets a different personal letter from the candidate depending on his or her response. If the response is enthusiastic enough, the voter is asked to work for the campaign on his or her block. In this way more people are contacted and involved, more telephones manned. During this time the candidate is also on television; but the essence of the campaign is the constant local contact. It's the old-fashioned technique mated with the modern electronic technology of phones, computers, and direct mail.

Reese stresses the elimination of the "why-don't-we's" in a campaign. This occurs when the candidate and his top advisers waste time and money debating in the vital closing weeks "why don't we" do this or do that: have a parade down Main Street, appear on an all-night black DJ show, hold a fund raiser. With a professionally managed campaign, the candidate's time and effort are planned in advance. Significantly it is planned from V day (not D Day but Vote day) backward. What the candidate does V-day morning. What he does on V minus 1, V minus 2, V minus 67.

This whole effort is designed to move voters over the "want-to line" and on to a point where they want to vote for Reese's candidate enough to go to the polls. Reese points out that it is as silly to waste time and funds on those that are going to vote for you anyway, say your wife, children, and friends (Reese is a happily married old-fashioned West Virginian) as it is to waste time on those that won't vote for you under any circumstances. There are two groups important to a candidate. The first are those who normally vote, in elections or primaries, and would be for the candidate if they just knew more about him. The second are those that are already for the candidate but normally don't vote. These two groups usually live in separate parts of a state and the telephone pitch used to motivate them is different. The Reese organization has a complex computerized formula by which the election districts of the state are ranked on the basis of polling and past election turnouts. From this ranking a candidate determines where to put his time and money. Then, by computer, a master calling list is prepared from voter registration records and the reverse phone book, which lists phones by address rather than name. Sections of the master list are distributed to those who will man the phone banks and the campaign begins. It is easy to appreciate how much of the important work is done during the invisible primary.

The volunteers begin to phone and recruit block and election captains. These captains get a personal computerized letter that looks handwritten from the candidate. (During Robert Kennedy's Indiana presidential primary, Reese sent out 20,000 personal, apparently handwritten letters with Ethel Kennedy's signature.) Next the block and election captains recruit more people into the organization and give small fund-raising parties and TV parties to watch the candidate on TV. Then more phone calls are made, and the organization grows apace—"Build from the voter up," being another Reese slogan.

Matt Reese sees himself as the inheritor of the political boss's role. The political party has dissolved, Reese believes, because civil service has removed the granting of government jobs from the bosses and given it instead to the bureaucrats of the knowledge industry with their tests for hiring and promotion. These tests are no more fair and produce no better government than the old referral by political bosses; they just work in different people's favor. Reese believes he is the repository of the new political knowledge. "One of the things you buy, when you hire me, is my past mistakes." At forty-eight, Reese has built up a tremendous amount of invisible primary experience. His analysis of the abortive 1972 Bayh campaign and how its lessons can now be applied in Florida seems to me to be a perfect blend of the best of old political shrewdness with computerized socioeconomics.

One swallow doth not a summer make; but one well-publicized political upset can go a long way toward making, or remaking, a campaign management firm. For gray-haired Doug Bailey and thin, nervous John Deardourff, the two soft-spoken, moderate Republicans who run Bailey, Deardourff, the collapse of the Percy campaign was a disaster. They began looking for smaller offices and laying off staff. Then John Deardourff managed the campaigns of James A. Rhodes in Ohio and William G. Milliken in Michigan and produced two Republican upset victories in the disastrous GOP year of Watergate. Meanwhile Doug Bailey successfully managed two easier, though by no means sure bets, in the successful Senate campaigns of Richard Schweiker in Pennsylvania and Charles Mathias in Maryland (over Barbara Mikulski of the Democrat's embattled Mikulski reforms).

"Strategy Gives Rhodes Upset," headlined the Washington *Post*. The *Times* was equally stunned. Bailey, Deardourff were out of the cold. Importantly, in the two upset races, Deardourff—or his candidate—had beaten candidates whose TV was managed by Charles Guggenheim (for Governor John Gilligan of Ohio) and David Garth (for challenger Sander Levin in Michigan). "I don't know what more we could have done for Levin," Garth told me later. "Deardourff," said Governor James Rhodes, "you are the king, because you have beaten the king."

"We were a firm born out of desperation," says John Deardourff. The desperation in question consisted in the fact that no one was providing any skilled media guidance for liberal Republicans. The firm originally had been Bailey, Goldberg, formed informally in 1964 when Bailey, who had been Henry Kissinger's assistant at Harvard for four years, and Goldberg engineered a surprise write-in victory for Henry Cabot Lodge in the New Hampshire Republican presidential primary. John Deardourff, who had worked as a research expert for Nelson Rockefeller, came aboard in 1967. The firm almost went down the tube in 1968–70 with George Romney's presidential campaign, followed by three other big losses in 1970. Then in 1972 they started to turn the corner with the successful campaign of Christopher Bond for governor of Missouri and the reelection campaigns of Senators Edward Brooke in Massachusetts and Charles Percy in Illinois. Today both partners are fanatical about advanced planning and insist on handling a total campaign or nothing.

"Winning campaigns are ground out week by week, month by month, over a period of years," intones Doug Bailey. Their report to Senator Percy three weeks after Nixon's overwhelming reelection victory told Percy that his winning the presidency in 1976 was "an impossible dream, except if you are willing to begin now."

The 1974 Ohio gubernatorial campaign, managed on the Republican side by John Deardourff, pitted James Rhodes, a lackluster Republican former governor, against the encumbent John Gilligan, an energetic Rhodes scholar who was already being talked of by liberals as a possible presidential candidate, but who had a reputation for arrogance inside his own state. It was Deardourff's genius—other political consultants and some reporters call it genius, Gilligan uses harsher words—that caught Gilligan and his hired media expert, Charles Guggenheim, completely off guard.

Instead of trying to bring out the vote by buying TV time in areas where Rhodes was strong, Deardourff took his limited budget and bought time in areas where Gilligan was strong, trying to hold down the Gilligan vote. The areas to hit had been carefully pinpointed by the polls of Robert Teeter.

"When we [Guggenheim and Gilligan] saw their media buys, we thought they were mad," said Gilligan later. In this Democratic heartland Deardourff ran anti-Gilligan television ads showing dirty, unpaved streets, deserted, crumbling schools, and highways that led nowhere. The gamble worked. In heavily Democratic Cuyahoga County around Cleveland, Gilligan dropped some 110,000 votes behind his showing of four years before. This, plus organized labor's dissatisfaction with Gilligan's early anti-Vietnam stand, put Rhodes over the top.

Whereas Matt Reese Associates and Bailey, Deardourff handle only candidates from one political party, David Garth Associates work both sides of the street. Before Garth takes on a client, the firm's six partners have a meeting and decide whether they can work with the candidate. Among politicians and their fellow gunslingers, the firm is regarded as one of the best and also one of the most controversial.

"All my clients love me," said David Garth, who then spends the next ten minutes telling why he is "suing that goy bastard Lindsay," whom he hates. Garth got ex-New York Mayor John Lindsay an apartment in the same exclusive West Side building as himself, and now both men make certain never to ride in the same elevator. Since there is a great deal of combativeness about Garth—in his TV commercials he goes for the jugular—it would be surprising if all his clients ended up throwing him roses. They don't, but he certainly has fans. "He's tough, but he's not insecure," says the campaign manager of one client who does like Garth. "He's got an abrasive personality but that's all to the good." When funds are limited, the manager points out, "you don't want someone around who just says, 'Yes, sir, yes, sir,' and takes your money."

Though he presents a total package to the political client, Garth remains primarily a media expert. Talk to Matt Reese and the expressions that occur and reoccur in conversation are "voter contact," "repetition," "personal involvement." John Deardourff talks of "planning," "grinding it out," "the total organization concept." Garth talks of "spots," "media time," "hand-held tape cameras."

Drawing on his own expertise, Garth sees TV, not pollsters or managers, as "breaking up the party. You can go to the tube and get your idea across for money, or in a debate for free, and you don't need the party." He holds, I believe correctly, that the management firms are an effect, not a cause. "I think the party today is a joke," says Garth. He is equally contemptuous of volunteers, believing that at five dollars a day for expenses, twenty thousand volunteers eat up all your budget and don't produce anything. He believes that Gene McCarthy might have beaten Robert Kennedy in California in 1968 if he had spent his money on media and not volunteers.

Congressman John Heinz, a liberal Republican and one of the brighter lights of the lower House, has used both Bailey, Deardourff and David Garth, all three of whom he considers his friends. "What Bailey and Deardourff can do," Heinz says, "is fine-tune a campaign. . . . They can take a campaign and tailor it to meet a limited budget requirement." Both

Garth and Bailey, Deardourff, Heinz stresses, look at "the product, that's the candidate, first." After that they design the campaign. Neither firm is wed to formulas. Garth's strength, says Heinz, is in making issues appear real to voters through the media ("He produces celluloid that is real"), while Bailey, Deardourff are strong in the overall management of a campaign.

Grown-ups believe the lessons of their childhood. Those consultants who come from media states like New York and California stress media. Those who come from the smaller towns and villages of the South and Midwest stress organization and contact. You pay your consultant and you take your chance. But whatever you do, it is, in fact if not in name, outside the party.

From the thirties through the sixties, political scientists and crusading reporters kicked the bosses. Now it's kick-the-campaign-managers time. "The professional managers are weakening democracy by their perceptions of what politics ought to be and through the techniques they are introducing to American politics. . . . They . . . minimize and discourage political participation rather than maximize it, and . . . they have failed to account for the social impact of their technological innovations in politics." So writes Dr. David Rosenbloom, of Hamilton and Kirkland colleges, in *The Election Men.*

A detailed piece in *The Village Voice* about David Garth's handling of Hugh Carey's successful campaign for governor of New York in 1974 concludes: "In a Watergate year, a year when voters should be particularly sensitive to manipulation, Garth's broadly true, but purposefully misleading, commercials might become inoperative."

Such criticisms seem to me part of our American tendency to look for scapegoats, to find villainy anywhere but in ourselves. Where an ancient Greek would see individual tragedy or a modern European the *condition humaine,* we see malefactors: big government, crooked bankers, scheming labor unions, yellow TV networks, manipulative campaign consultants, biased journalists. Are we really that gullible? Do we not get the politics and the electioneering we deserve? The political parties are breaking up. The candidates in the invisible primary as well as elsewhere have a problem: to get organized, to find out what's going on, to get known. To do this they turn no longer to the party professionals but to reporters, pollsters, and campaign consultants. These categories, being people, perform much as people always have.

> *So, when the crowd gives tongue*
> *And prophets, old or young,*
> *Bawl out their strange despair*
> *Or fall in worship there. . . .*
> *Say neither in their way,*
> *"It is a deadly magic and accursed,"*
> *Nor "It is blest," but only "It is here."*

CHAPTER 8

The Close of the Invisible Primary (I)

A hot August sizzled into a cold and wet September. Secretary of Agriculture Earl Butz almost saw his optimistic wheat predictions of spring shrivel on the stalk beneath the endless blazing days. President Ford vacationed in the Rockies and took political trips on the weekends, much as he had when in the Congress. While on the rubber-chicken circuit in California in an effort to head off Ronald Reagan at the pass, Ford looked down the barrel of a real gun from a distance of two feet. The .45 Colt automatic was held by a redheaded, red-caped, red-cowled cult follower of ritual murderer Charles Manson, Lynette Alice "Squeaky" Fromme. "The country is a mess. This man is not your President," she yelled. Fortunately for Ford the gun did not go off. Fromme learned a lesson appreciated too late by many a dead soldier: under stress it's easy to forget to put a round in the chamber.

Seventeen days later and eighty miles northwest, Sara Jane Moore's .38 Smith and Wesson revolver was properly loaded. Shooting from across the street in front of the St. Francis Hotel in San Francisco, she missed Ford by five feet, thanks in part to the alertness of an ex-Marine standing by her who saw the handgun. There is a seventh track in the invisible primary: Chance.

On the six conventional tracks, the processes of the invisible primary worked over the candidates, grinding some down, building others up. None of the announced candidates, Democrats or Republicans, finished the summer of '75 having done particularly well. And that, too, was part of the process. For in both parties, as some of the early starters showed definite weakness, off stage other men sought ways to take their place. In offices, pressrooms, TV studios, kitchens, auditoriums, over the phone, anywhere people met, the race went on.

By now the selection process was both gaining intensity and coming more under public scrutiny; a "mere" half year away were the first state caucus in Iowa and the first state primary in New Hampshire. In both parties the final shape of the invisible primary had taken form, though its details remained amorphous. It was like a new play whose director has set the main thrust of the action and blocked out crucial scenes, but whose individual moments of pain and joy, triumph and defeat, still remained to be discovered by the actors and judged by an audience.

Outside the central action of the play, the courts made a critical decision. On August 15th the Appeals Court in the District of Columbia, six to two (with one justice disqualifying himself), declared the Campaign Financing Act of 1974 constitutional. The suit against the Act had been filed in January by Senator James Buckley, the Republican Conservative from New York. Later, strangely, he was joined by ex-Senator Eugene McCarthy of the anti-war movement, and the American Civil Liberties Union. The Justice Department couldn't decide where it stood on the issue, so Common Cause, which had lobbied for the law, retained its own counsel to argue against the suit.

Lawyers for Buckley and McCarthy argued that, quoting the late Justice Brandeis: "The greatest dangers to liberty lurk in insidious encroachment by men of zeal, well meaning but without understanding." (A curious way to categorize the United States Senate.) The plaintiffs further held that the Campaign Act violated the first amendment's rights to free speech: ". . . restrict[ing] the political freedom of individual citizens by limiting political activity, circumscribing speech, institutionalizing advantages for incumbents, authorizing unprecedented government surveillance over political association and establishing broad investigative powers of doubtful constitutionality. . . . The end result we fear will not be fairer elections but rather a restriction of dissenting points of view. . . ."

In defense of the law, Lloyd Cutler, retained by Common Cause, argued: "Money has always corrupted elections, but by 1972 money had become a habit-forming drug. The preoccupation with raising and spending money corrupted not only a President but a significant proportion of all politicians and all voters who gave."

The District Court agreed, holding that:

> . . . We have not been sufficiently vigilant; we have failed to remind ourselves, as we moved from the town halls to today's quadrennial Romanesque political extravaganzas, that politics is neither an end in itself nor a means for subverting the will of the people. The excesses revealed by this record—the campaign spending, the use to which the money is put in some instances, the campaign funding, the quid pro quo for the contributions—support the legislative judgment that the situation not only must not deteriorate further, but that the present situation cannot be tolerated by a government that professes to be a Democracy.

After the decision, the two groups immediately filed briefs before the Supreme Court. Most court watchers believed that the near unanimity of the lower court decision, the lack of time for the Supreme Court to go into the case before the first state primaries, and the reluctance of the present Supreme Court to politicize itself meant that the Appeals Court's ruling would be reaffirmed and the law upheld. Candidates with programs that appealed to those of enormous wealth would no longer hold a decisive advantage.

Meanwhile, back in the invisible primary, Senator Edward Kennedy withdrew one giant step further. After the explicit wording of his official withdrawal announcement, this should hardly have been necessary. But such are press suspicions these days, of politicians in general and perhaps of this politician in particular, that Kennedy found he had to do something more. The rumors and reports that Kennedy was secretly running were fueled in two separate ways, even though key members of his staff were emphatically indicating their belief in his sincerity by taking other jobs. On the Georgetown cocktail party circuit, an alleged girlfriend kept reporting that Kennedy had told her he was running. That's all it takes to make the media today in pygmyville on the Potomac, where a senator's hairpiece is news and his programs, if he has any, are only measured for political "sex appeal."

The second person to raise doubts as to Kennedy's sincerity carried far more weight: Congressman Tip O'Neill, Jr., the majority leader of the House, friend of the Kennedys, trusted by the press, and one of the most astute politicians in the land. O'Neill kept insisting, both privately and publicly, that Kennedy had never told him he wasn't running, even when asked. Finally on July 30th, O'Neill repeated that statement over national television. He said Kennedy had replied "Keep me alive, Tip" when he asked Kennedy if he were running. Four days later, Kennedy called O'Neill on the phone and after a few friendly preliminaries said pointblank: "Tip, I wish you'd stop saying I'm a candidate." O'Neill stopped.

While Kennedy moved backwards, another long-time Democratic warrior edged forward: Hubert Horatio Humphrey, "Dear old Hubert" to his friends, a napalm-scarred Vietnam apologist to his foes. Humphrey was still insisting publicly and privately that he would not enter any state primaries and that he did not want the nomination. But not entirely without his knowledge, a group of friends began to organize a committee on his behalf, led by Governor Wendell Anderson of Minnesota, I. W. Abel, chairman of the Steelworkers, and friendly senators such as George McGovern and Fritz Mondale. Humphrey himself sent an emissary to Robert Strauss to get a detailed briefing on the rules and dates of every state primary. A few weeks later, in October, he demonstrated at an off-the-record breakfast with reporters that he had, with his remarkable blotting-paper memory, mastered the incredible intricacies of the state primary-caucus system in 1976.

But those urging Hubert Humphrey to run came up with a conclusion that ran totally counter to Humphrey's plans. They decided that the ultimate winner at the Democratic Convention was almost certain to be a candidate who had entered at least a few primaries. They rejected as unrealistic their previous strategy: to lie back and wait for a deadlocked convention to nominate Humphrey practically by acclamation. But Humphrey was unwilling to enter any primaries.

So, for a time at least, the Humphrey Committee died aborning, though its members continued to keep in touch with each other and hope. As a holding action, some Humphrey supporters threw their prestige and the votes of the organizations they controlled behind minor candidates. Their strategy was to whittle down the votes of the leaders and elect as delegates people who would switch to Humphrey after supporting the minor candidate on the first ballot. For example, Humphrey's long-time supporter, George Hardy, president of the Service Employees International Union, threw his support in mid-October to Fred Harris, with a broad wink in Hubert's direction.

Not all of those supporting Hubert Humphrey saw him as the man they most wanted for President. Some of them merely wanted a Democratic President and were alarmed by the failure of any of the candidates in the invisible primary to gather momentum. Many of Hubert's supporters were older, and they naturally turned to Humphrey as a symbol of the good old days when they were all more united. Some were merely hungry and saw in the Minnesota senator the easiest way to climb back to power. Others were dismayed by the announced policies of some of the new candidates and reached toward Hubert out of fear.

How did Senator Humphrey feel about all this? What was his standing on the psychological track? All his friends agree that he remains terribly upset by the financial hosing many of his friends had to take during his primary campaign against McGovern. He had been totally unable to pay back the vast sums he had been loaned. In politics Humphrey has a reputation for telling the truth, but as seeing the truth differently from day to day. He has repeatedly gone to bed firmly believing one thing and on waking been equally firmly committed to another. "I am not going into the primaries," he was still saying publicly in October. Mike Berman, a close friend who is back to practicing law in Minneapolis after the Mondale caper, described Humphrey's stand against running as being, "As firm as anything I have ever seen him take in his political life."

Still, with powerful friends trying to involve him in the presidential race, and with no one emerging clearly in the lead, the question remained—would he find the strength in himself to stay out this time? He had sworn up and down that he would never enter the primaries in 1972, that he was going to leave the way open for his old friend Muskie. Then on his sixtieth birthday, May 27, he got a group of reporters together at breakfast, and after sloshing catchup on his omelet, almost shouted: "I've got the sails up. . . . I'm occasionally licking my chops." Would his ego defeat his brain once again? He was older now, sounding a bit wiser, and his fabulous energy had begun to ebb. "I'm not entering the primaries. I just don't want to," he told a group of reporters. "I've been through that route. . . . If I was an avowed candidate I'd let you know. Since I'm not, I am letting you know. . . . I find them [the primaries] financially, politically and physically debilitating."

Despite Humphrey's impressive popularity in the polls, it seemed to me that he would stay out of the invisible primary and the state primaries for so long that he would not be a potent factor. He might get in later, in time to hurt himself, but not in time to change the outcome.

On the Republican side of the invisible primary the view from August to

October was mixed. Ford's popularity, which had risen to an all-time high of 51 percent after he sent in the Marines to free the crew of the Mayaguez, dropped to only 38 percent by the end of August. Then it began to rise slightly after the two attempts on his life. But even as his popularity dropped, Ford continued to hold a decisive lead over Ronald Reagan among Republican voters, 60 percent to 32 percent.*

The bad news for President Ford began in New Hampshire, where Reagan supporters, following the identical strategy of several Democratic candidates, were concentrating their forces, hoping to provoke an early and decisive battle. In September, Reagan strategists John Sears and James Lake persuaded Republican ex-Governor Hugh Gregg to head the Reagan drive. At the same time, Stewart Lamprey, a former speaker of the New Hampshire House, came on board as an assistant. Though neither man was presently active in politics, both were considered Republican moderates. Gregg had run Nelson Rockefeller's primary campaign in New Hampshire in 1964, and Lamprey had been chairman of Nixon's campaign in 1968. The presence of these two moderates in Reagan's camp mitigated some of the extreme right-wing flavor implied by his most vocal New Hampshire supporter, conservative Governor Meldrim Thomson. No longer could it be said: "Only the nuts are for him."

Ronald Reagan continued to keep silent about his intentions, for, among others, excellent financial reasons. As soon as he became a declared candidate, he would lose the estimated one million dollars a year he made from his daily five-minute radio programs on more than two hundred stations. The stations would be forced to cancel his program or give equal time to all the other political candidates. Also, as long as he was a non-candidate, none of his traveling expenditures counted against either the ten-million-dollar total spending limit or the fifty thousand dollars he was allowed to spend on himself. Some of the money he received for his banquet speeches came from tickets purchased by corporations, an illegal fund source once he became a candidate. Such economic losses, plus his own psychological disinclination to campaign, must have made tremendously attractive the role of a non-candidate who merely went, as Reagan calls it, "Paul Revereing" around the nation for conservatism.

Yet, during October and November, the Citizens for Reagan for President Committee, led by Senator Paul Laxalt of Nevada, ex-Governor Louie B. Nunn of Kentucky, ex-Representative H. R. Gross of Iowa, Mrs. Stanhope Ring, a former California Republican National Committeewoman, and George B. Cook, a Lincoln, Nebraska, insurance executive, slowly pushed a genuinely divided Reagan towards his candidacy. Their principle argument

---

*Several commentators and Reagan supporters looking at these figures believed they showed Reagan strength. "If McGovern had been that close to Muskie," said one observer, "six months before New Hampshire, he'd now be President." Not so. McGovern was then an unknown with a vast pool of undecideds to work on. In the invisible primary, Republican undecideds numbered less than 10 percent.

was Ford's declining popularity, particularly in three early primary states: New Hampshire, Florida and North Carolina. They were also encouraged by Ford's poor showing in Reagan's home state of California, a "winner-take-all" primary for Republicans. Ford's chief accomplishment in October appeared to be his acceptance of a copy of the *Declaration of Independence* made out of alphabet noodles. "The big change," said Reagan staff leader Mike Deaver, "was that between then [July and November] the nomination became possible." The committee felt, and to some extent Reagan's personal staff agreed, that Reagan could savage Ford quickly, as Kefauver had savaged Truman, or Eugene McCarthy had Johnson. Reagan's high UQ (unacceptability quotient) in the polls and the power of the television-augmented imperial presidency, they brushed aside.

In the last week in October, Committee and candidate secretly set November 20 as the date for a Washington announcement, followed by a one day whirlwind tour of six key primary states. This frenetic media event would exploit Reagan's mastery of television and, they hoped, start the vital snowball of excitement within the conservative constituency. President Ford was no longer home free.

At the same time, two and one-eighths more candidates officially entered the Democratic side of the invisible primary: Senator Birch Bayh of Indiana, and Sargent Shriver, Kennedy in-law and former director of the Peace Corps.* George Wallace was in Europe proving both that he could deal with heads of state and that his health was up to the ordeal of the presidency. Before he left, his staff had arranged for the Waldorf ballroom for his official announcement of entry on November 10th. Later this was switched to a Montgomery announcement on November 12th. Four other Democratic candidates, James Carter, Fred Harris, Lloyd Bentsen, and Terry Sanford, had been reduced to the status of minor players. Only two possible champions remained, Morris Udall and Scoop Jackson; and they were both scarred, though also wiser.

Jackson's strategy of staying in the Senate and gaining national TV exposure and headlines through legislation and investigations had not proved successful. His standing had improved slightly in the polls, up three points, but now stuck at around 10 percent, well beneath Hubert Humphrey or George Wallace. His efforts to broaden his constituency from the few labor unions and Jewish organizations that had supported him since '73 had proven unsuccessful. He still had problems with the media, whose members admitted his Senate power but doubted his ability as a political campaigner. To win, he was going to have to prove himself as a vote-getter in

---

*The one-eighth candidate was millionaire Governor Milton Shapp of Pennsylvania, who flopped into the race suffering from advanced Stassomania. He may have been seeking the answer to the question: Can a lackluster governor whose campaign finances are under grand-jury investigation and whose campaign manager has been convicted of extortion, along with four other members of his administration, escape to the presidency? If your answer is, "Yes," you are a Pennsylvania politician suffering from Stassomania.

some early primary. His staff were divided on just where that primary would be.

Interestingly, both Senator Jackson and Governor Wallace had made the strategic decision to bypass the New Hampshire primary. Further, Jackson was uncertain whether to enter the second state primary, Massachusetts, though Wallace would make a major effort there. The media and other politicians accepted these decisions, by and large, as an example of wisdom rather than weakness. Previously a candidate practically *had* to enter New Hampshire to be considered "serious." I mention this to show how candidates, press, and public make their own adjustments to the irrationalities of the invisible/state primary system. These adjustments, made without fuss, legislation, or litigation, often prove far more effective than changes in party rules and federal laws.

On one track, money, Senator Jackson was the outstanding candidate, though even he had found fund-raising more difficult than anticipated. He had $1,242,345 on hand by October 1, 1975, and had raised $2.8 million since 1974, whereas he had hoped to have over $3 million by this time. Still, this placed him miles ahead of his closest competitors—George Wallace with $744,208 cash on hand in October, and Senator Lloyd Bentsen of Texas with $195,000. In fact, with Scandinavian frugality, Jackson was even investing his money in government notes to raise extra cash.

In late August, Robert Keefe, Jackson's campaign manager, gave a blackboard briefing for the staff on where their candidate stood now. His graph of the money track showed a climb through May, then a gradual decrease as contributions fell off during the summer, when political expenses mounted. Then came a sharp upturn in the early fall as fund raising got under way again; after that, another drop as the expenses of Jackson's effort in the early primaries of Florida and New York would begin to mount. Finally would come the decisive spurt as the matching federal funds arrived and private contributions surged after early primary victories.

"What happens if the federal financing is overturned?" asked an aide.

Keefe swept his chalk up the graph and released at the ceiling. "We go through the roof," he said.

Keefe was right. On the money track, no matter how the rules changed, Jackson ended up ahead. If the law held, he would receive more matching federal funds than any other candidate. If the law was repealed, his enthusiastic and wealthy Jewish backers, with their tight fund-raising organizations, stood ready to make his the best financed campaign in the race within the week. He and his staff had been the first to figure out that the proliferation of primaries plus proportional representation meant that all the primaries might well become almost equally important and that candidates could run out of money before they reached the later primaries. His top staff, Robert Keefe, fund raiser Dick Kline, and treasurer Walter Skallerup, had laid out a tightly controlled, detailed budget to make certain they had enough cash left for the final primaries: California, New Jersey, and Ohio. Other candidates might snicker publicly, but privately they were impressed. Yet the overall question remained: Could Jackson find a way to translate his financial lead and expert staff work into votes in the state primaries?

The other early candidate who had survived was Morris Udall. Like Jackson, his position was a bit shaky, but he still stood out on the center-left as Jackson stood out on the center-right. Udall also was having trouble on the constituency track. He had not been able to expand his following beyond the initial group of former Muskie and McGovern liberals who saw him as both an idealist and a winner. No major political figures or labor leaders had come aboard to give his campaign the bandwagon effect beloved of the press. In both New Hampshire and Iowa, those who had signed on early had not had the expected success in persuading other more nervous politicians fearful of supporting a loser. As Governor Michael S. Dukakis of Massachusetts put it at a meeting of liberal Democrats in Springfield in late September: "The Muskie experience has made some of us more reluctant to move early."

John Gabusi, Udall's campaign manager who chose marriage over politics, was replaced by Jack Quinn, a former New York lawyer and a deceptively innocent looking professional from McGovern's personal staff. (Sargent Shriver had wanted Quinn as his campaign manager.) Also to solve staff problems, Mo's older brother Stewart, who had proved better at theory than political follow-through, was moved sideways to special contacts and ideas. The staff, which had almost foundered in mid-October, got back to speed by mid-November—another advantage of an early start.

On the financial track, Udall edged close to disaster, being $127,435 in debt at the end of September. He had found fund-raising harder and volunteers more expensive than expected. Both he and his staff had to divert blocks of time planned for campaigning to fund raising. Still, he had raised enough cash to survive until the arrival of federal funds in January. But unless he won in New Hampshire and Massachusetts he seemed dead. He lacked the funds to battle in the later primaries.

On the psychological and media tracks, Udall had made substantial progress. His speaking style and personality had toughened. He had obviously decided he wanted the presidency. The jokes were still there, but they were fewer and more pointed. He was using his House record to highlight his early efforts—almost alone—for causes that later became popular: against Vietnam, in favor of civil rights, land use, environmental protection and congressional reform. The media began to drop their initial reluctance to believe a congressman could make it to the White House and started to treat him as a "viable" candidate.

The other four Democratic candidates had been shaken down to minor candidate status. Lloyd Bentsen had found that the votes he had to take in the Senate to retain his eastern constituency of conservative labor leaders and politicians lost him his money in Texas. Further, those votes jeopardized the constituency he would need back in Texas to gain reelection to the Senate. On September 10th, Bentsen voted to sustain President Ford's efforts to decontrol oil. Two weeks later he announced he would vote against common situs picketing. Both votes had been demanded by his Texas money, angered over reports that he was in favor of limited federal help for New York City. Since he had failed to raise an adequate amount of cash outside of Texas, he had to obey his Texas money. With these votes his eastern constituency vanished. Bentsen found that after spending $1,610,389 he was back where he started: a candidate with southern and southwestern backing who had a chance at the vice-presidency to balance a ticket headed by a northern liberal.

Bentsen's campaign manager, Ben Palumbo, the chief architect of Bentsen's national strategy, vanished—just the way Lloyd Hackler had vanished when his strategy of playing for the vice-presidency had lost out to Palumbo in early 1974. Besides, Bentsen and Palumbo, who both were detail men, found they spent a great deal of time issuing and reissuing differing orders to accomplish the same task. Probably by trying to become a national candidate and failing, Bentsen had killed his chances of being a regional candidate and succeeding as Vice-President. But he had enough money and media strength to hang on grimly to the end with a reduced staff and schedule, trying for the second prize.

Former Senator Eugene McCarthy, leader of the anti-war movement in 1968, had never been a serious candidate in this invisible primary. His presence in the race at all served as a grisly reminder of how easy it is to fall from candidate to joke, to descend from politics to paranoia. He was not even running as a Democrat any longer, but as the candidate of the Committee for a Constitutional Presidency whose aim was to revive the Electoral College. McCarthy was petitioning the states to get his name directly onto the ballot. His campaign was being managed by Ron Cocome, a former health-food store employee who called McCarthy's followers "militant independents" and vowed that they would never sell out to the system. The committee was originally funded by a $15,000 contribution from William Clay Ford, the auto heir who had hoped to give more later but was prevented by the campaign financing law from doing so—which is why McCarthy had joined Buckley in attacking the legality of the law.

"There is not much I could do within the Democratic Party," said McCarthy when setting up his Committee in the fall of 1974. He was sitting in his Georgetown house, a torn rug on the floor, threads dangling from the furniture. The house was cold at ten in the morning, and there was an oppressive, doggy odor in the air. McCarthy had just gotten up. He had a bad cold and remarked that the heating system was too complicated for him to work. The dank room was decorated with kitsch antiques: a child's bugle, a child's steam engine, an old-fashioned scooter.

The Kennedy people didn't like him, he said, "because they feel I am responsible for Bobby's death." I must have looked surprised, because he added: "Oh, yes, some of them do." He asked me if I remembered how the

Kennedys had sabotaged him at the Worcester convention in 1968. I didn't. He began to explain with real bitterness, a long and rambling story full of names I didn't know. McGovern was against him, too, he said, because, "I am more right on the issues." He pointed out that in 1972 he was the only candidate talking about the CIA, troops in Europe, poverty and inflation. He added that there had been a lot of Kennedy money secretly behind McGovern to prevent McCarthy from getting the Democratic nomination in 1972.

I asked him why, with all the abuse he had taken, he wanted to subject himself to the process again. "I don't anticipate the same type of physical commitment as if I were going to run in the primaries," he said. He felt that once he had his committee established, his ideas were so sound and right that "more and more people come to you."

By October of 1975 McCarthy had been reduced to abusing the Advisory Committee on Protection of Presidential Candidates, chaired by House Speaker Carl Albert, for not granting him Secret Service protection. "He is better known to the American public than five of the six candidates recently offered Secret Service protection," said Cocome in an official release. He went on to call on each member of the Advisory Committee "to take personal responsibility [for] . . . any harm to Gene McCarthy."

Perhaps the poet in McCarthy was remembering the final temptation of Archbishop Thomas Becket in T. S. Eliot's "Murder in the Cathedral": "Saint and martyr rule from the tomb."

Another candidate culled by the invisible primary was Fred Harris, the former senator from Oklahoma. Once he had been one of the golden boys of the Democratic party; appointed Chairman of the Democratic National Committee in 1969, his future seemed bright. But he was a loud and ineffective chairman, alienating almost everyone; and there were signs of instability. In 1971 he ran for President as a people's candidate and in six weeks blew $300,000, advanced him by two millionaires, on Lear Jets and high living. Now, the second time around, fatter and flakier, he was again the people's candidate, only this time nickel-and-diming it and living in a Winnebago camper as he politicked across the states. In between living in the camper, he flew first-class to speaking engagements.

"There are two parts to my campaign," Harris yelled. "One, people are smart enough to govern themselves. Two, there is a need for widespread diffusion of power in the country." He was Wallace without racism or executive experience and money. At Democratic party rallies his followers were the one group immediately identifiable, still wearing the uniform of the sixties' protest, shoeless, long-haired, defiantly dirty; dressed in jeans and Mother Hubbards. For them, Harris was not a candidate but a cause. Unfortunately for Harris, the courtship of purist constituency had left him with few supporters elsewhere. "Those people we have on the coast," said Harris's Iowa organizer, John Freeberg, "they would rather vote for Dick Gregory if he were on the ticket."

There was a third part to Harris's campaign: his wife LaDonna, a striking

Comanche Indian with flowing dark hair who often travels resplendent in her turquoise and silver jewelry. With her effective speaking voice and great energy, plus her reputation as a force in both the women's movement and Indian affairs, she probably drew more votes to Harris than he gained himself. They ran their campaign out of their home in McLean, Virginia, augmented by two trailers parked in the yard. Harris's strategy was to concentrate on the early Iowa caucus and New Hampshire primary to launch him as they had launched McGovern. But his forced mixture of simplistic thirties rhetoric and sixties protest drew little notice and less money.

Probably his most important function in the invisible primary was to indirectly aid Udall. With Harris out there on the purist left, no one could attack Udall as an extremist. This left Udall free both to remain left-liberal and exploit the center. Harris cast a glow of moderation over Udall from the left, just as Bentsen cast a glow of liberalism over Jackson from the right.

There is even less to say about ex-Governor Terry Sanford of North Carolina than about Fred Harris. He could not raise money, he could not recruit able staff, he could not find a constituency and he never showed at most rallies. He had a certain following among students. I believe the reason for it was that he is an imposing father figure who is easily pushed around, thus reminding some few of their ideal daddy. Sanford, now the 56-year-old president of Duke University, had also made the attempt in 1972. Then he spent $700,000 and was beaten by George Wallace in his own state.

In late September 1975, he had $7,000 in the bank and was $78,000 in debt. He hastily cut his staff's salaries in half; yet he was still spending $40,000 a month and had twenty-six people on his payroll plus the largest set of offices of any candidate after the well-financed duo of Wallace and Jackson. His strategy, that he would be the one candidate who would challenge Wallace in the South, was no longer valid since ex-Governor James Carter was making the same claim. There is a political saying: "You can't make a soufflé rise twice." In Sanford's case the soufflé had not risen once.

The minor candidate who almost made it out of the ruck was James Earl Carter, Jr., former governor of Georgia. He didn't have any spectacular success on any of the six tracks, but he didn't have any great weaknesses either. This solid, if minimal position, might have stood him in good stead if everyone else had been devoured in the invisible primary or slipped on one of the state primary stepping-stones.

"The country is ready for someone like me," said Carter, "a farmer, an engineer, a businessman, a planner, a scientist, a governor and a Christian." The latter attribute seemed particularly important in Carter's campaign. He was a deacon in his local Baptist Church and often delivered the sermon. He also had courage; he voted to desegregate his local church several years before such an act was popular. The fifty-one-year-old Carter was a Naval Academy graduate who went on to become one of Admiral Hyman

Rickover's nuclear submarine hotshots. Upon his father's death in 1953, Carter left the Navy, a puzzling episode in his career, and went from successful officer, commander of the nuclear submarine *Seawolf,* to peanut farmer. In a short time he proved he could handle nuts as well as "nukes," succeeding as both a peanut grower and a politician.

As a governor, Carter was certainly in the tradition of southern progressives—in fact, you can leave out the sectional adjective. He reduced the 300 state agencies to 22, instituted zero-base budgeting, raised the number of blacks in executive positions from three to fifty-three, passed an ecology measure, pioneered local community centers for mental health care, and pushed other pieces of progressive legislation through the often recalcitrant Georgia House. Outside the state, Carter benefitted tremendously from his 1974 appointment as head of the Democratic National Committee's Campaign Committee. This gave him a base from which to travel around the country speaking on behalf of Democratic candidates. Unable by Georgia law to succeed himself, Carter spent a great deal of time on this DNC plum. Not surprisingly, many of the states where he spoke and handshook often turned out to have important early primaries and caucuses: New York, New Hampshire, Iowa, Florida.

While not particularly effective on television or with large groups, Carter is an able speaker before a small gathering. He is obviously a man in command of himself, one who knows where he wants to go. His fund raising—$500,000 by October of 1975, with $14,545.61 cash on hand—while not spectacular, was adequate. His staff was his weakness. They were nice people, but they lacked the knowledge and fire found on the staffs of other candidates. In fact, Carter appears to have trouble establishing relationships with his peers. His New York organization seemed to have discovered the delights of Greenwich Village and disappeared. "By the middle of August I might have something for you to look at; I've only been here since July," said Knox Pitts, his New York coordinator, when I woke him one balmy summer morning.

Carter's strategy of focusing on Iowa and New Hampshire for early wins, gaining national recognition there, and then successfully taking on Wallace in Florida was both rational and suited to his means. It was also suited to his obvious fallback position, the vice-presidency. For Carter, like Bentsen, had a coldly calculating eye for the modern world. He could count. After eight years as Vice-President he would be sixty, with plenty of time left to run on his own.

In the invisible primary, Carter's had been a campaign of "ifs." If the national media had paid a bit more early attention to governors—particularly southern ex-governors. If he himself had been a bit better speaker. If Terry Sanford hadn't split his constituency by being in the race. If his staff had been just a tad more knowledgeable. If he had not been such a prominent part of the anti-McGovern drive in 1972. If his fund raising had produced a little more money. If a few more activists had been impressed by his folksy competence and icy drive. If he wasn't so self-contained that he sometimes reminded thoughtful people of Nixon with his distance and self-confidence. It had been close, but he hadn't quite made it for the first spot. However, with some substantial wins over Wallace, which were possible, he would be in a strong position as a vice-presidential candidate.

Everybody loves a parade, especially a Kennedy parade, and Sargent Shriver tried to bring back that parade with his politics. At the close of his ten-page announcement speech which he delivered, immaculately groomed as always, in the grand ballroom of Washington's Mayflower Hotel, he said, speaking of his brother-in-law: "His legacy awaits the leader who can claim it. I intend to claim that legacy, not for myself alone but for the faith that John Kennedy brought into being for the millions whom he called to public service, for the billions around the world for whom John Kennedy is still an inspiration."

Even the jokes he made showed how conscious he was of his Kennedy status. "You've got to vote me in office or I'll always remain in-law," he said in St. Louis. He didn't repeat that wincer often.

As befitted a man trying to get the Kennedy parade going again, he came trailing clouds of famous names as supporters: Arthur Ashe, James Caan, Morton Downey, Frances T. Farenthold, Aaron E. Henry, Cloris Leachman, Dr. Walter Menninger, Arnold Miller, Robert V. Roosa, Orville Schell, Ray Stark, Kurt Vonnegut, Jr., were among his 102 New-Frontier-type names. Everywhere he went, aides made certain his wife was introduced as Eunice *Kennedy* Shriver.

Not all of the names were quite as supportive as they appeared. Cyrus Vance, former deputy secretary of defense who was named as the campaign manager, explained that he wasn't. "I told Sarge I'd be glad to help him out over the phone." Another prominent supporter on the list opined, after making certain it was off the record, "If Sarge would cut his hair, learn as much about domestic affairs as he knows about some phases of foreign affairs, and learn not to shoot from the hip, he'd make a hell of a candidate. Besides he is the only Catholic in the race." And then there was Tip O'Neill, Jr., and other close friends of Teddy Kennedy spreading the word: anybody but Sarge. With help like that from his friends how could the other candidates hurt him? How would he ever rise to the ranks of major candidate?

In building his constituency, Shriver had three valuable assets. He had been around the track once before as vice-presidential candidate—though this didn't help him on the media track where he was viewed as having been an ineffective campaigner. However, it meant he had supporters who had worked with him once before and would be on lists where they could be reached and used again. Then he was, as he and his followers pointed out endlessly, the only Catholic in the race. His wife Eunice was active in the Right to Life movement against abortion. In August of 1975 Shriver had sent out a fund-raising letter with Right to Life advocates on the letterhead. Later, in September, he had said he would stand by the Supreme Court abortion decision. Abortion and busing are the two most explosive issues in politics today, and the Right-to-Lifers would certainly work and vote for Shriver—though the support of this constituency would cause problems with liberal groups and the women's movement, in which Shriver also hoped to find support. Shriver also had a constituency among former members of the Peace Corps and the Office of Economic Opportunity, for whom he brought back forgotten days of glory.

Then there would be those who were for him because of the Kennedy connection. Though here his opponent Birch Bayh had succinctly capsulated Shriver's problem: "He is too close to the Kennedys to be perceived as an independent candidate. But not close enough to fully benefit from the family association."

Shriver entered the presidential race in a rather insouciant fashion. He said that he hadn't bothered to look over the other candidates or figure out their strengths relative to his. He just came back from a lecture trip and felt that none of the other candidates had caught on and that people out there were waiting for him to make a move. Shriver then went up to Hyannis and asked Teddy if it were really true that he was not going to run. According to Shriver, Teddy was quite shirty about even being asked. He repeated in no uncertain terms that he wasn't going to run, and he wished people would take him at his word and stop asking him all the time. This was in the fall of 1974. Shriver began to call up old friends and got Patrick Caddell to poll for him. The poll turned up an 80 percent name recognition factor. So Shriver hired a fund raiser and press secretary and began to put together his list.

By July 1975 he had Washington office space and had officially formed his committee. By the time he announced two months later, Bill Kelly, a former Peace Corps executive who was his fund raiser, had qualified him for federal matching funds with $186,352, an impressive early show of strength on the money track. In other areas Shriver had trouble. After several of those he had counted on to be his campaign manager or to fill other important posts politely told him, "No," he finally picked up Richard Murphy, a smooth, middle-aged executive with a young, hip, aware look to his clothes and tinted glasses. Murphy, an old friend of Shriver's, was an assistant postmaster general under Lyndon Johnson.

On the psychological track, Shriver, still youthful and bouncy at sixty, is cursed with an inability to control his tongue. Even close friends who say that they think Shriver will go all the way, pause, and then add "unless he goofs it up." He has a speaking style that makes "Scoop" Jackson appear to be a legendary spellbinder. The harelike enthusiasm of his commitments tends to outdistance the more tortoiselike pace of his logical thought. He is in many ways a Gerald Ford with a bigger income and better-cut clothes. As an example, at an off-the-record luncheon for reporters, he recited proudly a list of famous brains who were producing ideas for his campaign. The list contained not a single woman.

On the media track, Shriver had serious problems. He was liked by the press, but he was regarded as a lightweight. Everywhere he went there hovered over him the Polish sausage story, casting darkness on him like the little clouds of gloom that follow depressed comic strip characters. He was a perfect example of the media track rule: to be taken seriously by the press is far more important than to be liked. His staff was certainly professional, and Shriver's rapid raising of the qualifying funds showed financial strength. But his constituency was reduced by his late start in the invisible primary; many of the activists who might have supported him out of memory were committed elsewhere. Besides, he suffered from a definite hostility to his candidacy among politicians in his home state. And many of his supporters were far more willing to make public pronouncements than do the necessary political work.

Still, having been round the track once before, with the Kennedy aura and black and Catholic support, Shriver appeared to have the power to compete in selected primaries till the end. I believe that sometime in the future, strong presidential candidates will come from the federal bureaucracy: secretary of the treasury or of state, or energy czar. But not yet, and not Sargent Shriver. He appeared not enough of a bureaucrat, a Kennedy, or a political personality to mobilize the necessary media acceptance, constituency, and voting mass for a successful candidacy.

The final late, official entry into the invisible primary had also been a candidate on the Democratic side once before: Birch Bayh of Indiana. In 1971 Bayh had jumped into the presidential race without much thought. His wife, Marvella, whose support and advice are usually crucial in Bayh's life, didn't want him to run. "I felt it politically unwise. Birch needed another term in the Senate. He needed to be a few years older, to be taken more seriously." The national press found Bayh's staff efficient but the candidate plastic. His fellow politicians, an important part of his planned constituency, were polite but unenthusiastic. When calamity struck his private life—Marvella developed cancer, fortunately curable—Bayh quickly dropped from the race.

In 1975 his entry into the invisible primary was totally different. His administrative assistant who later became his campaign manager, Jay Berman, described the decision to enter as "long and tortuous." Bayh's 1974 Senate campaign against Mayor Richard Lugar of Indianapolis had left him and his staff limp. "They hit us with busing, abortion, all the tough ones," says Berman. ". . . [it] may have been no harder; but perhaps we are just a little older," said Marvella. Bayh had seen the 48-to-27 percent lead he held over Lugar in May, when the campaign started, dwindle to a bare 2 percent difference. On election day in the year of Watergate, when other Democratic incumbents were rolling up impressive majorities, he had just squeaked by. In 1968 Bayh had allowed the same thing to happen. Then his 63-to-13 lead over Republican William Ruckelshaus (later, with Elliot Richardson, a hero of the Saturday night massacre) dwindled down to one percent on election day.

Bayh's supporters claimed the reason for the close campaigns was that the liberal positions which he courageously maintained in Washington were not liked in conservative Indiana.

"You have to give Birch credit for a great deal of courage," said John Brademas, Rhodes Scholar and congressman from South Bend, Indiana. "Even his fight against Clement Haynsworth and Harrold Carswell [two Nixon Supreme Court appointments Bayh successfully blocked] didn't help him in Indiana." Bayh's detractors, including surprisingly many Democrats who have worked with him and still support him vociferously in public, believed the drop came because Bayh's campaigns have no substance. "Deep down he's shallow" was the cliché, given off the record, that occurred three times in my notes. Both friends and foes agreed completely on two aspects of Birch Bayh. One: He is a master politician. Two: Marvella, his wife, is a key part of his success. And neither Washington nor Indiana are places overly inclined to give women credit.

On January 10, 1975, Bayh made his first post-election speech outside of Indiana. By March his staff was regularly scheduling out-of-state engagements. The speeches went over well. More requests for appearances followed, particularly from unions. Berman, a political scientist from City College in New York (he was the first member of his family to attend college), said of that time, "We believed there was room out there. . . . We began to think seriously about running."

I got the impression—it's hard to be more precise—that in the beginning Bayh's staff was a good deal more enthusiastic about his running than Bayh. The Senator's relationship with his staff was different from that of the other candidates. It was relaxed and informal but at the same time distant. They talked, he listened; but there often seemed to be an invisible shield between their words and his head. Ex-staff members complained of being exploited, ordered to perform petty tasks. His staff in return could be pretty cavalier about Bayh's ability. I remarked to Berman that Bayh was going to have to learn to budget his time better if he was to be a successful candidate. "It's to teach him things like that I go on the road with him," said Berman.

Bayh's strategy was to build a constituency of labor, liberal activists, women, and blacks. Or to "position himself correctly on the issues to maximize chances of support," as his associate campaign manager, Ann Lewis, put it. Particularly important was labor, with Mike Miller of the Communications Workers, Martin Gerber and Steve Schlossberg of the Auto Workers, Helmuth Kern of the Meat Cutters, all coming aboard early. Labor leaders are comfortable with Bayh. They can take off their ties and shoes and talk to him. They are certain he understands them and owes them one for their hard work in Indiana on his behalf.

The staff was also building on its own and the senator's strength, for both are known on "the Hill" for their excellent grasp of politics but sometimes sloppy work on the issues. Bayh has the ability to appeal to widely varying segments of the Democratic party. Bob Keefe, who used to be Bayh's administrative assistant and now manages Jackson's campaign, remembered standing on the floor of the Democratic Convention in 1972 with two Californians, one an old-line labor leader, the other a far-out member of the state's Office of Economic Opportunity. The only thing the two had in common was that they were both for Bayh.

On issues in 1974–75, Bayh's staff let him down by not adequately checking out S-1, the measure to reform the judicial processes of the United States. Bayh was an early and important sponsor of this bill. On close reading, parts of the bill turned out to be highly damaging to civil liberties of Americans. "I am watching that bill closely," Bayh told an audience in Minnesota. "If it's not improved it should be defeated." A little better staff work would have saved the need for such fancy footwork.

Besides building a constituency, the strategy laid out by the staff was similar to Udall's and Carter's. First Bayh would do well in the Iowa caucuses in January to start the ball rolling. Then he would win in New Hampshire and Massachusetts and use that momentum to take New York, where his union support would give him an edge. The union base would be used again to score heavily in Indiana and Michigan to show strength in the midwest against Wallace. The capstone would be victory in California, fashioned with labor support and the women's liberal coalition again.

Senator Bayh campaigned with the relaxed air of a man enjoying himself. He is one of the new breed of politicians who enjoy the campaign more than the office. The only psychological lift he apparently gets from legislation is in battling it through. These modern politicians are more actor than statesman. Rather than enjoying the rewards of wielding power, they have a deep psychic need to be reassured that people still love them, and so must continually play Russian roulette with their futures.

Bayh's performance before the young Democrats in St. Louis in August 1975 showed both the strengths and weaknesses of his campaign. He wowed the young Democrats, largely a crowd of professional junior politicians in their late twenties, with his speaking technique. He roamed the audience, jacket and tie off, mike in hand, like a daytime game-show M.C. His staff had skillfully lobbied the convention and, with union aid, bused-in Bayh supporters so that he made media mileage by winning the delegate straw poll.

However, some of his quickback answers caused the jaws of the listening press to drop. "I'm convinced that if you locked Sadat and Rabin in a room . . . they could solve their problems in half a day. . . . We have a federal deficit not because of extensive spending but because of a decrease in revenue." He answered the question about the illegal $3,000 he had received from Ashland Oil during his senate campaign by demanding to know, in view of his record against monopolies, why they had sent him the gift. Before a fund-raising group at lunch, he answered a question on Israel's defenses by saying: "I would have sent them [Phantom jets for Israel] in crates through the Mediterranean in the dark of night . . . no one would have known." (His campaign theme was to restore morality in government.) Also in St. Louis he said he was not in favor of unconditional amnesty: "I see nothing wrong with being asked to perform reasonable service." Two months later, when speaking before a group of liberals in Springfield, Massachusetts, he would be for total amnesty.

Two days after St. Louis, Bayh was in French Lick, Indiana. The Indiana Democrats meet there in August of each year for booze and politics. The great, rambling, turn-of-the-century resort hotel sits in the foothills of the Cumberlands that rise suddenly—lush, small, and steep—out of the flat farmlands in picturesque jumble. French Lick used to be a nationally famous resort, the "in" watering place for the nation's political bosses. The great rail lines passed through the one-block town. Eastern and midwestern politics roared down from Chicago on the Wabash Cannonball. The southern grandees steamed up the Spirit of St. Louis, and the westerners came in on private cars behind the Golden State Limited of the Atchison, Topeka and Santa Fe. It was here, in 1932, that Franklin D. Roosevelt officially announced his intention to run for President to the assembled state governors. In the ballroom of the hotel, Bayh discussed his coming campaign, off the record, with Indiana's Democratic leaders: ". . . I ask myself, Birch, can you do it? . . . I can tell a good man from a bad. . . . I have a responsibility to take my best shot. . . . We decided to really go out and try on the shoes. . . . To see if we can have a Democrat who is a Hoosier sitting in [the White House]. . . ." He went on to lay out for the audience his biting impressions of the other candidates, the names of his secret supporters around the states, details of his strategy. I promised I wouldn't report that part of the speech as it would give away to others much of his secret game plan. But I can say that for half an hour there was no mention of principle, idea or issue.

Two months later, at the start of October, I am flying with Bayh, still an unannounced candidate, though he's set the date, from Washington to Iowa, then on to a convocation of liberal Democrats in Minnesota. Our first stop in Iowa is to be Burlington. In college, as an agricultural student at Purdue, Bayh had dreamed of making his way in the world by playing baseball, starting in the minor leagues with the Burlington Bees. If the Bees had made an offer he wouldn't have gone to law school. They didn't. He's a senator.

I am reminded again of what an important part sport has played in the lives of so many recent Presidents and presidential candidates. Both John F. Kennedy and his brother Robert harked back to football days at Harvard. Richard Nixon did the same about the Whittier football team. Now there are Jerry Ford, the Michigan captain and Yale coach; Bayh, who played college baseball; Udall, who played college and professional basketball; and George Wallace a tournament winning boxer. If the battle of Waterloo was won on the playing fields of Eton, perhaps the invisible primary may be won in the sports arenas of the American universities.

We change planes in Chicago and pick up Judge Joe Anderson, another

college athlete and Indiana politician who has been advancing Iowa for
Bayh. Anderson, a big, slow-speaking man of thirty-four, worked his way
through college and law school supporting himself and his family. He
is concerned because he must spend so much time away from home
campaigning for Bayh. He started in Iowa nine days ago, with two names
from the Washington office and one contact of his own, and started building
the organization from there. Birch and Joe slap each other around and
punch each other in the time-honored greeting of politicians who haven't
seen each other for five minutes or five years. The three of us go up to the
airline VIP lounge and, while the television blares "Gilligan's Island," Bayh
and Anderson sip coffee and talk the real guts of politics, names: a county
secretary here, a Communications Workers local leader there, a United
Automobile Workers steward somewhere else, a powerhouse from the
League of Women Voters elsewhere.

"It's the women who make the difference at this stage of the game," says
Anderson. "The men will sit all night and drink with you and tell you how
they will get this good little-ole-boy on your side; but it's the women who go
out and make the phone calls." Anderson sees the situation in Iowa as
fluid—he's right there—with "plenty of good people floating around
waiting to be picked up. . . . It's going to be all organization in Iowa. If we
can get two hundred people to meet you [Bayh] tonight in Iowa City, we'll
take the county." He is certain Bayh can take the state, and the two men
punch each other happily—a pair of scouts who have discovered next
Saturday's opponent isn't all that tough.

Iowa City will be our third stop tonight. We get there an hour late, and
there are seventy-five people still waiting. I guess that gives him a fair shot at
taking the county.

Late in the afternoon we fly into Burlington in a six-seater plane. The air is
blue-green and dramatically clear to the lip of the horizon. Beneath us the
edges of the little towns eat inexorably out into the farmland, bulldozed
fields and new buildings etched around the edges of the little squares of
human life over which we fly. That afternoon the Iowa legislature, faced
with fiscal crisis like the rest of America, had increased the taxes on farmland
33 percent. There's a political event: food, pocketbook, family tragedy. But
it won't be mentioned. That's the *real* world. We're here to campaign for
President and that means talking about "the greed of OPEC and the oil
companies. . . every American who is able to work ought to have a job . . .
I am concerned about the moral fiber of this country, the number of people
who have lost faith. . . ." No wonder only 37 percent of those eligible
actually voted in the last election.

It's a quiet, orderly crowd in Burlington, some 120 people seated at
wooden tables, eating a barbecue, in the American Legion Park behind the
town ballfield. Mostly older people, the men in windbreakers, the women in
sweaters and pantsuits. The children run and swing in the rear. The county
chairman, Harry Baxter, is for Carter. His wife, who is running for mayor, is
uncommitted but leaning towards Udall. Bayh charms her into his camp.

Then he stands beneath the hickory and butternut trees in the slanted rays of the setting sun and delivers his standard speech against Ford, inflation, cancer, big oil, and unemployment. His suit is electric blue and the Legion shed behind him is bright green. The scene looks like a badly reproduced Hopper painting.

Three stops later it's just past midnight, and we're in Bayh's hotel in Iowa City. Here he makes his big mistake. First, he agrees to get up early to make an appearance at 6:00 A.M. at a local farmers' market. He doesn't want to get up that early, particularly as it means he will be up at five to do his exercises before the appearance. But his local organizer puts him on the spot, saying she has to live here after he has gone and that he must go. Bayh changes his mind several times but in the end agrees to the appearance.

Next morning at six, there will be some sixty people at the farmers' market. At the four-state Democratic Caucus in Minneapolis the next afternoon there will be some 4,000 liberal party leaders and other activists. Bayh's energy will be at its low point of the three-day swing. He will bomb. My doubts that he is strong enough to be his own man are reinforced.

Having decided to get up at five, he makes a second error. He sits and pores over the intricacies of local politics with Judge Anderson and his four supporters for another hour: What part can the communications workers play, who should come up from Indiana and talk to the local labor convention, who should work the women's caucus? There is nothing said that his staff should not have been able to handle, bringing the decision to him at another time. To me it seems that Bayh's county organizer, who is a woman, is making the most sense. She also keeps suggesting he needs sleep; but her words don't seem to get through.

One of the keys to Bayh's strategy to corral the women's movement is his sponsorship of the Equal Rights Amendment (ERA) to the Constitution that guarantees women the same rights as men. Bayh's leadership on this amendment is, again, the work of his chief political strategist and adviser, Marvella. She is proud she got him out front on the issue, because: "He really had no idea what women were about." I point out that his reputation on the Hill for women in responsible staff positions is not good. "He could do a lot better with women," she says. Good politician that he is, Bayh is learning fast. He no longer says, "So glad to see all you gals here," as he did to a group of activist women Democrats at a Democratic National Committee forum a year earlier.

After the "event" at the farmers' market at six, we flew to Minneapolis from Iowa City. I tried to draw Bayh out about his childhood. He likes to talk about growing up on a farm; and being a farmer is an important part of his self-image that, like Carter and Udall, he uses with political effectiveness.

Bayh himself speaks often of "being born in Indiana and growing up on a farm" and "Can a farm boy from Shirkieville, Indiana, ever be President?" The trouble is that both of those statements, while accurate in detail, are untrue in effect. He knows this but continues to present the false image. Even such a cautious reporter as Joseph Kraft, covering Bayh's formal entry into the race in late October, was taken in and wrote: "Mr. Bayh emphasized [his] quality of plainness anew last week by opening his campaign in his birthplace, Shirkieville, Indiana."

Not true. "That Bayh was born in Terre Haute and grew up in Washington, D.C., not Shirkieville, Indiana, is one of the most carefully kept secrets in the Senate," says a former aide, shaking his head. Which is too bad because Bayh's actual life reveals a more interesting character than the myth he has constructed. And the series of little deceptions about who he has been casts doubt about what he will be, should he become President.

Bayh was born in 1928 in Terre Haute, Indiana. His father was a teacher and physical education instructor, first in the Terre Haute school system and later in the District of Columbia school system. Like so many of the other candidates, Birch was much closer to his mother than father. Until he was fifteen, Birch and his sister grew up in suburban Washington. Roger Mudd, the TV reporter, remembers going to school with Birch: "We both had a strange name." He also remembers Bayh as an intense competitor on the basketball court in junior high school.

When Bayh was fifteen, his life underwent a total change, which must have been tough to handle along with adolescence. His mother died; and his father, a reserve officer in the Army, was called up to help handle the physical training of the early draftees flooding into the Army just before Pearl Harbor. Birch and his sister went to live on the 320-acre working farm of his maternal grandmother and grandfather in Shirkieville, Indiana. "Life on the farm completely changed me around," says Bayh. From what to what?

Bayh remains grateful to both grandparents for "taking two strangers into their home when they were over seventy." He found himself closer to his grandmother than to his grandfather. It was she who got his grandfather to let him grow the famous prize-winning tomatoes that form the centerpiece of his official early years. He was then seventeen. There was no gym for basketball or any indoor sports in the small, rural high school he now attended; his mouth hardened at the bitter memories. He took up baseball instead and excelled there too. During this time, he and his father drifted apart, a break that was never repaired. His father was against his political career; like so many in the military, he considered politics dirty.

Bayh took to farming enthusiastically enough so that he went to agricultural college at Purdue. While there he entered the debating contest in which Marvella Hern, from Enid, Oklahoma, finished first. Shortly thereafter, when she was nineteen, Bayh married the champion. A year later, driving home one night with Birch at the wheel, another car slammed into them, leaving Marvella with a chronically painful back and, friends report, genuine psychic fears.

One of the ways a young man can advance fastest in politics is to have the skill, courage, and luck to take on a seemingly unbeatable ancient champion whom no one else cares to attack, when that champion is actually over the hill. In 1962, Bayh, a relatively unknown young speaker of the Indiana House, took on Senator Homer E. Capehart, the aging, three-term Indiana

Republican dragon, a man judged invincible. Here once again Bayh showed both his political skill and courage. Helpfully, Homer Capehart ran a terrible campaign, to put it mildly. His TV ads showed him feeding a bunch of pigs to prove he was a more consistent farmer than Bayh, which he was. The problem was that old Homer looked something like the pigs and ran into all sorts of jokes about which twin has the Toni, or which piggy is in the trough.

On the other side, Bayh had "the jingle." "The jingle" has since become a political legend. It won a prize for the best locally produced television commercial that year of 1962 when TV was new across the land. Since by general agreement among Republican and Democratic politicians and reporters it won the election for Bayh and started him on the road to the invisible primary, it deserves to be recorded here. Not, I hasten to add, to put Keats to shame, but to say something about the making of a senator in 1962. The tune is: "Hey, Look Me Over."

Hey, look him over,
He's your kind of guy.
His first name is Birch
His last name is Bayh.
Candidate for Senator
From our Hoosier state,
For Indiana he will do more
Than anyone has done before.
So hey, look him over,
He's my kind of guy.
Send him to Washington
On Bayh you can rely. . . .

Once elected senator, Bayh got off the blocks fast. The Senate had been about to close down the Constitutional Amendments Subcommittee of the Judiciary Committee. Bayh persuaded the southern leadership to let the committee live and make him chairman. Two months later, President Kennedy was assassinated, Lyndon Johnson was President, the next in line for the White House was the aged, dictatorial Speaker of the House, John McCormack. Bayh grabbed the opportunity and helped create the 25th amendment, which is why Jerry Ford—and not Carl Albert—is President today.

In 1968 Bayh had the first of his reelection cliff-hangers when he almost blew a 63-to-13 percent lead over William Ruckelshaus. Ruckelshaus' pollster had advised him to fake illness and quit the race. This '68 battle saw the famous two letters on gun controls. These, like "the jingle," have become the stuff of legend. The Ruckelshaus staff found that Senator Bayh was sending out two different letters about his stand on gun controls, one to those who favored gun control, the other to those who were against. The letters appeared at a glance to be almost the same. But not-too-subtle changes in wording gave the impression in one letter that Bayh was fighting for stiff gun-control laws and in the other that he was battling against their extension. The deception only came to light because a fumble-fingered Bayh staffer stuffed both letters into the same envelope to an anti-gun constituent.

"Birch's problem," says a friend who has been in Indiana politics with him from the beginning, "is that he has had to be retroactively self-righteous." Bayh had just been an ordinary Indiana politician before he led the fight in 1972 against the nominations of Clement Haynsworth and Harrold Carswell for the Supreme Court. The friend points out that Bayh was quite able to clean up his future, but he had a bit of trouble with his past. He had some trouble with his future also. In 1974 he accepted $1,239 worth of freebies from Mount Snow during a New Year's holiday with his family. Mount Snow, now bankrupt, was in difficulties with the SEC. Nothing really bad; other senators do far worse, but they are not running for President on a ticket stressing morality two years after Watergate.

Back in 1967 Bayh had put pressure on the Department of the Interior to enable friends of his chief financial backer, Miklos Sperling, to dredge the Potomac River halfway between Washington and Mount Vernon. Fill was needed as the foundation of a high-rise apartment building to be erected on the scenic site.

"Mike Sperling always was a good friend," says a disenchanted former Bayh staffer, adding that in the 1968 campaign Sperling put five members of Bayh's campaign staff on his company's own payroll so they wouldn't show up on Bayh's accounting.

On *Face the Nation,* Bayh told the American TV audience: ". . . as far as my personal finances, I've made them public. And when I ran for the Senate the law required, and I didn't hesitate for a moment, to make all contributions available."

Well, yes and no. A senator has to fill out a form with the secretary of the U.S. Senate indicating what he spent and received to get elected. The form reads: "I hereby certify that the following is a correct and itemized account of each contribution received by me or by any person for me with my knowledge or consent from any source." On the form for 1968 Bayh listed his campaign contributions as "none," his expenditures as $3,000 for a filing fee!

How does he get away with it? Well, on TV he was talking about personal contributions, and that is what the Senate asks one to list. Bayh gladly makes his public because, he says, he never accepts anything or spends anything himself. All his campaign fund raising and expenditures are done by committees. It's a common dodge, no longer possible under the new campaign law. The late John F. Kennedy and Richard Nixon were masters of it. If you ever try to check the finances of the committees, good luck.

In a fine piece of investigative journalism, two reporters from the Dayton, Ohio, *Journal Herald* finally tracked down some of the sums raised and spent by the network of Bayh committees. They uncovered roughly $150,000 in contributions and expenditures for which there was no record at all. Again, other senators have collected and spent such slush-funds. But, again, it is Bayh who is running for President two years after Watergate.

I asked Bayh if he thought any of his financial problems in the '68 campaign would hurt him now. "No," he said, not surprisingly. Unless he continued running up such a big debt, which was a problem. With the campaign already in debt, he went up to New York for a meeting in Averell Harriman's East Side townhouse with a group of New York liberals who had, he said, guaranteed him $50,000. The meeting netted him $15,000. But Bayh, realizing how close the election was, went ahead and bought the local TV time anyway, running up a debt of $150,000. For the first time in a campaign, he and his wife had trouble sleeping at night.

Looking at Bayh's legislative record, one sees again and again his political timing. On Vietnam he changed from super hawk to cautious dove more slowly than most "liberals," but not slowly enough to offend many people. In 1967 he was "not going to turn tail and run in Vietnam." In 1968 he did not support the anti-war plank at the Democratic Convention, but he would open his Washington office so that protesting students coming to town would find a place to stay. By 1969 he had decided the war was wrong. When quizzed about his support of the war in 1970, he reminded the questioner that ". . . the two men who opposed the Tonkin Gulf Resolution* are no longer in the Senate."

On abortion, Bayh quite simply had not been on the floor when the votes came up. In 1974–75 he missed the key votes on the Helms, Bartlett, and Church amendments. The abortion issue obviously gives Bayh a great deal of psychological trouble. He rambles and stutters when he talks of it, which is unusual for him. He mentions "those itty-bitty little fingers and hands" and how he personally is against abortion. Pressed in St. Louis by the Young Democrats, he came out in favor of the Supreme Court position and later, in mid-September in his Senate subcommittee, voted with the pro-abortion forces.

In 1972, national political lightning struck Birch Bayh. A loose group of Americans for Democratic Action liberals and labor leaders were looking for a member of the Senate Judiciary Committee to lead the fight against the appointment of Judge Clement Haynsworth of the Fourth Circuit Court of Appeals to the Supreme Court. The group objected to what they considered conservative and anti-labor rulings made by the judge. Senators Eastland of Mississippi, McClellan of Arkansas and Ervin of North Carolina, the three senior members of the Judiciary Committee, wanted no part of the job. Philip Hart of Michigan had led the battle for the confirmation of Abe Fortas, who later had to resign; so he was scratched. That left Edward Kennedy, Joe Tydings of Maryland, and Bayh. Kennedy was out because

---

*A nifty little motion flimflammed through the Senate by President Johnson in 1964 that gave him the authority to run the war in Vietnam any way he wanted. Hardly a true test of opposition to the war, since even William Fulbright and George McGovern voted for it. Wayne Morse of Oregon and Ernest Gruening of Alaska voted against. The defeat of neither man turned on this vote.

of Chappaquiddick, Tydings didn't want in. That left Bayh. He took a lot of persuading; the action would definitely hurt him in Indiana, but with political courage he finally decided to lead the troops. Once in, he gave it everything he had, all his skill as a debater and politician. He not only blocked Haynsworth but went on to defeat the appointment of Harrold Carswell, Nixon's far more second-rate second choice.

Earlier Bayh had protected his right flank back in Indiana by voting to support Nixon's appointment of Otto Otepka to the Subversive Activities Control Board. Otepka, who allegedly used to slip information from the state department, where he worked, to congressional Red-hunters, is a darling of the conservatives. "Justice for Otto" has long been a right-wing crusade. Said Bayh, "It's unrealistic to expect to get the support of the kind of people who like Otto Otepka, without putting someone like Otepka in the government."

The national publicity Bayh received as a result of his successful fight against the Haynsworth-Carswell appointments caused him to leap blithely into the 1972 presidential race, a race from which he withdrew when his wife developed cancer.

"Birch always had the presidency in mind from the very first day he came to the Senate. It was something that was understood but never discussed," says a fellow Indiana politician who preceded him to Washington. So now it's 1975, Bayh is in the race again; and our plane is letting down into Minneapolis.

The meeting here is the brainchild of Congressman Don Fraser, he of the weighty briefcase and infinite faith in reforming plans. Under Fraser's prodding the Americans for Democratic Action and several liberal unions have gotten together to hold five Democratic Forums around the country. All the Democratic candidates are invited to appear at these forums and have their liberal credentials tested by knowledgeable activists asking detailed questions. Since in several of the early state primaries —Massachusetts, New York, and Wisconsin—these liberal activists may well hold the balance of power, the forums play a key role in the invisible primary. The candidate who consistently scores best before their audience will have gained an important constituency.

The four thousand Democrats gathered in the Leamington Hotel ballroom in downtown Minneapolis are middle-aged and serious. Fred Harris has cannily tried to pack the hall with students from Macalester College, where he spoke the day before. But the strategy backfired; his barefooted supporters with their long hair and Mother Hubbards merely emphasize the monochromatic tone of his support. As usual, Harris, with his driving populist harangue "to get the rich off welfare" and the country moving again, gets the most applause for his speech. But he doesn't do as well with his rhetorical answers in the question period.

Bayh is met by his two campaign managers, Jay Berman and Ann Lewis.

Lewis, a women's-movement activist, used to field hot political grounders for Mayor Kevin White of Boston, and then handled the unsuccessful Senate campaign of Barbara Mikulski of the Mikulski rules. Her brother, State Representative Barney Frank, is a leading Udall supporter in Massachusetts. You get family strands like that crisscrossing the invisible primary. Berman and Lewis have been lobbying the assembled Democrats for their candidate. They have also cleverly stacked the panels of neutral activists who will be asking the questions so that those questioning Udall will be largely Bayh supporters armed with specially prepared zingers.

Bayh takes off his shoes and loosens his tie and listens. Jay lies back on the bed, and Ann takes her shoes off also. The whole scene is relaxed, as his aides try to explain to him the stands he must take on the issues to "position himself differently" from the other candidates. But again there is a short circuit someplace. They explain one thing to him, and he answers with questions about something completely different. Puzzled, I look out the window at the decaying downtown Minneapolis. The cars whizz by, their drivers unconscious of any energy problem. Maybe it's just that Bayh is having energy problems after his late night? Maybe all that interests him are the nuts and bolts of politics: where he should stand on the stage, who is supporting whom? I realize, looking out the window, that I first came through Minneapolis covering General Eisenhower's campaign against Adlai Stevenson. We were traveling by train. Christ, I have been at this work an awfully long time. And the more I learn, the less I'm certain.

Bayh leaves to go downstairs for a disastrous press conference—long disjointed answers that ramble on. He has no staff with him to end the conference, and it just peters out. Berman and Alan Baron, a McGovern staffer who is helping Bayh, go into the other room of Bayh's suite and put the pressure on a key Udall organizer in Iowa to turn him around. Bayh comes back up and slaps the Iowan in friendly fashion, telling him he has a great future in the Bayh administration. The guy had given his word to Udall and sits on the couch desperately trying to have it both ways like any red-blooded American politician.

Bayh goes back into the other room and begins to work up his coming speech on 3 x 5 cards, writing with a squeaky felt-tipped pen. Just before going down to face the crowd in the hotel auditorium, he has three-quarters of an hour with a group of women activists who are suspicious of his stand on abortion. The group is hostile because Bayh has held hearings on a constitutional amendment to prohibit abortion. Again Bayh does a superb political job, winning the women to his side as he explains the inside pressures in his subcommittee and how, as chairman, he will use these to control the order in which the various amendments are called up and so defeat the anti-abortion legislation. He asks the women to help him. They are flattered and impressed.

But the conference has been a tactical error, draining Bayh of his last energy. Ten minutes later in the auditorium he is bland and slow, his speech rambling, his answers to the questions disjointed and full of laughable platitudes. Besides, his staff, in their successful maneuvering to load both his and Udall's panel of questioners with Bayh supporters, have actually done him a disservice. They have created a kind of reverse jujitsu situation in which their own strength becomes a liability. It's the tough questions that enable a skilled candidate to look good while the easy floaters make for dull answers.

There is no way a man can answer the question: "Tell us about your well-received proposals for solving the energy crisis, Senator," without sounding like a self-serving jerk. Udall is asked why he had voted to deny welfare mothers the right to have abortions. He not only proves he hadn't, but draws a round of applause with his answer. Bayh is asked if the present levels of foreign aid are adequate and answers, "If you want to make a friend an enemy, lend him money." He is also against "the United States support of tinhorn dictators overseas." He sounds as if he is secretly training to be the Hubert Humphrey of the dimwitted. By the time he finishes, the hall, jam-packed when he began, is barely half full. A weekend of politics is over. We race for the airplane.

From Bayh's first campaign to enter the Indiana legislature, none who knew him well have doubted the not so hidden source of his strength. The petite woman with the iron will, with back stiff from the automobile accident, fluffy blond hair always in place, has been at the very least an equal partner in his career.

"My wife has a better political head than anybody who works for me," says Birch.

"Politics is all-consuming to us both," says Marvella.

"It's hard to remain loyal to both," says ex-staffer Robert Keefe.

While still in high school, Marvella Hern was governor of Oklahoma Girls State and president of Girls Nation. She met Birch at the famous debating contest sponsored by the National Farm Bureau. A year later, at nineteen, she was married, an only child and a refugee from a family life that would have destroyed most. In its final violent act her father was to murder her stepmother and then commit suicide.

Marvella clipped the newspapers for Birch, wrote his speeches, guided him on issues, campaigned for him, tried to change the way he thought, the way he dressed. "I live completely through him," she told Sally Quinn in a Washington *Post* interview in 1972. By 1975 Marvella Bayh had discovered the unconscious resonance in the adverb "completely." She had her own life. Birch Bayh campaigned alone.

"We talked over what was going to happen in this campaign for a long time, because we live out our life in phases. . . . I was twenty-nine when he was elected to the Senate. . . . I am forty-two now. . . . I know more. . . . I have always wanted to do my own things . . . the thrill of doing my own work. . . . Now I'm forty-two, I can't give up [my own life] any more." She leans forward out of her straight-backed chair and cracks her knuckles as she talks, left hand torturing the right. "I had a really terrific job offer in 1967 which I turned down. I won't do that any more." Now she has her own life flying around the country organizing and speech-making to mobilize women in the battle against cancer.

Marvella stresses that she and her husband are still close. Nothing could happen that could destroy the marriage; she knocks on the wood of her chair and falls silent. I remark that traditionally men have not treated well women who gave them everything. "Yes, they disregard them, don't they," she says softly.

She draws a deep breath and out it comes. "Last year right here in this room, I told him this was it. Life was not endless. I was forty-one." She pauses for a long moment. "We had quite a time. He kept on telling me—reciting—all the things he's given me. Asking what more I wanted. What more? I said, 'Even if you were John Paul Getty there were things I wanted to take for myself. That I must take.'" She went on to talk about her cancer and being close to dying and realizing life was not endless, what she had lost, never known.

I shut my notebook. In 1962 I had the joy of watching a superb actress, Marion Seldes, stand on that center of magic energy called a stage and say lines I'd written about a woman at such a crisis. I'm still proud of those lines because in 1962 few women and almost no men had seen the truth about such female loss. But I realize now, watching Mrs. Bayh relive her moment, that I had only skimmed the surface of that agony.

We switch back to the present and she says, "So many have the impression that I am ambitious, that I am pushing him all the time to run. That is not true."

I register disbelief and give a few examples.

"I was twenty-nine when he was elected. I wanted that then. Today is different. I'm very ambivalent."

"Even about winning?"

"I am very ambivalent," she repeats. ". . . personally I don't really want him to run." Again she adds that she doesn't want to hurt him, that she is helping him campaign by taking care of the house. "Though he could do more there too." If he gets the presidential nomination she will campaign with him then. But the primaries he does on his own. Birch understands all this, she says; they are not fighting about it. They are still happy with each other. But "life goes in cycles."

There is a dead tree outside of their house. He thinks she should take care of it because it's part of the house. She thinks he should take care of it because it's outside. The tree has been dead for six months now.

She wants to know if I think she will hurt her husband by not campaigning with him. Like most reporters when faced with a tough one I duck. Besides I'm not sure it's a genuine question and not a stroking. I say: If he can't make it through the primaries on his own then he doesn't deserve to be President.

"Thank you," Marvella says. "I wouldn't want to think I had hurt him. But I must be true to myself too."

So for the first time in his life Birch campaigns without the support of Marvella. Even with everything else breaking for him, that alone would put the outcome in doubt.

Brooding over all the activities of all the Democratic candidates in the invisible primary loomed the Alabama dragon, Governor George Corley Wallace. Birch Bayh was in trouble with the liberals because he had said during his desperate campaign for reelection in 1974, "I can see circumstances where there might be a balancing effect; I would support him [Wallace] for Vice-President." Morris Udall was making a campaign issue out of the fact that he had been the first to say he would not have any part of a Wallace ticket. Carter and Sanford were saying they were going to beat Wallace in his back yard in the South. Bayh, who now wouldn't support Wallace, vowed to lacerate the Governor in Indiana. Scoop Jackson was merely saying he would defeat Wallace in the primaries. Lloyd Bentsen used the same line. Fred Harris was claiming he was the only candidate besides Wallace who could reach the Wallace constituency. And what was Governor Wallace doing about all this?

"I'm just sitting here not saying a thing, and not straining," said Wallace in the summer of 1975, with a smile into which you could read anything. "And it seems I'm the one all the others are talking about. . . . And some of them are beginning to sound more and more like me."

In September 1975, Wallace was the strongest Democratic candidate in the invisible primary. NBC's polling of Democratic voters as they left the polls in New Hampshire, after the rerun Senate election between John Durkin and Louis Wyman, found more voters favorable to Wallace—11 percent—than to any other candidate. And Wallace had not even been in the state since 1968. The candidate closest to Wallace was Jackson, with 8 percent. And like Jackson, as the invisible primary went into its last lap, Wallace was a well-financed candidate. The compulsory October accounting revealed he had $744,208 in the bank. In the last two years he had raised over four million dollars, more than all the other candidates put together, including President Ford.

In the red brick executive building in Montgomery, Alabama, where the Wallace for President Committee has two spacious floors of modern office space—computer terminals, data retrieval units, a mail sorting operation, plus the staff command post—Alton Dauphin looked at me across his executive desk and said, "Even in June we didn't have the money. Now [September 1975] we have the money and the people." Dauphin is Wallace's brother-in-law and deputy director of the campaign. Down the thick-carpeted hall from his office, a woman at a computer console was separating out Wallace contributors in a Michigan congressional district by use of zip code information and reverse phone books. "We're building an organization congressional district by congressional district," says Dauphin, a pleasantly open man, though a bit jumpy when dealing with the press.

Wallace had been round the track twice before. He had funds and a constituency and the rapt attention of the press every time he spoke. He was a most formidable candidate, up to a point. "The tragedy of George Wallace," says Ray Jenkins, editorial page editor of the Alabama *Journal*, "is also the tragedy of the South. Wallace ran for governor in 1958 as a moderate. He got beaten by John Patterson, the only election he's ever lost. At that time he got over 50 percent of the black vote." But in the 1960s the forces in the South were moving away from moderation. And so George Wallace moved. For he is part of the South and quite naturally proud of it. (One of the unanswered questions of 1976 is whether the country as a whole is moving away from moderation. Or is it, as seems to be more likely, moving back towards "normalcy," as we have after our other wars?)

Wallace realizes full well the importance of his southern tap root, and not just in the South. "A lot of people in Illinois and Indiana came up from here or got kinfolk here," he says. True indeed, and even when those transplanted southerners are northern liberals as far away as New England, they still often harbor a secret admiration for George Wallace. The courage, the scrappiness, the country smarts as distinct from street smarts, the ability to shove the stinking facts of northern bigotry beneath the nose of pontificating Yankeedom. I am convinced that in the privacy of the voting booth Wallace picks up a fair amount of support that is neither populist, conservative, nor racist, merely southern.

One cannot cover Wallace for long without being close to overwhelmed by the southern connection. In the noon heat the green lawns that ring the Alabama Capitol are immaculate. The Capitol itself, and the low buildings around it, gleam as white as the windmills on Greek islands. Over the Capitol dome flies the Alabama flag. The American flag is relegated to street level and one side. This is Dixie. To claim, as many do, that in today's homogenized America the differences between North and South are more mythical than real is to miss the emotional point and therefore the political impact. As I walk up the deserted white marble steps that shimmer in the blazing sun, a small bronze plaque set in the steps winks out at me. The inscription tells me it marks the spot where Jefferson Davis stood with his right hand on his family Bible and received the oath as President of the Confederacy.

Designed by Frederick Law Olmstead, the Alabama Capitol, though smaller, is both visually more impressive and better kept up than the Capitol of the United States. The bronze doors are burnished to gleam, the dark woodwork polished to high gloss, the tile floors unpitted and immaculate. No idiot architect has been allowed to "improve" the building's basic structure as has happened in Washington. For that matter, the food at the Elite (pronounced "eelyte") Cafe, where the "good ole boys" from the legislature come to deal, is at least the equal of any in Washington. It is a combination of southern and Greek that is both simple and memorable, whereas official Washington gorges on pseudo-French dishes that are complicated and forgettable.

The anterooms of the governor's office are full of people waiting for a moment with "him." There are legislators in sports jackets or double knits and white shoes; there are "long-time friends" up from the country; there are folks who just drop by hopefully and go away satisfied with a picture.

Down the corridor a filibuster is in progress as the black members of the Alabama legislature protest a new bill restoring the death penalty. Members of the legislature, including the blacks, surge in and out of Wallace's office as he hammers out a compromise. "In our kind of politics you can't be too organized. You learn to take things as they come," Wallace says, looking at me over the top of his heavy-frame glasses with a hard stare that is one of his trademarks. Aides drift in and out to talk of people and legislation. He interrupts to take a phone call on a state police problem. I notice again his selective deafness. At times he catches exactly what is being said to him from a far corner of the room. At other times he doesn't hear what is being said up close. It appears to be a function of the noise level. In small groups or one-on-one, he is okay.

The legislative day's work done, Wallace becomes semi-relaxed. He still is maintaining the fiction that he hasn't decided whether to run in 1976; but he isn't trying very hard to make that cover story believable. "I might get out [of the race]. I wish I could get out. I talk to my wife and family." He feels that people want him to run. More than that, that the tide is turning for him. Back in 1968 and 1972, he points out with a bitter grin: "It wasn't too fashionable to support me . . . now people are glad to have their picture taken with me."

The week before, Nelson Rockefeller has had his picture with Wallace prominently displayed around the country. At the time, Rockefeller said: "George and I didn't always agree, but we always respected each other, and were the two who stood up for what we believed."

Wallace rings for a cigar, and his office manager, Margaret Andrews, brings one. Wallace lights up again and remarks how he doesn't talk to politicians much anyway. "Most politicians have friends on all sides." He'd rather go directly to the people. As he explains his methods of political action, I am again reminded of how much politics is like jujitsu—take the thrusts made by your adversary and use them to throw him. Wallace has taken the political slogan used first by radicals and later by reformers —"power to the people"—and decked the liberals with it. While most other candidates just talk about it, Wallace has an actual people's campaign. He knows this, and the bitter irony amuses him.

"My organization is mostly folks who are dedicated and interested and philosophically involved with me, as in Florida and Michigan [two Wallace victories in 1972]. . . . In '72, as far as mapping out strategy, we had some brochures and some pictures . . . what we did was go right to the people." He talks about the importance of political rallies in getting people fired up to support you. This is part of the thirties and forties aspect of his campaign, the emphasis on rallies and meetings rather than television.

Part of Wallace knows this, for a few minutes later, still commenting on strategy, he says: "I feel we have the best TV of any of the candidates." And, he adds, it is not some slick New York job but is made right here in the South. But he is not really interested in TV. He wants to make certain that I understand he is politically strong because he says what the "common people," the "middle class," has "wanted a politician to say." Only other politicians have not had the guts to speak out about issues like crime in the streets or "bad people" because "it was not the social thing to do." Though he adds, "I am not one of your exotic noisemakers. . . . If you organize in the sense of ideas, you will find that the organizations just naturally spring up. . . . Organization and strategy are necessary when all the candidates behave and sound about the same. . . . But a man with ideas organizes the people; or rather the people organize themselves. . . . [Then you have] a movement in which there are masses of people, and that is a strategy and an organization in itself."

George McGovern describing the mobilization of his anti-war constituency could not have been more eloquent. But Wallace has told only a two-thirds truth. Those people that rally to a candidate still have to be gotten to caucuses, have to sign lists, have to run as delegates, man phones. There must be both an organization and a strategy to place the energy of the people in effective channels. This grassroots work doesn't interest Wallace. He is a candidate of ideas and emotions; like Ronald Reagan, an ideological rather than a political campaigner. Again, Wallace knows this in part because he tells me several times that "in '76 we are better organized . . . have better people." But he really doesn't care about that compared to his message and his constituency.

"Were you at Lynchburg when I was there?"

"Yes." Lynchburg, Virginia, was a trip he made to the Thomas Roads Baptist Church, "America's fastest growing church," in August of 1974. He'd been in New Mexico the day before at the National Association of State Legislators and when he got off the plane he looked old and tired, in much less good health than today. In the church with all the organ music and singing he had great difficulty hearing.

The New York Times wrote about those people who came out to see me. They said: 'God help us if these people ever run the country.' Now why did they say that? Those people are honest, God-fearing people; fought their country's wars; raised good families. They should run the country."

The New York Times didn't cover Lynchburg; but Wallace still made his point. He had his people and they were his strategy and his constituency. And he used the attacks on himself (political jujitsu again) to increase his hold on his people, increase his political power. When in March 1975 an article in *New York* magazine on Wallace's administration of Alabama triggered a whole series of political attacks on the governor, Wallace replied that the reason Alabama ranked 48th in per capita income was that Wall Street was stealing from the state. As for the low funding of hospital care: "We look after our own. . . . We aren't broke like New York [City]." Wallace vaults higher on adverse publicity the way Ralph Nader used the General Motors' attacks on himself to shove himself upward. On the media track, Wallace runs a canny race.

"Wallace is at his best when challenged," said Robert Gambacurta, Atlanta TV personality and TV director of the campaign. "It triggers his sense of humor and his answers."

On August 17, 1975, a year after his trip to Lynchburg, Wallace was in Graves County, Kentucky, for the annual Fancy Farm town barbecue that kicks off the Kentucky political season. Once this part of western Kentucky was wild, backward, and Republican. The New Deal changed all that. It built dams, strung electric wires, sent in county agents, pegged farm prices, and brought this region from shoeless poverty—shacks, outhouses, and kerosene lamps—to well-kept lawns, ranch homes, and small family farms of beans and corn. The crossroad town of Fancy Farm isn't as opulent as the big spreads with their swimming pools and split-rail fences that you'll see in central Kentucky. But it isn't the hard-scrabble living of eastern Kentucky either, with the mining towns smeared into the Cumberlands of "Harlan, bloody Harlan!" In Graves County there are now 14,003 registered Democrats and 523 registered Republicans.

But in 1945 at the close of World War II, progress stopped for the people of Fancy Farm. Other sections of society started their march ahead—the blacks began their climb from poverty; loans and highway funds built up suburbia; the industrial unions won larger and larger wage increases. But the big subsidy money went to the larger farms in the midwest; the developers' bulldozers began eating into the Graves County farmlands and the wild lands, the stands of spool wood and the bramble thickets that held game. The beautiful, blue Ohio where I used to swim as a World War II private now flows brown and polluted, the color of the Brassac in Vietnam. In the lonely little hollows and valleys that hide the houses from one another, middle-aged men remember the progress of the New Deal and pass the word to the young men who sit in front of the general stores and filling stations, blankly staring down the cracking roads. It's Wallace country. The votes he gathered in Kentucky in 1972 came almost entirely from this part of the state.

For Wallace is the candidate, even more than Hubert Humphrey, about whom the nostalgia of the New Deal still clings. He doesn't just talk about the great days of Roosevelt rhetorically, he still lives partly in them. Charles Azbell, a former southern newspaperman, now Wallace's director of communications, thought up the '72 slogan, "Send Them a Message," and the '76 slogan, "Trust the People." Azbell is also proud of his friendship with Martin Luther King, recalling that he testified *for* King when King was tried for advocating violence. A couple of Wallace workers and I sat in Azbell's office wedged among the clippings, letters, magazines, and newspapers piled everywhere.

"In our shack in Texas," says Azbell, "we had a picture of Roosevelt and a picture of Jesus over the bed, and my mother and father's wedding picture. The reason they were over the bed was the walls shook when the wind blew and the pictures fell down. They didn't break when they fell down." Another Wallace worker nods, "My folks had tarpaper walls too."

As I pause at the door of Wallace's office and thank him for his time, his last words are: "I'm going to win like Roosevelt did. He came at a time when people's hope was gone and saved this country from a revolution."

Today at Fancy Farm it's hot and close and the sky spits rain from time to time, but not enough to call off the speech-making or the eating; 120 sheep slowly smoke in a row of pits back of St. James parochial school. "Got to stop someday. Got to get some rest," says seventy-two-year-old Sam Grey, who has been doing this barbecue for forty-five years. He is to barbecuing what the legendary Kentucky marksman is to shooting: unbeatable.

Beside the school there is a Wallace Headquarters set up in a camper. People come by and sign their names on yellow legal-size pads and give money: one dollar, five dollars. The Wallace advance team of two hasn't arranged this camper. Some local people put it together and purchased the buttons from Wallace's Alabama headquarters—an example of Wallace's thesis that local organizations just spring up if you have the right message. The crowd, about 4,000, young and old, male and female, stand on the sloping hill beneath the two huge oaks in front of the school and wait for Wallace, the men in short-sleeved, pastel-colored sports shirts, the women in pantsuits. They are silent and respectful as they wait. There is one black man in the crowd. He is wearing a Wallace button. The hand-painted signs say: "Welcome to Kentucky, George." "Stop busing." "The working people stand behind you, George." "Save America—Wallace for President."

Wallace looks little and wizened as he waits in his wheelchair to be rolled up the ramp to the speaking platform. He seems tight and in some pain. His two legs stick out stiffly in front of him because he recently, without realizing it for a time, broke the right one while doing his daily exercises, probably by hitting it on the pedal of his exercise cycle. But once he starts to speak, holding two microphones in his right hand, he comes thoroughly alive.

Wallace delivers his standard speech, leading into it by telling how he used to sell magazines through this area when he was broke and just out of college. It's a speech against things. It's against the "intelligentsee" and the "bureaucrats with briefcases who make more than the working man." It's against Washington, "hypocrisy city" where the bureaucrats make laws during the day telling the working man how he and his children shall live and then go home to Virginia so "they" don't have to obey their own laws. It's against *The New York Times* which has bankrupted New York City. It's against big government, elitists, all of the "theys" who do bad things to "you" who are good. "You pay the taxes; and you do the jobs; and you fight the wars; and you hold the country together. . . . You are too busy to make yourselves heard. That's going to change."

The speech is in an old and honorable American tradition of hate the powerful; and its theme has been mated to violence many times before—Senator Pitchfork Ben Tillman, waving his fork aloft and yelling he'd march on Wall Street and stick the bankers. Only now the bureaucrats, the knowledge industry and the media are more powerful than the bankers, so Wallace is marching on them. The speech is constantly interrupted by applause, enthusiastic, respectful, above all powerful.

Wallace ends with his tire iron story, the finest example of a pure code message in the invisible primary. This little fellow and this great big fellow are drinking in a bar. The little fellow is not doing anything, just minding his own business. All of a sudden the big fellow reaches over and slams the little fellow to the floor. When the little fellow picks himself up, the big fellow says: "What I used on you, son, was jujitsu, and it comes from Japan." The two go back to drinking and pretty soon the big fellow reaches over and decks the little fellow again. Bam, he hits the floor. And the big fellow says, "That was karate, and it comes from Korea." Well, the little fellow gets up and leaves the bar, and after awhile he comes back and sidles in kind of silent and comes up behind the big fellow. And kapowee! There is the big fellow lying on the floor out cold. And the little fellow says to the bartender: "When that big guy comes to, you tell him that was a tire iron, and it comes from Sears and Roebuck."

The crowd goes wild.

That's the violence bit that fuels so much of Wallace's campaign. Not fascism; even his enemies in the state say that's a bum rap to lay on Wallace. In spite of being shot, he goes around followed by fewer state police and other trappings of power than, say, Governor Jimmy Carter of Georgia, who will be his liberal southern opponent. What Wallace exploits is plain old American rage: rage at being southern, at being poor, at being left out, at being small, at being a press target. Wallace runs to get even. His supporters vote for him so they can get even.

"I was shot running for President," Wallace said to me. "What the Democrats have done against me violates the law. . . . You know how the Republicans went after me on that taxes thing. . . . I don't owe either party anything." He is perfectly capable of forming a third party. He's done it before.

As of November 1975, he was number one in the polls among the candidates. (But remember his UQ, unacceptability quotient, the 40-odd percent who wouldn't vote for him under any circumstances.) He and Jackson were the best financed. He had a constituency. His staff of twenty-four full-time members was the largest and the best financed in the campaign, spending more than Jackson and Bentsen combined. And they had been in place for six years. Charles Snyder, the director, Alton Dauphin, the assistant director and finance manager, Joe Azbell, the idea man, all held their jobs in 1972. Why wasn't he further ahead?

The first answer usually given to this question was that his staff was not able. The press and other politicians had a tendency to degrade those around Wallace.

Said Democratic Party Chairman Robert Strauss, ". . . We're helping all of the candidates. We're giving all of them lists and information and advice on delegate selection and everything else. But the truth is we're giving Wallace more help than any of them. We have to. They don't know anything. I told Wallace the problem with him is that his people are too damn dumb."

This country contains many kinds of smarts, and a wise reporter from one area of the country makes judgments about other areas and groups slowly—as those old-timers who wrote off George McGovern's "kids" learned to their sorrow. But still the Wallace campaign operated in such an erratic fashion that questions about staff competence were inevitable.

Take Wallace's appearance at Fancy Farm. Why did he go there? He spent no time with local politicians. Nor did his staff; they flew into the state the night before and ate alone. Wallace got no national press or TV coverage, nor did his staff make an effort to obtain such coverage.

"Why the appearance at Fancy Farm?" I asked Billie Joe Camp, who is Wallace's press secretary and the more or less official liaison between the Governor's Capitol staff and his campaign staff in downtown Montgomery.

"Because the governor of Kentucky has been asking him for three years," Camp replied. It got harder and harder to say no and this year they went. "Maybe if he got a new staff every three years," said Camp. The staff members, the pilots and security men at the two tables where we were breakfasting all laughed.

When the state of North Carolina moved to abolish its primary and go back to the caucus system of presidential candidate selection, the Wallace staff didn't learn this was taking place till the national press called for their reaction. At first, the Wallace campaign was perpetually in debt and only later became wealthy, thanks to the independent brilliance of Richard Viguerie, the direct-mail magician who came to them. The efforts of Wallace's supporters to organize a block of delegates to the midterm Democratic mini-convention at Kansas City failed completely. "We didn't have the money to organize back then," said Alton Dauphin, who added: "This primary thing is frightfully complicated. It's hard to know just what to do."

One could almost hear the good folk of the antebellum South complaining of the Yankee traders with their wooden nutmegs. But Dauphin had a valid point. The present primary rules are arcane, complex, and ridiculously tortuous. They were devised by people light-years removed from the attitudes and thought processes of the Wallace staff, by people who were afraid of voters. Many politicians frankly used the rules to screw Wallace anytime they could. One must therefore measure the effectiveness of the Wallace organization with a certain tolerance.

The two floors that made up Wallace's campaign headquarters had a totally different feel from Wallace's state offices nine blocks up the arcaded, broad avenue. Wallace's Capitol offices and staff were of the past: heavy, dark furniture, oak paneling, paintings of Venice on the walls. The Capitol staff dressed in traditional suits or dresses, they were older; the phones were old-fashioned buzzer intercoms: the office rolled with the slow deliberation of southern politics. In the campaign headquarters the furniture was square and modern-functional, the staff and secretaries younger, the clothes modern, their colors lighter, the intercom system was dial, the men and women slimmer, everyone walked faster.

What both campaign and state offices shared deliberately was their southernness. All were proud that the headquarters is in Montgomery, not in Washington. "You get out of touch with people there," said Dauphin. (Jimmy Carter made the same point in his campaign. "I want you to help me overcome two handicaps I have in my race for President," he told his followers. "I am not a lawyer, and I don't come from Washington.")

When the Wallace headquarters wanted a campaign film, they deliberately went to Atlanta for a producer—not New York. The film was "deliberately unslick," said Azbell. It had a grainy thirties quality about it, one-eighth home movies and one-eighth WPA social commentary—that New Deal heritage again—the rest "March of Time." It opened with shots of people working, both white and black, while underneath a band played "America, the Beautiful." What has gone wrong with America? the film asked. George Wallace, seated at his desk, answered: "The politicians don't trust the people anymore." The viewers were then shown how to become Wallace volunteers.

Into this Montgomery headquarters every week came some 3,000 letters containing money. They were opened by bonded staff members, the contributions logged and deposited, the letters answered within the week. All pertinent information about the contributor was telefaxed to Viguerie in Virginia for his master tapes of future contributors and workers and for statistical analysis. The contributor or writer was further cross-filed within the computer by state and congressional district for future help in creating local campaign organizations. This had been going on full-scale since mid-1974.

One of the main uses to which Wallace's new-found wealth was put was to create an efficient network of regional organizers and advance men. "They are a group of young men who are trying to get it together and will get it together as an organization," said Azbell, speaking with his soft lisp. Sitting at his cluttered desk behind a terra-cotta statue of a boy holding a floppy-eared bunny rabbit, Azbell went on to explain the campaign with shy care, like an old-fashioned craftsman framing a house:

"You might say your average man today is involved only in his own involvement. He goes from womb to tomb in considerable distress. He is in flight and in fright from what is happening to him and to his happiness. . . . From the bureaucrats that interfere with him. . . . and the media that put pushers on TV. . . . Now these people don't want to send a President to Washington. They went to send a man with a message who will be President. . . . Wallace is like John F. Kennedy. He sees the people the other candidates don't see. . . . The waiters, the bellboy, or a desk clerk or the airplane mechanic, these are non-persons (to the other candidates). But these non-persons that no one else sees, George Wallace sees . . ."

This explanation was like so much of George Wallace's campaign, including the candidate himself. Nine-tenths of the time, though I might disagree with what was being said, it was logical and made sense. Then came the one-tenth that dropped my jaw. Azbell would say: "Barry Goldwater came close to winning. With a different candidate and technique he might have been successful." But Barry Goldwater, next to George McGovern, was the most overwhelmingly defeated candidate in our history. What does it mean to say that if he'd been different he might have won?

Talking about the origins of World War II, Wallace told me that it was the French seizure of the Ruhr and the stringent provisions of the Versailles treaty that made General Hans von Seeckt turn to Russia for arms. That's a sophisticated and debatable point; not too many people are aware of this secret pre-Hitler deal by the German General Staff. But Wallace went on to argue if it hadn't been for the Treaty of Versailles, Hitler would have died in Vienna babbling about wallpaper. Maybe. And maybe he just would have had a wealthier power base and won. Either generalization is equally valid and invalid.

The regional organizers and advance men that Wallace had on his staff this time around were certainly more impressive than those with him before. In the key, early primary state of Massachusetts was Frank Sullivan, for four years head of the young Democrats there. Handling Florida and the neighboring Gulf Coast states was Paul McCormick, who advanced for Muskie in the '72 primaries and later was an assistant to Florida's present senator, Richard Stone. Many of the other regional directors were similar—younger men, new to the campaign, soft-spoken, confident about themselves though nervous in their dealings with the press. They were concerned about their relationship to God and the passing of an older, more traditional, better America. They were interested in cars and mechanical things, and very, very proud of being southern even when they had just moved there. It was no longer Wallace, broke, with a few old friends against the world. His staff was better than before, and determined to prove that Dexter Avenue in Montgomery can outsmart Madison Avenue in New York.

George Wallace's performance on the psychological track was obviously a psychosomatic question—and the question everyone asked: How is his health? On the basis of research and first-hand observation: adequate at home, only so-so on the road. Since he was shot on May 15, 1972, Wallace has been paralyzed from the waist down. Having no control over his muscles below the waist, he cannot control either his bladder or his bowels and must use a catheter and catheter bag. This is both a physiological problem—the danger of bladder and bowel infections—and a psychological problem. The bag has to be changed several times a day. Wallace can never be certain when he may defecate, though the time at which he defecates can be controlled to a certain extent by regular eating habits and drugs, particularly when he is at home in Montgomery.

In addition, since the moment he was shot, Wallace has suffered constant pain from the shock dealt the spinal cord. Always present, sometimes this pain rises in nearly overwhelming waves. For this pain Wallace takes daily dosages of a drug called Tegretol, usually used in the treatment of epileptic seizures. Tegretol is not mind-bending or habit-forming; but it can have serious side-effects. When the pain occasionally drives Wallace to insomnia, he uses Dalmane, a tranquilizing drug that is practically never habit-forming. And even his enemies don't claim Wallace moves about like a zombie.

Wallace talks and thinks continually about his health. That's quite normal and understandable; the man has been involved in a genuine tragedy. It also takes up a lot of his time. With his exercises and special medical preparations, it takes Wallace about three hours of most mornings to get ready for his day. In addition to the drugs he takes for pain, he needs medication against the possibility of infection. He even has to worry about common colds because he has taken so many drugs over the past few years that he may have become immune to certain types of antibiotics. In short, Wallace's health is a constant problem, particularly when he goes on the road and is away from his usual routine and equipment.

Travel also must enhance his psychological problems: his feelings of helplessness and dependency as he is carried from planes and cars, pushed from strange room to alien hall in a wheelchair. And always the fear that the excitement and change will bring on an unexpected bowel movement or surge of pain. All this, plus the constant vulnerability to accident. He broke his leg in the spring of 1975 while exercising at home, and did not realize it for several days.

I have great sympathy for George Corley Wallace, having been wounded and having to spend two years either in bed or on crutches and in braces myself. And my problem with one leg is literally nothing compared to the paraplegia that has struck him. Still I have been in pain enough to know the total pull towards "La belle indifférence," the desire to retreat forever behind the protective glass shield of morphine, every four hours, like a bank teller's window, and watch languidly while my pain and the world's agony take place somewhere else. I remember my rage at trying to get a cab on New York's Fifth Avenue. The smartly dressed women who kicked my crutches out to get to the cabs first. The men who would pull me out as I was getting painfully in the cab door and dump me on the sidewalk. The tears of pain and impotent anger as I would pick myself up. The days, later in life, sitting at some table in some meeting, knowing people were moving to cut me up, but being too slow from drugs or lack of sleep to effectively fight back. The bastards who passed me in this way. I can still tap this rage to fuel myself today and have to watch it in my writing. And, again, I have been through nothing compared to Wallace.

But though I can sympathize and forgive and, yes, admire the man's physical courage, I do not have to condone the political use to which he puts his often unbottled anger. From Electra and Orestes through the Hatfields and McCoys to Syria and Israel, hatred is a destructive way to run a life, a family, or a nation. And from my experience in the minor leagues I know that to fight serious pain doesn't leave much time for other activity. On most days Wallace could do the work of governor for eight hours. But his campaigning for the White House had already been curtailed. And so would be his presidency.

I am certain Wallace knows this and that it does not concern him in the least. He doesn't want to be President. He wants to run for President—and secondly to reach people with his message. Just as Norman Mailer and William Buckley ran for mayor of New York City partly because they had something to say, but mostly to gain attention, so Wallace runs to be where the action is. In that way this spokesman for the old New Deal coalition is a very modern candidate.

Further, in Wallace, I believe, his campaign and his message fuse into one act. He runs and he speaks to get even, to fight back for himself and his constituency. He exists to give the establishment the eternal punch in the eye.

It appears that the 1976 election is largely a holding action. And George Wallace, entangled in his past bigotries and crippled by an assassin, will not be able to succeed, even though his constituency of the dissatisfied is growing, his staff has greater ability and his funds are large. But in the next election, the watershed of 1980, when it appears that America will not have worked for the majority of us, who will speak to Wallace's constituency then? Is Wallace with his southern preacher's fire the John the Baptist for some still unrecognized coalition? I don't know. And I am fearful. Not of George Wallace. But of who may next come crying down the highway he now makes straight through the wilderness of American anger.

CHAPTER 9

The Close of the Invisible Primary (II)

In the weeks following Thanksgiving, normal men, women and children turn to thoughts of Christmas with varying degrees of rapture. During the same period in a pre-presidential-election year the thoughts of politicians, political activists and reporters begin to swing towards the presidential hopefuls. Like so many human events, there is no clearly defined moment when one political phase ends and another begins. The press, electronic and written, devotes more time and space to the "making of the President." At the same time, growing numbers of people make their political commitment; the constituency track takes final shape. Sometime around Christmas, the end of the invisible primary merges imperceptibly with the start of the state primary-caucus race.

On the three days comprising the long weekend of November 23, 1975, there was a total of twenty-three articles related to the candidate selection process in *The New York Times* and the Washington *Post*. Six of these were on the front page. This number of articles was greater than had appeared on the invisible primary for the entire month of June 1975 in these two political bellwethers. Simultaneously, Ronald Reagan made the cover of both *Time* and *Newsweek*, the first candidate to be given such treatment coincidentally with his announcement. That week, the Sunday news interview shows on each of the three major networks featured presidential candidates: Udall, Carter, and the media master, Reagan. A week later, CBS assigned a reporter to each of the major candidates personally. Yet the candidates themselves had not significantly stepped up their activities between mid-September and the end of November.*

Nor was there a decrease in other news. A variety of important events jostled for front-page space and network program time. Justice William O. Douglas, bent beneath pain and the infirmities of age, resigned from the Supreme Court. The Portuguese revolution lurched between left and right, anarchy and fascism. In New Jersey, Karen Quinlan's inert body asked questions from which most recoiled. The third world pushed a resolution through the United Nations condemning Zionism as racist. Nelson

---

*See Appendices One and Two.

Rockefeller found the Vice-Presidential game not worth the midnight petroleum. The Big Apple proved financially rotten at its core. And President Ford called into question his competence with a series of maladroit Cabinet firings and reshufflings. In emphasizing campaign politics that old shiboleth, news judgment, was at work again. The time had come to talk to Presidents and candidates.

Inside the invisible primary itself the bulk of the activity was confined to the constituency and money tracks. Indeed, the two had now more or less merged, as candidates used the mechanism of fund raising to draw commitments from this or that individual or groups to their cause. (All the candidates were virtually locked into position on the other four tracks—another sign the period of time covered by this book was drawing to a close.) But everyone's constituency was building, though some a lot more rapidly than others. The politically active and aware, and those committed to this or that cause, including many committed quite properly to the cause of their own economic welfare, were choosing up sides. Every day from the candidates' offices came announcements that some national, state, or local figure or organization had endorsed their man. And the press and other candidates would analyze the names like diviners of old and wonder if they meant new strength in camp or if the candidate was, to use the language of the time, "going the Muskie route." Which meant: Were the endorsements from people of zeal who commanded followers who would work and vote, or were they merely names such as Muskie had relied on in 1972, officials doing their duty but lacking commitment or followers?

It is hard to analyze the effectiveness of the various names. Yesterday's wallflowers may turn into today's prom queens, while the man who put it together for Wombatt in Snopesville in 1974 may now be into the money and only a name. Some of the most potent forces within the small area they control are unknown on the national scene, while a big gun with the national media may possess little local clout. How is one to evaluate the fact that in New Hampshire Earl Borden and Arthur Cilly of the Steel Workers are supporting Birch Bayh? Or the news that Lucille Kelly is with Carter or that Maria Carrier and Dudley Dudley organize for Udall? And what to make of the fact that in New York Jackson has Morris B. Abrams and John Roe, while Bayh goes with Richard N. Gottfried and Mark A. Siegel, and Udall sports A. B. "Pete" Grannis and Ronald A. Scott?

One could say that when Harris' New Hampshire manager left the state without telling anyone, so that for two months Harris supporters were calling a disconnected phone number, this crimped the Harris campaign. Further, if one had to balance out the various people—and as a reporter one had to—it appeared that for the Democrats, Udall, Jackson, and Bayh were drawing the ablest people to their constituencies, with perhaps a slight edge given to the first two. While on the Republican side, Ford, though floundering about at times, was on the whole drawing GOP activists away from Reagan.

For example, in New Hampshire Udall by the last week in November had the most volunteers—four hundred—actually at work in the state. Carter was second with two hundred. In addition, Udall had a montly newsletter going to 12,000 people, while the other candidates were still making their first mailings. At the same time, Shriver was announcing the start of his New Hampshire drive in Manchester before a crowd of nine—count 'em, nine people. This was less of a crowd than that drawn by the cross-carrying minister, Arthur Blessit, running for President on the "God loves you" ticket. Shriver pointed out to the crowd, the nine citizens plus five reporters plus eighteen Secret Service men and twelve campaign workers, that he was starting his New Hampshire bid two months earlier than the late President Kennedy. "Hell, I beat John by two full months," he said. At which point one of his staff whispered to a reporter, "It's a damn good thing you've started earlier, because you've got a hell of a lot less to say." Even Van Lingo Wombatt has more support than that.

Before turning to the increasingly visible events on the Republican side of the invisible primary, we should take a final bow toward the Supreme Court of the United States. Precisely at 10 A.M. on November 10, to the cries of "hear ye, hear ye," eight Justices—Justice Douglas, bombarded with pain, was by now usually absent—took their places to hear arguments on the appeal from the District Court's favorable decision on the legality of the Campaign Finance Act. Again the key question was whether the limitations on giving and spending were merely limits on money or also infringements on freedom of speech.

This writer, who had by then covered sixteen candidates in the invisible primary, was puzzled by the freedom-of-speech argument. Candidates certainly had been prohibited from hiring Madison Avenue firms to do a barrage of slick commercials. But restrict their speech? If there had been any staunching of the flow of bull across the land, no instrumentation of mine has been delicate enough to record the diminution.

For the Republicans the major event of this time period was the official announcement by Ronald Reagan of his candidacy. Reagan was both drawn in by Ford's apparent weakness in the invisible primary and forced in by his supporters. They felt Reagan's moment was passing as Ford nailed down more and more commitments from leading Republicans around the country at the same time that Reagan's strength was rising in the polls. It also seemed to me that Reagan had been seduced into the battle in part by the press. The media has a financial interest in hot political fights. As long as only the Democrats appeared ready to tear each other apart, there was a whole battlefront on which nothing was happening. But if the Republicans started gouging each other also, then reporters would go out on the trail, advertising would be sold, readership and viewership would rise. And the coverage would appear to be more balanced, not just about Democrats, a consideration that delights editors, publishers, and TV station owners. I'm not saying this was done consciously. However, I know that I, myself, writing this book, often hoped that the Republican side of the contest would heat up again from the gelatinous coagulation to which it had cooled after the withdrawal of Charles Percy, Elliot Richardson, and Nelson Rockefeller.

Certainly President Ford was setting neither the prairies nor the cities on fire—nor was much blaze observed in the suburbs. But if Ford could be made to seem just a bit weaker than he was, the Republican discontent a bit deeper than actual, and Reagan's strength a bit stronger than apparent, why then there might be a fight. So it was "Go! Go! Ronnie!" and if Reagan came in and won, why then Ford was proven as weak as predicted. But if Reagan got cut to pieces, then the press had done its job and proven he didn't really have it on the national level. In any event there was another candidate to cover and analyze. "Let's you and him fight," had worked once again.

As always, Reagan's strength on the media track was his most impressive asset. At 9:31 on November 20, the three television networks covered his entrance into the race live from the conference room on top of Washington's National Press Building. When another ex-Governor, Terry Sanford, had stood behind the same podium in the same room five months before, in May, to announce, he had drawn no such attention. Indeed no candidate had been so honored by live television since Nelson Rockefeller declared in 1968. On the tube Reagan appeared alert and vigorous. With him was his wife, Nancy, in her red, white and blue "campaign dress." His announcement speech was little changed from the on-the-stump litany he had long been delivering across the nation.

"Our nation's capital has become the seat of a buddy system that functions for its own benefit—increasingly insensitive to the needs of the American worker who supports it with his taxes." Here Reagan took the stance of the non-politician campaigning against the machine, probably the strongest position of attack for a politician to take in the mid-seventies. (Democratic candidate Jimmy Carter was making effective use of the theme in his campaign.) Reagan's staff, also showing their media astuteness, had the candidate announce the week of interviews for the final Gallup Poll for 1975. When released on December 12, these figures would devastate President Ford. Reagan would surge from 23 points behind Ford in October to 8 points ahead. He would now lead Ford by 40 percent to 32 percent; and in the same period Ford's popularity would have dropped 16 points.

In the half-hour press conference following his speech, Reagan fielded most of the questions with non-answers. What would he do about New York City? "The only difference between the national government and New York City is that the government has a printing press." How did he feel about the hounding of Dr. Martin Luther King by the FBI? He hadn't had time to read the papers yet. How big should the military budget be? "The military budget is what you have to spend." He didn't have a specific figure. His press conference was a media, not an information, event.

The Washington TV event over, Reagan and his Secret Service escort raced off to Florida and New Hampshire in the same day, then North

Carolina and California in the next, to manipulate local television by the pace of the journey. Outside an airport motel in Florida his campaign got added notoriety when a man pointed a toy pistol at the candidate. Interestingly enough, ABC News considered this incident the most important news of the day, leading all its evening news shows with the toy gun. NBC reported the incident in a 35-second segment buried in the center of a more detailed report on not only Reagan's activities that day but also of his record as governor of California.

His two-day media blitz over, Reagan retired back to California for two weeks of rest, rather than return for constant contact with voters and political leaders in the key primary states of New Hampshire, Florida, North Carolina, and Illinois. Again this emphasized Reagan's distance from the other candidates, whether Democrat or Republican. Reagan alone relied primarily on the media track. Any success Reagan obtained would not only measure his own strength, but also test the degree to which the primary process is dominated by television.

Not that Reagan's campaign was only media. He had political experts on board who knew the value of organizational muscle. For example, in Massachusetts, where President Ford had been expected to garner every delegate, the Reagan forces, led by a former Massachusetts state chairman, William Barnstead, pushed through proportional representation by two votes, 26 to 24, at a sparsely attended Republican state meeting at which thirty of Ford's supporters failed to show up. The Ford Massachusetts team, led by Congressman Silvio O. Conte, seemed, like so much of the Ford campaign, to be playing 1930s ball against the professional formations of the 1970s, to use a Ford-like metaphor. From being sure of all the votes of Massachusetts, Ford had, in a moment of error, gone to being sure of perhaps 66 percent.

Even with his lead in the polls the question remained: How hard would Reagan be willing to campaign? Could he change his psychological set of recent years? What Reagan had to do—sometimes it's necessary to state the obvious because it's overlooked—was win Republican primaries. What he had done so brilliantly in his two successful campaigns for governor of California was win the votes of ticket splitters and independents. He had been particularly effective with the second group, among high-school graduates and those with some college who were drifting out of the Democratic party. But most of this group could not even vote in Republican primaries unless they were registered in that party first, and by December there was still no sign of any Reagan effort to achieve that. And both independents and ticket splitters are less likely to vote in primaries than loyal party members. This left Reagan relying on the right wing of the Republican party to produce his primary victories. Though vocal, they amount to only about 30 percent of the Republican party in most states.

This 30 percent is highly motivated by ideology; also, it is older and against things—all attributes that make a voter more likely to go to the polls. Still, pollsters agree that, unless there is a major emotional issue like Vietnam, the important reason why people turn out in primaries is party loyalty. Running against an incumbent President, Reagan needed such a major issue. There was a possibility that he could develop it from the anti-Washington, anti-government feeling seeping up through the land. If he could exploit this successfully, he could overcome his handicap of running from a minority base against the party loyalists who were supporting a personally popular President. Also, in the late stages of the invisible primary, Reagan was aided by incompetent blunders on the part of both the President and his inadequate staff. Towards the end of November, it sometimes seemed that Ford and those around him were determined to give Ronald Reagan every boost that they could.

Thus in November occurred the "Halloween massacre" and Nelson Rockefeller's formal withdrawal as a vice-presidential running mate for Ford in '76. Over the weekend of November 2, President Ford fired Defense Secretary James Schlesinger and CIA Director William Colby, and accepted the resignation of Rogers Morton as secretary of commerce. In a game of musical chairs, he shifted his White House chief of staff, Donald Rumsfeld, to be secretary of defense, while ambassadors Elliot Richardson and George Bush came from London and Peking to head the Commerce Department and the CIA respectively. The suddenness of the move, the lack of new talent, the bumbling nature of the shift—the participants left mad and the details leaked in the press first—raised questions whether the pressures of the presidency had become too much for Gerald Ford. Was he isolated inside the White House, too weak to tolerate dissent?

The President hurt his case in the televised White House press conference that followed. He stood before the press, smiling affably in his customary blue suit and vest, his bald spot glistening a bit more than usual. Looking square and stolid, like the figure on a Dutch Master cigar box, Ford insisted that there were "no basic differences" between himself and the departed Schlesinger. He also claimed he had consulted no one about the shifts. "I did it totally on my own," because he wanted his "own team." But the differences between himself and Schlesinger were well and publicly known. And if he really had consulted no one about such an important shift, he was admitting to an isolation in the White House more complete than even Richard Nixon's. It was more charitable to Ford to believe he was not telling the truth than to credit him with behavior of such singular arbitrariness. A week later, Ford admitted that differences between himself and Schlesinger over the size of the defense budget and détente had led to the firing. With this belated admission Ford was able again to achieve the worst of both possible worlds.

As for Rockefeller's denial that he wanted a vice-presidency in his future, that was, as we have seen, psychologically in keeping with the erosion of his interest in the presidency itself. Under increasing attack from the right, and with Ford listening to him less and less, Nelson Rockefeller simply decided that the vice-presidency was a job he did not need. He wasn't given the opportunity to attack those problems that he'd charmed himself into believing he would be called on to solve. Instead he was expending his energy in defending a regime that increasingly had scant use for him, and his reward was to be beaten about the head by bombast. "I didn't come down here to get caught in party squabbles," he told the press. His staff let out a collective sigh of relief. They, like the Vice-President, had become increasingly irritated by an administration that neither listened to them nor protected them. Rockefeller and his staff had not been working that hard anyway. Rockefeller's weekends away from Washington with his family grew longer and longer—two days, three days, three days and a half. In the end the private man called it quits for the public figure. Another candidate in the invisible primary defeated on the psychological track.

Still the question lingered: Was Rockefeller out for good? As he left the chamber in the Executive Office Building where he'd held his resignation press conference, the reporters and members of the staff pressed informally around him. Rockefeller had been uptight at the beginning of his press conference, but after the first five minutes he had relaxed happily, licking his lips after a good answer. Now the atmosphere was easy. One of the reporters asked if this was really the end. "You never know what's in the tea leaves," said Nelson. But the man who had gotten all that tea all those years didn't act as if he'd spend much time peering into the bottom of his cup to find a political future.

President Ford's weak staff, both at the White House and on The President Ford Committee, led to his total failure on the strategy track. Like Mondale before him, the President went anywhere an attractive invitation beckoned, and as a result his campaign went nowhere. His genial campaign manager, the breezy "Bo" Callaway, wanted him to concentrate on the south. Donald Rumsfeld and Ford's personal friends wanted him to take on Reagan in the west and midwest. Other congressional friends called up the alternate White House power center, Robert Hartmann, and urged Ford not to forget the early primaries in the northeast. There was no rational screening of speech invitations. In the White House eight speech writers worked on Ford's texts, but the committee-produced end products lacked both themes and personality. He was briefed for press conferences often for half a day, but no consistent policies emerged. He had his own TV advisor, but came across just as he always had—pleasant, honest, marginally competent. The result was that he was away from his desk every weekend and parts of some weeks jerking about the country in a frantic Brownian movement that appeared, and probably was, unrelated to any concerted political or governmental purpose.

Moderate and liberal Republicans complained of Ford's shift towards the right and lack of political direction. Senator Charles Mathias, Republican moderate from Maryland, called a press conference to announce that he might run in the GOP primaries as a liberal. Later he even talked of running as a third party candidate. From the farthest reaches of the politically possible, big John Connally of Texas boomed about coming in if ". . . greater confusion than now exists" befell the Republicans. In the election of 1976, primarily a holding action, such threats were unimportant. But who could tell what these little dust devils presaged in the way of tornadoes for 1980. At the start of November, Donald Rumsfeld planned to ease out "Bo" Callaway as campaign manager; he hadn't even been able to raise money, usually the Republicans' strongest track. But the shambles resulting from the Halloween massacre caused at least a delay.

Yet with all his failures and faults, Ford was still able to deploy against the charm of Ronald Reagan, not the might of the imperial presidency, but the media omnipresence of the electronic presidency. For example, at 9 A.M. Friday, November 7, Ford left Washington for a one-day spasm of politics, this time in Massachusetts. Massachusetts was now the second primary in the nation, part of the continual minuet of shifting dates as warring Democratic factions tried to seize the advantage by scheduling primaries to suit the strengths of their candidate. Massachusetts' liberal Democrats, who engineered the date shift had also inadvertently set up the Democratic side of that state's primary for George Wallace. I could explain how this came about, but it would take five pages—and in the end you would risk dying of rage or laughter, depending on your reaction to watching Harvard-trained boy scouts throw banana peels before old ladies—for the ladies' own good, of course. All that's really important is that now Massachusetts came early so Ford went to Massachusetts. And we came with him, the fusilage journalists of the electronic press.

The early morning mist curls about Andrews Air Force Base; the trees in this remarkable Indian Summer have just begun to turn. There are sixty-two of us covering this presidential jaunt; 6 wire service reporters, 18 newspaper reporters, 2 magazine reporters, 1 book writer, 16 radio and TV commentators and executives, 5 still cameramen, and 14 television cameramen and assorted technicians. Most of us do not even have to worry about where we sit: There are little names already stuck to the back of the seats, and a White House staffer to record those of us who may have overslept. The chartered Pan Am 727 blasts into the morning towards Westover Air Force Base at Chicopee, Massachusetts. We are served steak, eggs, French champagne, bloody marys, tea, and coffee by six stewardesses. Since we are, most of us, men and women of purpose, not to mention people with the normal fears about job security, no one proceeds to get bombed on Pan Am so early in the morning. But already we are being placed, and we know it, in a cotton-wool lined box in which we will journey partially isolated from reality.

In describing the press that day, I do not use the words "men and women of purpose" cavalierly. I'm parochial too. One of the reporters on the plane that morning joined the press on graduation in part because of a speech I gave on press power at his college newspaper banquet in the mid-fifties. I am always sobered by such examples of personal responsibility. I bristle at such denunciations of the press as that given by George McGovern in England in 1973, ". . . perhaps the most discouraging development of recent years is the exhaustion of the institution of the press," McGovern said then. "Much of this can be blamed on the incestuous character of the White House press corps itself. Ask one wrong question and a reporter may find himself cut off altogether, thus ending his repose in one of the cushiest assignments a journalist can draw. . . ."

That's a cheap shot, and what is worse, it hurts rather than helps solve the problem of covering presidential politics, which is a major one. The fear of losing the White House beat, or any good beat, is not the fear of losing the steak and champagne—few give a hoot about that; the fear is that of losing the ability to command air time, get on the front page, in the magazine. It's the fall from power to impotence; a fear few men or women know themselves well enough to control. Then there is the strain of the symbiotic relationship a reporter has with his sources; and this strain is increased because today the media often finds itself, as in fusilage journalism, isolated from the world with only itself and its sources. Where is reality then?

Politicians feel the press is power-mad, weak, and corrupt. The press feels businessmen are stupid and crooked. The businessmen believe the bureaucrats are shakedown artists out to paralyze the country and line their pockets. The bureaucrats are certain that politicians are cynical exploiters of public passions bent on climbing to power over a twitching citizenry. So we all dance round and round, screaming. And the citizens, after a while, tune us all out. In this book I have stressed that I think the Senate, for many reasons, is a rotten training ground for the presidency. But this doesn't mean that I believe senators to be made of different hydrocarbons than you and I; or that Harry Truman was not a great President.

The meal is whisked away, and we land at Westover Air Force Base. Here there is a roped-in press area with ten long-distance phones. The report of the pool men, the three reporters riding with the President on Air Force One, has been mimeographed up on the President's plane and is now distributed to us. It is not even necessary to open a notebook except perhaps to record the weather, 62 degrees with a few scattered clouds, the name of the obligatory high-school band, Chicopee, and the size of the crowd, 1,000-plus. After watching Ford shake hands along the fences (will there be a Fromme or a Moore in the crowd?), we pile into the waiting buses and, sixteen cars back from the President's car, follow him into the town of Springfield. There in Albert's Restaurant we have been granted another pressroom with food and a cash bar and junction boxes for the phones and tape recorders. Since the President is speaking to newspaper editors, no reporters are allowed in to hear what he has to say. Were he to so restrict his remarks before any other group, the room would be explosive at the insult. But since it is our own bosses who are shafting us, we are resigned.

Besides we have the controversy of the day to enliven us: Was Ford struck over the right eye by a "young kid" waving a twenty-inch-long stick with a pointed tip to which was attached a small American flag? A number of these toy flags and staffs had been patriotically distributed by the local high-school principal. Two of the pool reporters believe he was hit. One heard Ford say, "Oops." Certainly Ford stooped suddenly. But the Secret Service believe he tripped over the foot of an old lady in a wheelchair (I'm not kidding). And the NBC film unit hastily reviewing its tape does not believe the boy's flag made contact with the presidential flesh. Now there's a controversy to delight the cymini sectores of medieval scholasticism. Should the story lead with the flag, bury the flag, ignore the flag, treat it with professional distance, or scrutinize it closely as part of Ford's accident proneness? His English breaking down under the strain of "le deadline," the reporter from Agence France Press (Ford would visit France next week) appeals to me for help. *"Avec cette question de coup de drapeau?"* As befits a man who remembers Kissinger when he was merely a sergeant, I try to reassure him in labored French that I think the Republic will survive at least this coup.

After the flag incident it's all downhill for the rest of the day—and we weren't up very high before. We are bused back to the airplane. Served a quick lunch. Land in Boston. Another motorcade to the Sheraton-Boston Hotel, where Ford goes to his suite to relax and the press goes to the Cafe Riviera, converted into a pressroom, to relax. It is now 2 P.M. At 3 P.M. the President speaks to the New England Council, a group of serious citizens who meet once a year to worry about the future of New England. Before Ford speaks to the Council, they hear from one life insurance company vice-president, one dean, and one college president, Jerome B. Wiesner of MIT. That's a tough act to follow. The press troops upstairs to the ballroom to watch the President from the side of the hall. We already have the advanced text of what he will say. He sticks to the text.

This is the Friday after the Halloween massacre, the sudden departure of Schlesinger and Colby, and in some quarters Ford is being criticized for cutting the defense budget too far. The speech is largely a reply to his critics. Its theme is: It's not me cutting the defense budget, it's the bad guys in Congress. "Defense is the only part of the Federal budget the Congress cuts with a vengeance. If this trend continues to the year 2000, according to mathematical projections, the United States defense will be reduced to one soldier carrying one rifle. . . ." That's the high point.

Back down to the makeshift pressroom to file and wait for an hour. Someone thinks they hear a bomb go off. We surge into the street. No bomb. By now it's dark and we cavalcade across the river to Cambridge for a meeting with Republican fund raisers. A closed meeting for those who gave $500 per person, an open reception and speech for those who gave $100; then back to the airport for a massive fund raiser and reception for those who gave $15. At each stop there are carefully constructed platforms on which the television cameras are set up and plugged in. They are the real purpose of the trip. At the $15 reception, before some 400 people gathered in the international departure lounge of the Boston Airport, the President is sweating and wilted. It's 8:15 P.M. The perspiration is dripping off his eyebrows and chin. The white collar of his otherwise blue shirt is crinkled and compressed. He has trouble pronouncing the word "Massachusetts." He sways a bit as he talks. "I know a fellow," he tells the nine motion picture and television cameras across the incidental audience, "I know a fellow that is going to enter New Hampshire, Massachusetts, Florida, and every other primary, and I know he is going to win."

The little phrase "every other primary" in an extemporaneous four-page speech—we get the text shortly after takeoff—is the only meager ration of meat we have gotten all day. And it seemed to slip out by accident. What does it all mean, we ask ourselves as we jet back to Andrews Air Force Base outside of Washington, again sipping champagne and eating steak if that's our pleasure. (It was mine.) Does Ford really intend to campaign in every primary state? Was he indulging in hyperbole? Had he perchance had an extra martini? We believe that's been responsible for late-in-the-day slips before.

Traveling with the President on Air Force One are the President's two Massachusetts campaign managers, Congressmen Margaret Heckler and Silvio Conte. Also, Ambassador John Volpe, a former Massachusetts governor who has flown back from Italy to get in on the day's events. And Ford talked about how he would campaign. Who will then pay for Ford's trip? (We are paying for ours, $187.) The Federal Government, the Republican National Committee, or The President Ford Committee, or some combination of these three?

The next day on *Meet the Press* Ford clarifies what he meant by "every other primary." He didn't mean he would actively campaign in all the primaries. Just that he would not be ". . . entering some and ducking others." As for who picks up the check for the President's trip, that was still being argued as this book went to press.

In spite of its lack of content, this electronic jitterbugging accomplished Ford's purpose. The President dominated the local TV news for two days in Massachusetts and even got on national network news. And what of the suave challenger, Ronald Reagan? Right after he announced at the National Press Club in Washington, when he raced for his chartered plane to fly to Florida and New Hampshire to announce again in both places, he could not take off as scheduled. His plane was held up for half an hour. Why? All flights into and out of Washington National Airport were being slowed down and diverted. The President was speaking in the courtyard of the Pentagon and airplanes were being rerouted as a result for "reasons of security." If Ford could do that to Reagan when he just took his limousine across the Potomac to see his old friend Rummy at the Pentagon, think how he wasted Reagan when he cranked up the presidential jet and went to Peking at the start of December followed by over three hundred members of his staff and the press.

At the end of November, a group of President Ford's supporters got together, in part under the guidance of Melvin Laird, in a suite at the Mayflower Hotel in Washington, and gently took the White House staff to task for letting the campaign committee maul—rather than handle—the President. After the meeting, Jerry Jones, Cabinet secretary and a political advisor, was heard to say that President Ford had made "his last speech to a Republican fund raiser for a long time and maybe forever."

Next, the Federal Election Committee ruled that any traveling Ford did after the first of the new year in 1976 would be presumed to be in support of his own candidacy. This meant those trips would have to be paid for out of Ford's campaign committee funds and would count against his $12 million spending ceiling. Robert Teeter, the Republican polling wizard, came up with figures that showed the public wanted the President to spend more time as Chief Executive and less as candidate. These hard facts, coupled with the advice from his friends, caused a sharp cutback of presidential travel. At least for a few months those around Ford had finally agreed on a strategy of staying in Washington and governing the country.

Meanwhile the Democrats were closing the year with a surprising show of unity. Or perhaps it would be more correct to say they were doing a Strauss waltz. With only one dissenting vote out of 362, the Democratic National Committee agreed to limit challenges to delegations at the national convention in New York in June. Those challenging now had to show damage; they had to have taken part in the political process of their state, and they could only challenge the actual implementation of the approved state plan for electing delegates. Where in 1972 it had only taken 10 percent of any committee to bring a minority report to the floor, now it would take 25 percent. The key vote on this provision was 143 to 90. One of the Democratic hopefuls questing across the land was going to receive a nomination worth something. "You know what my reward is going to be?" asked Strauss. "The first thing the winner is going to do is fire me."

Like the weird sisters playing cards on a Harz Mountain summit amid the shriekings of Walpurgis Night, here and there—as the Democratic candidates frolicked in their mad pursuits—occurred a few moments of relative order. The Democratic Party of Iowa decided to invite all the candidates to the annual Jefferson-Jackson Day Dinner on October 25—Colonel Sanders chicken and Cokes at the Hilton Coliseum in Ames, Iowa. Two thousand people came, conservatively dressed, middle-aged and serious; four thousand had been expected. And seven candidates showed; Shapp, Wallace, and Bentsen staying home. The main problem of the meeting, which took place at night, was that the candidates were restricted to ten minutes of speaking. There is very little about a man that can be learned in a ten-minute speech except whether he can deliver a ten-minute speech. All the candidates except Shriver can. He introduced his wife okay, "Eunice KENNEDY Shriver"; after that he floundered.

By now the press had begun to play what we called "candidate of the week." Three weeks earlier Birch Bayh had been the fair-haired boy, the real comer. Then for a time it was Sargent Shriver. After Iowa it was Jimmy Carter's turn. He did remarkably well on a straw poll taken by the Des Moines *Register* at the convention, winning 256 or 23 percent of the votes cast—the next closest being that favorite non-starter, Hubert Humphrey with 135. Reporters interviewing around the state confirmed the poll reports. Carter's strategy of concentrating on the early caucus states of Iowa and Oklahoma had been successful. In both states he had built a well functioning, grass-roots organization. "Carter gets ball rolling in Iowa," headlined the Washington *Post. The New York Times* saw Carter picking up strength in New England as well as Iowa.

The Udall camp, which had been expecting to do well in Iowa on a modest effort while concentrating on New Hampshire, took the severest beating in the poll. They now grew concerned that the Iowa caucuses in 1976 might become the decisive first event, as the New Hampshire primary had been in 1972 and 1968. When in December, NBC decided to cover the night of the Iowa caucuses, January 19, live, Udall's new campaign manager, Jack Quinn, budgeted ten days of the candidate's time to Iowa and also sent three full-time workers into the state, including the famed Rick Stearns who put together the non-primary states for McGovern in '72. Bayh in turn brought in Richard Sikes, who had been handling Wisconsin. In Bayh's 1974 Senate race, Sikes carried Mayor Lugar's home county of Marion for Bayh. Carter was forcing the other candidates to play his game.

But there was another interesting trend in Iowa: Even the politically active were getting fed up with the length and intensity of the nominating game. "I probably have the highest tolerance for politics of anyone in the world, and I can't stand this much politics. I get sick of it," said Gertrude MacQueen, an Iowa Democratic leader. That seemed to sum it up for a lot of people. The cheers at Ames for any of the candidates or for George McGovern were brief and perfunctory. Fewer people showed up at turnouts than expected, fewer people were willing to commit themselves. Not just Indian summer but also apathy shimmered across the land.

Fred Harris had hoped for 100 at the opening of his Iowa headquarters; about 30 showed. I questioned the people coming into a Jackson reception at the Ramada Inn outside of Ames. Were they for Jackson? "We're just looking around," was the answer of the vast majority. Polling at the end of November, Patrick Caddell found the same mood nationally. "The degree of noncommitment is staggering," he said. "There is no intensity of support for anyone. Even the staffs of the candidates aren't really committed." Perhaps some of the excesses of the invisible primary were curing themselves.

Beyond apathy, there was also hostility to the whole process of politics, and this included definite hostility towards the press. At the Coliseum a group of ticket holders surged towards the TV cameras to pull them down so they could see better. "This whole thing is just arranged for the press," I heard over and over. "Why don't you all go home and let us see the candidates." The press had switched from being viewed as the medium through which the candidates were displayed to being seen as a barrier between the candidate and the people. Iowa voters resented the facts that the press had the best seats in the house, the best location for their cameras, events scheduled for their convenience.

It seemed to me, also, that people were becoming more guarded in their communications with reporters, less open, more inclined to say "I don't know," or even, "What's it to you?" "Why don't you all go home and let us have our own politics?" "The press is part of our problem." I began to think I might be growing paranoid until pollsters reported that they were finding the same reaction among potential interviewees throughout America. The pollsters call it "the twitching curtain phenomenon," in which, when the pollsters come to call, they know there is someone home, maybe even the whole family, but no one comes to the door. "It's a very serious problem that threatens the long-term viability of the survey profession," said Irving Crespi, one of Gallup's vice-presidents.

Just as an over-preoccupation with self can make an individual disturbed, so it seems too much self-examination is disturbing America. A Gallup survey reports that one out of seven Americans over the age of eighteen has been interviewed at one time or another in his or her life. Back in the sixties, when the University of Michigan Survey Research Center began making its in-depth interviews to find out who we as Americans are and what we feel, it took five hours to obtain each one-hour interview. Now it takes seven. Interestingly enough, it is hardest to get interviews with the young, the well-educated, the very rich, and the very poor. These are the same groups that tend to be in the ranks of the independents and not to vote—another indication that Americans are not just alienated from politics but from society as a whole.

That the media has become part of the political process is obviously true. We help create the image that makes the candidate stand out and which often divides him from the people. Just as the security force of Secret Service men both guards the candidate and draws people to him. Since the press is part of the process, those in America who are turned off by our present politics—and they are a growing number—are critical also of the press.

On the 7 A.M. United Airlines flight from Des Moines to Washington the next (Sunday) morning, the first-class section was exclusively full of "us": reporters, TV technicians, candidates and their staffs. We stood a bit apart in the airline terminal as if clustering together for safety as Americans used to do in jungle clearings in Vietnam. We were members of the same profession, though on different sides. (And how different do our "sides" appear to an outsider?) Some of us, politicians and reporters, had known each other for twenty years. Are we, the press, talking to America or to each other? Are we a transmission belt or a barrier? Do we see or are we part of some on-stage ritual? Most likely, being human, we are now one thing, now another.

Nine little Indians sitting on a Democratic wall. George Wallace joined them officially on November 12. There was also one Indian at the wall's base hammering the final nails into his ladder. Senator Frank Church was winding up his CIA investigation as rapidly as possible, leaving to the committee staff the serious work of drafting legislation to regulate the CIA without destroying it. His hope was that spook-watching would do for him what Mafia-watching had done for Estes Kefauver in the fifties. He was another senator using a sexy investigation to grab the media and gain name recognition.

At the same time one big chief stood back from the wall, arms folded on his chest, and insisted he had no intention of climbing up, even if his friends brought him a tip-proof ladder. "I've learned you cannot be a good senator and a good candidate. You can't do it," said Hubert Horatio Humphrey. In those states, such as Florida and Massachusetts, where a candidate mentioned in the media had his name automatically placed on the ballot unless he officially withdrew, Humphrey mailed in affidavits of noncandidacy. For the time he seemed out of it. But in mid-December, when the Gallup Poll showed Humphrey by far and away the most popular of the Democrats (he had 30 percent, ten points more than his closest rival), the press took off in an orgy of speculation about candidate Humphrey.

There were two scenarios on how Humphrey would wind up the Democrat's nominee. The first, and most popular, had him being offered the crown at a hopelessly deadlocked Democratic convention. Humphrey himself said that under those circumstances he would accept the nomination. The second had his name being written in by voters in a large number of primaries so that he received both delegates and press momentum. In effect he would be a primary winner without having to enter the primaries.

The steadily decreasing possibility of a brokered convention that truly chooses a candidate has been one of the major themes of this book. Conventions are becoming media events that ratify the results of the state primaries, demonstrate party unity or factionalism on television, and choose a Vice-President. By December, even Hubert Humphrey himself had come to accept this view. "There was a time when I thought it would be a brokered convention," Humphrey wrote a friend, ". . . (but now) it's very unlikely that a nonprimary candidate will get the nomination."

This left scenario number two: a write-in campaign in several state primaries that would gain Humphrey media attention, increase his popularity and, most important, win him delegates. Those who leaned to this strategy continually cited the knockout blow dealt Rockefeller's 1964 campaign for the GOP nomination by the large write-in vote in the New Hampshire primary for Henry Cabot Lodge, then Ambassador to South Vietnam. But the new campaign financing law now made such write-ins difficult. Any committee organizing for an undeclared candidate was limited to $1,000 in expenditures. As soon as a group trying to organize for a candidate without his permission, opened an office, made ten long distance phone calls and sent out their first mailing they would be either broke or illegal. When Robert Shaine of New Hampshire tried to organize a write-in for Hubert Humphrey in that state's primary in November, Humphrey, through an aide, disavowed the drive. Shaine said he would go ahead anyway. Then he ran into the new campaign law with its complex accounting procedures and its $1,000 limit. He also learned that any literature he sent out had to be prominently labeled "unauthorized." Shaine's write-in effort quietly faded. While the provisions of the new law were always complex and sometimes vague and subject to future legal challenge, write-in campaigns had taken a quantum jump in difficulty.

Those organizing for Humphrey had to be careful to comply with every jot and tittle of the law. Having been around the track three times before—1960, 1968, and 1972—Humphrey had a number of advantages, particularly on the media and constituency tracks, but past weaknesses on the staff track had left him vulnerable to any signs of hanky-panky. Jack L. Chestnut, the manager of both Humphrey's 1970 Senate campaign and his disastrous 1972 presidential primary campaign, had been sentenced in May to four months in jail and fined $5,000. He had allegedly arranged for a Madison Avenue advertising firm handling part of Humphrey's campaign to be secretly paid by the Associated Milk Producers, Inc. Humphrey had defended his old friend Jack L. Chestnut as ". . . a man of rigid integrity . . . [who] would not have intentionally violated the law." Norman Sherman, a former press secretary to the senator, had pleaded guilty the year before to aiding and abetting another illegal contribution from the Milk Producers—this one for payment of a computerized political mailing.

Robert A. Maheu, Howard Hughes' chief operative in Nevada, testified under oath that he left $50,000 in cash at Humphrey's feet in his vice-presidential limousine outside the Los Angeles Century Plaza Hotel in 1968. Humphrey has said he has no record of the money or any memory of the incident. Since the money came from Howard Hughes personally, the gift would not be illegal, provided Humphrey performed no service in return. This is all part of the freewheeling before-Watergate politics when big money talked and most leaders of both parties listened and some few jumped when the money whispered.

Then there was the question of Humphrey's taxes. Humphrey is slowly paying off the $240,000 in back taxes and interest he owes the government as a result of a technical violation of the tax laws over the donation of his private papers to the Minnesota Historical Society. While there is no question of fraud involved, as there was in the alleged back-dating of President Nixon's donation of his papers, the type of violation is still the same: a gift that turned out not to be a gift because the senator kept control over the papers.

While capable of moments of vast self-delusion, Hubert Humphrey is no fool. He was aware that as long as he remained on the sidelines, he would not be asked questions about these past incidents—just as Teddy Kennedy, while out of the race, was spared questions about Chappaquiddick. Once Humphrey started to campaign, he would in many places, turn from being good old Hubert to an old, corrupt, pro-war blabbermouth. "You may count on Hubert to carefully examine both sides of an issue before endorsing all possible viewpoints. . . . He is a worn out old retread in a time when many Americans are tired of old flat tires, Model T Fords, and indifferent political mechanics," wrote Larry L. King in *New Times*, pawing the earth at this "terrible nightmare" that Hubert Humphrey might be running again.

When anyone has been famous as long as Hubert Humphrey, people may not know the man as he appears to his creator, or as he appears to himself, but they are willing to choose up sides on the man as he appears to them. The rich, full mosaic of Humphrey's often controversial life is there for all to judge according to their needs. There is the constant talking, the love of people, the desire to please, the ambition, the blotting paper memory, the fabled energy. "There are very few men in the world who've got what he's got, genes that few other politicians have," says Dr. Edgar Berman, his old friend and physician, who campaigned with Humphrey in the disastrous battles of 1972.

The frieze begins with the boy growing up poor in Doland, South Dakota, son of that small town's (500 people) druggist, working in the drugstore himself, finally being able to go to college, becoming a teacher at Macalaster College, organizing everything in sight. The young man, rejected by the draft because of hernia, color blindness, and calcified lungs, helps to put together the Democratic Farmer Labor Party, presiding over the key merger meeting in April 1944 the night his first son is born. At 34 he becomes mayor of Minneapolis. "Hurricane Hubert" cleans up Minneapolis and reforms its civil service. Then finding that the Communists had taken over the Democratic Farmer Labor Party, he turns around and purges them in a tough and still controversial campaign.

At the Democratic convention in Philadelphia in 1948 occurs what may be his finest hour, when he speaks for forty minutes in favor of the minority report for a strong civil rights plank. He receives an ovation and the convention votes in his plank. Famous now, he is swept into the Senate in 1950 where he introduces legislation like Medicare long before its time and supports Truman's attempts to limit the Korean War. Yet he is ineffective, alienating his fellow senators by his constant jabber, and is considered an unfortunate joke. "That Minnesota," cracks Vice-President Alben Barkley, "first they sent us their ball (Senator Joseph Ball), then their thigh (Senator Edward Thye) and now they've sent us their goddamn ass."

Three years later he has worked his way back from purdah to become a respected member of the Senate's inner club. It was at this point that I began to see Humphrey for extended periods of time. I remember the first of these, in 1953, when Humphrey was talking to a small group of about ten reporters at a private dinner. He was justifying his stand in favor of high price-supports for farm products by insisting that there was no grain surplus. "Do you realize," he said, (I am paraphrasing) "there really is no grain surplus. Why if every man, woman, and child in the United States was to start eating our so-called surplus, they would eat it all up in two days. Yes sir, in two days." Suddenly in my mind appeared the picture of every man, woman, and child in America chomping at the base of gigantic silos for five minutes and then giving up, while the giant maxillae of Hubert Humphrey heroically ground on to finish the rest of the surplus on their own.

In 1960 Humphrey mounts his first campaign for the Democratic presidential nomination. Under-financed and badly staffed, he is blown out of the water in West Virginia by PT-boat-hero Jack Kennedy. He returns to the Senate, where he pushes many of his liberal programs into reality, is tapped by Lyndon Johnson to be his Vice-President in 1964, and in 1968 runs for the presidential nomination himself, against fellow senators Robert Kennedy and Gene McCarthy.

While Kennedy and McCarthy battle it out in the primaries, Humphrey, the former populist, now Lyndon Johnson's surrogate, lines up the boss-controlled delegations in the back rooms. Then follows the assassination of Robert Kennedy, the divided convention in Chicago, and the provoked police riot. In the presidential campaign itself Humphrey, starting far behind and with his party shattered, closes fast and barely loses*. He retires, bitter, to teach again at Macalester College, then runs for Gene McCarthy's vacant Senate seat and wins overwhelmingly. After swearing it won't ever happen again, in 1972 he swigs too much ambition and campaigns once more for the presidential nomination, reminding listeners that "the last four letters of American spell I can." He is defeated by the legions of George McGovern for whom Humphrey's support of Lyndon Johnson and the Vietnam War is unforgiveable.

What does he do now?

I have always thought of Hubert Humphrey as fickle; basically a good man, with an extraordinary memory, who genuinely loved people and wanted to help them—but plain, old-fashioned fickle. The same need to be loved that leads to his incessant chatter, that makes him try excessively to please every group he is with, causes him to hop from issue to issue and stand to stand. He is that flawed, romantic hero who betrays himself for love—a man who breaks up his marriage, not out of basic intellectual or emotional difference, nor even because of a serious affair, but because he must always conquer someone new to prove his own attractiveness.

Does he realize his age, 64—three months younger than Ronald Reagan? Does he acknowledge to himself that we have never inaugurated a President as old as he is now, except for James Buchanan? Is the dye in his hair

---

*One more pro-Humphrey vote in every precinct of the nation would have given him victory over Richard Nixon. A fact to warm oneself with when suffering from the my-vote-doesn't-count blahs.

cosmetic or psychological? In short, can his need for love be satisfied with the role of revered senior statesman? Will he listen to his reason this time? Or will he find himself in battle once again? Will men say of him, as courtiers did of the declining Lear, "Even at the best he hath but slenderly known himself"?

I don't know. He is sending out those affidavits demanding that his name be taken off the ballot. I believe without too much conviction that this time he will remain constant and stay out of the primaries, and that therefore he will not be the candidate. But I am also certain he thinks of himself as the man most fit to be President, and I remember his past. And the head start he has from having been a candidate before on so many of the invisible primary tracks must be tempting.

While Humphrey remained in part an enigma, the announced candidates sought their constituencies whenever and wherever they could find them: at the Democratic Forum meetings, at political clubs, in parties and coffees, among delegates at labor conventions, and through the press and television. The difference was that now there was more movement as politically-aware people chose up sides and went to work. In New York, Robert Abrams, the reform boss of the Bronx and unsuccessful candidate for attorney general, came aboard the Bayh wagon. This meant that Ethan Geto, Abrams' former manager, came on as Bayh's New York manager. He proceeded to mount an energetic, well-financed effort against Udall and Harris on the left and Jackson on the right. Hiring half a storey on Lexington Avenue near Grand Central Station, and a printing press, Geto was spending around $15,000 a week by the middle of December "mostly on mail and phones."

"We made the first contact ourselves," said Geto, rubbing his unshaven face beneath the red, white and blue bunting and the pictures of Bayh that formed his office frieze. A big mailing had gone out at four o'clock that morning. "Abrams and I felt that Abrams should play a major role in a presidential year. . . . Udall had been in New York for a year and never done anything. . . . Harris was running a campaign that could not get outside support. . . . We were looking for a broad-barrel liberal. . . . We made the decision to jump." Money played a part too, though Geto didn't say so. Only the Jackson people were offering the same kind of cash that would keep part of a New York organization happy.

Geto's first goal for Bayh was to lock up the endorsement of the New Democratic Coalition—our old friend the NDC, or "November Doesn't Count." The NDC, a group of liberal purists, has been described "as a splinter of a splinter." But its endorsement is a media event and also a trail blazer for other liberals seeking a candidate. Here Bayh's labor constituency gave tremendous help. Five respected leaders of the UAW, led by General Counsel Steve Schlossberg, sent a letter to all NDC members urging them to support Bayh: "Of all the declared or potential Democratic contenders, Senator Bayh best combines a record of consistent and outspoken liberalism with a proven ability to appeal to all segments of low- and middle-income working men. . . .," they wrote.

Bayh's New York organization printed up a throwaway showing the senator glaring out of an Israeli bunker at presumed Arab positions in the distance, making Bayh even more pro-Israeli than Scoop Jackson. More important, Geto arranged a series of coffees, receptions, and political club meetings. "By the time of the meeting [the December 6 NDC nominating convention] Bayh will have seen every NDC member," said Geto.

In mid-November it seemed as if Bayh had a lock on the NDC, a fact his managers were incautious enough to admit. Bayh was also doing well with the NDC's mirror image in Massachusetts, CPPAX (Citizens for Participation in Political Action, called "C-P-Pax" in the talk circles). Then Bayh tripped over himself. His Massachusetts campaign manager was John McKean, a likable hot-dog who graduated from Harvard in '71 and then went up to New Hampshire with Joe Grandmaison to organize for McGovern in '74. McKean was caught printing 1,200 CPPAX memberships on his own in order to pack the CPPAX meeting. The ruse came to light when Boston Photo Service, Inc., which was doing the printing for Bayh, called CPPAX to tell them the printing was ready. At that moment the liberals hit the fan; and blood, gore, and mimeograph releases filled the air around Cambridge, with bits of quivering nonsense even landing as far away as New York.

To further woo the NDC, Geto had put out a flier on Birch Bayh: "The candidate with a proven record of accomplishment." And what accomplishment led off the issues list? "An early opponent of the Vietnam War, Senator Bayh cosponsored the original End-the-War Amendment. . . ." Since Bayh had voted against the anti-war plank in the '68 Democratic convention, this claim seemed a bit overblown. After much probing, the Bayh staff explained that this vote referred to the Cooper-Church Amendment of June 30, 1970, which passed the Senate 58 to 37. One of those who voted for that amendment was Senator Jackson. Bayh, who was not one of those who introduced the amendment, though he came aboard early, was running as an anti-war liberal on the basis of his support of some mid-1970 language—voted for by a majority of the Senate including hard-liner Henry Jackson.

In the end, on December 6 in the Stuyvesant High School auditorium, Bayh lost the NDC endorsement by one vote on the sixth ballot. The convention adjourned without endorsing anyone. Second was Fred Harris with close to 30 percent of the vote. Decisively defeated was Udall, with less than 11 percent of the ultra-liberal group. Bayh claimed a victory anyway, since he had failed by less than one-tenth of a percentage point to gain the necessary 60 percent. But a wise man would have been inclined to remark with Pyrrhus, "One more such victory and I am lost."

It seemed that Bayh, like Sargent Shriver, was suffering from his late start in the invisible primary, though Bayh because of his brief 1972 race suffered less. At the liberal Democratic Forum held in Atlanta, Shriver said that he didn't know where he stood on the right-to-work law. Udall, Harris, Carter, and Jackson had made mistakes, but they had made them early and out of sight of the media. Udall's campaign had practically come apart in late September in a series of staff shuffles and shake-ups, but the mess had been invisible and he had been well enough established to have recovered by the time media attention began to focus on his campaign. Jimmy Carter and Fred Harris, tramping the cornfields of Iowa and the woods of New Hampshire, had signed up supporters and obtained commitments before the former was asked publicly to explain his support of Lt. Calley and Lester Maddox, and the latter his votes to increase the oil-depletion allowance or continue the Vietnam War. When they finally were asked, at major news conferences or on national television, they had their effective explanations well rehearsed. Similarly the Jackson organization in New York faltered in early September, had time to bring in Terry O'Connell, the badly wounded veteran of both the Hobo Woods in Vietnam and the Michigan anti-war movement. O'Connell, who wrote the handbook on primary campaigns for the Democratic National Committee, put his fabled charm and energy to work and stitched most of the pieces—though not all—back together again, invisibly.

As the press begins to pay attention earlier to the state primary-caucus system, the invisible primary takes on an additional function: to let the candidates make their mistakes out of sight without serious consequences. Good campaigns are forged like good combat units. They need a few easy victories in a quiet sector to shake down, get the kinks out of their system. The First Infantry Division and the Second Armored went from their initial minor battles in Africa to become fabled outfits. The Twenty-Ninth Infantry never recovered from having its first taste of combat at Omaha Beach on D Day. So Jackson, Udall, Harris, and Carter had the advantage over Bayh and Shriver. And among other strengths, President Ford had the same edge over Ronald Reagan, though the publicity focus on the White House minimized this advantage.

Of all the constituencies forming at the end of the invisible primary, the strength of George Wallace's was the hardest for me to judge. What was I to make of Frank Sullivan, the pleasant, open, 22-year-old high-school graduate who was running the Wallace campaign in Massachusetts out of his mother's home? "I'm running a people's campaign. Not even any bumper stickers. Spending maybe $350 a month, though that's about to increase," he told me. He'd run the campaign of the Massachusetts secretary of state in Brockton and New Bedford. From Viguerie he had the names of those people in the state who had contributed to, or offered to help Wallace: "Two hundred fifty people ready to work for us in New Bedford alone. . . . People kid me that I'm running this like a local race for alderman. And I say, 'You [sic] damn right I am.' Yessir, that's what I tell 'em, 'You damn right I am.' . . . I'd rather have ten good high-school students working for me then a hundred politicians any day."

Sullivan hadn't intended to go to work for Wallace. He contacted several candidates and sent off his résumé to Joe Napolitan, the political consultant.

He had a copy of the résumé left over and thought, why not? So he sent it down to Wallace Headquarters in Alabama. Mickey Griffin, Wallace's national coordinator, got on the phone. Sullivan flew down and talked to the staff in Montgomery. They signed him on.

Sullivan, who was president of the Young Democrats in Massachusetts for two years, looks like a sincere management trainee, or a slightly nervous platoon leader before his first action. Are his troops really there? At the end of November he did not yet have any headquarters to show me; but he insisted that his people were ready to go. His father was mayor of Brockton and "I grew up in politics." He is short and wiry, pleasant, anxious to please, much like Wallace must have been when he was young. He was putting himself through Suffolk College working nights but had to give that up for the Wallace campaign. Everyone in the organization was under forty. He assured me, "This isn't the John Birch Society." It certainly wasn't that.

"Will you get help from the Right-to-Life troops?" I asked him.

"They'll come aboard later. But this campaign isn't going to be about busing. It's going to be about jobs. Liberals care more about fish than people. That's why fishermen are out of work in New Bedford. That's what Wallace is going to talk about."

I wished I had time to go out with him for a week and watch his people work, if they were working. But the deadline for this book was lunging at me, so I am forced to be more superficial. I don't think Sullivan and his troops can do it; they lack the political and sociological wisdom, and the burning issue or the leisure time of McGovern's soldiers. Busing does not have the force of Vietnam for the same numbers of people. Besides, by December '75 I'd grown increasingly skeptical of Wallace's claims to vast funds. I believed there might be far less gold and more overhead in Richard Viguerie's list than he and Wallace's staff would admit. But, but, but . . . I will be watching the Massachusetts returns on March 2 with a great deal of interest.

In their more conventional search for constituencies, the "liberal" Democratic candidates went through the ritual of appearing at each of the five Democratic forums sponsored by several liberal unions and the ADA (Americans for Democratic Action). By forum number three they all had their acts down pretty well. By forum number five one could make a judgment as to who was where. The winners were Harris and Udall. Harris gave the best ten-minute speech, a stem-winder hitting all the tried and true bases. Udall gave the best answers to questions—liberal, but stressing unity. The big losers were Bayh and Shriver.

Bayh was a surprise. He was well briefed and there was nothing in his answers that the liberal listeners didn't want to hear. But, except in Massachusetts, his energy level was always low; he seemed to be dragging his answers out of himself with effort after an inner battle with his feelings over the words. He would flap his hands and his coattails in the middle of a lengthy response. His voice rose strangely at the end of his declarative sentences, giving them more the effect of questions. At the final conference in Baltimore, as at the first in Minneapolis, the hall which had been full when he started was half empty at the end of his allotted hour. My feeling is—I can dignify my conclusions with no more precise term—that Senator Bayh, a superb consensus politician, is emotionally upset by questions. He genuinely does not know where he stands on a number of issues. He is waiting to hear from the people: to be told. He grows anxious when forced to define his position outside the context of politics, to state what he himself feels. This inner tension saps his energy, and the audience feels the confusion and is let down.

Shriver was easier to fault. He was not a politician and didn't know what he was talking about. His answers to too many questions were: "I have a position paper on that." The press took to keeping track of his more quotable malapropisms. In Baltimore the favorite was: "These complex issues are not simple." I think I preferred: "Abortion is not a viable solution." In Baltimore, Shriver was reduced to a stutter on the abortion question, about which he obviously feels deeply, even while trying to pick up votes by taking positions that are uncongenial to him. "We spend more money on pregnant cows than we did on pregnant women." Followed by a wonderfully Freudian sentence: ". . . a woman is being subjected to pressures [on abortion] that men are not subjected to." The crowd tittered. Shriver pressed on to a disjointed lecture on adoption as an alternative. I thought again of presidential candidate Arthur Blessit carrying his cross through the New Hampshire snows. The line between a serious candidate and a man damaging himself is perilously thin.

At the last conference in the first week in November, Harris had also been hurt by allegations in the press that Gulf Oil had supplied covert money to finance his 1964 Senate campaign. "You may have heard that back in 1964 Gulf tried to slip a Gulf Oil contribution to me," yelled Harris. "Neither I, nor LaDonna, nor my campaign treasurer . . . have any record or any memory of a contribution from anyone connected with Gulf." He went on to add that if they had given him money, "They made one of the worst investments they ever tried to make." He had fought big oil, was an opponent of the depletion allowance, and wanted a "public energy corporation." Not all true. In 1969 Harris not only voted to keep the 22 percent depletion allowance but to restore it to its former level of 27.5 percent, a move rejected by the Senate, 30 to 62. Maybe, as he claimed, he hadn't been bought; but the suspicion remained that he might have been rented.

By mid-December, other visible signs of a presidential campaign began to spring up. In a shift of tactics, Jackson opened two store-front headquarters in Massachusetts, a state he had planned to avoid. He also began to mount a mail campaign under the direction of Bill Ezekiel, who had built up the little city halls around Boston for Mayor Kevin White. In New Hampshire there were Udall inserts in the state newspapers. In New York Bayh had sent out over 100,000 pieces of mail. The Wallace organization remailed to their list of 200,000 who had already contributed (which seemed to me a surprisingly small number). Ford's trip to China was being critiqued as much for its impact on his presidential chances as for any possible diplomatic accomplishments. Harris took a half hour of national radio time to talk up his campaign and raise money. Each day Ronald Reagan announced some new politician as a convert to his cause.

There was no longer much room for change and maneuver on the parts of the candidates. They were in position, staffs and strategies set, constituencies either forming or too amorphous to ever form. From Harris on the left to Reagan on the right, they had staked out their turf on the issues. Now that the contest was going public, further shifts would be costly, bringing clucking noises from the press and cries of anguish from some groups of supporters.

As for the issues themselves, they were, now that the war was past, much as they had been since the mid-sixties. There was the economy: jobs and inflation. There were civil rights and civil liberties which reduced to busing, an issue still present but fading in intensity. There were the intertwined issues of electability and character: What sort of a man was the candidate; could he be elected President? Questions of particular force in 1976 because of the past failings of Nixon in one category and McGovern in the other. Finally, there was the issue often called "energy" but which, it seemed to me, should be more correctly called "future." Americans felt things were going wrong in ways not accessible to normal political solutions. Energy, which was getting scarcer and more expensive, was the first symptom of these self-doubts. It was the forerunner of other potential nation-dividing issues, all parts of the "politics of the shrinking pie."

Who then won the invisible primary? As I write in Christmas week it is impossible to say. The "final" Gallup Poll that first caused me to suspect the existence of the primary is still a month away, to be conducted at the end of January. Since the constituency is the final track on which a candidate gathers momentum, these thirty days are always of tremendous importance. But never more so than in this strange election year of 1976. Our nation is now more politically divided than it has been since 1932, perhaps since the Civil War. The explosive forces of Vietnam, Watergate, the abdication, and the deteriorating quality of life resonate in our politics as in ourselves. The polls find us full of apathy, resentment and distrust, and the results of the polls are becoming inconsistent and volatile, less useful as a tools for analysis and forecast. Lacking commitment to the personality, politics, or policies of anyone, voters ricochet from candidate to candidate. "You can't measure something the respondent doesn't know," says Robert Teeter, properly emphasizing the often overlooked obvious.

So it is a month too soon to name the winners, and yet I owe it to you and myself to try. Very well then:

For the Republicans the constant sudden shifting of the polls is both important and potentially misleading. The problem is that there are so few

Republicans out there. From 1952 to 1972 the number of people calling themselves Republicans dropped only four percentage points, from 27 percent to 23 percent. Now, four years later, it has dropped five percentage points, to 18 percent. To get a statistically reliable sample of such a small number of Americans is difficult. Polling only two weeks apart, the Gallup and the Harris polls came up with estimates of President Ford's strength differing by ten percentage points: a result closer to guesswork than science.

While the December Gallup Poll gave Ronald Reagan a significant eight point lead over President Gerald Ford, more detailed polls taken around the same time showed Reagan's lead very much more slender. More significantly, while Reagan was ahead among *all* those who called themselves Republicans, President Ford was substantially ahead among those Republicans who were registered and voted regularly. Unless Reagan's staff were highly sophisticated or his campaign exceptionally successful, the Reagan effort would in part be sending Ford supporters to the polls. This would be true in both the key early primaries: New Hampshire and Florida. In Florida, where Reagan was strongest, his position would be further complicated by the presence of George Wallace. Many Independents and Democrats who might be persuaded to register Republican and vote for Reagan would instead become or remain Democrats and vote for Wallace. At the same time Gerald Ford would have all the power of the electronic presidency at his disposal, assuming that he and his inept staff learn how to control that monster.

I see no walkaway for either man. But measuring their relative strengths on all six tracks, President Ford now seems to me to have an edge that will carve out his final victory.

As for the Democrats, what should one say when the top four candidates in the December Gallup Poll—Edward M. Kennedy, Hubert H. Humphrey, George McGovern, and George C. Wallace—all have either withdrawn from the race or, with George Wallace, have an unacceptability quotient far higher than indications of their popularity? This has left the actively campaigning frontrunner as Scoop Jackson, at 10 percent, down from 11 percent two months before. The only other candidate on the Gallup Poll who even showed was Birch Bayh at 5 percent; the rest registered under 3 percent. More precise polls of voting Democrats revealed the same bunching of active candidates at the low end of the scale. Jackson had the overall lead, but it was slim. Birch Bayh was slightly ahead of Morris Udall in favorable mention; but also in unfavorable mention. When the factors were balanced Udall was a whisker ahead of Bayh.

There now appear to be three candidates who have sufficient strength on all six tracks to give them a chance: Jackson, Udall, and Bayh. I believe the initial race will be between Udall and Bayh to see who can capture the constituency of the liberal center. The victor in this battle will then go on to challenge Jackson. Wallace will run his own private and reasonably effective race, but he will not win above 20 percent of the vote. In the Udall–Bayh race both have advantages. Bayh is a Senator and has the more potent public image: the farm boy behind whom labor and liberals can unite. Udall has the abler staff, slightly better funding, and the reputation, recognized by the media, for thought and integrity.

Whoever wins the Udall–Bayh contest—I give Udall a slight lead as of now—will nevertheless find many of the tangibles still pointing to Jackson as the eventual winner: money, organization, his Senate position, the length of time he has been campaigning, the new rules dividing the delegates proportionally. And the events are breaking Jackson's way: Detente is deteriorating, Henry Kissinger has postponed his trip to Moscow, the Mideast is unquiet, the Russians have intervened in Angola. All this benefits a man whose image is that of a hard guy for a tough time.

So, on the strength of the tangibles, it should be Jackson. But I am all too well aware of the importance of the intangibles—the uncertain mood of the country, the influence of the media, the makeup of those who will vote in the primaries, the *deus ex machina* of chance. It is not an easy time for forecasters.

The end of the invisible primary and the start of the state caucuses primaries can be compared (if you will indulge me in an extended metaphor) to the situation along the French-German border at midnight, May 9, 1940. All sides were in position, their alliances made, their strategies set, their staffs trained, their forces deployed. Some weaker candidates —Spain, Poland, Czechoslovakia, Finland—had been knocked from the race. Holland and Belgium were still neutral, planning to fight it out as favorite sons. One side, last time's winner, had put its faith in lines of concrete, backed by artillery and masses of infantry, with tanks dispersed to stiffen the infantry. The other had a flexible strategy of concentrated tanks supported by dive-bombers and mobile infantry.

On that still, foggy night, an expert could venture a forecast. Indeed, many did, choosing one side or the other but usually deciding in favor of those they admired. Since this book is, in a sense, a test of its own thesis, I have made a prediction at the end of the invisible primary on the basis of the candidates' relative strengths on the six tracks. Honor and my own curiosity permit no less. Yet I should be sorry if my prediction, right or wrong, were to be taken as the point of this enterprise. What I really have wanted to do is indicate the nature and location of key early battles, the state primaries and caucuses which, read correctly, will show *how* the invisible primary was fought and won. Just as a military expert that Spring would have been wiser (and less full of journalistic "hype") to say: If the Germans reach Rotterdam in a week, take Fort Eben Emael on the Albert Canal in two weeks, and force the line of the Meuse-Oise in a month, the Anglo-French alliance is in trouble. If they don't, the Nazis are in trouble.

Eben Emael, "the strongest fort in the world," fell on the first day, May 10. Rotterdam was reached in three. The Meuse was crossed in three; the Oise in six. It was then May 16. It was not necessary to wait for the fall of Paris on

June 14 to know who had won the ten-year arms race between the Anglo-French alliance and Germany, though wise men went on deluding themselves to death for some time to come.

It will probably not be necessary to wait for the Republican and Democratic national conventions in July and August to determine the winner on both sides of the invisible primary, though people, including those in the media, will go on spending energy and money to prove the race still open. By April 6, the day of the New York primary and also of some sort of a primary-like event in recalcitrant Wisconsin, we will, barring handguns and acts of God, know the winners in both parties—just as we knew the victor after that balmy week in May when, for a terrifying historical moment, the blitzkrieg created by the genius of Heinz Guderian and Erich von Manstein first revealed itself.

Here are seven dates, from January 19 to April 6, at the close of each of which we shall know with increasing certainty who won the invisible primary for 1976. Other experts may use, perfectly logically, other dates; but these seem the most conclusive to me.

January 19, 1976: The Iowa caucuses. This is a date crucial for Jimmy Carter. He has stated so often that he plans to do well in Iowa and so generate momentum that he has committed himself to excel here. Of course just what "do well" means is going to be the subject of much media interpretation and counterclaims from the other candidates. But this in turn will indicate how well Carter has mastered the media track. Iowa is critical for Carter only; a strong showing by any other Democratic candidate there would be a straw in the wind—and only that, certainly not a telephone pole in a tornado. The other candidates have marshalled their troops on other terrain. On the Republican side, Ronald Reagan's local-boy status—he got his start as a broadcaster in Des Moines—gives him a slight advantage. But the state is not significant for either Ford or Reagan, because, again, both have decided to battle elsewhere.

February 24: The big opening media event, the New Hampshire primary. On the Republican side, New Hampshire is critical for Reagan but not for Ford. As the challenger, Reagan practically has to win here or come close enough to cause the media to pant a bit. However, since it is generally accepted that New Hampshire Republicans are conservative, and since Reagan is the challenger, Ford can afford to lose this one, though he cannot afford to drop it on his toes and break his foot. If Ford wins in New Hampshire, Reagan is in that painful political posture of having his back to the wall before his foot is off the mark, a contortion that may, to push the metaphor, break his back.

On the Democratic side, Udall *must* win here. If any Democrat— any—edges Udall out, his campaign is almost through. His strategy and staff have focused on New Hampshire, and as I write, he is as much ahead there as Carter is in Iowa. All Carter needs in New Hampshire, provided he has led Iowa substantially, is a strong third, though a strong second would be more helpful. If he has not won in Iowa, then he must place at least second here. Let me try and protect the verb "win" from the winds of the electronic moment and the gas from the candidates. I define "win" in Iowa, as gaining close to a majority of the delegates; and in New Hampshire as both gaining a majority of the delegates and being number one by five points in the preference poll. Anything less in either state, while it can and will be claimed as a victory by somebody, cannot be classed as a definite win.

As a sub-issue, watch the votes in southern New Hampshire between Jackson and Bayh. If either pulls decisively away from the other, or if Udall runs strong there as well as in the north, it will indicate the probable direction of the labor vote. Neither Jackson nor Bayh have to do well in New Hampshire, since their strategy has been to focus elsewhere, and the press has conceded the validity of this tactic—though any strength either shows in this primary is a definite plus. New Hampshire is not only significant in itself, but the "winner" can probably count on a five-point lift in the Massachusetts primary ten days later, particularly if he has been garlanded with the TV-bestowed crown of "runaway winner."

March 2: The Massachusetts primary. Coming ten days after New Hampshire, this is the second major event. But it represents something entirely different from New Hampshire for most of the players. On the Republican side, the Ford-Reagan positions are reversed: Massachusetts is critical for President Ford, but not for former Governor Reagan. Reagan plans largely to bypass Massachusetts and head for Florida. In that conservative state he'll attempt to capitalize on what he hopes is a New Hampshire victory. If, having lost in New Hampshire, Ford falters here, gaining a bare majority of the delegates, he probably will not get the nomination. He may last until Illinois, but he will have demonstrated, even to me, that an incumbent in this electronic age is still capable of squandering his massive initial advantage.

On the Democratic side, Massachusetts is again critical for Udall. Having planted his flag in Massachusetts, he and his staff plan to put together two substantial victories here and in New Hampshire. If he brings this off, he will have swept the liberal side of the Democratic party. If he is the only "liberal" who finishes ahead of Wallace in this primary, he is obviously far enough ahead on all six tracks so that his eventual "victory" at the convention becomes probable. Conversely, if Bayh finishes ahead of Udall in Massachusetts, it is he who will capture the liberal constituency. Carter can sit Massachusetts out since he, like Reagan, intends to leap over Massachusetts on his way to Florida to give battle to George Wallace. This primary is also critical for Sargent Shriver; if he can't make it in Massachusetts with the Kennedy connection he can't make it anywhere.

While Massachusetts is not as vital to the other candidates as it is to Ford and Udall, it contains further auguries for the future events. The sexiest of these, journalistically, is the strength of George Wallace in the north. It seems possible to me, though not likely, that George Wallace will gain more delegates in Massachusetts than any other candidate. This is not merely a function of Wallace's strength, but also of the fact that the mechanism of the Massachusetts primary favors candidates with great appeal in a few congressional districts over candidates relatively strong throughout all the state. A strong showing by Wallace will help not only himself, but also any candidate who finishes close to him, as dismayed Democrats scramble for a man to stop the Alabama dragon. Conversely, if Wallace doesn't do as well in Massachusetts, Jimmy Carter will suffer; there will be little media gain from slaying a weakened Chimera two weeks later in Florida.

Massachusetts will also be the first test of the new Democratic Party proportional representation rules. Can states still be decisive, or will all the candidates get their 20 to 30 percent of the delegates in state after state? No one knows. One of the major historical changes in our political processes rests on hazard. As I write this, I have just spent a whole day checking with the "experts," from David Broder to Robert Strauss, and we all admit that the best we have is an educated guess. If Massachusetts indicates that there will be no series of decisive state primaries, this greatly benefits Jackson, since his campaign is predicated on such a result.

Should Massachusetts split every which way and Jackson get his fair share of the delegates, in effect he has won. Why? Because his strategy will have been proven correct: to be financially flush and adequately staffed for the long haul, so that one can pick up parts of everything while other candidates, desperately short of funds, scramble for little pieces of this or that. Jackson is in a no-lose position in Massachusetts. He isn't expected to do well in a liberal state, so any strength he shows will help his cause. If any of the other candidates I have so blithely or intelligently written off carries Massachusetts, the laugh is rather painfully and publicly on me. Still, I wish them well—even though there are some out there who still remind me of Lear, self-garlanded and slightly mad.

March 9: The Florida primary. This is another of those events that is crucial for Ronald Reagan and not for Ford. The roles have reversed from what they were nine days earlier in Massachusetts, returning to the New Hampshire pattern. In this conservative state Reagan must win over Ford to prove he can oust the incumbent. Ford must merely stay "reaonably close," i.e., Ford should be closer to Reagan in Florida than Reagan was to Ford in Massachusetts. If Ford tops Reagan in both Florida and New Hampshire, his invisible primary strategy will have prevailed. If Reagan has topped Ford in both and stayed close in Massachusetts (or won) then he in all probability has the prize.

On the Democratic side, Carter must beat Wallace in Florida to keep his candidacy alive. The smaller the showing Wallace makes in Massachusetts, the greater the lead Carter must show against Wallace here to prove he is an effective vote-getter. This is particularly true if Carter has not done well in Iowa and at least fairly well in New Hampshire.

Jackson must demonstrate that he can carry the urban areas around Miami in the south, Tampa in the center, and Jacksonville in the north. If Jackson does not do this and has not shown some strength in Massachusetts, he is hanging on by his fingernails going into New York. For the other Democrats, Florida is a bye, as they have all declared they will be campaigning elsewhere; and again the press has accepted that declaration as a sign of wisdom, not weakness.

March 14: This is a strange and almost invisible date, important, as I write, to only one man, though conceivably it could become critical for two or three more. This is the last day on which a candidate can file to enter the California primary. In effect, although there are possible exceptions like New Jersey and Oregon, this is the last moment at which a candidate can decide to enter the primaries. One of the theses of this book has been that the eventual winner will come out of the invisible primary and the state primary process, rather than from the convention. Therefore no one who is not in the race by this date, close to the last chance to enter a primary, holds, in my opinion, more than the faintest hope of being his party's candidate for President. This is D-Day particularly for Hubert Humphrey, but also for any other hopeful toying with the idea of a last-minute blitz campaign. If Humphrey enters after this date, he cannot do himself any good, though he will still have ample time to savage himself once again.

March 16: The Illinois primary. This date has importance only if Ronald Reagan has won in either New Hampshire or Florida. If Ford has won in those two states the results of the Republican invisible primary have already been confirmed and, always with a bow to chance, that race is over. Ford will be the victor. If the two men have split the two states, or if Reagan has won both, this will be Ford's last chance. Ford must win Illinois, or Ronald Reagan will have demonstrated that the electronic presidency is not as strong as some of us have presumed. Both Ford and Reagan have strong organizations in the state, with Ford's, co-directed by former candidate Charles Percy, given a bit of the edge. On the other hand, Reagan, who was born in Illinois, will capitalize on being a native son. However it turns out, the Republican invisible primary winner will be clear when the TV tube darkens that night.

The Illinois primary lacks impact on the Democratic side because, until November 25, it appeared that the last of the old-time bosses, Mayor Richard Daley, was planning to run the last of the old-time favorite sons, Senator Adlai Stevenson III. Daley believed that the Stevenson campaign would make one of the eventual front-runners come to him at the convention. With limited time and funds available, the major Democratic candidates were therefore planning to bypass Illinois. Holland, in 1940, believed that she was protected by neutrality. There's always someone standing on today's ground sporting yesterday's strategy. When Stevenson, not Daley, finally figured out how expensive and politcally dangerous the new rules made favorite-son campaigns in 1976, he dropped from the race the last week of

November. But this late withdrawal, plus Mayor Daley's determination to run slates of uncommitted delegates, means that on the Democratic side Illinois will be too confused to provide anyone with a "win." The final, decisive Democratic primary is therefore New York.

April 6: The New York primary. This is a purely Democratic event since the Republican winner will have been determined by March 16. Again the significance of this date is determined by what will have happened in Massachusetts and New Hampshire. Of the Democratic candidates, only Udall can afford not to finish either first or a close second in New York. If he has had earlier successes, he can afford to let a strong showing in the Wisconsin media event (held on the same day) offset a third place showing here.* The chief battle in New York is between Bayh and Jackson. The results may be hard to determine, as the state organization under Governor Carey plans to run its own slate of candidates in all congressional districts. Also, in this state alone, the candidates' names will not be on the ballot—just the names of their delegates—and this will tend to skew the results. However, even with those caveats, there should be enough evidence in after this test to indicate the eventual Democratic candidate.

Bayh, short of funds and, except in Iowa, not catching on with the speed and enthusiasm he has envisaged, must finish first or a strong second in New York to stay in the race. His Massachusetts showing is a factor here; the weaker his race in Massachusetts, where he will have tried to mount a strong drive, the better he must do in this primary. He doesn't have to get more votes than Jackson and the organization combined. But unless he has done well in Massachusetts, he needs better than a three-way split—not just for the media effect, but for the practical political reason that parts of the Carey ticket are also loyal to Jackson.

Jackson and his bits-and-pieces strategy does not have to forge so strong a win to emerge as number one. However, he must do well enough—again this is a subjective judgment on the part of the media and other politicians—so that both experts and the public start to believe his grind-it-out strategy will lead to victory. He must break his image as a man who can't win primaries. If the early primaries on the Democratic side have all been indecisive, paradoxically this can make New York decisive for Jackson, provided he has picked up his share in the other states. If he has done well in Massachusetts and the urban areas of Florida and now ends up with the most delegates in New York, he has blown the race wide open.

In fact, if any candidate has won in either Massachusetts or New Hampshire (or in both, as I personally believe will happen) and now "wins" in New York, that candidate is the eventual nominee, again barring chance.

---

*At present the Wisconsin primary will be a "beauty contest" only, with no delegates selected. The Democratic National Committee has ruled that the delegate selection rules in Wisconsin are illegal since they permit Republicans to vote in the Democratic primary. The delegates will be chosen in a series of caucuses probably held in June.

For by the evening of April 6, the winner of the Democratic side in the invisible primary may well no longer be in doubt.

If everything is totally confused after New York—say Carter has won in Iowa, Udall in New Hampshire, Shriver in Massachusetts, Wallace in Florida, and Bayh and the organization split in New York, and Jackson has not shown real strength anywhere—what then? Then there will have been no victor on the Democratic side and I shall have chosen a very bad year to propound my thesis about the invisible and visible primaries. All I can do if that happens is admit that I am as confused as anyone. The Democratic race will go down to the wire on the night of June 8, when California, New Jersey, and Ohio hold their primaries. After that, since there are no favorite sons to hold the balance of power, two of the candidates with enough votes to put one of them over the top will combine forces *before* the convention, and, naturally, make a deal on the vice-presidency. Right now such a situation would seem to benefit Jackson and/or Udall, since Jackson has the staff and money for the long haul and Udall is the second choice of most "liberals." But here I am pushing past even informed guess to pure conjecture. Birch Bayh may have put together his labor and liberal coalition to be the chief beneficiary of the long haul; or Hubert Humphrey may have entered some of the late, late primaries and have some delegates to bargain with. All I can say is I don't think this will happen. I believe that even the traditional confusion of the Democrats will have cleared enough to reveal the candidate by the morning of April 7.

There you have my signposts toward who has won the invisible primary. Believe me, printed prophecy, like being hanged, concentrates a man's mind wonderfully.

CHAPTER 10

The Future

Look in the bathroom mirror and slowly say out loud: "Our present system for choosing Presidents selects the best among us." Try to keep a straight face. We choose our Presidents from two candidates. These two candidates are winnowed from the state primaries. The state primary winners are largely determined during the invisible primary, when from all the talent in the nation the five or six men who will run seriously in the state primaries are selected and ranked. Perhaps once this selection process, or candidate rummage sale if you prefer, is better understood, we can be more rational about whom we select and how we choose him or her.

Publicly the candidates place their hands over their hearts and proclaim that the invisible primary-state primary system functions to perfection. Would he change the system, candidate Lloyd Bentsen was asked. "Hell, no. It's not easy. But then neither is the presidency." With more words, Governor Jimmy Carter said the same thing. "The long, tortuous path that must be walked through, the primaries, has a positive value in our system because the unending and varied types of physical, mental, and in some cases moral stresses that are going to confront a candidate are going to become only greater once that person becomes President of the United States." Morris Udall sees the value of a "testing ground," though he has a bill in to change it. And no wonder. In the entire 1952 election, General Eisenhower broke precedent and traveled a then unheard-of 53,000 miles making 228 speeches. With still just under a year to go in the invisible primary, Udall had already made 400 speeches and traveled 250,000 miles. What does that test but a man's ability to absorb jet-lag?

Ex-candidate Edmund Muskie had a contrary view of the present system. "As a test of leadership it misses the target by a mile. It boils down to a race to get on the tube. It's a race to shake more hands. It's a race to get headlines, to get attention, to be dramatic and sensational; and none of those things have a hell of a lot to do with the qualities of leadership that this country is looking for. . . . The primaries are an endurance race. But twenty-four-hour-a-day physical activity by a candidate is not proof of his national leadership ability."

One of the deans of candidate watchers, reporter David Broder, was even more contemptuous. ". . . We have concocted not the sanest but the longest, most convoluted, and bizarre system of selecting our maximum national leader that any presumably civilized culture has ever devised . . . [this] hideous, ludicrous endurance contest course that now passes for a presidential selection contest."

I weigh in on the Broder-Muskie side of the argument. What we have done is to create a new job category: "Running for President." Little that a man has done before is given much weight in judging him in this new line of work, though what he has said may occasionally be used for or against him. What is important is how a candidate threads himself through the intricate maze of the invisible primary. Character is judged on the basis of television appearance. Past performance is seldom mentioned.

It would be nice if candidate Jimmy Carter were correct when he said, "The physical and mental strain of a tough campaign has an important role in our political system. The pressures and fatigue tend to strip away even the most carefully constructed facade and reveal basic strengths and flaws of character. . . . Confrontations with angry, dissatisfied voters and hostile questions with no easy answers are what an election in a democracy is all about. . . ."

Unfortunately it doesn't work that way. Look at our choices in the last two elections. Listen to today's candidates give simplistic answers from their well-rehearsed stock of snap-back with quick-back at shopping center after shopping center, living room after living room. *Q:* "Senator Bayh, how do you explain that $3000 gift from Ashland Oil?" *A.* "What I want to know, in view of my record against monopoly, is how do they explain their gift to me?"

This is not to be against all travel. Candidates should be seen personally, examined and tested, especially by those interested in becoming part of their constituency. But to race from place to place for three years is lunacy. A system that puts a premium on simple answers and flesh-pressing hardly seems designed to produce executives who must handle power at the birth of the twenty-first century.

In faulting the present system, I am not looking back at our political past and seeing a sun-drenched landscape painted by Thomas Cole. There have been times in the past when the selection system worked and times when it produced odious choices. "A crooked stick has been made available to beat a mad dog," remarked acerbatic Gideon Welles, Lincoln's secretary of the navy, of the 1872 election which pitted General Ulysses Grant against Horace Greeley. The elections of 1876, Hayes versus Tilden, or 1880, Garfield versus Hancock, can hardly inspire students of democracy. But in those "good old days" the country had distance and time in which to recover from disastrous choices.

The past forty years have given us Franklin Roosevelt, Harry Truman, Dwight Eisenhower, John Kennedy, and Lyndon Johnson. While one may disagree with some of the things all of these men did and most of the things some of them did, it seems to me they were all men of size. Their reasons for being in the presidency made sense. There was a rational, albeit invisible and little understood system at work. In some states the people picked the candidates in primaries; in others the party regulars picked the candidates in caucuses. From judgments made on the basis of these twin indicators of relative popularity, a final decision was made at the party convention. At least until the time of Dwight Eisenhower, campaigns were relatively short.

But towards the end of this period there were indications that the system was breaking down. The amount of time the candidate had to spend campaigning began to increase. In 1942 Wendell Willkie became the first presidential candidate since Theodore Roosevelt to actually enter a state and campaign in a primary. In 1946 Harold E. Stassen, the former boy governor of Minnesota, declared himself a candidate 18 months before the election and a year before the first primary. He went on a 476-day speaking tour which took him 160,000 miles, a bagatelle by today's standards but a cause for wonderment and laughter at the time. In the late fifties Senator Estes Kefauver, the first TV candidate, prodded the sleeping giant of the state primary system awake. After Kefauver, Barry Goldwater and Richard

Nixon for the Republicans and John Kennedy and George McGovern for the Democrats, made campaigning for President a separate job, one that lasted at least four years.

As the campaigns lengthened, big money became too important a part of presidential politics. Before the recent campaign financial disclosure laws, there was little way to measure the dollars flushing down the political sewers; but the sums spent by Nixon, Rockefeller and Kennedy are the stuff of legend. As Matt Reese, who was himself part of the Kennedy operation, remarked, "You know, Jack Kennedy's operation wasn't all that efficient. They just had so much money and so many balls in the air that parts of it were bound to be successful."

While all this was happening, the political parties began to break down. Complex issues arose, like school busing and local control of spending, that cut across party lines. Television gave senators an ideal public forum on which to run for the presidency, even while actual power was passing from the Senate—in part to the House, but more to the federal bureaucracy. The number of state primaries, which had been growing slowly since the early 1900s, began to rise rapidly. Meanwhile, back in the state capitals, the job of governor became so complex that a governor had no time in which to campaign in the ever-increasing number of primaries. Our system has not yet shifted to successfully accommodate these changes.

As campaigning to win state caucuses and primaries, particularly the latter, increased, the importance of the invisible primary increased also. A candidate was no longer running primarily on his record but rather on his ability to run. And it is in the invisible primary that he both demonstrates and perfects this ability. Long before the state primaries start, the candidate's funds must be raised, his staff recruited, his strategy integrated, the media wooed, and his constituency organized and energized. All this during a three-year mad scramble while the candidate is supposedly holding down some other important full-time job.

The process of reform is continuous—so continuous as to lead to a suspicion that what we see is change, while reform, like beauty or myopia, exists only in the eye of the beholder. How to choose our President has vexed this nation since its beginning. And it remains, today, a large, sticky bicentennial problem. The Constitutional Convention wrestled long and hard over the method of selecting America's Chief Executive. In his famous "Journal of the Federal Convention," James Madison, later to be the nation's fourth President, recorded his own doubts. He quoted his fellow Virginian, George Mason: "In every stage of the question relative to the Executive, the difficulty of the subject and the diversity of the opinions concerning it have appeared. Nor have any of the modes of constituting that Department been satisfactory."

A whole host of suggestions were put forward, primaries, direct election, election by the Governors, by state legislators, by special electors, by the Congress, even by a lottery among the final candidates—an interesting anticipation of modern game theory that found few takers among the Founding Fathers.

Finally, after sixty ballots, the Electoral College system was agreed on. This became part of the Second Article to the Constitution, whose outward and visible form still governs our selection today. However, as a functioning reality the Electoral College broke down in the political feud between Thomas Jefferson and Aaron Burr. The selecting power *next* passed to the Congress and the Congressional Caucus. This method in turn broke down beneath the maneuverings of Andrew Jackson to assure Martin Van Buren as his successor. After some years of confusion, the party convention, still nominally in effect today, was created to choose the party's candidate.

Since Theodore Roosevelt, a candidate's selection at his party's convention has been slowly shifting to his selection in the state primaries. The shift towards state primaries had its start in the reform movement at the turn of the century and got its first impetus in 1912 when William Howard Taft and the regular organization stole the Republican presidential nomination from Theodore Roosevelt. In the last three presidential elections the feuding between extreme right and left (or purists versus cynic-pols) in both the Republican and Democratic parties has accelerated the drive towards an ever-increasing number of primaries.

I believe—though here I am almost a minority of one, among both the press and the social scientists—that the party convention has passed as a method of selecting presidential candidates. Conventions have become largely ceremony and TV entertainment, their principal political function the selection of the Vice-President and a demonstration of party unity for television. Almost, but as yet not quite, the convention has gone the way of the presidential Electors. If I am right, by the seventh of June 1976, the day after the California, New Jersey and Ohio primaries, the candidates of both political parties will be obvious. There may be some preconvention maneuvering as, say, candidates one and three put it together to shaft number two. But with the votes all known, and with most favorite sons excluded by the new system, the days of convention wheeling and dealing will be over. Indeed, hoopla and myth to the contrary, the conventions of 1952 in which Eisenhower defeated Taft and Stevenson defeated Kefauver were probably the last two conventions where the outcome was in serious doubt.

There will of course remain overtones of excitement, which the news media will do their best to amplify. NBC and CBS expect to spend 10 million dollars apiece covering the conventions. For that kind of cash you can't admit to covering a non-event. Passions of the moment will be overly recorded and dissected. What will George Wallace do? Who will win some obscure rules battle? Which group of extreme purists will take a walk? But the function of nominating a presidential candidate will have passed to the primaries. And the two primary victors have been decided largely in the invisible primary.

So we have arrived at our present method of presidential choice: the unending round of travel and speeches that demonstrates nothing but a candidate's stamina; the neglect of a candidate's present job and the lies he must tell to make it appear he is not neglecting that job; the discontinuity between what a man has been or done in the past and how he is judged as presidential candidate. Do you think issues get debated? Listen critically to the candidates on local television or in their personal appearances. Indeed both Democrats and Republicans as they cross the land in the invisible primary pledge themselves not to attack others in their own party. Many Democrats still regard Hubert Humphrey as somehow dirty because during the California primary he exposed George McGovern's welfare program as poorly designed and forced from McGovern the admission he hadn't studied his own programs carefully.

We choose our automobiles by their styling, our wives by their figure, our husbands by their income, our clothes by their status, our liquor by its lightness, our food by its packaging, and our Presidents by their telegenic smile and their willingness to utter platitudes in southwest nowheresville two years before the election. We turn from our TV sets to exclaim: "I'm for Van Lingo Wombatt, by God. Here he is in our state again. And he's going to lower taxes and bring back twenty-cent gas." It's not Wombatt who is a menace. It's ourselves.

And the press? Do you think we are doing our job as we scramble to interview candidates on planes; as we frantically check with one another to see if what the candidates said today before one group bears any resemblance to what they said last week before another; and all the while worrying that we may be scooped by our competitors or spell Wombatt with one *t*? We are trapped, in part quite properly, in a tradition that demands objectivity.

When Carl Leubsdorf, a thoughtful and brooding man, who is the chief political correspondent for the Associated Press, a veteran of fifteen years' reporting, wrote a roundup piece about President Ford's barnstorming trip through the midwest over the weekend of July 13, 1975, his lead began: "President Ford's hectic 'nonpolitical' three-day weekend in Michigan and Illinois enabled him to show the strengths he will carry into the 1976 presidential campaign. It also showed some weaknesses." The AP editors in New York and Washington deleted the last sentence as "editorialized comment." This left Ford showing only strengths. The editors had not done this because they are Republicans—they probably are not—or because they like to censor, which they certainly don't. They did it out of genuine conviction that Leubsdorf had not supported the "weaknesses" in his story. One of the weaknesses Leubsdorf had cited was Ford's lackluster speaking style. But if the AP's chief political correspondent is not in a position to comment with precision on a man's speaking style, who is?

Somewhere between objectivity and partisan journalism in the French style there must lie a happy middle ground. I have no wish to see a lead go out over the AP wire: "Dumb-dumb struck again today when President Ford came to town." But falling back on quotes is no help either. Give me an audience of five hundred and I'll find ten who say Van Lingo Wombatt puts them to sleep and ten who say he sets them on fire.

Writing this book, I face the same problems of partisanship and objectivity as anyone else. In the course of two years I've come to like some candidates better than others, to put it mildly. Some of those I like I don't think would make good Presidents; and to a certain extent vice-versa. One candidate I regard as instant Watergate. What am I to say about him? And is it judgment on my part or merely prejudice? Some candidates have given me a great deal of access to their professional and personal lives. I know more about them. How do I balance that surfeit of information, both pro and con, against the lesser amounts of information I have been able to lever out of more secretive candidates and staffs? And I have had space and a reasonable amount of time. A daily journalist, and in particular a TV journalist, has little of either. And the candidates take knowing advantage of this.

To describe the problems inherent in our present method of selecting candidates for President and to criticize where we are is relatively easy—but small help. When we know where we are, we may not be certain what to do next; but at least we won't be hit from the north while staring to the south. Nations are like men. Their strengths and weaknesses twine to weave their successes and tragedies from the same threads. From the beginning we Americans have been a people who put our problems behind us to turn to new ones. We solve problems by taking the risk of leaving them. The Pilgrims left religious persecution at home to brave the ocean and the dangers of the new world. Those who didn't like life in the new colonies grabbed axe and rifle and went out to the frontier to war on nature and Indians. Our successive waves of immigrants were composed of men and women who had elected to leave the problems of the old world and brave the trials of the new.

If in the new world the family farm got worn-out with overplanting or reckless grazing, why there were homesteads in Ohio or even gold in California. We Americans revere people who move on. They are our heroes and the substance of our myths. Everyone can get ahead—leave where they are and their present problems and rise to new glories, and of course new trials. But the new problems are seldom mentioned. After all, they, like the old ones, can be left behind while we go somewhere else. No wonder we were the first to reach the moon.

This attitude, and the people it bred, the leaders it selected, the energies it released, accomplished miracles. We are the country of the future, with all that implies. Where we are is where the rest struggle to come. Only now we who have been trained to solve problems by moving away from them have reached the end. There is no place else to go. Like those who stayed at home in the "old country," we have to stand and patiently deal with problems that go on and on. So it is with the problem of presidential selection. The difficulties of it stay with us and will stay with us. But we still refuse to admit this and rush about frantically changing laws and rules to make the problem go away. We do not apply history to ourselves.

This is not a call for hesitant inaction. Rather, a plea to realize that we do not now know enough about today's system of choosing candidates to perfect it through new rules and laws. We need to leave the system alone awhile, until we understand it and can adjust our attitudes towards it. When things go wrong in America we have a tendency to cry, "There ought to be a law." Or perhaps we create a new government department. Do we really need a new law to keep us from voting for people who take the time to come into our local supermarket and chuck us under the chin—not once but four times? Every time Senator Wagglejaw, Governor Fourflush, and even our hero Van Lingo Wombatt appear in that supermarket to tell us we are the greatest, instead of yelling, "Right on! We are!" we should yell back, "Why aren't you in your office doing your job?" They will get the message. And the message will be reinforced if the press also asks such questions. This does not require a new law. Rather a moderation of our egos by our intelligence.

Restrictions on the franchise are restrictions on the franchise, and they are no less odious if they are deployed by a corrupt political boss or levied in the name of social good. The rules for "affirmative action" with which a candidate in the Democratic party must comply run to 36 pages of pettifoggery. And that's just one step. Unarguably some restrictions and special effort are necessary to redress past wrongs and aid those too long excluded from the vital basic processes of democracy. But there is no point in crying "Tally-ho, Goodness!" and rushing into a numbing complexity of legalistic social theory.

Reformers, when they are restructuring the election process (jargon for changing the rules to help themselves), are always appealing to Jefferson. They have the wrong man. The current crop of reformers are Hamilton's descendants. Jefferson believed in passing power down to the people. His objective in designing a political system was to have it work so that people would be as free as possible within it to do what they thought right. He was against any system that constricted human energy. Hamilton was more distrustful of people. He wanted a system wise enough to restrict people when they did wrong. That's what today's reformers want in spades. They hedge the selection processes with legal and sociological restrictions because they believe that people (other than themselves) will abuse power. People will. But so will rule-makers. And the rules cramp the energy in the political process. Then the reformers wonder why Wallace gets such an enthusiastic response when he says "Trust the people."

Worse, the increased laws and the changed rules do not even accomplish the good purposes for which they were created. Wistfully writing of the part he played in drawing up the 1972 rules of the Democratic party, University of Wisconsin political science professor Austin Ranney said:

> I well remember that the first thing we members of the
> McGovern-Fraser commission (1969–72) agreed on—and about the

only matter on which we approached unanimity—was that we did *not* want a national presidential primary or any great increase in the number of state primaries. . . . But we got a rude shock. After our guidelines were promulgated in 1969 no fewer than eight states newly adopted presidential primaries . . . [and] Congress was considering a national presidential primary more seriously than ever before.*

He might have added that his new rules had almost destroyed a political party preferred by voters in a ratio of three to one. But he needn't have gotten that "rude shock." We are told we live in a complex, interdependent world so often we forget what that means. It means most of the time we don't know what will happen when we change something.

Our experience in changing, "reforming," politics shares the fate of other recent social experiments. We build highways and create ghettos and start riots. We pass laws to improve the air and the air gets worse while we throw people out of jobs. We start a program to aid poor families and break families apart. We win a war to make the world safe for democracy and end up defending the remnants of French imperialism in Vietnam. Our housing programs actually decrease the amount of housing available to the poor. The Democrats labor to open their political party to anyone, restrict participation in it to the idle and set it up for the man on horseback. It goes without saying that none of these things happened because the people initiating the programs were ignorant, vicious, or conniving. They were merely being American: trying to do the difficult immediately.

The mixture of state primaries, party caucuses, favorite-son candidates and national conventions from which we picked our presidential candidates from Coolidge through Eisenhower and Kennedy functioned as it did because only a few people understood the process. From the last high tide of reform, which began to ebb in the early 1920s, to 1956, only the professional politicians, "the bosses," understood the rules. By 1960 the bosses had begun to get tired, the world had changed without their realizing it, their control over the political process began to weaken, their knowledge of it became fuzzy. The rules began to be understood by lawyers, social scientists, activists old and young. By 1970 this new group understood the rules better than those few bosses who remained.

"In 1972 no one knew what the hell was going on," says Democratic party chairman Bob Strauss. "In 1976 I want to make certain people know the rules." That's not true. In 1972 the activists and reformers knew just what was going on. And everyone isn't going to understand the rules in 1976, in either party, because the rules are too new, still being tested and formed. But to have everyone know the rules is a good goal for 1980. Leave the old rules alone—the campaign financing act, the delegate selection processes. After all, they are only one year old. Perhaps by 1980 we can all understand them. And more important, we will have begun to learn what actual effect these

---

*Barber, James David (ed.), *Choosing the President;* Prentice-Hall, Englewood Cliffs; 1974; p. 73.

changes and new laws will have brought about; not in theory but in the real world.

Right now nobody is quite certain how the complex campaign and financial laws will affect this coming election and elections thereafter. I'm meant to be one of the experts—at least my phone rings and people ask me questions—and I know I don't know. And when I confer with other "experts," either in the press or in politics, we gather over drinks or coffee and swap ideas and end up shaking our heads. I've got some educated guesses; but it is so hard to separate myth from fact.

Take the widely held belief that the increase in primaries means the death of the local political party and therefore the death not just of "bossism" but of national political parties and party responsibility. I see no evidence this is true, though it may be. When the bosses knew the rules, they won the primaries. When the reformers knew the rules, they won the primaries. The same was true of caucuses. McGovern won the nomination not by winning primaries, but by winning caucuses, the very area where "bosses" were meant to be strongest.

In 1976 there is so much confusion that the political parties probably *are* hurt. But I don't think this will be true in 1980. What I have observed leads me to believe that the proliferation of primaries, combined with the curtailment of funds, is working to strengthen the local party structure. The local party has the lists of voters, the detailed knowledge of the area, the volunteers, the funds raised locally and the indigenous workers with tangible things like jobs to gain and lose. If the local party has the same energy level and dedication as the candidate's staff (often a big *if*), primaries will probably turn out to strengthen political parties. Were I a campaign manager for a presidential candidate with limited funds, time and energy, I would far rather try to pack a caucus for one night than spend the weeks necessary to grind out a primary victory against a strong local organization.

Also, state presidential primaries are not the bastion of citizen choice we hold them to be in myth. In terms of numbers participating, a frighteningly small portion of the electorate is deciding the future candidate. Using voter statistics from past elections, Lance Tarrance points out that in a precinct of 1,000 eligible voters less than 230 will decide an off-year election for Congress. And presidential primary turnouts are even lower than those in off-year elections.

At present there are before Congress four bills aimed at changing the system of presidential candidate selection. In addition, various other legislators and social scientists have plans in their briefcases to "improve" the system. The thrust of these plans is to simplify the process by creating larger primaries with standard rules: either a series of regional primaries or one overall national primary. Or else the plans contain some spectacular mystery ingredient guaranteed to produce perfect Presidents without being habit-forming or unpleasant to swallow. As the reader will have gathered, I believe to pass such laws at this time is profoundly, even dangerously, the wrong way to proceed.

Congressman Albert Quie of Minnesota has introduced a bill frankly labeled "A National Primary Act." Under this bill all states would hold primaries on the same day, the first Tuesday after the first Monday in August of the year before the incumbent President's term is finished. (For openers, think what that would do to the travel and resort industry and the vacation patterns of Americans.) Republican Senator Robert Packwood of Oregon has a bill to hold five regional primaries, the regions to be selected on the basis of population and media coverage. A "nonpartisan" commission would determine the order in which the regions held their primaries. The commission would also decide whose names should be on the ballot. The names would be those "who are generally recognized in national news media throughout the United States as a candidate for nomination." While there are ways in which a candidate can get on the ballot without commission support, basically this legislation would take power away from the people and give it to the press and some undefined group of "good guys." In the name of reform, Hamilton wins again.

A presidential candidate himself, Representative Morris Udall has introduced a plan similar to Packwood's. It recommends the establishment of three primary dates, one in April, one in May and one in June, on which the present state primaries would be held. States would be free to pick one of the three dates on their own. Udall assumes that this would provide cross sections of the country on all three dates, rather than represent merely regions. What would happen if the states all clustered on one date is veiled in mystery. Any party that had received 10 percent of the vote in the previous Presidential election could pick a candidate to enter the primaries, and the mandatory "nonpartisan" commission also could put forward and approve candidates.

Several other legislators have filed, or are planning to file, legislation to create a national primary. Often these proposals are coupled with direct election of the President. In talking to the bills' sponsors, one gets the feeling they have not spent much time or thought upon the legislation. Rather, they have heaved some quickly dictated measure into the hopper to tell the folks back home they are wrestling with the broad problems of Democracy.

Americans for Democratic Action chairman, Congressman Donald Fraser, was a key member of both the McGovern-Fraser Commission and the Democratic Charter Commission. In a sincere effort to strengthen both political parties, he pushed the reforms that are in large part responsible for the proliferation of complex primaries. Now he says, "I have created a system [that makes it] enormously difficult for a good guy to get a chance at the Presidential nomination." After this appealingly honest admission, what does he propose to do next? Patting his briefcase beside his chair, he says he has a new plan for a national primary. But this time a party convention would endorse a candidate before the primary. And how would the delegates to that convention be selected? He has some rules, for that too. We have not quite gotten to a point where a citizen can only vote after consulting his lawyer, but we are getting close.

Farther out are those perennial suggestions that we abolish the fixed-term presidency and assume instead a system more like that of Great Britain, in which the President could call an election at any time. This suggestion has recently gained fresh support among social scientists who believe that if elections coincided with debates over national issues, the number of non-voters would be reduced. There are many arguments against this plan, not the least of which would be the magnitude of the political and constitutional changes necessary to take it from theory to substance. One basic question is: At a time when we are wisely reducing the power of the imperial presidency, do we wish to enormously increase that power by giving the President the ability to define the issues and circumstances under which he will campaign?

The common trend of all these reforms is towards a national primary. By this is meant that all the voters in our nation would go to the polls on the same day and select two or three people, nationwide, who would then run later in a national presidential campaign. Gallup reports that the majority of Americans, 72 percent, favor a national primary.

In politics there are no final answers, only trade-offs. Remembering this, it is hard to see how the benefits from a national primary come close to offsetting its evils. We are becoming a homogenized society. The precious differences of personality among our people and our national regions are already being lost. I don't want to get up on the mass-culture soapbox—its planks are weary from having supported countless cheap sociological jingoists—but it is a fact that we are just beginning to appreciate the unique benefits of our pluralism: national, sectional, ethnical, and personal. We are glad San Francisco isn't New York, isn't Mobile, isn't Boston, isn't Las Vegas, isn't Minot, isn't Anchorage. A national primary pushes us a step closer to national sameness. Even if every other argument led to the conclusion that a national primary would be best for America, the extra shove towards uniformity still might be too high a price to pay.

But the practical results of a national primary seem to me solidly negative. A national primary is a media primary, a television primary. Its proponents argue this as one of its advantages. Candidates won't have to travel about the country so much; instead they can stay on their jobs and appear before the voters on the tube. But you don't see real work on television. You see candidates performing actions that give the illusion of work. Not Shakespeare creating but Andy Warhol being pop. Senators interminably investigating oil companies instead of writing legislation to deal with both the oil companies and the energy crisis. We all know what gets on television news and what makes headlines.

"You lie, Van Lingo Wombatt!"

"You're a crook, Senator!"

"WOMBATT CAMPAIGNS RIDING GIANT TARANTULA!"

We don't need it.

In post-Watergate America the press has a great deal of power. I, for one, am reluctant to take more. Not that I am a shrinking violet. I just don't want to get so far out in front that all the other power centers rightfully gang up on me as they did against the imperial presidency. Even now, the press has enormous power to focus the attention of the public on this or that candidate. But at least under the present system candidates not taken seriously by the press can still win. They can concentrate their resources in a small area or on a few issues, cultivate an active constituency, and surprise us—as George McGovern did. Under a national primary the media, particularly television becomes the whole ballgame. The surface man, the plastic smile, the facile answer, the gimmick issue, become the roads to the White House.

A national primary reinforces the power of money in politics, which power we are just beginning to lessen. Instead of organizing a staff, mobilizing a constituency, having a variety of ways to power, the candidates would be forced into buying as much TV time as possible. A candidate with little money but programs that appealed to one or more groups has a chance now; but no chance in a national primary. Proponents of a national primary argue that it would reduce the amount of time spent campaigning. It certainly would reduce the amount of time spent traveling, since fund-raising and getting on national television would become all-important. But this is not the same as giving candidates more time at work.

The present scattering of primaries give the voters everywhere a chance to learn how the voters of a candidate's home state feel about him. John Lindsay, New York's ex-mayor, isn't mentioned as a candidate anymore because he can't carry his home state. Ex-Governors Jimmy Carter of Georgia and Terry Sanford of North Carolina know they are through if Wallace beats them in their home states. Birch Bayh is paying a great deal of attention to the Indiana primary, while the usually voluble Fred Harris falls silent when asked how well he'll do in Oklahoma. In a national primary we would lose the priceless pilotage brought by local knowledge.

Many of those boosting a national primary have a great deal of self-interest in its adoption. Again this is natural; but it should be recognized. The media, particularly television, has the most to gain, both in power and dollars. They can be expected to push the national primary as a wise way out of the present complexity. Pollsters and advertising agencies also have a lot to gain. So do candidates with a Washington base and easy access to the national television outlets, especially senators. So do those who might want to transfer from one highly visible profession to another without ever having to prove themselves as politicians or administrators in the process: generals, entertainers, sports figures. Remember that the two people overwhelmingly preferred by Americans for the presidency are Walter Cronkite and Billy Graham. Of all the presidential candidates, only one gives his vocal, wholehearted support to a national primary: George Wallace. And with good reason. If such a national primary were held today among declared Democratic candidates in December of '75, every poll shows that Wallace would win.

Somewhere between the national primary and the present system is the regional primary: an informal or legal grouping of states in one area, which would all hold their primaries on the same day. Here again one must look closely at the trade-offs. The candidates will be able, if they wish, to economize on their television and newspaper buys because the same TV station or newspaper often serves an audience in more than one state. A candidate's travels would be more efficient, if not less exhausting, because he or she could hit several states in one trip. Since the primary is by a region and not the whole nation, the benefits of diversity and pluralism would be retained; the all-pervasive use of national TV avoided.

On the other side, a candidate doesn't have enough time on most of his swings to meet all those he wants to in even one state, let alone a whole region. What really do, say, Massachusetts, Vermont, New Hampshire, Maine, and Connecticut have in common except contiguity and Yankee jokes. If the activists and politicians from a region want to join informally, that's one thing; but do we want the federal government stepping into yet another local issue? And if, in an effort to be first and make their region the determining factor, all the regions produce primaries at roughly the same time, then we have a national primary by another name—which may just be what many supporters of the regional primary want.

And there is something else that disturbs me. Some of the proponents of the regional primary see it as a means of accomplishing another, less obvious, objective. This is always dangerous in politics, witness busing. What the supporters of the regional primary are fighting is the extraordinary influence of the first presidential primary, New Hampshire, on the nation's political process. But they can't make New Hampshire the twentieth primary, or even the second, since the wily granite men hungry for the tourist buck will be first if they have to quit drinking and vote at 12:01 New Year's eve as the last notes of "Auld Lang Syne" die out in the blizzard at the town hall door. Unable to change New Hampshire, reformers try and group New Hampshire in with other states or create rival combinations of states that will hold their primaries close to the date of New Hampshire's and so dilute the importance of that state.

I sympathize with those who feel their choices overly determined by what happens in New Hampshire. Were I a politically active Texan, Californian or Pennsylvanian, I would want to be first sometime. Why should the national press and all the candidates focus always on New Hampshire, not on me? For there is no doubt about it: in the invisible primary the five early primary or caucus states—Iowa, New Hampshire, Florida, Wisconsin, and New York—get the candidates' time, staff attention, and money.

But again, are not we rushing to formalize a rule change, when all we need is recognition of the problem? If other states strongly object to New Hampshire's primacy, they can advance their primary dates as close to New Hampshire's as possible. Massachusetts has done this for 1976. And there are signs that both public and press are coming to realize that they focus too much on New Hampshire. Two of the major candidates, Wallace and Jackson, have no plans to campaign there. Nor is President Ford making a drive on the Iowa caucus.

Lest I begin to seem the apostle of *dolce far niente,* let me repeat that I do not mean to confuse the present system with perfection or inaction with reform. But I do believe that understanding must come before action—in part because it sometimes relieves the need for action.

For example, this book has stressed the great advantages enjoyed by senators in the invisible primary. They have so little important work to do that they can easily take time off to campaign, and they have the staffs, the political base, plus the all-important access to national television. If a governor, a cabinet officer and a senator were racing one another in the invisible primary, one candidate would be in a tracksuit, the other two in chains. "I never could have spent so much time campaigning like this when I was governor," said Ronald Reagan on one of his midwestern exploratory swings.

But the immediate answer to this inequity is not to change the rules or pass a law to handicap senators, even assuming that were possible. Once again we would be constricting the political process, in effect denying ourselves access to potential candidates. We would simply be exchanging one set of problems for another. Rather the answer is to understand the advantages a senator enjoys campaigning in the invisible primary, along with the disadvantages he suffers in preparation for the White House, and then compensate for these in our attitudes and actions.

The reason candidates get out on the road three years before the state primaries start is obvious. It's to get known locally and sew up workers and party activists. The candidates want *you.* As they troop from state to state and mug on TV, they will get the message very quickly if your answer is: "I'm sorry, I never make up my mind before the January of the presidential year, after I've seen all the candidates, including those who are doing their job." This is not to fault Senator Walter Mondale or Congressman Morris Udall or Elliot Richardson or Scoop Jackson or anyone else. Given our expectations and the effects of the funding limitations and the new rules, they were all following a wise and necessary strategy. Our irrational demands lead to their irrational campaigns which in turn feed our irrational demands.

In the political game—an unfortunate noun for such a vital process (who refers to the brain surgery game?)—each faction tries to advance his presidential candidate by changing the rules. Undoubtedly this extends back into pre-history. In the days when chiefs were chosen by athletic contest and Lord Vombatus of Lingos could throw the hell out of the javelin but was a trifle slow of foot, the priests backing him would argue with conviction that the gods favored fewer races but an increase in the quota of javelin events: the light javelin throw, the heavy javelin throw, the mounted javelin throw, the javelin target contest.* And the partisans of the other candidates would argue for more races or wrestling. While the crowd, ahead of the politicians once again, wondered if there were not some more rational method of selecting leaders.

"Wombatt cares about me. He looked me in the eye when he shook my hand."

"Mummy loves me. She always gives me what I want."

There is no way to correct beliefs like this through law. One can only hope to acquire enough knowledge to learn what Wombatt and Mummy really are after.

Already, formal rules and regulations aside, our system for selection of presidential candidates is working to adjust itself. Several state parties—the Iowa Democrats are an outstanding example—have scheduled day-long rallies where leaders, activists, and other interested citizens can meet all the presidential candidates, hear them speak and respond to questions. A group of politically active unions, the Machinists, the Auto Workers, the Electrical Workers (IUE) have combined with the Americans for Democratic Action to hold five regional caucuses at which all the Democratic candidates could speak and answer questions. These informal gatherings gave "liberals" across the country a mechanism to help them select a candidate. Undoubtedly other groups of varying political hues will likewise move to try and make the invisible primary more rational. This is how our system has always adjusted.

In one of his brilliant departures from fiction into contemporary fact, *The Long Week-end,* novelist and poet Robert Graves indicts the British press for allowing the rise of Hitler. He cites them for a concentrating on sensation and trivia while fascism rose in Europe. I do not feel the American press, specifically including television, deserves such an indictment. But increased press attention to the invisible primary and the rest of our mechanism of presidential candidate selection is at least as necessary as the shift in public attitudes.

When a candidate arrives in a local area to campaign for President, that is certainly news and should be covered. Trips are legitimate. Candidates need to travel both to be seen and to learn. Those who are planning to spend time, energy and money, and risk their political futures on a candidate should meet him personally and probe him or her, if not face-to-face, at least without the electronic filter. But the free ride a candidate gets from most of the local press should end—especially those non-press conferences where a candidate standing before a TV camera gets fed soft queries.

---

*Count Fishsock of the Sislik Isles, who on rather slight evidence is believed to have been an early humorist, reportedly broke up those assembled with his suggestion that chiefs be chosen in a contest to see who could shake the most hands in a week while chanting praises to the ancient gods with a mouthful of cold hen.

Candidates need to be asked detailed and informed questions about their record and their future plans. What is happening to their jobs while they are campaigning should be investigated and reported. Editors, in both television and print media, should give their reporters time to become familiar with the candidates, what they have said on other trips, how they have voted, how their colleagues regard them. We all need the knowledge that good local reporting from a candidate's home state can give us about his or her beginnings, successes and failures. Each year, as the structure of the political party breaks down, the press becomes more a part of the candidate selection process. We too seldom bring detailed knowledge, serious purpose, and the necessary expense of time to that task.

The best of those who now argue for further rule changes in the invisible primary/state primary system believe new laws and regulations are needed because attitudes shift too slowly in America. They hold that legal change is necessary to speed additional change. That may sometimes be true, but I have not found it true about the politics of presidential selection. Writing this book, I have generally found the people to be ahead of candidates, politicians, and reformers. People realize the present system isn't working, that it is too lengthy and overly complicated, that it provides scant substance on which to judge the fitter man. They are looking for ways to find better candidates just as you and I. They *are* you and I.

It seems to me attitudes change quite fast today in areas of public policy. Ten years ago, few people believed we would be safe unless we had many more nuclear weapons than the Soviet Union. Now the balance of terror is accepted. Ten years ago Red China was seen as all threat. Now she is accepted as another superpower. Ten years ago the idea that we could run out of some natural resources before the end of the century was regarded as alarmist. Today we are all concerned about next winter. As late as the 1960s we still regarded the creation of a new federal agency as a valid answer to a problem. There was also the little matter of Vietnam. Indeed our attitudes seem at times to shift with close to dizzying speed; but perhaps that's speaking from the perspective of old-fogeysville.

Bugle blowers turn me off—all those high notes ringing in my ear while I am trying to figure out what to do next. So there have been few bugles in this book. But I hope that what I have written may have provided some help in judging not just this invisible primary but also the next.

Though its contours are still mere outlines, 1980 already begins to emerge as an historic and frightening election—probably the most important presidential selection since 1862. The period of America's rapid growth is over. Our two political parties are breaking apart. Both voters and candidates face the new nation buster: the politics of the shrinking pie. Fewer and fewer of us vote: By 1980 it appears that 60 percent of us who are eligible to vote will never have voted at all. Does government by such a small minority qualify as democracy? Can it successfully respond and adjust to the modern needs of us all?

To call the present process of selecting presidential candidates irrational, ridiculous and wasteful is a banal understatement of the obvious, like calling war deadly. Presidential politics today repels most voters and a good many politicians. I believe we can best change the present system—even improve it—first by understanding it, then by changing our attitudes toward it, becoming involved in new ways ourselves. The next country we make safe for democracy might be our own.

A typical invisible primary schedule for a long weekend. Congressman Morris Udall campaigns eight states plus a fund raiser in the District of Columbia during the Veterans Day weekend in late October 1975.

Wednesday, October 22: District of Columbia

6:30 P.M. **A Salute from the House of Representatives to Mo Udall,** Shoreham Hotel, Regency Room

7:30 P.M. Dinner

8:50 P.M. MKU introduced by Senator Hubert H. Humphrey

9:00 P.M. **MKU Remarks**

Thursday, October 23: Pennsylvania

4:50 P.M. Wheels-up "Tiger" en route to York County, Pennsylvania—Capital City Airport, Harrisburg, accompanied by Rusty Mathews and Ron Pettine

5:30 P.M. Arrive Capital City Airport—proceed to Wisehaven Hall, Prospect Rd.—**York County Democratic Committee Dinner**

6:00 P.M. Arrive Wisehaven Hall—**Press Conference**—contact: Don Paul 717/843-9968

6:30 P.M. **MKU Remarks**

7:00 P.M. Depart hall en route to airport

7:30 P.M. Wheels up en route to Pittsburgh—Greater Pittsburgh International Airport

8:35 P.M. Arrive Pittsburgh International—proceed to Pittsburgh Hilton, Gateway Center

8:55 P.M. Arrive Hilton—proceed to Main Ballroom—**Allegheny County Democratic Committee Dinner**—contact: Mickey Berger

9:00 P.M. **MKU Remarks**

10:00 P.M. Depart dinner en route to adjoining suite—**Press Conference**

10:20 P.M. Depart press conference en route to airport

10:50 P.M. Arrive airport—proceed to "Tiger"—wheels-up en route to DCA

11:30 P.M. Arrive DCA

Friday, October 24: Arkansas, Iowa

7:15 A.M. Wheels-up DCA en route to Jonesboro, Arkansas accompanied by: Ella Udall; Jane Watkins, Trip Director; Bob Neuman, Press Secretary

10:00 A.M. Arrive Jonesboro Municipal Airport, Ed Goode, Station Manager, proceed to Arkansas State University

10:30 A.M. **Press Conference,** College of Communications Building, Arkansas State U. campus—contact: Charles Rasberry

10:55 A.M. Depart Press Conference en route to Student Center, Arkansas State U. Campus

11:00 A.M. Arrive Student Center, **MKU Remarks**—meeting of University students (Student Government Assn., host)—contact: Tom McClain

11:45 A.M. Private Time, Guest Room, Student Center

12:15 P.M. Depart Student Center en route to Wilson Hall, A.S.U. Campus

12:30 P.M. **Meeting with Democratic Officials and General Public**

1:45 P.M. Depart Meeting en route to KAIT-TV studios, Highway 141 N. —contact: Darrel Cunningham

2:00 P.M. **Taping of "In Focus,"** KAIT-TV studios

2:45 P.M. Depart KAIT-TV studios en route to Jonesboro Municipal Airport

3:00 P.M. Arrive Airport

3:15 P.M. **Wheels-up** en route to Adams Field, Little Rock

4:00 P.M. Arrive Adams Field (Central Flying Service—Proceed to Holiday Inn, 617 Broadway

4:15 P.M. Arrive Holiday Inn, **Press Conference,** Flintstone Hall

5:00 P.M. Arkansas State Democratic Committee Meeting, **MKU Remarks,** Flintstone Hall

5:15 P.M. Depart Holiday Inn en route to Governor's Mansion, 1800 Center St.—contact: Ann Pride

5:25 P.M. Private Time, Governor's Mansion

6:00 P.M. **Arkansas Democratic Committee Reception,** Governor's Mansion

8:00 P.M. Depart Reception en route to Adams Field

8:15 P.M. Arrive Adams Field (Central Flying Service)

8:25 P.M. Wheels-up en route to Des Moines, Iowa

11:00 P.M. Arrive Des Moines Municipal Airport, proceed to Johnny & Kay's Hyatt House, 6215 Fleur Dr.

11:05 P.M. Arrive Hyatt House, proceed to suite

R.O.N.

Saturday, October 25

7:30 A.M. Wake-up (breakfast in suite)

8:45 A.M. Depart hotel en route to Salisbury House, 4025 Tonawanda Dr.—contact: Norma Mathews

9:00 A.M. Arrive Salisbury House, Iowa State Education Assn. Interview

9:55 A.M. Depart Salisbury House en route to home of Lois Beh, 5400 Waterbury Rd.

10:00 A.M. **Udall for President Coffee,** Beh home

11:50 A.M. Depart Beh home en route to Goodwin-Kirk Dormitory Lounge, Drake University, 1215 30th St.

12:00 NOON **Udall for President Student Rally,** Goodwin-Kirk Lounge

1:15 P.M. Depart Goodwin-Kirk Lounge en route to Hyatt House

1:30 P.M. Private Time, Hyatt House

3:45 P.M. Depart Hyatt House en route to Ames Udall Headquarters, 155 Campus Ave. Ames, Iowa

4:30 P.M. **Iowa Udall for President Committee Meeting,** Udall Headquarters

4:35 P.M. Depart Udall Headquarters en route to Unitarian Center, 1015 N. Hyland, contact: Clif Larson

5:30 P.M. Arrive Unitarian Center, **New Frontier Club Reception**

5:40 P.M. Depart Unitarian Center en route to Hilton Coliseum, Iowa State University

6:00 P.M. Arrive Hilton Coliseum, **Jefferson-Jackson Day Dinner**

10:25 P.M. Depart Hilton Coliseum en route to I.S.U. Memorial Union

10:30 P.M. Arrive Memorial Union, Regency Room, **Udall for President Reception**

11:30 P.M. Depart Memorial Union en route to Hyatt House, Des Moines

12:00 P.M. Arrive Hyatt House, proceed to suite

R.O.N.

Sunday, October 26: Wisconsin, New York

8:15 A.M. Wake-up

9:00 A.M. Depart Hyatt House en route to airport

9:15 A.M. Wheels-up en route Milwaukee, Wisconsin

11:00 A.M. Arrive Milwaukee, Mitchell Field, proceed to Pfister Hotel, 434 E. Wisconsin Ave.

11:15 A.M. Arrive Pfister Hotel, Private Time

12:00 NOON **Meeting in suite with local Udall supporters**

12:35 P.M. Depart Hotel en route to Milwaukee County Stadium

1:00 P.M. Arrive Milwaukee County Stadium, **Football Game, Green Bay vs. Pittsburgh**

3:30 P.M. Depart Milwaukee County Stadium en route to Pfister Hotel

3:45 P.M. Arrive Pfister Hotel, Private Time

4:30 P.M. Depart Hotel en route to home of Cathy Carlin, 1209 N. 46th St.

4:50 P.M. **Udall for President Reception,** Carlin Home

6:15 P.M. Depart Carlin Home en route to VFW Memorial Hall, 6151 N. Sherman Blvd.

6:35 P.M. Wahnerfest, VFW Memorial Hall

7:30 P.M. **MKU Remarks**

8:00 P.M. Depart Wahnerfest en route to Mitchell Field

8:15 P.M. Arrive Mitchell Field

8:25 P.M. **CDT** Wheels-up en route to Schenectady, N.Y.

12:10 A.M. **EST** Arrive Schenectady, proceed to Holiday Inn, 100 Knott Ter.

12:25 A.M. Arrive Holiday Inn, proceed to suite

R.O.N.

Monday, October 27: New York, Massachusetts

8:15 A.M. Wake-up (breakfast in suite)

9:15 A.M. **Meeting with local labor leaders,** Holiday Inn

9:45 A.M. **Press Conference,** Holiday Inn

10:30 A.M. **Udall for President Reception,** Holiday Inn—contact: Gene Zeltman

11:45 A.M. Depart Reception en route to Schnectady County Airport

12:00 NOON Arrive airport

12:15 P.M. Wheels-up en route to Syracuse, N.Y.

1:00 P.M. Arrive Syracuse-Hancock International Airport, proceed to Conference Room, Airport Terminal Building, **Press Conference**—contact: Dick Schecter

1:30 P.M. Depart airport en route to Syracuse University, Hendrix Chapel

1:45 P.M. Arrive Hendrix Chapel, **MKU Remarks,** Q&A

3:00 P.M. Depart Hendrix Chapel en route to mayor's office, City Hall

3:15 P.M. Arrive City Hall, **Conference with Mayor Lee Alexander**

3:45 P.M. Depart City Hall en route to airport

4:00 P.M. Arrive airport, proceed to Conference Room, Meeting with **Assemblymen Jim Tallon and Ron Stott**—contact: Dick Schecter

4:30 P.M. **Meeting with local labor leaders,** Airport Conference Room

5:00 P.M. Wheels-up en route to Boston, Mass.

6:35 P.M. Arrive Logan International Airport, Boston proceed to home of Hale Champion, 19 Francis Street

7:00 P.M. **Private Dinner** at Champion home

9:20 P.M. Depart Champion home en route to Kirkland House Senior Commons, Harvard University Campus

9:30 P.M. Arrive Kirkland House, Meeting with Nieman Fellows—contact: Mike Fernandez

10:00 P.M. Depart Kirkland House en route to Logan International Airport

10:25 P.M. Arrive Logan Int'l

10:40 P.M. Wheels-up en route to DCA

12:45 P.M. Arrive DCA

Tuesday, October 28

11:20 A.M. Depart office en route to University of Maryland, College Park accompanied by: Ron Pettine, Trip Director, and Julie Ferdon, Youth Coordinator

12:00 NOON Arrive University of Maryland—proceed to Room 1133, main floor, Student Union—Student Government Association Speakers Series

12:05 P.M. **MKU Remarks,** Q&A

12:50 P.M. Depart campus en route to Baltimore-Washington Airport

1:25 P.M. Arrive airport—proceed to lunch with Baltimore County Executive, Ted Venetoulis

2:20 P.M. Wheels-up en route to Staunton, Virginia

3:05 P.M. Arrive Staunton-Shenandoah Valley Airfield—proceed to ground transportation en route to Lexington, Virginia— Washington-Lee University

3:55 P.M. Arrive Washington-Lee—proceed to Lee Chapel—**Mock Convention Candidate Series**—contact: Dan Westbrook,

4:00 P.M. **MKU Remarks,** Q&A

5:00 P.M. **Udall for President Reception**—University Bookstore

5:30 P.M. Depart Reception—Private Time—dinner

6:20 P.M. Depart Washington-Lee en route to Staunton

7:00 P.M. Arrive Staunton-Shenandoah Valley Airport—proceed to "Tiger"

7:10 P.M. Wheels-up en route to Charlottesville, Virginia

7:45 P.M. Arrive Charlottesville-Albemarle Airport (804/973-8341)—proceed to University of Virginia, Old Cabell Hall

8:05 P.M. **MKU Remarks,** Q&A, University Union Speakers Program—contact: Carl Deaner, Andy Purdy

9:00 P.M. **Udall for President Reception**—Newcomb Hall, Commonwealth Room

9:45 P.M. Depart reception en route to airport

10:00 P.M. Arrive airport—proceed to "Tiger"

10:10 P.M. Wheels-up en route to DCA

11:00 P.M. Arrive DCA

APPENDIX II

POLITICAL EVENTS AND INVISIBLE PRIMARY DATES

November 7, 1972: Richard M. Nixon and Spiro T. Agnew are re-elected for the office of the President and Vice-President.

Senator Hubert H. Humphrey launches the Senator Mondale for President campaign.

November 8, 1972: Senator Charles Percy's chief political aide, Joseph Farrell, hires a campaign firm to manage Percy's Presidential drive.

December 28, 1972: Percy decides to run.

January 15, 1973: Agnew's name is first mentioned before a Baltimore grand jury.

January 17, 1973: Senator Henry "Scoop" Jackson makes his first public appearance in 1973 outside of Washington State.

February 7, 1973: Percy and his exploratory committee hold their first meeting.

February 15, 1973: Governor George Wallace continues filing required financial reports as a Presidential candidate. His reports began in 1960.

May 17, 1973: Senate Watergate hearings begin.

June 10, 1973: Percy announces an "exploratory" candidacy for 1976.

July 1973: Wallace hires mass mailing expert Richard Viguerie to handle his 1976 effort.

Senator Walter F. Mondale has visited over twelve states including New Hampshire and California.

July 4, 1973: Wallace and Senator Edward Kennedy appear on the same podium in Decatur, Alabama.

July 16, 1973: In a Harris Poll asking "Who would be your first choice in 1976 between Kennedy and Percy?" Percy gets 46% of the vote to Kennedy's 44%.

September 10, 1973: The Senator Charles Percy Exploratory Committee files with the General Accounting Office, a legal requirement for all such committees.

October 6, 1973: The "Yom Kippur War" begins.

October 10, 1973: Agnew pleads no contest to a charge of income tax evasion. He resigns.

October 12, 1973: Gerald Rudolph Ford is nominated for Vice-President.

October 17, 1973:	The oil-producing Arab nations impose an oil embargo on the West.
October 20, 1973:	The "Saturday Night Massacre." Archibald Cox, Elliot Richardson and William D. Ruckelshaus are out.
October 30, 1973:	The House Judiciary Committee starts consideration of possible impeachment procedures.
November 2, 1973:	"A Fall Evening with the Bentsen's" in Houston raises $365,000.
November 13, 1975:	A letter with Milton S. Eisenhower's signature is sent out to Percy friends asking for money.
November 25, 1973:	In a Gallup Poll of possible Democratic nominees Kennedy leads with 41%, Wallace 15%, Muskie 9%, Jackson 6%, McGovern 6%, Bayh 3% and Mondale 2%.
November 27, 1973:	Ford is confirmed as Vice-President.
December 17, 1973:	Ford announces he will not run in 1976.
January 18, 1974:	The Walter F. Mondale Committee registers with the GAO.
January 29, 1974:	The Lloyd M. Bentsen Jr. Committee registers with the GAO.
February 1974:	Richardson makes his first trip as a possible candidate.
	Mondale makes his first visit to Florida.
March 1, 1974:	The Mikulski Commission rules are adopted by The Democratic National Committee.
March 13, 1974:	The John Connally Committee registers with the GAO.
March 23, 1974:	Percy makes his first New Hampshire trip.
April 1, 1974:	A Gallup Poll shows Kennedy leading prospective candidates for the Democratic nomination in 1976 with 44%, and Wallace at 17%, Jackson 8% and Muskie tied with McGovern at 7%.
April 21, 1974:	Kennedy goes to Moscow.
April 30, 1974:	The White House releases 1,239 pages of edited transcripts of White House conversations related to Watergate and its personalities.
May 10, 1974:	Congressman Morris K. "Mo" Udall takes his first trip to Florida.
May 20, 1974:	Students for Duke University President Terry Sanford file with the GAO.
May 28, 1974:	Twenty-nine Democratic members of the House petition Udall to run in 1976.

June 1, 1974:	Kennedy's office confirms Joan Kennedy is a patient in a New England sanitarium. The Senator also releases his income tax returns.
June 10, 1974:	Nixon leaves for the Middle East.
June 13, 1974:	Connally terminates his John Connally Dinner Committee with the GAO.
June 25, 1974:	Nixon departs for Moscow.
July 1, 1974:	Jackson hires the first of his staff for 1976.
July 8, 1974:	Jackson rents office space for campaign.
July 14, 1974:	*The New York Times* prints Robert Sherrill's scathing article entitled "Chappaquiddick plus Five."
July 18, 1974:	Jackson files a Jackson Planning Committee with the GAO.
July 24, 1974:	Former Senator Fred Harris hires his first staff member with a 1976 race in mind.
July 30, 1974:	The House Judiciary Committee charges Nixon with abuses. Ford stands behind the President.
August 2, 1974:	John W. Dean is sentenced to one to four years in jail.
August 8, 1974:	Nixon resigns as President. Gerald R. Ford is sworn in the next day.
August 10, 1974:	Percy folds after visiting 26 states and raising $215,000. Udall's first trip to New Hampshire.
August 14, 1974:	Kennedy's exposed for failing to file receipts of a fund-raising dinner.
August 15, 1974:	Senator Eugene McCarthy's Committee for Constitutional Presidency files with the GAO. They start with $15,000 in a private donation and a three-person staff.
August 17, 1974:	The Democratic Charter Commission's meeting in Kansas City ends in a right-left walk-out.
August 20, 1974:	Ford nominates Nelson Aldrich Rockefeller for Vice-President.
August 21, 1974:	Ford decides to run in 1976.
	Udall registers a committee with the GAO.
August 25, 1974:	The Committee for a Constitutional Presidency opens a three-person office in Washington.
September 8, 1974:	Ford pardons former President Nixon.

September 20, 1974:   Harris decides to run. Makes his first visit to New Hampshire with 1976 in mind.

September 23, 1974:   Vice-President designate Rockefeller begins hearings on Capitol Hill for possible confirmation.

September 24, 1974:   Kennedy holds a press conference in Boston and folds.

October 10, 1974:   Mondale assembles a campaign staff of three.

October 14, 1974:   Udall and Mondale share a podium in New Hampshire. Liberals decide for Udall.

October 15, 1974:   Campaign Finance Reform Act of 1974 becomes law.

November 4, 1974:   Richardson makes the last trip of his pre-primary campaign and folds after covering 36 states.

November 5, 1974:   Senator Birch Bayh is reelected in Indiana.

November 6, 1974:   Bentsen passes the 200,000-miles-traveled mark.

November 8, 1974:   Governor Jimmy Carter of Georgia Committee files with the GAO.

November 16, 1974:   Udall's strategy group of 28 representatives from all party factions meets privately in Washington.

November 17, 1974:   Mondale goes to Russia. In 1974 he campaigned for 51 Democratic House candidates, 11 Senatorial and 11 Gubernatorial candidates.

November 20, 1974:   Mondale folds after eleven months and $100,000 spent.

November 23, 1974:   Udall announces in Bedford, New Hampshire, that he is a candidate.

December 1, 1974:   Robert Keefe officially becomes Jackson's campaign manager.

December 5, 1974:   A Gallup Poll survey of Democratic voters, who were given a list of 31 potential candidates, shows Wallace 20%, Humphrey 11%, Jackson 10%, Muskie 6%, McGovern 6%.

December 6, 1974:   The Democrats met in Kansas City for their first mini-convention.

December 7, 1974:   Carter sends out his first mass mailing soliciting funds.

December 12, 1974:   Carter announces he is a candidate.

December 19, 1974:   Rockefeller is sworn in as the 41st Vice President.

                      Harris goes to Iowa for the first time.

January 1, 1975:	Jackson raises his first million; Wallace has raised two million.
	Udall takes office space for his candidacy.
	The Federal Election Campaign Reform Act of 1974 takes effect.
	Carter hires staff of three and rents office space.
January 11, 1975:	Harris announces for the Presidency.
January 12, 1975:	McCarthy announces he is a candidate.
January 14, 1975:	Carter becomes Former Governor Jimmy Carter.
February 1, 1975:	Loyd Hackler, a chief Bentsen aide, resigns.
February 6, 1975:	Jackson announces he is a candidate.
February 11, 1975:	Carter makes his first visit to New Hampshire.
February 16, 1975:	Ronald Reagan meets with John Sears and Lyn Nofziger in Washington to discuss his 1976 role.
February 17, 1975:	Bentsen of Texas announces he is a candidate.
February 26, 1975:	Carter makes first visit to Iowa.
February 28, 1975:	Richardson heads for his new job as Ambassador to Great Britain.
March 17, 1975:	*New York* magazine's detailed article on Wallace's Alabama administration.
March 29, 1975:	Bayh makes his first trip as a tentative candidate.
April 1, 1975:	Udall campaigns in his 44th state.
April 30, 1975:	Wallace, still a non-candidate, qualifies for government matching funds for 1976. The first declared or undeclared candidate to do so. Followed later in the month by Jackson.
May 25, 1975:	Gallup Poll break down among Democrats: Kennedy 36%, Wallace 15%, Humphrey 9%, Jackson 6%, Muskie 4%.
May 29, 1975:	Terry Sanford, former Governor of North Carolina, says he is a candidate.
June 1975:	Bentsen raises his first million dollars.
	Bryce Harlow, Melvin Laird and Dean Burch meet with other Ford supporters in Washington to plan Ford's campaign.

June 18, 1975:	Howard "Bo" Callaway, Secretary of the Army, named to head Ford's campaign.
June 19, 1975:	Bentsen qualifies for Federal Election funds.
June 23, 1975:	Senator George McGovern writes his key 1972 backers to ask whether he should run. They say no.
July 1, 1975:	Sargent Shriver hires Pat Caddell to poll for him. He also confirms with Kennedy that Kennedy is out of the race.
July 14, 1975:	A Gallup Poll of Republicans and Independents show Ford with 61½% and Reagan 33%.
July 15, 1975:	Citizens for Reagan open an office in Washington and filed with the GAO.
July 27, 1975:	Udall is hospitalized in Phoenix with pleurisy and viral pneumonia from overwork.
July 30, 1975:	Harris leaves on a cross country camper tour.
August 1, 1975:	Shriver hires the first of his staff.
August 5, 1975:	A Birch Bayh for President Committee registers with the Federal Election Commission (which took over the duties of the GAO.)
August 6, 1975:	Shriver rents office space in Washington.
August 7, 1975:	Ford qualifies for Federal matching funds.
August 23, 1975:	Bayh privately tells a few supporters he will run.
September 5, 1975:	Ben Palumbo, director of Bentsen's presidential campaign, resigns for "personal reasons."
September 12, 1975:	John Gabusi, campaign manager for Udall, announces his resignation; replaced by Jack Quinn.
September 19, 1975:	The Federal Election Commission votes unanimously to allow Wallace to accept royalties from his presidential campaign's sale of watches, medallions and the like with his picture.
September 20, 1975:	Shriver announces for the Presidency.
September 25, 1975:	Milton J. Shapp of Penn. says he is a candidate.
October 1, 1975:	Shriver hires political consultant Matt Reese.
October 10, 1975:	Three candidates in debt: Sanford $78,000, Udall $127,435, and Harris $12,151.

October 11, 1975: Wallace rents a plane, at the cost of $500,000 plus operating costs, for the next 11 months; visits Europe.

October 30, 1975: Humphrey says he will not enter any primaries.

November 9, 1975: Ford fires James Schlesinger as Secretary of Defense and William Colby, Director of The Central Intelligence Agency. Roger Morton, Secretary of the Interior, submits resignation. Vice-President Rockefeller announces he will not seek Vice-Presidency in 1976.

November 10, 1975: The Supreme Court hears oral arguments on the Campaign Finance Reform Act of 1974.

November 11, 1975: Bayh becomes the sixth candidate to accept Secret Service protection. The Secret Service has budgeted for fiscal 1976 (March, April, May, June, July) five million dollars for a possible fourteen candidates.

November 12, 1975: Wallace announces his candidacy, eighteen days after his return from Europe.

November 15, 1975: The last of five Democratic Forums held around the country meet in Baltimore. Udall and Harris are generally judged as winners.

November 20, 1975: Reagan announces his candidacy.

Index